Philadelphia Lawyer

FOREWORD

THIS is the life-story of a Philadelphia lawyer. Ostensibly it has been written for the pleasure of friends who urged me to record my experiences. Actually, of course, the dominant motive has been self-gratification.

I was born in the days when seven miles an hour was the accepted speed limit and when a telephone was only an unrealized dream. I have lived to see the annihilation of space and time and the incidental substitution of world chaos for world order. In the interval the world has been almost continuously in quick water.

As I write the words "quick water" there flash upon my inward eye streams in the woods of Maine which can, I suppose, be matched in charm by other streams in many parts of the world. But the memory of the waters of the Pine Tree State happens to be the bliss of my solitude. Accordingly, when trying to describe the course of my life, I have often had in mind the streams of Maine, with their amazing alternation of rapids and pools, of currents and backwaters, their seductive murmur and their terrifying roar.

As I bring my narrative to a close it is the terrifying roar of a world war which drowns all the other sounds and almost quenches the memory of peaceful days. Nevertheless I retain my optimism. Just as I am confident of personal immortality so I believe that through the grave and gate of death America will pass to a joyful resurrection. Perhaps it is only wishful thinking, but my belief is that as America goes so will go the world.

Independence Hall—designed by
Andrew Hamilton, lawyer and artist.

To
Andrew Hamilton
and all other
Philadelphia Lawyers
Past and Present

ACKNOWLEDGMENTS

Some of the material in this volume originally appeared in *The Saturday Evening Post* and, later, in a small book called *In the Senate*. For permission to use it, I am grateful to the Curtis Publishing Company and to the University of Pennsylvania Press.

CONTENTS

PART ONE

> "Sing me a song of a lad that is gone;
> Say, could that lad be I?
> Merry of soul he sailed on a day
> Over the sea to Skye.
>
> "Mull was astern, Rum on the port,
> Eigg on the starboard bow;
> Glory of youth glowed in his soul:
> Where is that glory now?"
>
> —ROBERT LOUIS STEVENSON

> "I heard a little water—and, oh, the sky was blue:
> A little water singing as little waters do."
>
> —R. C. LEHMANN: *Singing Water*

> "He that had never seen a river imagined the first he met to
> be the sea."
>
> —MONTAIGNE: *Essays*, Bk. 1, c. 26

PART TWO

> "Shallows where a lamb could wade and depths where an
> elephant would drown."
>
> —*Matthew Henry's Commentaries*,
> "Of Solomon's Song"

"When the sea is calm the careless sailor relaxes."
    —OVID: *Ars Amatoria*, Bk. III, l. 259

1. REAL WAR

"Know you are *bound to help* all who are wronged—
Bound to constrain all who destroy the law.
What else holds state to state but this alone,
That each one honors the great laws of right."
                    —EURIPIDES: *The Suppliants*

2. SHAM PEACE

"Do not think you are fighting for the simple issue of letting
this or that state become free or remain subject to you. . . .
Your empire is a tyranny by now, perhaps, as many think,
wrongfully acquired, but certainly dangerous to let go."
            —PERICLES—as reported by Thucydides

PART THREE

"The ship of State is a metaphor re-invented by the bourgeoisie,
which felt itself oceanic, omnipotent, pregnant with storms.
That ship was, as we said, a very small affair: it had hardly
any soldiers, bureaucrats, or money. . . . In our days the
State has come to be a formidable machine which works in
marvellous fashion; of wonderful efficiency by reason of the
quantity and precision of its means. Once it is set up in the
midst of society, it is enough to touch a button for its enormous levers to start working and exercise their overwhelming
power on any portion whatever of the social framework."
        —ORTEGA: *The Revolt of the Masses*, pp. 129, 131

1. I GET ABOARD
2. IN THE ENGINE ROOM
3. LEARNING THE MACHINERY
4. INTERNATIONAL UNDERTOW
5. THE ADMIRALS ON THE BRIDGE
6. I AM PUT ASHORE

PART FOUR

"They that go down to the sea in ships, and occupy their
business in great waters;
These men see the works of the Lord, and his wonders in
the deep.
For at his word the stormy wind ariseth, which lifteth up
the waves thereof.
They are carried up to the heaven, and down again to the
deep; their soul melteth away because of the trouble.
They reel to and fro, stagger like a drunken man and are
at their wit's end."

—PSALM 107: V. 23-27

"I knew all the swift importings
On the wilful face of skies.
I knew how the clouds arise—
Spumèd of the wild sea-snortings."

—FRANCIS THOMPSON: *The Hound of Heaven*

"There were pleasant parties and well-ordered homes and nice
lads and jolly hunters in war-wracked Greece. History never
takes account of such pleasantries, but they have their importance. The Greek world would have gone insane if
Thucydides' picture had been all-inclusive."

—EDITH HAMILTON: *The Great Age of Greek
Literature*, p. 210

PART FIVE

ILLUSTRATIONS

The drawings throughout the text are by
the author, except that on page 266, which
is by his son, George Wharton Pepper, Jr.

PART ONE

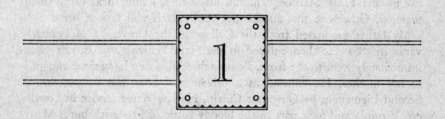

Childhood

"Sing me a song of a lad that is gone;
    Say, could that lad be I?
Merry of soul he sailed on a day
    Over the sea to Skye.

"Mull was astern, Rum on the port,
    Eigg on the starboard bow;
Glory of youth glowed in his soul:
    Where is that glory now?"
                    —ROBERT LOUIS STEVENSON

ALL biographies, whether sacred or profane, are wont to begin with a series of "begats." Following precedent, I record that a Philadelphia merchant, named George Pepper, begat a goodly number of children of whom one, William Pepper, was destined by smiling fortune to become my paternal grandfather. Another estimable Philadelphian, named William Fishbourne Wharton, did the like; and of his sons one, George Mifflin Wharton, became my maternal grandfather. In course of time Grandfather Pepper took Sarah Platt to wife. To them seven children were born, of whom my father, George Pepper, was the eldest. Likewise, in due time, Grandfather Wharton laid siege to the heart of winsome Maria Markoe. While this young lawyer was pressing his suit he wrote her a series of letters, some of which have been preserved and are in my possession. One, dated April 3, 1835, begins "My Dear Friend," but only a week later he is addressing her as "My Sweet Love." Shortly thereafter they were married. It was of this union that my mother, her two brothers and her five sisters were born.

Having thus in my narrative brought my father George Pepper and my mother Hitty Markoe Wharton into being, I must next bring them together. Otherwise this autobiographical sketch will lack a hero.

My father graduated from the College of the University of Pennsylvania in 1862. He then enlisted in the Sixth Pennsylvania Cavalry and immediately went to the front. Before taking this step he became engaged to my mother. He enlisted as a private and later was commissioned Second Lieutenant by Governor Curtin. He saw active service in Northern Virginia and took part in the bloody battle of Fredericksburg. Many of his letters to his father, mother and brother are in my possession. They are characterized by reticence, respecting hardships and dangers, but they are full of the detail of army life. In them my father has much to say about his beloved horses and not a little of the friendly contacts between Union and Confederate pickets. Here and there I find a trace of homesickness and now and then a reference to his fixed determination to win promotion by merit.

Among the later letters is one from my father's warm friend and comrade, Benoni Lockwood. It announced to my grandfather an injury sustained by my father. His horse fell on the ice and the rider's shoulder was dislocated. This was at first thought to be of little moment; and after some time spent in the hospital he returned to duty. However, the ensuing months of active service so greatly aggravated this injury, and so seriously incapacitated him, that an application for discharge became essential. This came through in May of '63 and he was invalided home.

After his discharge from the army he studied medicine at the University of Pennsylvania and graduated in 1865. He and my mother were married at once. Their wedding preceded by only ten days the surrender at Appomattox of the Army of Northern Virginia, against which he had for a time fought. Their first child died in infancy. I was born at 1215 Walnut Street, Philadelphia, on March 16, 1867. My only sister Frances was born some years later. I was baptized April 24, 1867, in St. Mark's, Philadelphia, by the Rector, the Rev. Walter Mitchell. His marine interests were evidently not limited to the waters of baptism because he wrote a poem styled *Tacking Ship Off Shore* which is to be found in the *Home Book of Verse*. It is one of the most spirited sea poems I know.

"SUB-FRESHMAN"

"FRESHMAN"

To be born on Walnut Street used to be, in Philadelphia, an evidence of social acceptability. It was the beginning of a career that might include an invitation to the Assemblies and end with burial in the churchyard of St. James the Less. In my case, however, the distinction was somewhat accidental. The house was the home of my paternal grandmother. My parents were merely sojourning there until they could acquire a home of their own. When they did it was on respectable but socially unexciting Pine Street, a neighborhood in which values were better suited to the slender resources of a young physician.

THE SINNERS OF WALNUT STREET

To mention Walnut Street to an old Philadelphian is to awaken memories of a departed glory. On bright Sundays, after church, there was always an informal parade of fashion on the south side of this thoroughfare. There the City's Four Hundred could be seen to great advantage. They were the blended congregations of half a dozen mid-city churches. They made upon the onlooker an impression of urbanity, of social experience and of entire self-satisfaction. If during church-time they had confessed themselves miserable sinners, by the time they appeared on parade their restoration to divine favor was seemingly complete.

Today the glory of Walnut Street is no more. Shops and apartment houses have replaced the homes of the paraders; and the paraders themselves, or their descendants, are scattered through the suburbs and the countryside beyond. As I look at the vacant city lots now used as parking places it gives me a bit of a pang to recall the fine old mansions which once stood there. The old saying that in three generations an American family goes from shirt sleeves to shirt sleeves might be supplemented by the lament that in a like period many historic homes have gone from dust to dust.

A package of my mother's letters lies before me. Many of them were written when I was only a few months old. They give delightful glimpses of life in Philadelphia in the late sixties. She waxes enthusiastic over Booth and Janauscheck. She looks forward eagerly to an occasional Italian opera. A projected Shakespeare Society is hailed with intense pleasure. And in all her letters are found such references to the charms of the new baby as a young mother might be expected to make. Here is one that is typical: "The baby is perfectly splendid. I only wish you could see him imitate the donkey. It is the funniest thing. He does it until his little throat is so dry he cannot articulate a sound." Such early interest in the Democratic symbol makes my later conversion to Republicanism all the more surprising.

FILIAL HERO WORSHIP

It is hard to resist the impulse to record at too great length my boyish admiration for my father. I still treasure his saber and pistols. His cavalry cloak, which has now seen service for nearly eighty years, I often wear in the evening instead of an overcoat. Although I was under six years old when my father died, I have vivid recollections of him. He had entered upon active practice and there are many evidences that he quickly attained unusual professional distinction. I can recall him distinctly. He was tall and broad-shouldered but slender. He was a superb horseman and I have before me a photograph of him and one of his horses, taken in 1871. He had much artistic talent. His sketches both in pencil and in India ink have unusual charm. One of his India ink drawings was the portrait of his Skye terrier, Wasp. Wasp, by the way, was the first of the many dogs upon which I have lavished affection.

My father never really recovered from the shock of his wartime injury. This predisposed him to the pulmonary phthisis of which, after a lingering illness, he died on September 14, 1872.

My paternal grandmother, Sarah Platt was, it seems to me, as lovable a woman as I have ever known. Her husband, Dr. William Pepper the elder, had died before I was born. His widow lived until after I was married. Her second son was my uncle, Dr. William Pepper the younger, who became in effect a foster father to me after my own father's death.

At Grandmother Pepper's country place at Chestnut Hill we spent the summers until my father died. It was named "Fairy Hill" after the much more notable family estate on the bank of the Schuylkill which had been sorrowfully abandoned when the damming of the river had (as was supposed) made the place malarial. This estate and many like it were afterwards incorporated into the big cemetery, called Laurel Hill. Where Dives had feasted he later slept. To me the lesser Fairy Hill seemed a vast estate. The shaded lane at the far end of the lawn was a region reserved for the fairies. Like other small children, I thought about all manner of things as I lay in bed at night. I remember confiding to my mother that in my opinion the two most sorrowful things I knew were the wind moaning in the trees in winter and a locomotive whistling through the woods at night. I also peopled the darkness with wild beasts and hostile Indians. A generation later, when my own boy was about three years old, I once suddenly turned up the light in his nursery to demonstrate to him that there were no bears present. Like so many demonstrations, however, this one proved unconvincing. "The kind of bears *I* see," he observed, "are the kind that only come in the dark." He, too, had danger zones which he approached reluctantly. "That's an awful dangerous place," he once remarked of a certain spot in my mother's garden at Strafford. Behind her tiger lilies lurked a peril.

My father died before he had had a chance to do more than earn day to day support for his family. After his death my mother and her two small children lived for a while with my maternal grandmother, who was then a widow. Grandmothers of today wear sport clothes and play tennis. In my youth, however, they appeared in pretty lace caps and wore immaculate kerchiefs crossed upon their bosoms. Of this type were Grandmother Wharton and her mother Hitty Markoe. I have a fine portrait of the latter painted by Sully in 1835 when she was fifty years old. My only picture of her daughter, my grandmother Wharton (other than a vivid memory of her as an old lady with cap and curls) is one painted when she was a young girl. With her hair built high upon her head and a wealth of material in bodice and skirt she appears to have been most entrancing. The family tradition is that she kept her suitor waiting a long time before that final week in which she suddenly surrendered. It appears not to have been an unconditional surrender, however; because according to the same tradition she held out until the suitor promised to be baptized and confirmed in the Episcopal Church.

HOMEWORK

After Grandmother Wharton's death my mother must have inherited a little money because she acquired a small house, 346 South 16th Street, and there, under conditions of utmost simplicity, my childhood was spent. Trouble with my eyes made it necessary for me to get most of my instruction orally, and my mother was for years (except for some French lessons) my only teacher. She was a woman of generous culture. She had read much and with discrimination. She was a convinced believer in the importance of verbal memory and she encouraged me to learn by heart many portions of the Bible and of the Book of Common Prayer, including many of the Psalms and a very considerable amount of poetry. She was a lover of music and had a strong and clear soprano voice. I have been told that during the Civil War she brought many an audience to their feet by her singing of war songs. Scotch ballads were favorites with her and she led me to memorize many of them. I also learned many of Aytoun's *Lays of the Scottish Cavaliers* and Macaulay's *Lays of Ancient Rome*. My valued friend Judge Learned Hand shudders at the mere mention of the *Lays* which to this day I like to repeat. However, he and I agree about Gilbert and Sullivan and when American Law Institute sessions become a trifle dull we often hum snatches from the operettas with much satisfaction to ourselves.

While I was led by Mother to take a deep interest in literature and in language as a vehicle of thought, my training in mathematics was most defective. Language consciousness has been of immense value to me in the teaching and practice of law. On the other hand, I have had to struggle to develop what mathematics would have stimulated, namely, a greater capacity for abstract thought.

As a boy I read much whenever the condition of my eyes permitted and at other times Mother read aloud to me. The arrival each month of the *St. Nicholas Magazine* was eagerly awaited. The Puzzle Box was as enthralling as the puzzle page in the modern newspaper and the stories were literally devoured. Some of them so impressed themselves on my memory that today I can recite large sections of them verbatim. In England Juliana Horatia Ewing was editing *Aunt Judy's Magazine* and publishing exquisite short stories, among which *Jackanapes, Madame Liberality* and *Lob-lie-by-the-Fire* made on me a lasting impression. The magazine itself was altogether admirable. It outranked *St. Nicholas* in quality and rivaled it in power of attraction. Fairy tales, of course, had a large place in my reading. Hans Andersen's tales, Miss Mulock's *Adventures of a Brownie* and Knatchbull-Hugessen's delightful stories were particularly absorbing. *Alice's Adventures in Wonderland* and *Through the Looking-Glass, Robinson Crusoe* and Hawthorne's *Tanglewood Tales* ranked among the leaders. Louisa M. Alcott's *Eight Cousins* was one of the thrillers. Cooper's books, especially the *Leatherstocking Tales,* were a source of unending delight. I recall, too, the thrill that came when I first read *Ivanhoe* and *The Talisman*. A series of books by Harry Castleman in which Frank, the hero, passed through hair-raising experiences in peace and war, had an important place in my little library. *The Boys of '76, Campfires of the Revolution, Campfires of Napoleon* and *Kenneth, or the Rear-Guard of the Grand Army* were particular favorites.

My mother kept my sister and me well supplied with Miss Edgeworth's and Miss Yonge's books. Miss Yonge's *Book of Golden Deeds* was a big help in forming worthy ideals. The style in which some of these books were written would seem stilted today but then it was altogether satisfying. My heart beat fast when, in *The Children of the New Forest* Edward, the young Cavalier, instructed to deliver a letter to a Roundhead, encountered Patience, the lovely Puritan maiden. As he was leaving she held out her hand and this time "Edward, like a true cavalier, raised it respectfully to his lips. Patience colored a little but did not attempt to withdraw it; and Edward, after a low obeisance, quitted the room." I quote from memory, not having seen the book for sixty years. But the quotation is accurate enough to mark the contrast between the thrill which such an incident then aroused and the ridicule with which modern youth would greet this account of it.

Fortunately I had little sense of isolation from other boys. There were many boys in our neighborhood with whom I played in the afternoons. One of them, a colored boy, named Willie Ryder, I considered my best friend. There was also, within a few yards of our house, a small "prep" school for boys and I quickly got on friendly terms with many of the students. I found out what they were doing in class and reported to Mother. She and I took some satisfaction in trying to outdo them. At the school they had adopted a mnemonic system devised (as I recall it) by a man named McHarg. He had a test of verbal memory in the form of the familiar nursery story of *Beauty and the Beast* translated into words beginning with "F." It was called "The Far-Famed Fairy Tale of Fenella." It began thus: "A famous fish-factor found himself the father of five fine flirting females—Fanny, Florence, Fernanda, Francesca and Fenella"—and so on, at great length. I took to Mother the leaflet containing the test and delighted her by memorizing the story within the time-limit but without the aid of the system.

I used to amuse myself by associating historical dates with the street numbers of certain houses. Thus 1215 Walnut Street, where I was born, is permanently associated in my mind with Magna Charta. 333 South 16th Street, the house of a friend, is paired with the battle of Issus. Marlborough's victories corresponded with numbers on familiar houses on Walnut Street above 17th. The date of Washington's birth and of many other historical events still have for me some such whimsical associations. In later life I have tried the same system with telephone numbers but they are for the most part too big and do not lend themselves to this use.

PHILADELPHIA IN THE SEVENTIES

Philadelphia in the early seventies was an overgrown village, badly paved and badly lighted. Our playground was the street.[1] It is true that we were little disturbed by the carts and carriages which passed now and then or by the semioccasional horsecars. But narrow streets, brick pavements, cobblestones and the protests of angry neighbors seriously complicated baseball games and marred attempts to do some roller skating on the few sidewalks smooth enough to be tempting. When I say "cobblestones" I mean it: not Belgian blocks but big pebbles, about the size of a 16 pound shot. The nearest city park, Rittenhouse Square, was surrounded by a high iron fence, the gates of which were padlocked at sundown. During hours of access the place was made pretty nearly intolerable for children by a custodian who kept us off the grass, sprinkled ashes on our slides and in general interfered with the normal use of the place as a playground for the children of the neighborhood. Nevertheless we managed to have a lot of fun there and I associate with the place the first thrill of loyalty that I ever experienced. Some twenty or thirty boys were wont to gather in the square astride velocipedes and primitive bicycles. We organized a troop and one of our number was chosen captain. One day somebody started a mutiny and tried to persuade some of us to secede from the organization. Our captain faced the hesitating crowd, reminded us that we had chosen him leader and called on us to follow where he led. He then wheeled about and started across the square. I shall never forget the flame of enthusiasm which instantly swept through me as we all wheeled into line behind him. I think it must have been of the same sort that Napoleon enkindled in Marshal Ney.

In 1876 a great change occurred and Philadelphia suddenly became a city. The Centennial Exposition was well-conceived and the plans were effectively executed. As a child of nine, I of course did not appreciate its significance. For me it was just a matter of parades and bewildering spectacles. A few things I recall distinctly. One was my glimpse of General Grant as he rode in an open carriage, the central figure in a great military demonstration. Another was the scene in one of the exhibition buildings when Alexander Graham Bell and his staunch supporter, the Emperor

[1] In later years vivid recollections of the conditions under which as a child I had to spend my playtime quickened my interest in playgrounds and in the Boy Scout movement.

Dom Pedro of Brazil, demonstrated the practicability of the telephone.'

In 1876 my mother married a second time. Her husband was Ernest Zantzinger, a member of the Philadelphia Bar, who had been Father's friend and classmate. This marriage too was a happy one. My stepfather was a man of culture and of deep religious convictions. He had caught the spirit of the Tractarian Movement which, originating in England in 1833, had profoundly affected religious life and thought on both sides of the water. He and my mother had similar religious convictions and were alike in their devotion to music, literature and art. He was, however, excessively shy and retiring. This reserve to some extent tended to quench my mother's natural gaiety and greatly restricted her social activities. It also prevented my sister from entertaining young people at home and seriously interfered with her opportunity to make new friends. Mother, however, never ceased to be a delightful companion and a lovable and inspiring personality.

CHURCH TRAINING

Mother was a woman of deep religious conviction. Her father, brought up as a member of the Society of Friends, had become a member of the

² Although I did not know it at the time, this incident had a dramatic background. The Emperor, during a visit to Boston, had been much interested in work that Bell was doing for children handicapped by speech impediment or by deafness and had spoken kindly to the young teacher. Soon thereafter Bell, who was laboring to perfect his telephone, had tendered his invention to the Centennial authorities. It was accepted and he was notified that the judges would pass upon its merits on a certain Sunday. All day he stood beside his precious instrument. Late in the afternoon Sir William Thompson and the other judges reached his part of the great building. To Bell's dismay, however, they decided to adjourn for the day after inspecting the very next exhibit to his. This was the death of all his hopes as he had made his arrangements to leave for Boston that night to keep faith with the members of his college class. It so happened, however, that the Emperor was in the group of judges and just as they were about to separate his eye fell upon Bell whom he recognized as his young Boston acquaintance. His cordial greeting gave the anxious inventor a chance to explain the situation. At once Dom Pedro asked the judges to make one more inspection. This they did and found themselves in the presence of the greatest invention of modern times. Years later, when I was representing the Senate on the Board of Regents of the Smithsonian Institution we celebrated the centenary of Bell's birth. As a bust of the inventor was being unveiled, the scene at the Centennial came again before my mind's eye. I realized that I was a witness both of the beginning of his career and of the crowning of its successful end.

Episcopal Church when he married my grandmother and he gave all his children regular and thorough religious instruction. St. James's was his parish and he represented it in Diocesan Convention. My father and mother, however, became parishioners of St. Mark's and St. Mark's has been my parish all my life.

The church structure, newly built, naturally attracted the younger generation. A site at Sixteenth and Locust had all the charm of the frontier: nothing much west of it but great open spaces. All of these spaces except Rittenhouse Square were quickly dotted with dwellings now replaced by shops and apartment houses. These in their turn have been thrown into shadow by surrounding skyscrapers. Today the once conspicuous steeple of the church rises only to the level of the lower windows of nearby office buildings. "It looks," someone has said, "like a lily in a canyon." Sometimes I wonder whether this is not an allegory and whether material interests have not for the time being cast eternal verities into shadow.

As I look back over my early childhood, I realize how powerfully my whole attitude toward life must have been influenced by Mother's precept and example. I suppose a cynical onlooker would say that I then and there became a narrow little Episcopalian. If so, later experience sufficed to widen my horizon. But I certainly have never outgrown the teaching that fixed beliefs are the foundation of a happy life and that in the Book of Common Prayer is enshrined the beauty of holiness.

Even as a small child my training must have given me a rigorous sense of decorum. On one occasion, although under seven, I was trusted to take my small sister to church. When a hymn was announced and the singing began, my sister, to my horror, in a clear childish voice, piped up a nursery song with which we were familiar, *Pretty Polly Perkins of Abington Green*. She refused to be hushed and I reported the matter to Mother. She sided with my sister but I insisted that we should consult Dr. Harris, in whose church (St. Paul's, Chestnut Hill) the disturbance had occurred. He too ruled against me, and assured me that God would accept such an unusual but well-meant offering. Then I was satisfied. I had carried the case to the court of last resort and I bowed to an adverse decision. If Franklin Roosevelt had had a similar training I doubt if he would have attempted to pack the Supreme Court.

My sister and I were, of course, often restive under discipline. We, however, always sought redress within the law. For years a saucer of oatmeal was an indispensable part of our breakfast. Growing very tired of it, we decided to agitate for relief. I drew up a petition to Mother in a form I had somehow happened upon in which we, the petitioners, prayed to be dispensed from eating oatmeal on Sundays, saints' days and holidays. The document was an impressive one, carefully written in black ink with initials in red. My sister and I signed it and solemnly presented it. The prayer of the petition was duly granted and so we rejoiced in our exercise of the constitutional right to assemble peaceably and petition for redress of grievances. Thus was another step taken in the training of a reactionary.

On Easter Even 1879 I was confirmed in my parish church, St. Mark's. Years afterwards I came to know Dr. Russell H. Conwell, Pastor of the Temple Baptist Church and Founder of Temple University. Contrasting the rite of confirmation with adult baptism by immersion, he once remarked to me that the former constitutes no such test of earnestness as does the latter. "It is one thing," he said, "for a young person, becomingly dressed, to be made an object of emotional interest to admiring relatives and friends and quite another to be willing to stand up and make a spectacle of yourself before the congregation." In this observation there is a profound truth. If it is merely a test of earnestness that is desired, I see no answer to Doctor Conwell's suggestion. Certainly I do not think that confirmation subjected me to any such test. It was simply a step in orderly church life and I took it in my stride. I even forget whether I initiated the step or whether my mother suggested it.

WAR AND OTHER THINGS

Listening to sermons was a less exciting experience than watching a war—even if the watching had to be done at long range. *The Illustrated London News* carried pictures of incidents in the Russo-Turkish War of 1877 and for me these had an absorbing interest. I waited eagerly for the arrival of the weekly magazine and I studied the illustrations until they were permanently printed on memory.[3] I used to pore over bound volumes of *Punch* in my Grandmother Pepper's library, and in Leach's drawings I found glimpses of the humor and charm of English life, and from the political cartoons I learned a lot of English history.

[3] This vivid recollection, after sixty years, of pictures in a magazine witnesses to the lasting impression which may thus be made upon the mind of a child. This seems to me to be an educational fact of capital importance. I am thinking, of course, of pictures which can be looked at again and again until they are photographed upon memory. I doubt whether motion pictures leave anything like the same impression, no matter how striking or beautiful they may be.

Even advertisements, in picture and rhyme, may come into a child's mind to stay. In the funny little Philadelphia horsecars of my childhood, the display of advertisements always fascinated me. In 1877, after Tilden had been nominated, and when a third term for Grant was a possibility, I got my political education from streetcar portraits of the two men and from these accompanying verses:

"Come all you true-born Democrats—you sturdy hearts of oak—
Who know a thing when it is good—and Blackwell's Durham smoke.
Gaze on this face and you will see
Your Presidential nominee—
The sage and statesman, S. J. T.

And all you true Republicans will surely be enchanted
When you behold the visage here and take the fact for Grant-ed
That he will win if he shall be
Your Presidential nominee—
The soldier-hero U. S. G.

But while you differ in your views political, we hope
You coincide when we remark the choicest brand to smoke
Is Blackwell's Genuine Durham—that
Suits ev'ry taste—no matter what—
Republican or Democrat." [4]

When President Garfield was shot on the second day of July, 1881, the only thing that really disturbed me, a boy of fourteen, and the children of my set, was the announcement that if he should die before the 4th of July the eagerly-awaited fireworks would have to be postponed. In point of fact he lingered until the autumn, and upon his death Vice President Arthur succeeded him.

Nothing happened in Arthur's administration that at the time affected me. Toward its close I was dimly aware that a political battle was impend-

[4] I often thought of those primitive conveyances when years afterward I was trying cases for the Union Traction Company which substituted for horsecars the cable cars and trolleys, and when, more recently, I have served as consulting counsel for the Philadelphia Transportation Company into which all transit lines have finally been merged. Now that Franklin Roosevelt is serving his third term, it interests me greatly to recall the Grant third-term controversy which was raging when those verses held my childish attention. If they were to be brought to Roosevelt's attention I can imagine with what delight he would proclaim that any limitation on his tenure of office would be as obsolete as a horse-drawn streetcar or an old-time buggy.

ing in which James G. Blaine would make a determined bid for the presidency. But it was not until after I had entered college that the storm actually broke. When in 1888 Grover Cleveland appeared as the Democratic champion I gave him my powerful support, as I had vainly given it to General Hancock in the campaign of 1880. "Support" meant vociferous shouting when political demonstrations took place and occasional roughhousing with Republican reactionaries of school age.

CRICKET AND LESSER SPORTS

Sports were even more fascinating than politics. The old English game of cricket had gained a foothold in the United States before the Civil War. A team of English professionals had visited Philadelphia in 1855 and easily defeated our local players, who at that time were more enthusiastic than skillful. The first international cricket match I ever saw was in 1878 when a celebrated Australian team played in Philadelphia. The game was played on the old Germantown Cricket Ground at Nicetown. Everybody assumed that the Australians would wipe up the field with the local team. I had all the enthusiasm of a novice and all of a boy's heroworship for the players. Breathlessly I watched every play. After the lapse of nearly seventy years I can recall the names of most of the players on both teams and their individual performances.

It was in 1881 or thereabout that I first heard of Gilbert and Sullivan. *Pinafore* and other operettas had made a great hit in Philadelphia. My aunt, Mrs. Thomas McKean, determined that there should be a performance of *Pinafore* by children, and this was actually brought to pass. I was a clumsy member of the crew; but I took great delight in Gilbert's versification. I memorized large portions of many of the operettas. My gleeful recitations of these and of some of the *Bab Ballads* have in subsequent years given more pleasure to me than to those who have had to listen to them.[5]

When college entrance examinations were not much more than a year away, my mother decided that she had carried my preparation as far as she could and that I should have a tutor. As my eyes, though much better, were still far from strong, there was always the possibility that I might

[5] On one such occasion at a Northeast Harbor picnic there was among the guests an English admiral whose ship was anchored nearby in Frenchman's Bay. "What was that you were reciting?" he asked of me. "A bit from one of Gilbert and Sullivan's operettas," I replied. "Do you mean," he inquired with a look of deep disgust, "do you mean the people who made fun of the British Navy?"

have to do much of my preparation through oral instruction. She accordingly selected a blind man, John F. Maher, to tutor me. This was on the theory that he would be (as indeed he was) most resourceful in devising substitutes for the use of the eyes. I studied Latin, Greek and mathematics with him.[6] I passed my college examinations in the spring of 1883.

THE PERIOD OF MY CHILDHOOD IN RETROSPECT

The stream of American life upon the bosom of which I was launched in the late sixties was turbulent enough; yet a frightful Civil War, Lincoln's assassination, a period of so-called "reconstruction" almost as devastating for the South as the war itself, the impeachment of Lincoln's successor—all these breeders of disaster had failed to unsettle the foundations of the Republic or to destroy American self-confidence.

To anybody born, as I was, in the year in which the historic Tenure of Office statute was passed, the record of the ensuing struggle between President Johnson and the Congress is, in retrospect, a matter of especial interest. In my own case this is particularly true, because sixty years later I was called upon to argue [7] before the Supreme Court of the United States, the constitutional point which had been involved in the impeachment.

The power of the President to remove officeholders at his pleasure had in the early days of the Republic been sparingly exercised. Jackson, however, made thousands of removals, and his example was, to some extent, followed by succeeding presidents. It was this assumption of executive power which, in 1867, incited the Congress to pass the statute which, in the case of presidential removals from practically all executive offices, made the consent of the Senate necessary. To test the validity of this effort to curb executive power, President Johnson, without the Senate's consent, proceeded to remove Stanton, his Secretary of War. Thereupon a resolution of impeachment was passed in the House. The Senate sat as a court to try the impeachment. The prosecutors failed by the margin of a single vote to secure the necessary two-thirds majority.

How quickly we forget even the most significant events in our history will become evident, I suspect, if I ask, "What was the Electoral Commission?" One way to find an answer to the question is to visit the Senate

[6] Long afterward, when I was teaching in the Law School, Mr. Maher decided that he would study law in order that he might enlarge the field of his own teaching. He who had been my teacher thus became my student, and a proficient one at that.

[7] *Infra*, page 361.

gallery, in the Capitol at Washington, and study a large painting which you will find there. It portrays the room in which, until recently, the Supreme Court of the United States sat for so many years. The bench is occupied by fifteen men of grave demeanor. The room is crowded to the limit of its capacity by an audience who appear to be listening intently to a speaker addressing the fifteen. Every face in the picture is the portrait of an individual of greater or less distinction. When I went to the Senate, in 1922, the only survivor in the entire assemblage was "Uncle Joe" Cannon, at one time Speaker of the House and at that date still a representative from Illinois. The grave fifteen that you see in the picture are five Justices, five Senators and five Representatives, sitting as the Commission which, by a Congress composed of a Republican Senate and a Democratic House, was created to count the electoral vote cast in the several States for Rutherford B. Hayes and Samuel J. Tilden. The speaker is William M. Evarts, that lawyer of national distinction who, ten years earlier, had succeeded in acquitting his client, President Johnson, in the impeachment proceedings. Here he is portrayed making the argument which led to the decision that Hayes was lawfully elected President over Tilden by the margin of one electoral vote.

The popular vote for Tilden, at the election in November of 1876, had been 4,300,000; that for Hayes, 4,035,000. As time passed and an official count of the electoral, as distinguished from the popular, vote became imminent, popular feeling became more and more intense. Talk of putting disciplined troops in the field to maintain the cause of the rival champions grew in volume and intensity. From what I have read I am satisfied that in January 1877 the country was on the verge of another civil war. Yet when the joint session of the Senate and House adjourned at 4:10 A.M. on March 2, 1877, after accepting the Commission's report, the crisis had passed. A result deemed grossly unjust by half the people was cheerfully accepted. Talk of resistance subsided. It was sixty years later that Franklin Roosevelt sensed danger in five-to-four decisions by the Supreme Court, and fancied that majorities of one would be done away with if he could substitute fifteen justices for nine.

In the late sixties there were economic and social forces quietly at work on both sides of the Atlantic which were destined within my lifetime to make of this old planet an entirely new world. I refer, of course, to the smoldering determination of the oppressed many to challenge the privilege of the dominant minority. In the days of my childhood, however, the existence and operation of these forces were, as far as I can learn, known and appreciated by few. The smug saw no wrong in a grossly inequitable distribution of privilege and opportunity. As far as we in the United States were concerned, the Civil War was over and the business of the moment was to resume a normal mode of living. To this business citizens everywhere addressed themselves and with surprising success. Except as it suited the purpose of political orators and of military biographers to fight battles over again, it appears to have been the effort of most people, at least in the North, to forget the war as soon as possible. As for the orators, Horace Porter at a later date wittily observed that the Democratic Party was the party that did not know the war had been fought and the Republican Party was the party that did not know it was over.

Scanning my early years I am tempted to generalize and to assert that happy childhood makes for conservatism in later years. On reflection, however, I doubt whether this is true. I know many apostles of change whose childhood years were sheltered and happy. I also know some thoroughgoing conservatives who in early youth were notably miserable. If a father lives for his children he normally wishes for them a repetition of his own happy childhood or an avoidance of his own early misery. But whether he will ascribe his past happiness to a certain social and economic order, or blame that order for his misery, depends upon facts of infinite variety. Moreover, if changing the old order seems on the whole the more hopeful course, there still remains the question of the rate of change. I have seldom met an impatient conservative or a patient liberal.

Student Years

"I heard a little water—and, oh, the sky was blue:
A little water singing as little waters do."
—R. C. Lehmann: *Singing Water*

In 1883 preparation for college entrance examinations more and more absorbed my energies and interest. It was predetermined that I should go to Pennsylvania. Those were days when the son went to his father's college pretty much as a matter of course. In our case the ties that bound us to the University were unusually strong. My grandfather Wharton had been a trustee and my grandfather Pepper a professor in the Medical School. My father, my stepfather and my uncle, Dr. William Pepper, had not only graduated from the College and its professional schools but had all been members of the same Greek-letter fraternity. Moreover, my uncle William had recently been elected Provost of the University. Somebody, in speaking of the Pepper family in relation to the University, has remarked that it has not been a mere succession but a dynasty.

If my early surroundings tended to develop provincialism, I soon outgrew it. This was particularly true respecting social distinctions. Students at Pennsylvania, in my day, were looked down upon socially by students at Harvard, Yale and Princeton. Athletic relations with those institutions were for this reason rarely satisfactory. What many disliked but what seems to me to have been wholly desirable was the fact that Pennsylvania was America in microcosm. Family and wealth counted for nothing. Everybody stood upon his own merits.

College life was for me an unalloyed delight. Never having gone to school I spent on the college a double portion of youthful enthusiasm and loyalty. Although only sixteen I was strong and in vigorous health and able to stand heavy strains. My eyes suddenly got well and have never since given me trouble. I entered into every possible college activity with what must have been almost ridiculous zeal. I delighted extravagantly in my classmates, with a score of whom I at once became intimate. I was fortunate enough, in September 1883, to be taken into Zeta Psi, my father's fraternity. I made up my mind to study for honors. I came out for the freshman football team and crew and gained a place on each. In the spring of freshman year I went in for track and field sports and began training for the half-mile run and the hammer-throw. All this must sound absurd to those who know only the highly specialized athletics of today. In those days, however, the student body was small (my class numbered only one hundred and sixty-seven) and everybody physically fit was expected to try his hand at everything.

I was fortunate enough to have in my class many men with whom it was an inspiration to work. George Flowers Stradling, William Romaine Newbold, James Alan Montgomery, Oliver Huckel and a dozen others generated an atmosphere that was essentially scholarly. Stradling was a mathematical genius; Newbold took more pleasure in intellectual work for its own sake than anyone I have ever known. Montgomery, with a remarkable gift for language, was not only proficient in Greek and Latin but became a master of Hebrew and Sanskrit as well. A direct descendant of William White, first Bishop of Pennsylvania, he entered the ministry of the Episcopal Church and became a teacher in the Philadelphia Divinity School and Graduate Professor of Hebrew and Aramaic in the University of Pennsylvania.[1]

Huckel introduced me to Walt Whitman and quickened my love of poetry. These men were not mere "grinds" but delightful companions.

Newbold after graduation became Professor of Philosophy in the University.[2] He was a deeply religious man. His was a character of utter

[1] His published writings have taken high rank in the world of scholarship. He is gifted with charm of style and casts his material into admirable literary form. It is one of my satisfactions in life that a son of his, James Alan Montgomery, Jr., has become one of my junior law partners.

[2] He attracted world-wide attention by deciphering the code in which the Voynich Manuscript of Roger Bacon was written. At the time of his death he was finishing a book (later edited and published by Professor Roland G. Kent) in which he described the cipher and set forth his conclusions. Some conception of his pure love of learning may be gained from the fact that he left in manuscript most elaborate and exhaustive notes to the Metaphysics of Aristotle written, I suspect, chiefly for the joy of the work.

simplicity and he had the humility of a truly great scholar. We had many long and earnest talks about Biblical study. I had accepted unquestioningly all traditional views respecting the authorship of the various books. He convinced me of the unsoundness of much that I had taken for granted. I remember how genuinely astonished he was when I admitted that I had really supposed St. Paul to be the author of the Epistle to the Hebrews.

Two of my classmates, Witmer Stone and Frank Keeley, were true nature-lovers and keen observers of life in the woods. Stone entered the service of the Academy of Natural Sciences, and at the time of his death in 1939, ranked high among ornithologists.

Our college curriculum in freshman year and thereafter would doubtless nowadays be regarded by expert educators with indulgent contempt. Those of us preparing for the degree of bachelor of arts had only five courses—Greek, Latin, English, History and Mathematics.

THEN AND NOW

Compared with the college life of my grandsons mine was highly concentrated. Automobiles and telephones had not made going and coming so easy. There were no movies to entertain us and no radios to enlarge our horizon. The young people of today know much more about current events than we did and have wider extracurricular interests. If we in our day learned more about the past they certainly know a lot more about the present. If they could have listened to our talk I am sure they would have dubbed us intellectual isolationists. They are socially more mature than we were. I suspect that they will become useful citizens much more rapidly than we did because their postcommencement world differs so little from their undergraduate experience. Whether they would be the better for a little more past and a trifle less present I am not able to say; but that we knew far too little about our contemporary world becomes more and more obvious to me as I grow older. We lived in a self-satisfied age. What we suspected to be amiss in the outside world appeared remote and altogether beyond our control. We were generally content to limit our dreams of reform to whatever within the University seemed to call for cautious criticism.

The contrast between then and now is as marked among teachers as with students. Our professors were more learned and less sophisticated. Living largely in the past they seldom expressed themselves on current issues and made no effort to influence our political or social views.

Among my teachers those to whom I owe most were Francis Aristides Jackson in Latin; Morton W. Easton in Greek; George S. Fullerton in Logic and Philosophy; and John Bach McMaster in American History. Professor Robert Ellis Thompson, in the field of economics and sociology, was witty, widely-read and as charming as only an Irishman can be. He was one of those teachers whose assigned subject is merely a starting point for stimulating discussion in a variety of fields. His teaching was exceptional in that he did not hesitate to be a partisan. Thus he tried hard to convince us that the protective policy was the only one for us to accept. The laissez-faire school came in for no end of caustic criticism.

These men managed to arouse in many of us a real intellectual enthusiasm. Jackson was as stimulating a teacher as I have ever met. His enthusiasm for Latin was whole-souled devotion to art. He admired Livy as a historian and he was happy in the companionship of Horace and Juvenal. Tacitus and Cicero were his friends. But it was their use of language in which he delighted rather than in the men themselves. A Latin word in his estimation was a thing of dignity and beauty, to be treated with respect and translated with something like a caress. The student who proved able to get his point of view became his friend and was ever after treated with indulgent injustice. In my freshman year we were reading Livy. When he first called upon me to recite he asked me to translate the first part of the XXI book in which occurs the account of the second Punic War. From some upperclassman I had learned that for Jackson *vis* meant power of attack and *robor* strength of resistance. When in translating I used those words to characterize the warfare between Hannibal and the Roman people Jackson's grim features relaxed and he fairly beamed appreciation. From that moment he treated me as if I were really worth teaching.

In our freshman year the college paper was the old *University Magazine*. Many of us had the temerity to think that it had ceased to be an adequate student organ. A mass meeting was accordingly called to consider the launching of a new paper. At this meeting I drafted and introduced resolutions providing for the publication of a newspaper to be called *The Pennsylvanian*. This was a daring proposal for a freshman to make but, notwithstanding their source, the resolutions were adopted and publication began the following year. I was elected an editor in both sophomore and junior years and editor in chief in my senior year. The paper, now a daily, was at first a weekly. We passed through the usual vicissitudes of college journalism, but finally established the paper on an enduring basis. Our office, in College Hall, was scarcely larger than a coat closet. To its equipment I contributed a huge pewter tankard won in a tennis tournament. It soon became the duty of the junior editor.to get this noble receptacle filled with beer at Otto's, a neighboring tavern, and carry it back foaming for the inspiration of his betters. It was good beer and it tasted all the better because to bring liquor on the premises was something in the nature of a felony.

AN ECHO OF GETTYSBURG

While Doctor Pepper was Provost he was wont to assemble many in-teresting people at his dinner table. In those days he lived at 1811 Spruce Street, where two Philadelphia dwelling houses had been thrown into one. To his office on the ground floor came throngs of patients who quickly developed a confidence in him due partly to his great medical knowledge and partly to the spell of his personality.

He was a charming host and in his home literally radiated hospitality. On one occasion he was giving a dinner to James Russell Lowell when, at the last minute, another guest sent word that he could not come. To fill the place at the table Doctor Pepper hurriedly sent for me. As I took my seat beside Judge Craig Biddle I asked whether he objected to thir-teen at the table. "No," he replied, "unless the hostess has made prepara-tion for only twelve." During the dinner Mr. Lowell raised the question whether anybody present had ever heard a speech so eloquent that he was transported during its delivery and entirely deprived of his capacity to criticize. With one exception all declared that they had never heard such a speech. The exception was Judge Biddle. He had heard one such. It was Lincoln's Gettysburg Address. Pressed to relate his experience the Judge gave a fascinating account of it. He described the place, the crowd, the platform, the speakers. What Edward Everett said he barely remem-bered. When Lincoln rose to speak he came forward slouching somewhat and with the air of a man about to tell a funny story. There was an uneasy movement in the crowd. Suddenly Lincoln stood still and appeared to grow in stature. He began to speak in a voice which suggested intense but suppressed emotion. Instantly all movement in the audience ceased and perfect silence fell. The Judge felt himself lifted from the earth and seemed to be poised in space. Each of the speaker's words burned itself into his consciousness. Presently he realized that the speaker had ceased speaking. Lincoln shrank to his former height and returned to his seat with the air of a defeated man, evidently attributing (as the Judge thought) the perfect silence of the crowd to the failure of the speech to impress them. The Judge was of opinion that all others, like himself, were in fact spellbound and that it was an appreciable time before they returned to earth.

I assume that Judge Biddle's tribute to Lincoln was music to Lowell's ears. He had written a discriminating appreciation of the great War President when criticism of him was loudest and when it required courage to express admiration. It meant a great deal to me to hear such talk as that dinner-table conversation. I was particularly delighted to see Mr. Lowell as I was familiar with *The Biglow Papers* and with many of his poems and had occasionally recited *The Country Courtin'*. He was one of the relatively few authors who upon acquaintance fully measure up to expectations.

A book that made a great impression upon me in college days was Shorthouse's *John Inglesant*. If it were not to be regarded as an affectation I should like to have on my tombstone the perfect epitaph which was carved on Inglesant's: *Sub marmore isto Johannes Inglesant, Peccator, usque ad judicium latet, expectans revelationem filiorum Dei.*

BOY MEETS GIRL

In the summer of 1884 we sojourned at Lake Minnewaska, in Ulster County, New York. Among the exceptionally cultivated and agreeable people who gathered there were Dr. George Park Fisher of New Haven and his daughter Charlotte Root Fisher. He was Titus Street Professor of Ecclesiastical History at Yale and a Congregational clergyman of great distinction. His wife had died many years before and he and his daughter were most congenial companions. I was irresistibly drawn to her from the moment of meeting. He had written and was about to publish his *Outlines of Universal History* and she was making the index. I volunteered my help and she and I spent many hours together ostensibly occupied in index-making. Although I was not yet eighteen years old and entirely without means of support, I nevertheless opened my heart to her and somehow succeeded in arousing her interest. Before we parted we had reached an understanding which in due time ripened into an engagement. This, of course, could not be (and was not) formally announced for several years. In the interval we did a vast amount of letter writing and I was supplied with a powerful incentive to make the most of college opportunities.

Professor Fisher was one of the most delightful men I ever met. Of old colonial stock, he had been born in Wrentham, Massachusetts, in 1827.

He had graduated at Brown in the Class of '47, had prepared for the ministry at Andover and had studied at the University of Halle. On his return from Germany he had taught school for a while at Worcester and thence, in 1861, had been called to Yale. He was a deep student of history and theology. His *History of the Reformation* is one of several of his books that have been translated into Oriental and other foreign languages. His *History of Christian Doctrine* has maintained a place high on the list of the products of American scholarship. These are only a few of his many writings. He was a profoundly religious man and though he had definite theological convictions was never a polemic. He had remarkable calmness of judgment and a nice sense of historical perspective. His was a seemingly inexhaustible source of anecdotes, most of them of men and events in the life of New England. I wish it were possible to recount some of them with the added quality given by his voice and expression. Wendell Phillips, he recalled, was once busily reading on a railroad train when a stranger poked into his hands a religious tract, remarking briskly, "My business is to save souls from hell"; to which, without looking up, Phillips replied, "Go there and attend to it."

Stories about old-time New England lawyers were among Doctor Fisher's favorites. Such was one of old Roger Minot Sherman, who in the course of an argument in court, declared that his listening adversary could no more make good an attempted distinction than he could split a hair with a penknife. His adversary, plucking a hair from his own beard and splitting it with an exceptionally sharp pocketknife, silently held it up to the speaker. Sherman glared at him and exclaimed, "I said a *hair,* sir—not a bristle."

Doctor Fisher's house in New Haven where his daughter presided was a gathering place for men of culture who came both from Europe and from all parts of America. Edward A. Freeman, the English historian; George Adam Smith of Aberdeen; John Brown of Bedford (the biographer of Bunyan); Dr. John Watson (Ian MacClaren); James (afterward Lord) Bryce; Dean Stanley of Westminster; Doctor Freemantle, Canon of Canterbury and Dean of Ripon, are among the visitors from abroad whom I recall.

Freeman was something of a boor. On one occasion his bad manners at some social gathering had irritated Professor Thomas Lounsbury who had been at pains to show the distinguished visitor the utmost consideration. Lounsbury immediately afterward burst into Professor Fisher's library exclaiming, "That man Freeman strongly resembles an Anglo-Saxon swineherd." A shout of laughter greeted this explosion, for it happened that just before Lounsbury entered those present had agreed that the bearded Freeman and the bearded Lounsbury looked strikingly alike.

Among Doctor Fisher's household guests were Phillips Brooks, President Eliot of Harvard, President Seth Low of Columbia, Andrew D. White, sometime president of Cornell and for a while our diplomatic representative, first at St. Petersburg and then at Berlin. Mr. White talked interestingly of his German and Russian experiences. He had happened to arrive at St. Petersburg in time to attend one of the Czar's brilliant receptions at the Winter Palace. As he came down the great flight of marble steps to be ushered into the presence of royalty he was conscious of a feeling of loneliness amid barbaric splendor. Two splendid-looking Nubian guards of immense stature and wearing gorgeous livery made him feel all the more a stranger. What was his amazement when, as he passed, one of them called out cheerily, "How do, Mister White!" The Nubian turned out to be a Southern negro who had been doorman at Mr. White's New York Club.

At Berlin he had received many impossible requests from Americans at home. One of these was accompanied by a package containing a lot of triangular pieces of cloth sent by a western woman who explained that she was making an autograph quilt for a country fair and wanted the Ambassador to secure for her the signatures of the Kaiser and all the members of the Imperial Family. On another occasion an ambitious mother wrote to him asking that her son be selected to execute the equestrian statue of Washington which German citizens were then planning to present to the City of Philadelphia. "He has never worked in bronze," she said, "but has done some beautiful things in butter and putty."

In Doctor Fisher's library you were sure to meet such men of distinction and culture as Edward J. Phelps, our Minister to the Court of St. James, Professor John Weir, President Timothy Dwight and President Arthur T. Hadley. From Doctor Fisher I learned (among other lessons) to set a high value on comprehension of the other man's point of view and I have always tried to heed his injunction to "verify your quotations."

I was unlucky enough, at the beginning of my sophomore year, to fall ill with typhoid fever. I thus lost an entire term and spent the second half of the year in an unsatisfactory effort to make up back work. This I managed to do but sophomore honors of the first class were of course out of the question.

DIKAIOPOLIS

BACK TO ATHENS

In my junior year came the most interesting experience of our college life. Under Doctor Easton's leadership we gave, in the original, a Greek play. Harvard had recently produced the *Oedipus* of Sophocles with marked success. We were ambitious enough to undertake the more exacting task of producing a comedy and we chose *The Acharnians* of Aristophanes. The Protagonist's part, that of Dikaiopolis, was assigned to me. The cast was a large one. The chorus in Greek comedy numbered twenty-four as against half that number in tragedy. The comedy was set to music by Dr. Hugh A. Clark, Professor of Music at the University. At last, in May of 1886, the two long-rehearsed performances actually took place. The Academy of Music was twice crowded to the roof. Everything went as it had been planned. We were elated and Doctor Easton was ecstatic. We subsequently accepted an invitation from Columbia University to repeat the play in New York. This we did the following November at the old Academy of Music in Irving Place. The box office receipts were given to the American School at Athens.

Looking back at our work I imagine it to have been somewhat crude. Much depended upon the principal actor and I know that my rendering of the part could have been greatly improved in many respects. Nevertheless, viewed as an educational experience, the production was highly successful. The strengthening of memory, attention to the use of the voice and the development of a habit of thoroughness were the least of its benefits. The transformation of Greek from a dead to a living language was for many of us a joyful experience. But even more important was the comparison we were led to make between the nineteenth century after the Christian Era and the fifth century before it. With Gilbert and Sullivan's comedies fresh in mind, it was natural that many resemblances to the comedies of Aristophanes should suggest themselves. Years afterward, when reading Edith Hamilton's delightful book *The Greek Way,* I was interested to find that she had not only perceived the resemblances but had justified the comparison by a careful and convincing analysis. Her chapter on "Aristophanes and the Old Comedy" begins with Voltaire's illuminating definition of true comedy as "the speaking picture of the follies and foibles of a nation." With such a picture Aristophanes regaled Athens when the Age of Pericles was coming to an end and with such a picture Gilbert and Sullivan delighted London audiences at the height of the Victorian Era.

SPORTS OF SORTS

Sophomore typhoid and Junior Greek had interfered sadly with the serious business of athletics. Nevertheless, indoor scholastic sports by no means displaced the others. I captained the class football team and the class cricket team for two years, and during the same years played on the Varsity cricket and football teams. I also rowed on our freshman four-oared crew and in junior year on our class eight. In the University handicap track meets I won the half-mile from scratch in 1885 and 1886 and the hammer-throw from scratch in the latter year. This, it must be understood, is a quantitative rather than a qualitative record; I was never a star performer in any branch of athletics but no college player ever got more fun out of competitive sports than I did. A number of my contemporaries were really fine athletes. William Byrd Page, though only 5 feet 7 inches in height, established in the running high jump a record of 6 feet 4 inches, which stood as the world's record for many years. Fred Graham, as a fullback, excelled all his contemporaries and was as great a drop-kicker as I have ever known. All our competitive sport was on a primitive basis. Much of the time we paid for our own uniforms and met our own traveling expenses when playing away from home. This is not recorded as an evidence of superior virtue but merely as an indication that, naturally enough, relatively few people were willing to pay for the privilege of seeing us perform.

In my college days walking trips were a favorite vacation pastime. One of the best was a tramp in June of 1886 through Civil War country. To this we were inspired by the historian John Bach McMaster. Four of us, James Alan Montgomery, Charles Cooper Townsend, Edwards Sanford Dunn and I, walked from the outskirts of Philadelphia to Luray Caverns in Virginia, exploring the Gettysburg battlefield, following Lee's line of retreat through the Fairfield Pass, crossing the Blue Ridge at Buena Vista, visiting the battlefield of Antietam, making our way through the John Brown country in and around Harper's Ferry, and thence through Berryville, White Post, Front Royal and other hamlets to our ultimate destination. We carried packs and bivouacked as we could.

During our walking trip to Luray the cries of the vendors of "relics" at Gettysburg suggested a verse which the old *Life* was lenient enough to print. It was the first literary effort for which I was paid. A check for ten dollars made me proud and opulent.[3]

The first original speech that I ever made was delivered in chapel during February of senior year. Its subject was "Pennsylvania in the War of the Rebellion." If I had realized the vast array of utterances of mine which during fifty years were to follow this one, I might have hesitated to "sound off."

The favorite drinking place for students, and for some members of the faculty, was "Otto's," a gathering place comparable in charm to some of the old London taverns. Here we drank beer and sang lustily and thoroughly enjoyed ourselves. I discovered by pleasing experiment that I could drink heartily without losing my head. "The Widow McGlinchy's," in the city, was a place of the same sort but attended principally by those who liked the reputation of being rather "fast."

Our style in dress was somewhat grotesque. Stiff collars were often worn ridiculously high. Trousers (called "pants" only by the ill-bred) were worn as tight as the size of one's feet permitted. Shoes were pointed. I had a pair with dark green cloth tops in which I extravagantly rejoiced. There were a few wealthy men in my class but most of us were on slender allowances. Some were "working their way through" by tutoring and doing such jobs as were available. My mother was able to allow me three hundred dollars a year, with which I was to buy clothes, meet traveling

[3] This was the jingle as I recall it:

> "You take your stand upon the ground
> Where Hancock fought so well;
> You look with pity at the mound
> That marks where Cushing fell.
> You note the peaceful homes that dot
> The wide historic plain,
> A fascination haunts the spot
> Where Pickett charged in vain.
> You raise your eye and next espy
> Old Round Top's lofty head
> Across the fields now thick with rye
> But planted then with dead.
> Your heart is full; mayhap a tear
> To check in vain you strive—
> When nasal tones salute your ear
> With 'Bullets—two for five.'"

expenses, pay class and fraternity dues and finance my amusements. I supplemented this allowance slightly by tutoring. Fortunately I was always compelled to practice rigid economy. There were times when the sale of secondhand books at Leary's was the only method of financing a week-end trip to New Haven to get a glimpse of my ladylove.

COLLEGE COMRADES

Senior examinations, the preparation of a graduation thesis, the excitement incident to class elections and, in my case, the preparation of the

"OH! THAT GERMAN BEER!"

valedictory for delivery at Commencement, would have kept us busy even had there been no athletic activities in track and field. For my thesis I chose "The Poetry and Prose of Matthew Arnold." This was my most ambitious literary effort up to that time, saving that I had previously prepared for Professor McMaster an exhaustive monograph on Jay's Treaty.

During the four college years I had developed a feeling of friendship with classmates of every type. That they in some degree reciprocated this feeling was shown when they made me "Spoon Man," an honor which had something to do with being well liked. I was lucky too in attaining the grades which admitted me to Phi Beta Kappa. Almost before we realized it, Commencement Day was upon us. Again the Academy of Music was crowded to the roof, as it had been for the Greek Play a year before. My Valedictory was a discussion of what the relationship should be between students, faculties and trustees. Each of us tightly grasped his diploma—curatorum professorumque manibus subscriptum—and realized that we had actually achieved our great objective. We were a bit vague then (and I still am) as to what precisely are "the rights and privileges which throughout the world pertain to this degree." But we were sure that the great world beyond the University was waiting for us and, diploma in hand, we were eager to explore it.

Bidding classmates good-by on Commencement Day proved not to be so sad a business as it had been represented. Parting meant little because confidence in early reunion was so sure. Doctor Pepper had made it possible for me to take, with three warm friends, a three-month trip abroad and we were to sail almost immediately. No wonder that the stretch of still water behind was for the moment almost forgotten. Quick waters ahead had no terrors. Niagara Falls in a barrel might have daunted me but nothing short of that. D'Artagnan on his pony, with his trusty sword at his side, was not a whit more self-confident than I.

LINDBERGH ANTICIPATED

I should like to tell at length how Charley Townsend, George and Charley Frazier and I boarded the good ship *Eider;* how big she looked; how tiny, compared to modern liners, she really was; how charming everybody on board seemed to us to be; how we exercised and ate and slept—in fact all the details which everybody knows and nobody wants to hear.

The crossing in those days took all of nine days, but they passed swiftly. Among the passengers were some interesting Philadelphia Quakers; Robert Pearsall Smith, his young and attractive unmarried daughter and several girl-friends of hers. That I had never heard of these fellow-townsmen of mine was due to the fact that within the limits of Philadelphia we had lived in different worlds. The Quaker community, with its center in Germantown, was as effectually shut off from the social group into which I was born as if between us there had been a Chinese wall. Perhaps the barrier was all the greater because of the circumstance that my maternal grandfather and my paternal grandmother had ceased to be members of the Society of Friends and had been baptized and confirmed in the Episcopal Church. In the Quaker community our fellow passenger and his wife were eminent as preachers and revivalists and were recognized both at home and in England as inspired expounders of Scripture. As the result of a successful business career Mr. Smith had amassed a considerable fortune. At the moment he was headed for London to visit another of his daughters who had married a young barrister named Costelloe. When we struck up an acquaintance with the young people of his party Mr. Smith was careful to interview us and to subject us to a rather severe examination respecting our social qualifications. Apparently we passed because we found ourselves on friendly terms with them and upon arrival in London were invited to a reception at the house of Mr. and Mrs. Costelloe. I was somewhat puzzled, in Mr. Smith's case, by the combination of evangelistic ardor and an attitude not far removed from snobbishness. I was to find confirmation fifty years later for my boyish suspicion that worldiness may penetrate even a Chinese wall, when I read the reminiscences of Mr. Smith's son Logan Pearsall Smith, entitled *Unforgotten Years.* In this most interesting, if rather cynical, volume one reads of the social contacts between the Philadelphia Quakers and prominent English members of their Society.

YEAR OF JUBILEE

About all that we four knew of London hotels was that cricketers were apt to stop at Morley's on Trafalgar Square. We had accordingly written ahead and engaged a couple of cheap rooms. We were dimly aware that in a few days after our arrival there was to be a Jubilee Procession but we knew nothing of its route. Imagine our delight when we discovered that the windows of our rooms commanded an unobstructed view of the most impressive pageant which it has ever been my good fortune to witness.

I think that I should have given myself the sheer pleasure of recording here our impressions of London in 1887 were it not that A. Edward Newton has already done it better than I could. Nearly forty years later I came by chance upon his little volume entitled *The Greatest Book in the World.* At the moment I was in the heat of a bitter political campaign. I was sitting in my library waiting until it was time to board an evening train for a long and tiresome speaking tour. Wondering whether such an output of effort was really worth while, I picked up Newton's little volume and had my attention arrested by an essay called "London in the Eighteen Eighties." There I found his account of all the things that had delighted me, including the very plays that we had reveled in: Wyndham and Mary Moore at the Criterion in *David Garrick;* the musical comedy *Dorothy*—and all the rest. As I read I felt refreshed in spirit. I picked up the telephone, called Mr. Newton and, somewhat to his astonishment I think, thanked him for the service he had unconsciously done me.

THE EUROPE THAT WAS

The days between the Jubilee and our return to Philadelphia in September passed with bewildering swiftness. Old London, Oxford and Cambridge, a row on the Thames from Henley to Windsor, the Cathedral towns, Edinburgh, the Trossachs, Glasgow and a trip through the Cale-

donian Canal to Inverness—all these made vivid and lasting impressions upon us.

I rejoiced extravagantly in all that we saw and heard. The choirs at the Temple Church and the Abbey, at Magdalen Chapel, Oxford, King's College (Cambridge) and at York Minster were among the most beautiful of those that satisfied all the expectations which St. Mark's had kindled in me. I shall never forget the way in which the first lesson was read one day at Evensong in Magdalen Chapel. A splendid-looking young Englishman read with exquisite simplicity and rare impressiveness the story of Ruth and Naomi. The late afternoon sun shining through the stained glass windows added glory to the interior of that beautiful chapel. We, as part of the small congregation, had already been enthralled by the antiphonal singing of the Psalms. Then came the reading of the first lesson. After more than fifty years I can still recall the dramatic beauty of those words: "Whither thou goest, I will go; and where thou lodgest, I will lodge; thy people shall be my people and thy God my God; where thou diest will I die and there will I be buried: the Lord do so to me and more also if aught but death part thee and me."

Here (in the manner of Thackeray) I do some moralizing. Among the tragedies of life we ought surely to reckon the persistent failure of the vast majority of clergymen to read the Bible as it should be read. Out of the hundreds and hundreds of times I have heard the Bible read aloud in church I can count on the fingers of two hands the number of men who seemed to me to do it full justice. Among them I should include three men long since dead: Bishop Doane of Albany, Bishop Brent of the Philippines and Rabbi Krauskopf[4] of the Congregation of Keneseth Israel in Philadelphia.

THE STUDY OF LAW

On the return voyage from Southampton to New York my mind was full of the plans I had made to begin at once the study of law. I had reached this decision only after much consideration. I had been for a long time divided in desire between the church, architecture and the law. Although it was in medicine that my father's family had made their mark, I never had the least inclination to choose that profession. I am not able to make a clear analysis of the reasons that finally controlled me. Much of it was a subconscious process. At any rate I had made my decision before going abroad and my mother acquiesced in it. She had hoped that I would enter the ministry but was partly reconciled to my choice by the fact that the law had been the profession of her father.

In my Grandfather Wharton's day the process of fitting students for admission to the bar made them for the time being members of the preceptor's household. As a very young lawyer he had his office in the fine old Philadelphia house in which Chief Justice Marshall had died. Later when he was married and had a home of his own his office was

---

[4] I was once called upon to make in Rabbi Krauskopf's synagogue an address at the unveiling of a memorial window to Theodore Roosevelt. As Dr. Krauskopf read the twenty-first chapter of the First Book of Kings I realized that never before had I grasped half the significance of the story of Ahab and Jezebel, of Naboth and Elijah. The prophet, standing forth to champion the rights of the common people against the king, was of the sort who cannot die. Nothing will suffice in such a case but that the hero be caught up into highest heaven in a chariot of fire.

in his Fourth Street dwelling. The work now done by clerks and stenographers was then largely done by students. After the semiweekly quiz, which lasted from seven to nine in the evening, my grandfather would lead his ten or twelve students upstairs to the drawing room where my grandmother and her six daughters were waiting to receive them. Somebody would play the piano while the others danced. Cake and wine were

The Crim House (right) where C. J. Marshall died. To the left, my Grandfather Wharton's first Law office.

served and at half past ten the students went home. Mother often told me of these parties with a good deal of amusement. She and her five sisters were associated by the students with the six volumes of Wharton's Reports of Pennsylvania decisions. Each of the girls was given a distinctive number and they were referred to as "1st Wharton," "2nd Wharton"— and so on, in the way that law reports are cited.

Whatever may have been the educational shortcomings of this process it at least had a civilizing influence on the students. The head of the office, himself steeped in the professional tradition, was careful to impart to his students his own point of view. Naturally there were all sorts of offices, some of them far less admirable than others. But at its best the system worked well. The young lawyer came to the bar with a high ideal of his duty to his client and with a respect for the judges which was on the whole well deserved.

By 1887 the process of legal education had become a somewhat haphazard combination of office work and law school education. I was registered with the firm of Biddle and Ward and was also entered as a first-year student in the law school of the University of Pennsylvania. There was increasing co-operation between the offices of the bar and the law school. The race of full-time professors of law was in its infancy. In almost all cases the lecturers in the schools were active practitioners who had a flair for teaching. There really were only two branches of the profession, the practicing bar and the judges. Those members of the bar who did not teach sometimes affected an attitude of amiable contempt for those who did. In court I often used to hear a lawyer refer to his adversary as "my friend the professor" in a tone not intended to be wholly complimentary. I have lived to see the situations reversed.

In the firm of Biddle and Ward, Mr. George W. Biddle was the senior partner. He was an elderly man of distinguished appearance. About a dozen years younger than my grandfather, he had been saturated with the same tradition. He was highly esteemed in the community both for character and professional attainments. His eldest son, George, a lawyer of exceptional ability, had died shortly before I entered the office. The two younger sons, Algernon Sydney and Arthur, were members of the firm. The old dwelling house, 208 South 5th Street, in which they had their offices, had been adapted as well as possible to such a use. Law books were everywhere. Mr. Biddle and his brother-in-law, Mr. Richard C. McMurtrie, had edited an annotated edition of the *English Common Law Reports*. My own desk was surrounded, indeed, almost smothered, by books on crowded wooden shelves. The aspect of the place corresponded to my conception of what a London solicitor's office looks like. It seemed appropriate that the leading decision on feudal tenures in Pennsylvania should have involved a ground rent reserved (i.e., created) upon an early conveyance of this very property. There was an air of settled respectability about the place. Somehow you felt confident that no sharp tricks could ever be played there.

On my arrival at the office, at nine o'clock on a hot September morning, in 1887, Mr. J. Rodman Paul, one of the partners, took me in hand, introduced me to the office force and to the other students, assigned me to a table in a corner of the library and told me to begin the reading of the second book of Blackstone. I at once sat down and gave to the task every ounce of attention that I could muster and for nearly five hours kept my mind hard at work in an effort to master the technical phraseology and to learn what it was all about. At the end of that time Mr. Paul looked in upon me and seemed surprised that I had not gone out to lunch. I went out at his suggestion and, as I walked across Independence Square, my head felt light and dizzy. At Winkler's Oyster House on Sansom above 6th I sat down and ordered an oyster stew but before it came fell over on the sanded floor in a dead faint. When I recovered consciousness I found a waiter and a customer disputing over my prostrate form as to whether in such cases a man's head should be kept higher than his feet—or vice versa. I was all right again in a few minutes, went back to work and for some time kept my rather humiliating experience a secret.

It was natural that my admission to the Biddle office should be most acceptable to my mother. Her father, as I have already said, was a leading Democrat and all my home influence had predisposed me to that political faith. The year that I attained majority I voted for Grover Cleveland for the presidency. I chronicle this fact with some satisfaction because many people have assumed that my Republicanism was a matter of inheritance rather than of mature conviction.

In the office there were ten registered students. One came from Pittsburgh and one from Ohio. The rest were Philadelphians. We were assigned books to read and were quizzed at regular intervals. We were given some of the practical work of the office to do, such as filing papers in the court offices and reporting upon the state of the trial lists.

Our most systematic work, however, was attendance from four to six each afternoon upon law lectures at the University. The law school had been founded by James Wilson, one of the Justices of the Supreme Court of the United States appointed by President Washington. Soon after that it had ceased to function. It was reorganized in 1852 by George Sharswood, later Chief Justice of Pennsylvania. In my day the faculty consisted of J. I. Clarke Hare, who taught constitutional law and contracts; James Parsons, whose subjects were partnership and decedents' estates; George Tucker Bispham, who lectured on equity jurisprudence; Christopher Stuart Patterson, who taught property; and my office preceptor, Algernon Sydney Biddle, whose subjects were common law pleading and evidence. The course of study in the law school covered two years. Both first and second year students attended the same lectures, the subjects being offered in alternate years. Judge Hare, working independently of James Barr Ames, had arrived at the same conclusions as the Harvard scholar respecting the origin and history of the proceeding to recover damages for breach of contract—known to lawyers as the action of assumpsit. Two textbooks, *Hare on Contracts* and *Hare on Constitutional Law,* embody his University lectures on those subjects and were standard works in their day. I took a deep interest in the course on partnership under Mr. Parsons who, in opposition to Mr. Ames, insisted upon the individuality of partners and refused to recognize "the firm" as an entity distinct from its members. In later years, when I had the advantage of close friendship and intimate contact with Mr. Ames, I vainly tried in friendly discussion to dislodge him from his position both with respect to the nature of the partnership and of the corporation. Lamenting to Mr. Parsons my failure, I said, "If only you and Mr. Ames could meet and exchange ideas I am sure that you could convince him, although I cannot." "No," he replied, "discussion between two men of our settled convictions would be useless. We must compete for the allegiance of the next generation."

Mr. Bispham had an orderly mind and a remarkable capacity for clear statement. *Bispham on Equity* is an excellent textbook. One day he quite casually asked me to take every paragraph in that large book and turn it into the form of a question suitable for quiz purposes. This I did, working night after night till the manuscript of a sizable volume was ready. He had this printed and used it for many years. Mr. Patterson did his best to make feudal tenures comprehensible and to elucidate the distinction between executory devises and contingent remainders.

Mr. Algernon Sydney Biddle, as the basis of his courses, used *Stephen on Pleading* and *Stephen (Fitz-James) on Evidence.* With these books many of us grew so familiar that we could reproduce large parts of them verbatim. Our examination in pleading was nevertheless a melancholy experience. I entered the room prepared to answer in the very words of the book whatever question was asked. Unfortunately for us, Algernon Sydney Biddle, after his last lecture and before our examination, had visited the Harvard Law School. Fascinated by Ames's way of teaching, he had prepared for us an examination paper presupposing an entirely different training than we had in fact received. So few of us managed even to scrape through that Mr. Biddle realized what had happened and gave the whole class a re-examination, this time based on what had actually been the course of study. We were warned, however, that thereafter he proposed to conduct his courses on the Harvard system. Unhappily he soon afterward fell ill and died. The

bar thus lost an able lawyer; the school a teacher with contagious enthusiasm; and I personally a kind and considerate friend. His sons have
made the most of qualities inherited from him and his talented wife.

Since we worked partly in office and partly in school, our training
lacked symmetry. Some things we learned thoroughly, some things
superficially and some important things not at all. One of the most useful of my law school experiences was membership in the Sharswood
Law Club. This was (and still is) one of several organizations formed
to help students acquire experience in the argument of cases. The moot
court cases were conducted with the formality of actual proceedings
in court. Either a member of the faculty or a judge or a lawyer of distinction presided. There were also periodic arguments between representatives of different clubs.

The so-called "Harvard system" to which I have referred was nothing more than the laboratory method of the physical sciences applied
to the study of law. Actual cases decided by the courts were treated as
material for analysis. The teacher and the students together sweated
over the evolution of the law. All this was in strong contrast to the
system under which the lecturer revealed to the class the ready-made
generalizations which he alone had laboriously worked out. The trouble
with the lecture system was that the class got the answer without having first wrestled with the problem.

GRAND OLD MAN

The routine of the office was occasionally relieved by some mildly
humorous occurrence. Mr. George W. Biddle indulged the comforting
belief that all Democrats are endowed by the Creator with exemplary
character. The dear old gentleman no doubt would have been gravely
shocked had he heard Chauncey Depew's answer to the man who asked
him how he, Depew, got out of the Democratic party. "Nothing was
easier," Depew is said to have replied, "I quit drinking and I was out."
Democrats, in Mr. Biddle's estimation, were congenitally qualified to
become capable lawyers. He accordingly encouraged the professional
ambitions of a Democrat, no longer young, who had been a police
magistrate in Manayunk, a neighboring town on the Schuylkill apt
to be inundated by spring freshets. He commended the newcomer to
me, as senior student, with a rather solemn guaranty of capacity. Unhappily for Bob, however, his eye was attracted, on the third day of
his apprenticeship, by one of Mr. Biddle's favorite pictures, an immense

photograph of the ruins of the Roman Forum. As bad luck would have it, its admiring owner emerged from his private office just in time to hear Bob say to the office boy, "Jordan, what the hell is that? Manayunk after a washout?" That was the end of Bob's legal studies.

Mr. Biddle's fidus Achates was an elderly clerk named Morris, who enjoyed his unbounded confidence. He was very popular with the students, as he had a dry humor, a moist appetite and the capacity of an excellent mimic. One day a telegram from Pittsburgh announced that the Supreme Court of Pennsylvania had just handed down a decision in Mr. Biddle's favor in a very important case argued a short time before. Morris was at once dispatched to Mr. Biddle's house to report the good news. He was, however, confronted on arrival by Mrs. Biddle, who said that her husband had a cold and could not be disturbed. Morris thereupon explained his errand and announced the victory. "Very proper," said the old lady, "I shall write to the Chief Justice and tell him so." Whereupon, as Morris subsequently reported to the delighted students, Mr. Biddle, listening at the head of the stairs, shouted in tones of thunder, "For heaven's sake, Maria, do nothing of the sort."

CALLED TO THE BAR

There were awarded in the Law School annually several coveted prizes. One was the Sharswood Prize for the best essay by a member of the graduating class, and another the P. Pemberton Morris Prize for the best final examination in practice, pleading and evidence. I went in for both of these and was fortunate enough to win them. I put an immense amount of work into the essay. It was entitled *The Borderland of Federal and State Decisions*. The subject had suggested itself to me during one of Judge Hare's lectures. He was discussing Mr. Justice Story's opinion in *Swift v. Tyson*, in which case the doctrine was announced that federal courts might properly apply, in suits between citizens of different states, their own conception of general commercial law even when at variance with the law of the states of the parties to the litigation. I began to explore the authorities and found the subject fascinating. After the prize was awarded the essay was published and received a good deal of unexpected commendation. My fond uncle, Doctor Pepper, sent a copy of the essay to Mr. Justice Miller, at that time perhaps the strongest man in the Supreme Court of the United States. Young lawyers will appreciate my elation when the following acknowledgment was received from that distinguished judge:

"I have just risen from the reading of it (the essay) with peculiar pleasure. This pleasure may be enhanced by the fact that the writer has taken the same view that I had in regard to the most important points that he discusses, and has referred with approval to my opinions in the decisions of the Supreme Court on those subjects. Apart from this I have been delighted with the clear and vigorous manner in which he has stated views of public matters that deserve serious consideration. The delicacy with which he has treated the Supreme Court of the United States while differing with it in some of its decisions is very commendable. I am charmed with the essay, the only objection to it being that it is too short."

Nearly fifty years later, in *Tompkins v. Erie R.R.,*[5] the Supreme Court of the United States overruled *Swift v. Tyson* and reached the result contended for in my youthful essay. Mr. Justice Brandeis cited it in support of the Court's conclusion. The concurring opinion of Mr. Justice Reed accords closely with the principal contention which I had advanced.

I was asked to deliver the law oration at the University Commencement in June of 1889. As a subject I chose "The Rights of Married Women." I tried to make the subject interesting to a typical commencement audience. But the reward of effort which gave me the greatest satisfaction was my election as Teaching Fellow in the Law School, a position which I held until some four years later I became a full-fledged member of the law faculty.

After finishing law school in June of 1889 I spent the summer vacation with my fiancée and her father at Northeast Harbor, our engagement having been formally announced the year before. Mount Desert Island, the beauties of which I then saw for the first time, was destined to become our summer home.

Fifty years after I had bid the Biddle office good-by I paid a courtesy call on Mr. J. Rodman Paul who, as a partner in the old firm, had fed me my first ration of Blackstone and had conducted many of the office quizzes. There he sat in the modern suite into which in recent years the firm had moved. Around him were the furnishings of half a century before, including a familiar framed facsimile of Magna Charta. "Whatever happened to Morris?" I asked, referring to Mr. Biddle's clerk who in student days had seemed to us already an old man. "Nothing has happened to him," was the reply, "you will find him in an

[5] 304 U.S. 64 (1938).

adjoining room." I gasped. "There were three stenographers in those days," I said, "Miss Shubert, Miss McGarry and Miss McNutt. Whatever became of them?" "They are still with us," he said—and so they were. I doubt whether outside of Philadelphia such a delightful episode would be possible.

The Self-Confident Nineties

"He that had never seen a river imagined the first he met to be the sea."
—MONTAIGNE: *Essays,* Bk. 1, c. 26

IN the autumn of 1889 after returning from vacation I began the life of unremitting effort which I have ever since lived. As an assistant in the office of Biddle and Ward, as a teacher in the Law School and as quiz-master of a number of student groups, I found days and evenings filled to overflowing with interesting work.

In the office, in addition to work assigned to me by the firm, I was at liberty to take any cases that might come my way. One valued client was George Boker, executor of the will of his father, George H. Boker.[1] The testator had been our Minister to Turkey and to Russia. He was a poet and dramatist, whose *Francesca da Rimini* had been successfully

---

[1] His biography, by Edward Sculley Bradley, University of Pennsylvania Press, 1927, will repay reading. George Boker the son was one of those men who, without regular occupation, read much and stored his mind with more or less important facts. Some years after the time of which I am writing an English Colonel spent some months in Philadelphia and caused a good deal of irritation to his entertainers by constantly reminding them (after the manner of Sir Garnet Wolseley) that American military operations were on a small scale compared to those of England. Mr. Boker, having endured this talk as long as possible, finally staggered the visitor by this statement: that in the single battle of the Wilderness in our Civil War the Union loss alone, in killed, wounded and missing, was greater than the whole number of English soldiers killed in foreign wars from the time of William the Conqueror to the outbreak of the Boer War. This statement caused, of course, much spluttering protest but there was no effective answer. I believe it to be correct.

played by Booth. In making contracts for the performance of this play by Frederick Warde after the author and Booth were dead, I had my first contact with the theatrical world. I had been thrilled by Booth's acting in *Richelieu* and had heard from my uncle many interesting personal reminiscences of a man who had been his father's intimate friend.

George Boker had married Edith Wharton, one of my mother's younger sisters, not to be confused with the novelist of the same name. In the social life of Philadelphia she was a person of great influence. She was one of a small group of women who had the making or marring of social careers. To be invited by her to the Dancing Class was a distinction quite as great as to be permitted to subscribe to the Assemblies. She was a woman of much poise and discharged her social duties admirably. Indeed, as I look back at the Philadelphians of her generation many of them seem to me to have had real distinction. Such people are vulnerable to caricature; but they unquestionably established and maintained standards of good manners and exercised a civilizing influence on the younger generation. It appears to me that with their passing Philadelphia lost some of its traditional charm.

My earnings during my first year at the bar were enough to encourage me to get married. Toward the end of that year Bayard Henry, a lawyer ten years my senior, had invited me to share an office suite with him. Thus began a happy association which lasted until his death thirty-six years later. Some months previously my great uncle, George S. Pepper, had died and by his will had left me $10,000. Most of this was invested in a small house at 1711 Pine Street. Although I had no other capital assets it looked as if earnings of $3,000 a year could be counted on. Accordingly on November 25, 1890, we were married at Professor Fisher's house in New Haven by Dr. William R. Huntington, Rector of Grace Church, New York. He was my father-in-law's warm friend. His kindness to us, both then and in later years, we shall never forget.

BRIDE AND GROOM

When after our honeymoon we took possession of our tiny house we found ourselves under the careful guardianship of a kind-faced fat woman whom we had engaged as cook. Coming home after our first dinner party we were met at the door by Winnie who said reassuringly, "You will find everything safe, Mr. and Mrs. Pepper. All the doors are locked—and here is the key of the piano."

My wife and I realized, as much as young people could do, how lonely her father was going to be. Since her mother's death when she was a child, she had been her father's constant companion. He visited us frequently in Philadelphia and my wife paid many visits to New Haven, often going thither to preside at his table when he had some notable guests to entertain.

Doctor Fisher took great delight in poking fun at Philadelphia. "Twenty square miles of brick oven with a cabbage store on every corner" was his impression of our metropolis. "The University of Pennsylvania people are not at all the barbarians that Yale men think they are," wrote my wife after she had begun to feel at home among my friends. "My dear," was her father's comeback, "if you had married a Turk you would be massacring Armenians." All the same he found much satisfaction in his contacts with the people in our circle and he made many lasting Philadelphia friendships.

THE PHILADELPHIA BAR

From 1735, when Andrew Hamilton won in a New York court his battle for freedom of the press in the celebrated Zenger libel trial, down to the time of which I am writing, there had been in Philadelphia a long succession of lawyers learned in the law, resourceful in practice and of commanding influence in the community. I hope that the once-familiar expression "as smart as a Philadelphia lawyer" was suggested by no qualities other than those I have named. I prefer to ascribe the reputation of our Bar to the fact that in colonial days many Philadelphia lawyers studied in the Inns of Court in London, where they sat at the feet of Lord Mansfield. When they came home to practice they brought with them many of the English procedural customs and not a little of the terminology. To this day we older Philadelphia lawyers often speak of "paper books" when we mean briefs; and with us the name of the senior always appears last on the list of counsel.

Even as recently as fifty years ago the Philadelphia Bar was really a fraternity. While its members strove mightily in court, their relations were social and intimate and practice included to no small extent an exchange of courtesies.[2]

[2] That the early Philadelphia lawyers did wisely when they went to London to study has always been assumed as a matter of course. However, when Lord Mac-Millan visited the United States in 1938 and addressed the American Bar Association he suggested that in those early days better legal training was to be had here than overseas. Whether this suggestion was to some extent a gesture of courtesy rather

Two leaders in the Nineties were, I am sure, unique. One of them was Richard C. McMurtrie. The other was John Graver Johnson.

Mr. McMurtrie was, as I have said, a brother-in-law of Mr. Biddle and co-editor with him of the American edition of the *English Common Law Reports*. While he was a deep student of the common law, it was in the application of equitable principles that he found the greatest satisfaction. He had for the law a feeling of loyalty like that of a knight to the lady of his choice. Judicial decisions which seemed to him unsound were resented as insults. I never saw a man who could criticize as bitterly without causing anger or manifest such contempt for stupidity without inflicting serious wounds. His obviously sincere devotion to his cause and the equally obvious absence of anything like malice must have been the explanation. He had none, of the arts of the advocate. He spoke briefly and to the point but expressed himself with almost brutal frankness. To a judge who interrupted him to express dissent, I once heard him say, "Your Honor, I am addressing myself exclusively to those members of the court who do not make up their minds until the conclusion of the argument." Once when appearing before President Harrison to urge the appointment of Samuel Hollingsworth to a federal judgeship, he characteristically forgot where General Harrison had practiced law. "It is well known," said Mr. McMurtrie, "that nobody west of the Alleghenies knows any commercial law." "There may be two opinions on that point," observed the President, smiling. "Possibly," rejoined Mr. McMurtrie, "but only one of them is correct." Hollingsworth was not appointed.

Mr. McMurtrie had been favorably impressed by my graduating essay and this led him to take a friendly interest in me. I have before me a treasured note from him written during my first year at the Bar. It reads thus:

> "Dear Mr. Pepper: Will you do me the favor of selecting a day toward the end of next week or in the following week, avoiding Tuesdays, when you will dine with me at seven at my home 1104 Spruce Street. I will try and get a half dozen persons to meet you."

To this dinner, given in honor of a mere boy, he invited a number of the judges and some practicing lawyers of distinction. I thus acquired, almost overnight, a standing for which otherwise I might have waited

---

than a sound historical statement I am not at all sure. Certain it is that, apart from the legal instruction which they received, those men were profoundly influenced by the London environment in which they studied.

many years. I cannot imagine an act of greater kindness to a newcomer at the Bar by a man in his assured position.

Mr. McMurtrie, like many other gentlemen of his period, took housekeeping seriously and went himself to market. He might be seen on market days with big basket in hand going from stall to stall, as well qualified to select a tender saddle of mutton as an appropriate principle of law.

The other unique figure was John Graver Johnson. He was, all things considered, the most prodigious man I have ever known. Of humble origin, without educational advantages or powerful backing, he had forced his way to the front rank of the profession, where he maintained his commanding position all the rest of his life. He had a big frame and seemed to radiate power. When he entered a courtroom he at once dominated the situation. The judges treated him with the sort of deference more usually shown by the Bar to the Bench. He was a tireless worker and drove himself relentlessly, always carrying home after a long day in the office an old-fashioned cloth bag stuffed with papers to be worked on after dinner. During the daylight hours he was interviewing clients, trying jury trials, arguing before appellate courts, dictating opinions and conferring with members of the Bar who came in ever-increasing numbers to consult him. Prominent lawyers from New York and other large cities were frequently to be seen in his anteroom, waiting their turn to enter his private office. Perhaps "private" is the wrong word to use because his door was always open. Nobody was announced, people in waiting observed priorities among themselves as if they were approaching a box office; and as soon as one person came out, the man at the head of the line went in.

In court he usually selected some one point on which to stake his case and drove it home as if he were hitting a spike with a sledge hammer. He always played fair and never distorted the evidence or misstated an authority. He was, however, in his attitude toward the law, at the opposite pole from Mr. McMurtrie. The latter would rather lose a case than make bad law. Johnson, on the other hand, would take an impish delight in successfully making the worse appear the better reason.

His only interests besides law were baseball and collecting pictures. In pictures he took an extravagant delight. His collection was bequeathed to the city under a somewhat extraordinary will. Its terms indicated that he had given more thought to making the collection than to the plans for exhibiting it. It is a collection of unequal merit, containing a great many pictures of the first order and not a few that are definitely inferior. Of the inferior ones it must be said that in each case they illustrate a stage of the artist's development. Perhaps, quite unconsciously, he reflected his law practice in his collection; for he took cases as they came, making little effort at selection. It is for this reason that his record of cases won and lost throws no light on his capacity. Desperate cases were often brought to him as a last resort: but he fought them all with equal vigor.

Only once and then when I was new at the Bar did he make me wince. On a technical question of equity pleading—the responsiveness of an answer—I had made an overelaborate argument, discussing dozens of cases in law-school fashion, attempting to fit them into categories and to deduce an applicable principle. Mr. Johnson rose as if to reply; looked at me with withering scorn, turned to the Court, uttered not so much as a word but gave a great grunt like a bull moose, gathered up his papers, walked out of court—and won his case. I'm sure he regretted what he had done for he afterward went out of his way to be cordial.

After Mr. Johnson's death, which occurred in 1917, I had a talk about him with Chief Justice White of the Supreme Court of the United States. He said that when he first became a Justice and Mr. Johnson was constantly before the Court arguing cases of all sorts coming up on appeal from various jurisdictions, all the Justices regarded him as by far the most powerful advocate of his day. The Chief Justice added, however (and this at first surprised me) that when later Mr. Johnson argued the great antitrust cases, which in fact gave him his national reputation, all the Justices felt that he was not at his best because he had lived into an economic era which he could not understand. A number of years after Mr. Johnson's death I began to collect some material with a view to a biographical sketch. I wrote to Mr. Justice Holmes and asked him to comment upon such of Mr. Johnson's arguments as had made a lasting impression on him. This was his reply:

"Probably Mr. Johnson never knew how much I liked him when he appeared before us, but I am afraid that I cannot say much to help you. He did not always seem to me to go to the root of the matter or quite to come up to his reputation in Pennsylvania. On the other hand he delighted me by the force and brevity with which he drove home what he had to say. He argued the first case that I wrote on coming to the Bench: *Otis v. Parker*, 187 U.S. 606. The decision was against him, but I was impressed by the intellectual courage that he showed. His argument finished the afternoon and he did not come back in the morning when the other side had their innings. I respected him for it and later

told him so. But I have no specific recollection of his later appearances—
only the general impression that I have mentioned. I am sorry to dis-
appoint you but I have not the kind of memory that some Judges have
who when a name is mentioned can say—he argued such and such a
case, or, when the case is named, say 'Don't you remember Johnson's
argument?' So I have nothing worth quoting or otherwise of use. I am
sorry for I should like to help you in an interesting and noble task.
With the kindest regards, I am

Very sincerely yours,

O. W. HOLMES."

Holmes's reaction to Johnson's failure to return to court while his adversary was arguing was to me rather surprising. I had always supposed
that courtesy to your opponent forbade such a course; and it would have
been my guess that the judges would be irritated by it. I imagine that
what Holmes meant by "intellectual" courage was a certain virility in the
expression of contempt for the other fellow and all his works.

Life for me was now one of intense activity. My practice was growing.
I worked hard on my law school courses, had some private quiz classes
and undertook to write for the *American and English Encyclopedia of
Law* the title, "Pleading at Common Law and Under the Codes." I
worked on this at night. Besides appearing in the encyclopedia, the article
was published in a separate volume.

One of the social diversions which my wife and I as newlyweds most
enjoyed was the Open Question Club. This was a small group of men
and women who met fortnightly at one another's homes for an evening
of discussion of topics of current interest. Agnes Repplier, Talcott Williams, Herbert Welsh, Morris Jastrow and Rodman Paul were among
those who made our meetings delightful. Miss Repplier had already won
for herself an assured position as an essayist. She had a pretty wit and
was well able to hold up her end in any argument. Talcott Williams,
an eminent journalist, belonged to the era when the editorial was a form
of personal self-expression. He had a great fund of accurate information
and it was dangerous to take issue with him on any question of fact.
Herbert Welsh may have been right in his settled conviction that the
government was always wrong. Morris Jastrow, an Oriental scholar and
a man of generous culture, was sure to see the pending question from
some interesting and unexpected angle. Rodman Paul, with a well-stored
mind and a fund of good humor, could always be counted upon to turn
the edge of controversy if it seemed to be growing dangerously sharp.

In 1892, while I was still very young at the Bar, I became a Republican, a father, a vestryman and an editor. To the daughter who was born on March 11th of that year we gave the name of my wife's mother, Adeline Louise Forbes. Throughout life Adeline has been to us such a blessing as is vouchsafed to few parents.

It was of the *American Law Register and Review* that I became an editor, jointly with my friend William Draper Lewis. This monthly magazine had theretofore been styled the *American Law Register* and had at one time been prosperous. We attempted with some success to rehabilitate it and for several years I was a constant contributor to its pages. During this period Mr. McMurtrie used to favor the *Register* with comments upon current decisions which, if published as written, would have broken a good many judicial hearts. The day after the New York Court of Appeals decided the *Tilden Will* case I received by messenger a note from Mr. McMurtrie reading thus: "Please see me at once in regard to this decision. Is anyone competent to decide whether I or Judge Brown is an ass?" I hurried over to his office and on my way met him going in the opposite direction. He was such a figure of a man as Trollope would have delighted to describe or Sir Joshua to paint. I touched my hat and paused to speak. He nodded but did not stop. As he walked past me he observed absent-mindedly, "You need not come. I have decided that it is Judge Brown." Later the periodical was acquired by the law school of the University of Pennsylvania and became the *University of Pennsylvania Law Review*.

In 1893 I was elected Algernon Sydney Biddle Professor of Law, a chair which I held until my resignation in 1910. As I conducted my classroom work by oral discussion with the students, the amount of preparation was necessarily greater than if I had lectured or used a textbook. I think my law school experience was, on the whole, the most satisfying that I have ever had.

I MEET THE OLYMPIANS

In the following year I made my first bow to the Supreme Court of the United States. Mr. Morton P. Henry, a distinguished admiralty law-yer, represented the appellee in a pending case and he had invited me to look up the law and draft a brief. When the case was about to be reached for argument he was taken ill and sent me word that I was to make the argument in his absence. I shall never forget the thrill which the message gave me. There was, however, no time to be lost in self-congratulation. A telegram from the clerk announced that the case would be called for the following day. I had not been a member of the Bar of the Pennsylvania Supreme Court sufficiently long to be eligible for admission at Washington. It occurred to me that in this emergency I might invoke the powerful aid of Mr. George F. Edmunds, then a Senator from Vermont, with a large practice before the Supreme Court. Senator Edmunds had been living for some time in Philadelphia, where a member of his family was under the medical care of my uncle, Dr. William Pepper. In the summer he had been sojourning at Northeast Harbor, Maine. We had gone on many deep-sea fishing excursions together and I had come to know the Senator well. After a morning's fishing, a hearty lunch and a stiff drink of whisky, he was wont to light a long black cigar and before the afternoon's fishing began, to make an eloquent address on the advantages of a protective tariff. Our relation had thus been one of comradeship and I felt sure that he would somehow gain for me a standing to argue my case. With no concern whatever about my sartorial fitness and thinking only of my argument, I hurried to the station, clad in the dark-gray business suit which I happened to be wearing. Reaching Washington in due course I sped to the Senate and stated my case to my influential friend. "Mr. Justice Shiras is from Pennsylvania," he said, "he's the man whose support we must secure." We called that evening on the Justice, who promised to ask Chief Justice Fuller to permit me to be admitted *pro hac vice*—for the purposes of this case only. So far so good.

I spent most of the night working on my argument and the next morning met Senator Edmunds in the clerk's office shortly before the opening of court.

The opening of the Court, always impressive, naturally gave me an exceptional thrill. Eight of the nine Justices (Mr. Justice Jackson being absent) entered with traditional solemnity and with dignity took their several seats, Chief Justice Fuller presiding. All of the eight have long since passed away but the image of each is graven on my memory. The Court being opened the Chief Justice asked if there were any motions for admission. Senator Edmunds was about to rise when a page handed him a note from the Chief Justice. The Senator glanced at it, looked puzzled, beckoned me to follow him and together we returned to the clerk's office. "The Chief Justice advises me," said the Senator, "that the motion must not be made as one of the Justices has objected." We were both mystified but Mr. McKenney, the clerk, quickly explained the situation. The objection, he told us, was based ostensibly on a lack of precedent for a motion for admission *pro hac vice* but really upon the all-too-obvious fact that I was not clad in a black coat. "If you will find a precedent," I said to Mr. McKenney, "I'll undertake to find a coat." He

entered into his search with zest and soon found the record of a case
directly in point. Meanwhile I had cast my eye over the clerk's assistants
and espied a young man of about my size decently attired in a black
cutaway. I proposed a temporary exchange. He readily agreed and in less
time than it takes to write the narrative we marched triumphantly back
into the Presence, the clerk armed with a transcript of the pertinent
record, Senator Edmunds wearing an amused smile and I the borrowed
wedding garment. Having thus overcome all obstacles, we waited confidently for a nod from Olympus. Presently it came; the motion was made
and I was admitted *pro hac vice*. A few minutes later my case was called
and I made my first argument before the Supreme Court.

Some days afterward Mr. Samuel Dickson to whom I told the story
made it his business to inquire from whom the objection had proceeded
and how it came to be made. In a confidence which can now with propriety be violated in view of the great lapse of time, Mr. Justice Brown
explained that immediately after the Justices had taken their seats Mr.
Justice Gray cast his eyes over the courtroom, leaned over to Mr. Justice
Brown and whispered, "Who is that beast who dares to come here in a
gray coat?"

Thirty-five years later Mr. Justice Holmes, having heard of the incident
which I have just described, wrote me regarding an experience of his
own before the Supreme Court of Massachusetts, in the days when Mr.
Justice Gray was a Massachusetts judge. "I had," wrote the Justice, "a
somewhat similar experience. I addressed the Court in a gray sack coat
and a little later was told by a member of the Bar that the Chief Justice
(Gray) had said to him that some friend of Colonel Holmes should tell
him that he ought not to appear before the Court in a gray coat. I have
realized from the Bench that it looks slipshod and neglectful. Gray was
a martinet in such matters but could be magnanimous in more important
things."

"But what about your case?" somebody may ask. I lost it.

Sometimes winning cases and sometimes losing them I found my practice steadily growing. So too was my little family. In January of 1895 a
son was born to us and given my name. He was destined to be to me
throughout life both a companion and friend.

THE ORGANIZED BAR

At about this time the organization of the Pennsylvania Bar Association was taking place. In Pennsylvania, from the earliest days, each of

the County Bars had been leading its own separate and detached existence. Admission to one was not, and even now is not, a passport to any other. The need of establishing contacts between these scattered units was felt to be a real one. Accordingly, the State Bar Association came into being and held the first of its annual meetings at Bedford Springs in June of 1895. Since I had been an active promoter of the movement, principally because of my intense interest in legal education and of my hope that much needed reform in this field might give the new organization a major objective, I had been invited to prepare a paper on "Legal Education and Admission to the Bar." It aroused a good deal of comment, both favorable and unfavorable, but it became the starting point for salutary reforms.

SIXTEEN-TO-ONE

As Cleveland's second term drew toward its close it became evident that the presidential campaign of 1896 would be fought on a currency basis. I lived in a zone in which the Republican financial policy was so generally regarded as sound that I accepted it as a matter of course. I looked upon the Silverites as debtors who were in effect proposing a *pro tanto* repudiation of all debts and I felt righteously determined to oppose them.

Feeling ran high. When the smoke of battle cleared away McKinley was found to have a decisive majority both of the electoral and popular votes. Mark Hanna had proved himself to be a political strategist of the highest order. Bryan, however, led in the number of states carried, the count being twenty-two to twenty-one, with two divided. The difficulties of the count were very great because Bryan was the presidential candidate on no less than six party tickets: the People's Party, the Silver Populist's Party, the Democratic Party, the National Silver Party, the Silver Party and the National People's Party.

With traditional sportsmanship the result of the election was accepted in good spirit and the stream of national life appeared destined for an indefinite time to be smooth and unruffled.

A COSTLY VENTURE

At this time William Draper Lewis and I had somehow reached the conclusion that it would help us professionally and enrich us financially if we were to prepare and publish two Pennsylvania digests, one dealing with statutes and the other with judicial decisions. We greatly under-estimated the magnitude of these tasks but chiefly through his perse-verance we succeeded in pressing both enterprises to a conclusion. *The Digest of Statutes* was a poor piece of work, did the editors no credit and cost the publishers a lot of money. They brought suit against us for alleged breach of contract but were rather ignominiously beaten. *The Pepper and Lewis Digest of Decisions,* on the other hand, was really a good and useful work and was so regarded by the profession. Once fairly launched in its preparation, we found that we needed more and more editorial help and that, instead of four or five large volumes, the work would require more than twenty of not less than a thousand pages each. We had to borrow considerable sums of money to meet our editorial payroll and, financially, the enterprise ended in disastrous loss. I had to mortgage my house to pay the digest debts and for a good many years all that I could save out of my professional earnings went toward the reduction and ultimate extinction of that encumbrance.

GENTLE WINDS

It is a relief to turn from this melancholy enterprise in digest-making to a happy and carefree organization which was concerned with digesting of a different sort. At the southeast corner of 8th and Locust Streets the Penn Club was comfortably housed. The place was within a short walk from the law offices and the courts and this led to its selection as a home for the Lawyers' Lunch Club. A long table in a spacious room was spread each day at the luncheon hour and a simple system of self-service insured both cheapness and informality. Following my association with Bayard Henry who was one of the founders of the Club, I was honored with an election to membership. This gave me an opportunity for friendly contact with a group of companionable men all of whom were older than I and some of whom were of my parents' generation. Between one and two o'clock on any day you were sure to find at least ten or a dozen men in attendance. There was plenty of serious conversation and not a little badinage. A member who had recently lost an important case would not be apt to come to the Club for sympathy. The wittiest member was Joseph C. Fraley, a patent lawyer of distinction, who appeared to find in our companionship the element of exhilaration which patent law seems to lack. His verbal sword-thrusts were not easy to parry but somehow the touch left no wound. At the head of the table, smiling benignantly upon the company, sat Mr. Henry Flanders, who specialized in admiralty law and proclaimed himself a Jeffersonian Democrat. His age and the dignity of his deportment afforded him a measure of protection against merciless hecklers. When, however, he expatiated at length upon the consent of the governed as necessary to any sound constitutional system, somebody was sure to ask him how he justified Jefferson's Louisiana Purchase when there was such bitter opposition on the part of the inhabitants of the purchased territory. "You must understand," the old gentleman would reply in a tone of finality, "that Mr. Jefferson always recognized that there was such a thing as involuntary consent."

Theodore Etting was the gentleman in politics. His service in the City Council was meritorious and self-sacrificing. He was, of course, held responsible by the Club for all municipal extravagance, political graft and dirty streets. John Ridgway was never able to get much sympathy for his gout or for his enforced visits to the establishment run by a Miss DeVinnie who by baking and massage undertook to deal effectively with gouty extremities. Joe Fraley always referred to her as "the DeVinnie that shapes our ends." Walter George Smith and Percy Keating were apt to be kept busy justifying the teachings of the Church of Rome. A favorite target for witticisms was DeWitt Cuyler whose corporate connections made him vulnerable. He liked to give us reminiscences of Alpine adventure; but doubts were freely expressed about the authenticity of some of his first ascents. Bayard Henry brought with him one day a lawyer from the South who contended that in '64 he had fought against our fellow member, Major Carpenter. When, however, the two men met face to face, the guest failed to recognize the Major. Sussex Davis thereupon relieved the situation by suggesting that recognition might be facilitated if the Major would turn his back.

In my life at this time there were many cheerful avocations. My alumni activities, especially in the management of intercollegiate athletics, were bringing me into some prominence in the college world. Pennsylvania's notable victories on the football field during the Nineties compelled a certain amount of attention from colleges like Harvard, Yale and Princeton, which socially claimed a certain superiority over us. I represented Pennsylvania at various intercollegiate gatherings. Among others I attended and spoke at a big Harvard dinner in New York in February of 1897. One of the more important speakers that night was Theodore Roosevelt, at that time Police Commissioner of New York City. He defended himself vigorously against the attacks then recently made upon him for arming the police force with "night sticks." As I write these words I note the contrast between the present day and forty years ago.

Today policemen everywhere, park guards, "traffic cops" and watchmen privately employed are armed to the teeth and everybody takes it as a matter of course. Going in the other day to argue a case in the Supreme Court of Pennsylvania I noticed with mixed amusement and chagrin that the attendant who checked my hat in the anteroom had a murderous-looking pistol at his belt. In 1897 to have predicted such a possibility would have branded a man as prophet of evil.

On May 30, 1897, our third child was born and we gave her the name of Charlotte Eleanor. At the time of her birth we were making our annual visit to my mother's hospitable home at Strafford. The only telephone to which I could get access was several miles away in the Pennsylvania Railroad Signal Tower at St. David's Station. When at dawn the trained nurse told me it was time to send for the doctor I mounted my bicycle, rode to St. David's and summoned the doctor over the railroad telephone. During her life of thirty-three years Eleanor made all about her supremely happy. She generated such an atmosphere as is made possible only when beauty, intelligence and charm are present in unusual combination.

BREAKERS AHEAD

During the winter of 1897-1898 work in office and court was heavy and I put an immense amount of effort into my law-school courses. The blowing up of the *Maine* in Havana Harbor [3] brought us to the verge of war with Spain. Six European nations, through Sir Julian Pauncefote the British Ambassador at Washington, had submitted a friendly protest against hasty action on our part. Their fruitless efforts were strikingly similar to the activities forty years later of the seven neutral powers which then undertook to dissuade Japan from persisting in her military operations against China. Whenever the conduct of one nation is such as to cause irritation or indignation on the part of a neighbor there is certain to be an impulsive demand for a punitive war. Whether war actually follows depends, principally, on three factors: Whether the disturbance has been in the immediate neighborhood, whether the indignant neighbor is confident of easy victory and whether the more sensational newspapers sense the possibility of arousing an indifferent public. Japan by her treatment of China had aroused plenty of indignation and our Army and Navy authorities had made up their minds that her defeat would be easy. On the other hand, Manchuria was far away and to preach an overseas

[3] February 15, 1898.

crusade to help China would have been in 1937 a well-nigh hopeless task.

In 1898, however, Spain's victim was at our door; Spain was known to be weak; and her colonial misgovernment was an open invitation to inflammatory journalism. With all three prowar factors present, an aggressive President might in 1898 have led the country into war even if the *Maine* had not been blown up. A strong executive, resolutely opposed to war, might have found a peaceful solution even after the explosion. But with a president in the White House more disposed to follow public opinion than to mold it, the destruction of the American battleship was all that was needed to bring matters to a head and in April a declaration of war followed. Admiral Dewey's destruction in Manila Bay of the Spanish Fleet commanded by Montojo and the naval victory off Santiago over Admiral Cervera gained by the fleet under Admiral Sampson's command, aroused popular enthusiasm to a high pitch. During the brief struggle the Navy appeared to much greater advantage than the Army. This was not due to inefficiency in the regular service but rather to a woeful lack of preparedness on the part of the War Department.

After war had been declared, but before the whereabouts of Cervera's fleet had been determined, almost every port on the Atlantic seaboard anticipated a surprise attack. I saw at close range many evidences of this apprehension. Sure that Frenchman's Bay would be the Spaniard's objective, some terrified inhabitants of Mt. Desert Island besought the War Department to supply them with adequate coast defense. This plea resulted in the mounting on Schooner Head of an antiquated cannon that looked like a relic of the Civil War. I suspect that, if discharged, it would have done more harm to the gun crew than to the enemy.

A summer visitor at Northeast Harbor, just returned from Machias, reported the same perturbation at that far eastern point, except in the case of one old chap who 'lowed he warn't a mite afraid. "There's the Pettigrew boys on the Pint," he told my friend reassuringly, "and *they* kin pick off a Spanyurd fur as they kin see him."

Although our forces in general were not so well prepared as the Pettigrew boys, the weakness of the enemy made it possible to win the war in spite of all deficiencies. Humorous comments on the course of events were common. The New York *Sun* suggested a cablegram from Cervera to Montojo reading, "Yours is not the only squadron on the beach." Finley Peter Dunne, writing under the pseudonym of Mr. Dooley, set the country laughing over his comments upon certain army appointments and other incidents of an *opéra-bouffe* variety. His volume entitled *Mr.*

Dooley in Peace and War is a just, though whimsical, commentary upon the less-glorious aspects of the conflict.

Having neglected opportunities for military training I did not take so much interest in the war as did many of my friends who had served in the National Guard. This I now regret because it is part of a good citizen's duty to take up arms at his country's call. I say this although it is my present deliberate opinion that the Spanish War should never have been fought. Our superior strength would have enabled us to wring from Spain all the concessions necessary for justice to Cuba. Indeed there is evidence that such concessions had actually been offered by Spain and were known to our State Department before the President asked for a declaration of war. By finding a peaceful solution we could have made an enormous contribution to civilization. Nobody can assert even with plausibility that our will to peace in 1898 would have had an appreciable influence on international relations sixteen years later. But there are three assertions which may be made with confidence: first, that we are at least responsible for setting a bad example; second, that the Spanish War gave to the officers of our Army and Navy an absurdly exaggerated idea of our superiority on land and sea which persisted until this present war rudely dispelled the illusion; and, third, that we became hospitable to a policy of colonial expansion which is today proving itself a source of weakness rather than of strength.

After the Spanish War something like Guedalla's "rich blossom of imperialism" flowered in the United States. I look back ruefully at my own youthful enthusiasm over confident announcements that it had now become the manifest destiny of the United States to reform the world and to do great things all over the globe.

I was bitterly impatient at suggestions that danger lurked in centralized power, exercised to effectuate ambitious schemes. I chafed at all decisions of the Supreme Court which applied constitutional limitations to legislative experiments. In June of 1898 I delivered the Phi Beta Kappa address before the University of Pennsylvania and in it I "went imperialistic" with a vengeance. The utterance, if applied to international affairs, might have been voiced in 1919 by those who were dreaming the League of Nations dream. As applied to a federal government exercising dominion over the states the address might well have been delivered during Franklin Roosevelt's administration by some young and immature New Dealer. In the light of later observation of the terrible consequences of international meddling and of intimate experience with bureaucracies in action I should feel like apologizing for that boyish utterance were it not that it was scarcely more serious than a nursery disease.

When the Treaty of Paris was signed on December 10, 1898, I should have smiled incredulously if told that it would one day be my responsibility to see that effect was given to one of its provisions protecting Cuba's interests in the Isle of Pines.[4]

THE WARRIOR'S REST

It was during the Spanish War that my uncle William Pepper died in the fifty-sixth year of his age.[5] For years he had driven himself relentlessly. Naturally strong and well-knit, he was nevertheless overengined. His heart gave way under the strain of incessant work and the effort to inspire inert Philadelphians with a sense of civic responsibility. He had a vision of a great cultural center of which the University was to be a constituent part. But the struggle to secure co-operation between existing institutions with a view to the more abundant life was in those days a punishing struggle. When he died a most lovable man was gathered to his fathers. He had been a father to me since early childhood. He gave me many of the opportunities with which my life has been blessed. His life work was characterized by a remarkable union of imagination and practical wisdom, of tirelessness in the pursuit of an objective and a quality of leadership which energized everybody who came within reach of his influence. As a lecturer in the Medical School he was regarded by the students as "tops." His clinics were considered brilliant. His medical writings were accepted as authoritative. During my student days and while he was Provost I watched with delight the growth of the University. As a physician, his control over his patients was extraordinary. Forty years after his death I still meet people who will tell you that their parents not only thought him infallible but claimed him as a family friend. On occasion he "treated 'em rough" but they always took it. "Oh, Doctor," whined an elderly woman, "I have terrible dyspepsia: I can't digest a thing." "Let me see your teeth," he said sternly. After one look he ejaculated "Ugh!" and hurried her out of the office. "Go to a dentist," he commanded, "and don't come back to me till you've been fitted out with a good set of teeth." Anybody who thinks horse-and-buggy days were slow can never have seen Doctor Pepper on his round of calls. He would leap to the pavement before the carriage had stopped, burst into the

[4] *Infra*, page 183.   [5] July 28, 1898.

patient's house when the door was half-opened and run upstairs two steps at a time. The women of the family, not attired for male visitors, sought cover as best they could. One sensitive soul complained that she had had to hide for a half hour in her mother's clothes-closet. Sometimes, after prescribing for the patient, he would stretch himself out on a sofa and direct the nurse to wake him in ten minutes. In that brief interval he could snatch five minutes of restful sleep. When General Sheridan was desperately ill in Washington and Doctor Pepper was turned to as a last resort he made it his habit to visit the sick man in the small hours of the morning, going and coming in a special train which the Pennsylvania Railroad was glad to place at his disposal. For his prolonged and exhausting effort in this case he declined to make a charge. He regarded his service as a tribute of gratitude for what Sheridan had done for the Union.

The only man of his time who approached him in ability and charm was Sir William Osler, but Osler always impressed me as handicapped by a self-consciousness from which Doctor Pepper was wholly free. As Elihu Root said of Theodore Roosevelt, "If you wanted to dislike him you had to keep away from him."

Three sons survived him. The eldest, William Pepper, has made an ideal Dean of the Medical School of the University of Pennsylvania. He has set and maintained high educational standards, has knit together a faculty of individuals into a cohesive and co-operative fellowship and has won the affectionate regard of the student body. Benjamin Franklin Pepper, in his short career at the Bar, proved himself able and effective. When just before the Armistice he was killed while leading his battalion in the Argonne offensive there died as fine a man as I ever knew. Oliver Hazard Perry Pepper, the youngest of the three, early attained eminence in his father's profession. A brilliant teacher and a skilled investigator, he holds the chair in the Medical School which his father held with such distinction and is rendering, in wartime, medical service of national importance. Their mother, Frances Perry, was a lineal descendant both of Doctor Franklin and of Commodore Perry.

During the winter of 1898-1899 I awaited with impatience the construction of the Law School's new home. For some years the University had been permitted by Mayor and Council to occupy, for classroom and library purposes, the rooms in the wings of Independence Hall and in adjacent buildings after these had been left vacant by the migration of the law courts to City Hall. Our sojourn there was designed to give us time to raise money for a permanent building and actually to erect it.

The then Provost, Doctor Harrison, was the leader in the fund-raising movement. Dean Lewis and I, among others, co-operated with him. In due time the money was raised and such progress in construction was made that plans for a notable dedication were in order. It was determined to hold the exercises in February of 1901 and, in the meantime, to extend invitations not only to American educators but to representatives of the English Bench and Bar and of the Universities of Oxford and Cambridge. I was assigned the pleasant duty of presenting in person invitations to English guests. In June of 1899 I went to England for this purpose taking Mrs. Pepper along. I was armed with letters of introduction to various distinguished people including the Lord Chancellor, the Lord Chief Justice and the Master of the Rolls. Some of these letters were from my father-in-law's great friend, Edward J. Phelps, whose then recent service as our Minister at the Court of St. James had made for him many friends in London.

I presented to Ambassador Choate a letter from John Hay, then our Secretary of State, and he went out of his way to help me. There may be compensations in the life of a diplomat but they must needs be ample if they can make up for the dreary round of services which he must render to importunate fellow countrymen. If in my case Mr. Choate was bored he exhausted the resources of diplomacy to conceal it. He took me to the House of Lords to call upon the Lord Chancellor, Lord Halsbury. The plump and somewhat pompous jurist, splendidly bewigged and begowned, explained it would be impossible for a Lord Chancellor to make a trip to America at a time when Parliament was in session but he somehow managed to satisfy me that he would have enjoyed an American experience.

The various eminent jurists whom I approached all felt or feigned pleasure at the invitation I tendered, but like the Lord Chancellor they said it would be out of the question to absent themselves from London during February. Sir Nathaniel Lindley, Master of the Rolls, was pleased when, in discussing with him a case I had heard argued in his court that morning, I cited a former opinion of his in *Simm v. Anglo-American Co.* "God bless my soul!" he exclaimed, "are my judgments known in America?" I did not recall at the moment—and happily neither did he— that his judgment in the *Simm* case had been reversed on appeal. Anyway the reference earned me an invitation to dine at his house. There I met among other guests Sir Edward Fry, a distinguished Lord Justice and a member of the Privy Council. He too was able to resist my invitation.

While abroad we had a family reunion of some dimensions. My father-in-law, Doctor Fisher, was taking a European trip with his friend Archdeacon Tiffany of New York. In London their paths intersected with Mrs. Pepper's and mine and we had some happy days together. One morning Doctor Fisher said, "Yesterday I was talking with a man who has looked in the face of Henry VIII." Thirty-five years later I should have said "Oh, yeah!" But what I actually did (seeing that we were still in the nineties) was to ask politely for particulars. The story was this: Some years previously a doubt had arisen respecting the identity of the coffin of Charles I in the crypt of St. George's, Windsor. Queen Victoria appointed a commission to examine and report. The commission consisted of the then Dean, a surgeon selected by the Queen and a third person whose identity I have forgotten. The three opened a certain coffin and were able unhesitatingly to identify the skeleton of King Charles because the cervical vertebra had been severed. Moreover, the executioner's ax, coming from above and behind, had cut off the royal "goatee"—which had been carefully replaced. Yielding to a seemingly uncontrollable impulse and escaping the observation of his colleagues, the surgeon had abstracted the beard before the coffin was sealed up. Then he had remorse but was afraid to tell what had happened. He made his wife promise that if she survived him she would make an explanation and tender the return of the relic. She did survive him and kept her word. The Queen thereupon commissioned the Dean of Windsor in office at the time to restore the relic to its place. This he had done shortly before the day on which he entertained my father-in-law and Doctor Tiffany at dinner. He told them that after discharging his gruesome duty he turned aside and noticed that the lid of a neighboring coffin had warped and evidently needed attention. Upon examining more closely the lid was found to be loose. He raised it and found himself looking into the face of Henry VIII. There lay the monarch in a state of perfect preservation. The Dean said that he was a replica of the Holbein portrait.

As it seemed impossible to lure representative judges across the Atlantic, I turned to the Universities—and with better momentary success. Pleasant contact with Sir William and Lady Markby at Oxford and with Professor F. W. Maitland at Cambridge brought from both men an acceptance of our invitation. It seemed as if my mission had at last been crowned with success. I accordingly came home with a light heart. Unhappily illness shortly overtook both these distinguished men. Maitland was exiled to the Canary Islands and died not long afterward. Both Universities sent substitutes but I was grievously disappointed that so much effort should have failed to secure the guests whom we particularly wanted.

My visit to Maitland at Cambridge was a memorable experience. The way was made easy for me by a letter from James Barr Ames, between whom and Maitland there was a long-standing friendship. Maitland was Downing Professor of the Laws of England and as charming as he was learned. He and Sir Frederick Pollock had produced that monumental work, *Pollock and Maitland's History of English Law*. I suspect that it was Maitland who supplied the scholarship while Pollock lent his name. I was studying in connection with my law-school work the historical development of the corporation. Maitland had lately published his translation of *Gierke's Political Theories of the Middle Age* and had prefaced it with a brilliant essay on the evolution of the corporation. With these writings I was familiar and we quickly established a community of intellectual interest. On pilgrimage to the various colleges at Cambridge, Maitland was an ideal guide. At first he was a bit doubtful of my capacity for appreciation and, with English naïveté, made his anxiety clear. "Here," he said at one point, "you will see that King's and St. Catherine's are neighbors." Then, looking at me searchingly, he added, "I wonder if you can catch the point of this:

> 'They say that cats
> May look at kings—but that's
> No reason in the world why King's
> Should not look down on Cat's.'"

"A verse," I suggested, "more often repeated by the men of King's than by the students of St. Cat's." "Precisely," he said, with evident relief; and after that treated me almost as if I were a Britisher. I left him with keen regret. We promised ourselves a reunion in America which, unhappily for me, never took place.

Before sailing my wife and I had luncheon with Mr. and Mrs. James Bryce. While gathering material for his *American Commonwealth* he had been a guest at Professor Fisher's home in New Haven. On this occasion he made a characteristic comment on the easy-going failure of Americans to resent defects in public service. I had told him how on the preceding Friday morning I had bought a week-end excursion ticket to Oxford and, returning to London on an afternoon train, had been told by the guard that the return coupon was not available for use on the day of purchase. "How ridiculous!" Mr. Bryce exclaimed. "What did you do?" "Do?" I asked in surprise, "why, I paid the difference in fare as demanded." "There you are!" said he despairingly. "Just like you Americans!" "Do you know," he added, "what an Englishman would have done in similar circumstances?" "What?" I asked. "Three things," said he. "He would have written a letter to the *Times*, instructed his member to bring it up in Parliament and brought suit against the company."

TROUBLE BREWING

Almost before I realized it, the deceptively Gay Nineties had spent themselves and the nineteenth century had come to an end. The twentieth century arrived on time and was greeted everywhere by bells and whistles and cannon. Everybody seemed confident about the future. Imperialism throughout the world was thought of as a sign of strength rather than as a signal of danger. The United States had definitely established itself as a world power. A low growling fight was in progress between John Hay and the Senate over the ratification of the Hay-Pauncefote Treaty. However, these and all other untoward incidents were not serious enough to shake everybody's settled conviction that the new century meant bigger and better things for the world.

THE POPULAR CONCEPTION OF A LAW SUIT
(Hogarth Modernized)
The Plaintiff—the Defendant—the Lawyer

PART TWO

4

Law and Politics [1]

"Shallows where a lamb could wade and depths where an elephant
would drown."
— *Matthew Henry's Commentaries*, "Of Solomon's Song"

I NEVER dove into the political stream. At the outset I merely waded
in—when the water was still. Later, when I went off the deep end,
it was as the result of a friendly push.

When at twenty I entered the Biddle law office my mother's influence
had led me to classify myself as a Democrat. Soon, however, what I was
pleased to call my political ideas underwent a change. It is hard to give
an accurate account of the process. On the intellectual side Judge Hare
in the classroom powerfully influenced me by the exposition of his constitutional views. In particular, his advocacy of "sound money" proved
convincing. In the domain of psychology I had the impression that the
Republicans of my acquaintance were in general the Doers and the Democrats the Talkers. I was young and eager for effective action. Moreover
the community in which I lived depended for its prosperity upon the
tariff. My father's family, the Peppers, had long been Republicans. Dur-

[1] This account of political experiences necessarily overlaps the years covered by
Chapters 3, 5, and 6, 1.

77

ing the Civil War they had been intensely loyal to the Union. My grandfather Wharton, on the other hand, was far less of a Northern partisan and as I grew older I came to regret his lukewarmness. Despite my mother's influence (never aggressively exercised in this particular) I was conscious of eagerness to carry on the Pepper tradition. Taking one consideration with another I decided to join the Republican Party. Later, in the presidential election of 1892, my vote was cast for Harrison. Having voted for Cleveland in 1888 when he lost, I now found myself backing a losing candidate on the other side of the fence. So far my batting average was not high.

While thus a convert to Republicanism I was, like most young men, a bit too ready to fall in with any local project labeled "reform" no matter how ill-conceived and impotent it might be. Since my student days the Republican organization in Pennsylvania had been controlled by Matthew Stanley Quay who had become United States Senator in 1887. The Junior Senator was Donald Cameron. Quay's principal lieutenant in Philadelphia was Boies Penrose, then a member of the State Senate. Very little about the State was known to me except its history and I had a vague impression, common among young people, that political leaders are bad men and that politics is a dirty business. This impression, however, led to no thorough study of the political situation either in city or state. What I did not know I took no pains to learn. It is a fact, although not an excuse, that I was all the while working at high pressure in office, court and law school and constantly busy with church and university affairs. I had as yet developed no sense of obligation to pull my weight in the party boat.

During McKinley's first term I was retained in a case which gave me my first personal contact with state politics. The revolt against Quay which had been brewing was led by William Flinn, a member of the State Senate who had political ambitions of his own. He had a very considerable following all over the Commonwealth. Quay's term as United States Senator expired on the 4th of March, 1899. Balloting in the legislature to fill the prospective vacancy had begun in January of that year and daily ballots were taken until in April the legislature adjourned *sine die* without effecting an election. Immediately after the adjournment Stone, the Governor of the Commonwealth, signed and delivered to Mr. Quay what purported to be a temporary appointment to represent the State in the Senate until the next meeting of the legislature. A memorial signed by a large number of members of the State Senate and House of Representatives was presented to the Senate of the United States, protesting the validity of the Governor's appointment. The protest was, in due course, referred to the Senate Committee on Privileges and Elections which held a meeting for the purpose of hearing arguments pro and con. The protestants had retained George F. Edmunds, former United States Senator from Vermont, and Hampton L. Carson, a well-known member of the Philadelphia bar. These men entrusted to me the preparation of a brief in support of the protest. I thoroughly explored the whole subject and wrote the argument which was filed with the Committee. This brief contained, among other things, an analytical statement of all relevant Senate election cases from the beginning of the government down to the date of filing. A brief in support of the Governor's right to appoint was filed by Attorney General Elkin of Pennsylvania. Our contention, in reply, was that the vacancy caused by the expiration of Quay's term had "happened," once for all, when the legislature was in session and that, therefore, the case did not fall within that provision of Section 3 of Article I of the Constitution of the United States, which reads as follows:

> "If vacancies happen by resignation, or otherwise, during the recess of the Legislature of any State, the Executive thereof may make temporary appointment until the next meeting of the Legislature, which shall then fill such vacancies."

The opposing argument was based on the theory that a vacancy "happens" whenever it happens to exist; and that, as in this case, it happened to exist after the adjournment of the legislature (as well as before) the Governor's appointing power was exercisable and the commission to Quay was valid.

The case attracted a great deal of attention. It was argued before the Committee by Senator Edmunds and Mr. Carson on the one side and by Attorney General Elkin on the other. The Committee subsequently reported adversely to Quay's claim to a seat and the report of the Committee was sustained in the Senate by the margin of a single vote.

One of the members of the committee was old Senator Hoar, of Massachusetts, who strongly favored the right of the Governor to appoint. At the end of the hearing he approached me with more effusion than he was wont to manifest, shook me warmly by the hand and congratulated me upon my argument. He said I had demonstrated the soundness of the Quay claim. If I had taken part in the argument this would have been a bit disconcerting. In point of fact he had mistaken me for Attorney General Elkin and when his mistake was discovered there was a good deal of merriment among senators and counsel. The incident was the starting point of a friendship between Elkin and me which continued after he became a Justice of the Supreme Court of Pennsylvania and was terminated only by his premature death. He himself had aspired to be Governor of Pennsylvania after the expiration of Stone's term and he counted on the support of Quay who, by that time, had recovered some of the prestige temporarily lost. Quay, however, decided to endorse his kinsman, Judge Pennypacker, who was nominated and elected. Elkin's place upon the bench was generally regarded as a consolation prize. It was the belief of many that Quay had broken faith with Elkin and some attributed to this incident the gradual waning of the Senator's political power.

My first experience with a political convention came when I was selected to nominate a fellow member of the Bar for the office of District Attorney of Philadelphia County. I realized, although somewhat dimly, that the delegates who crowded the Academy of Music had had their orders and were there to execute them. I was more or less conscious that my speech was a mere formality but it was delivered as if on me alone the fortunes of the day depended. It was part of the game to give appointed speakers a "good hand" and to listen to their speeches with apparent interest. As I went through with my part in this theatrical performance there was loud applause for lofty sentiments with which "the boys" were not in the least sympathetic. My candidate was nominated and subsequently elected.

In 1904 Quay died and the Governor of Pennsylvania appointed Philander Chase Knox to succeed him. At a dinner given the new Senator, I recalled the fact that in former days men in Massachusetts, when asked for an opinion on a public question, were wont to parry the inquiry by asking, "What does Mr. Webster think?" I made the prediction that it would become the habit among thoughtful people to ask, "What is the opinion of Mr. Knox on this matter?" This prediction was abundantly justified for Knox became a great Senator.

In 1905 there was in Philadelphia a fierce local struggle between the Republican Organization and a reform group entitled the City Party. I must have been taking myself rather seriously at the time for I wrote and published a long letter explaining my position and justifying what later came to be known as "taking a walk." The victory of the City Party was sweeping but, as usual, the wave of reform soon spent itself. Lincoln Steffens was not altogether just when he called Philadelphia "corrupt and contented." The truth is that influential Philadelphians have never been content with corruption; but they have generally been prosperous enough to be contented with their prosperity and too deficient in public spirit to make a substantial effort for good local government. The under-privileged element in the population has never been organized in its own interest and has been exploited by both parties for the advantage of their leaders. We seem to be at least a century behind the English cities in this respect. Judge Willis Martin had a story about a colored voter who on the evening of election day proudly showed his wife ten dollars received from the Republicans, five from the Democrats and three from the City Party. "How did you vote?" she asked. "For the City Party," he replied, "because they was the least corrupt."

Before we knew it Theodore Roosevelt's second term was drawing to a close. He showed a natural disinclination to quit but probably never thought seriously of immediately seeking a third term. The plight of anybody selected as his successor and expected to carry on his policies was bound to be an unhappy one. In point of fact, Roosevelt could scarcely be said to have policies. It was rather the way a thing looked when he did it or sounded when he said it that gave it distinction.

TIDE-RIP

Taft, who was nominated and elected in 1908, was of wholly different mold. Roosevelt was always ready to crusade at a moment's notice—or without any notice at all. Taft was hard to arouse. Roosevelt got along well with his subordinates because he made himself felt through them. Taft gave his subordinates free rein and sometimes the very confidence he placed in them gave them the opportunity to get him into trouble. This happened in the case of his Secretary of the Interior, Richard Ballinger.[2]

Shortly after his inauguration President Taft offered me an appoint-ment as a Judge of the United States Circuit Court of Appeals for the Third Circuit. This tender came as a great surprise. Active practice at the bar or the life of judge and teacher were the alternatives. Mr. John G. Johnson and Dr. Weir Mitchell urged me to accept. Both had, I suspect, been asked to do so by Attorney General Wickersham. I decided, how-ever, to decline. Perhaps this was a mistake. My cast of mind is essen-tially judicial. I have always had the habit of weighing opposing con-siderations. Such success as I have had in advocacy has resulted, I think,

[2] *Infra,* page 82 *et seq.*

from always recognizing the strength of the arguments on the other side. Later I was to find that the habit of mind which qualifies a man for the judicial office is a handicap to him in politics. I never realized this clearly until I was called upon to deal with political questions in the Senate. Yet as I look back I think my decision was the right one. I have had a life of wider activity than would have been possible had I been garbed in a black gown.

As an advocate I was to become familiar with the political world if I was not to be an actor in it throughout my life. My participation in the Ballinger case, which came to be a *cause célèbre,* was in itself a political education. When Richard Ballinger was made Secretary of the Interior by President Taft, Gifford Pinchot was head of the Forest Service, one of the Bureaus in the Department of Agriculture. As long as James A. Garfield was Secretary of the Interior he and Pinchot had co-operated effectively in promoting conservation of natural resources. When to the great disappointment of Garfield's friends a new man was named to succeed him, it soon became evident that the era of good feeling was over. Charges were freely made by the Pinchot-Garfield group that the Roosevelt policies were being ignored by the new Administration and that important rights in the public domain were being handed over to great corporate interests. Counter-charges were made by the Secretary's friends to the effect that all was not well in the Forest Service; and the outcome was the appointment, at the request of Secretary Ballinger, of a joint committee of Senate and House to investigate both his Department and the Forest Service. The Chairman was Knute Nelson, Senator from Minnesota, and the Committee included many notable men, among them Elihu Root, then a Senator from New York, and Senator Sutherland, later a Justice of the Supreme Court. Of the twelve members six were elected by the House. The Senate members were appointed in the usual way.[3]

It was at this point that I became an actor in what proved to be a drama of considerable public importance. I was called up late in December of 1909 by my old friend Henry L. Stimson, who urged me to come at once to New York for a highly-important conference on a subject which he did not care to mention over the telephone. I went as requested and at an evening meeting in Stimson's house met for the first time two friends of Pinchot's, Louis D. Brandeis and Joseph P. Cotton, Jr. At that

[3] By the President of the Senate on the recommendation of the "Committee on Committees."

time Pinchot was the only one of the five of us in public life. In subsequent years every one of the five was to hold some important public office.

These men explained to me the situation in Washington, of which at that time I had little knowledge. They urged me to accept a retainer as Pinchot's attorney and, in co-operation with Stimson, to represent him before the Joint Committee. Brandeis and Cotton were to appear for one Glavis, a land agent, whose complaints and charges were the principal basis of the attacks that had been made on Secretary Ballinger. The plan was that Brandeis and I should be colleagues and map out co-ordinate courses of action for our respective clients. I hesitated to accept, both because I had had no previous experience in this sort of warfare and also because the proceeding was evidently going to last for months and would inevitably dislocate all my other work. They pressed me hard, however, speaking much of public duty, and I finally consented to go ahead. It was agreed that I should have as my junior Nathaniel A. Smyth of the New York Bar who proved to be a congenial and able colleague. At the moment nobody had even the foggiest notion of what the issues before the Committee would be and I quickly decided that the most difficult part of my job was to find out what my job was. However, public announcement of my retainer was duly made and with considerable misgiving I set about my preliminary preparation.

Almost instantly I had a foretaste of what I was in for. Pinchot in his eagerness for effective publicity wanted to get an immediate statement of his case before the country. With this in mind he insisted upon writing an open letter to the Secretary of Agriculture and much time was spent in drafting it. The letter was finally put into a form which Stimson and I approved. To our dismay Pinchot subsequently and without our knowledge changed it both in substance and form and, instead of sending it to his Chief, addressed it to Senator Dolliver and contrived to have it read in the Senate at about the time that a message upon a phase of the pending controversy was received from President Taft. The President interpreted Pinchot's letter as a reflection upon the President's own conduct and an attempt to excuse in advance an alleged serious breach of discipline by two of Pinchot's subordinates in the Bureau of Forestry. The President therefore immediately directed the Secretary of Agriculture to remove Pinchot from the office of Forester. This was done; and I thus found myself no longer the adviser of an important officer of the federal government but merely the attorney for a private citizen whose own conduct had brought about his summary dismissal. I seriously considered withdrawal from the case but as this would have seemed like deserting a client under fire I decided to stand by him. In Alfred Leif's biography of Brandeis [4] it is represented that I was retained by Pinchot after his dismissal. This is a mistake as is also the same writer's insinuation that Stimson withdrew when the dismissal was announced. On the contrary Stimson later came to Washington (whither I had preceded him), took part in the preparation of Pinchot's case and did not become inactive until much later when an overriding professional engagement made it necessary for Smyth and me to go it alone.

A letter written to my wife on January 25, 1910, the day after reaching the Pinchot mansion in Washington, gives a picture of what was found there.

"I arrived here yesterday at half past four. Pinchot, Price, Shaw and I talked till seven—nothing being accomplished. Shortly afterward the Congressional Limited brought Harry Stimson, Jim Garfield, Joe Cotton and Smyth. All were much excited because Mr. Root had talked to Harry on the train and had stated that the Committee would not waste time on dead issues but wanted the evidence presented in such a way as would give a basis for planning constructive legislation in aid of the Conservation cause. As Senator Nelson had asked for Pinchot's letter by noon today suggesting what he wanted the Committee to do, it was determined to prepare it at once on lines conforming to Mr. Root's thought. We went into session at about 9 P.M. I drafted the letter in about half an hour and all criticized it until 2 A.M. I then went to bed and slept well till 8. At 9 the crowd assembled, now joined by Brandeis. A draft of the letter was taken to Root by Harry and approved by him. By noon it was in final shape. Pinchot took it to Nelson—who said it was not what was wanted—that the Committee were going to investigate only past personal issues and had nothing to do with constructive legislation. More flurry. Harry and I found Root and reported Nelson's view. He went to a private meeting of the Committee to see about it. At 3 I got some lunch and worked on the case with Garfield till 5:30; slept till 6:30, dressed—and am now ready for 7:30 dinner. More pow-wow tonight in anticipation of a public meeting of the Committee at 2:30 to morrow afternoon. The situation is not in the least degree a legal situation but wholly political. Nobody in this crowd understands it—but I seem to be the only one who is willing to admit this obvious fact."

In the midst of distracting turmoil and with the minds of most of those about us focused upon publicity, Brandeis, Smyth and I did our

[4] *Brandeis* by Alfred Leif, Stackpole Sons, New York and Harrisburg, 1936,

best in private to sift the essential facts from the mass of undigested material submitted to us. A somewhat vague course of procedure was finally determined upon by the Committee. We shaped our course to conform to it. The hearings began and proceeded in the presence of an excited audience that crowded one of the largest rooms in the Senate Office Building. The principal reason for the excitement was that Pinchot was regarded as in some sense representing Theodore Roosevelt's administration; and both newspaper men and spectators were eager to have the proceeding develop into a sensational controversy between President Taft and his predecessor. The Pinchot publicity was high-powered and effective. Ballinger was soon on the defensive and proceedings in the committee room took on the appearance of a prosecution rather than of an inquiry. He found it advisable to retain counsel to appear for him. Col. John J. Vertrees, of Nashville, was selected. He was a lawyer of the old school, a fire-eating Southerner, experienced in combats of various sorts, but quite helpless when called upon to meet the more subtle strategy of Brandeis. One day, when the latter was on his feet, the Colonel suddenly rose from his chair and addressing the Chairman said with emphasis and deliberation, "The gentleman says what is untrue and what he knows to be untrue." Brandeis gave him a beaming smile and waited. "The gentleman," repeated the Colonel, "states an untruth and he states it knowing it to be an untruth." This time surely there would be an explosion—perhaps a challenge and possibly an old-fashioned free-for-all. Not a bit of it. Brandeis, with his arms folded and wearing an indulgent smile, looked silently at the old gentleman for a few seconds and then asked with an air of deference, "Anything further, Mr. Vertrees?" The Colonel, literally speechless with rage, sank into his chair and Brandeis resumed his argument at the point at which he had been interrupted. Two philosophies of life had confronted one another in dramatic fashion and one had evaporated.

One of the most interesting members of the Committee was Ollie James, a Democrat, then representing a Kentucky district in the House. He later became a Senator. He was a huge man for whom a special chair had to be provided. He spoke with a pleasing southern drawl. "Befo' I came to Washington," he one day observed, "I used to hear that the Republicans were the watchdogs of the Treasury; and I reckon they are—but they're like our Kaintucky watchdogs: they don't bark so loud at the home folks."

On behalf of Pinchot we consistently maintained three positions. One was that the Department of the Interior had been faithless to the public interest in respect to power sites, coal, forests and land. A second was that Secretary Ballinger was actually and substantially responsible for what had happened. The third, that at critical times the President had been deceived as to what was actually going on. An immense amount of testimony was taken and after sessions lasting through four months the case was finally argued by Vertrees, Brandeis and me during the last week in May.

A meeting of the Committee was called at Minneapolis during the following September. Some Republican members failed to attend so it befell that a majority of those present were the Democratic minority members of the Committee. These members brought in a report declaring that the charges made by Pinchot against Ballinger had been proved; but the Committee quorum was broken by the withdrawal of representatives of the majority party. Early in December a majority report was filed exonerating Ballinger from any wrongdoing but suggesting additional protection for the public Reserves. Congress took no action upon either the majority or the minority report. Public criticisms of Ballinger continued until he resigned his office in March of 1911.

Of all the difficult and disagreeable duties I have ever performed this was the most arduous and nerve-racking. From the December day when I reluctantly agreed to act till the middle of June when our brief was filed, the case, because of the conditions under which it had to be prepared and tried, was a constant and grievous anxiety. The only redeeming feature of the situation was association with Brandeis, which I greatly enjoyed. In a few instances our ideas differed both as to strategy and propriety. In at least one instance we agreed to disagree. In the main, however, we found ourselves in perfect accord. Leif [5] represents Brandeis as going to Pinchot behind my back and giving him advice different from mine. I am confident that such a thing never occurred and that Leif's statement is a grave injustice to an honorable colleague. My effort uniformly was to present Pinchot's case to the Committee in such a way as to win for him their respect and, if possible, their verdict. Pinchot's objective was (as he expressed it) "to win before the country." While, therefore, I was struggling to determine what was fact as distinguished from rumor and fiction, Pinchot's associates and his corps of journalistic friends were busy trying the case in the newspapers and incidentally making statements for which I often could find no adequate supporting evidence. The consequence was that the public were

[5] *Ibid.*, page 163.

always being led to expect sensational developments which actually could never take place. The brief, as finally submitted, was a demonstration of Ballinger's unfitness although without culpability and was so generally regarded by people of calm judgment. Judged, however, by the standard of seekers for sensation, my handling of the case might be described in Leif's words [6] as "polished but ineffectual": although another statement of his to the effect that I raised points of order and "rarely came to grips with the facts" is a flat contradiction of the record. Professional opinion was very different from that of the sensationalist— as indicated by a multitude of comments from those whose judgment was worth while. Among these Stimson wrote me as follows:

> "This is just a line to tell you what I meant to tell you some days ago—namely of my great admiration for the way in which you have put Pinchot's case. I am in a position to appreciate some of the difficulties under which you have labored and I have never seen a more admirable piece of work. The way in which the evidence on March 1st—the day when I was present to listen—went in, was enough to delight the professional hearer."

Brandeis generously expressed the same opinion. The truth, no doubt, lies somewhere between these two extremes.

The proceedings before the Committee were in form judicial but the judicial atmosphere was wholly wanting. The Committee was a political body, governed by political considerations. Even on questions of admitting or rejecting evidence the vote was a party vote. Day after day the great committee room was crowded with spectators whose attitude toward the proceedings was that of rooters at a football game. I personally was treated with marked consideration by the members of the Committee. Only on one occasion was there any unpleasantness. On that occasion (and its precise nature I have now forgotten) Senator Nelson interrupted me and spoke disparagingly of some statement of mine or of some proposition that I was trying to establish. Long afterward, and when the arguments were over, I wrote a courtesy note to him, thanking him and his colleagues for their patience and consideration during the months which the hearings had consumed. In reply I received the following letter, written in the Senator's own hand:

> "Your very kind letter of yesterday is at hand for which you have my hearty thanks. It was a source of regret to me that I did not have the opportunity to say good-by to you in person and to congratulate you—

[6] *Ibid.,* page 162.

as was my purpose—on the gentlemanly and able manner in which you conducted your side of the case and to further say to you how sorry I felt over the interruption I caused you on one occasion during the proceedings. I regretted the incident within 30 minutes after it occurred. I felt very much pleased over the well-deserved compliment Mr. Vertrees paid you. I can further say to you that the entire Committee were pleased with the manner in which you conducted the case."

The incident, whatever it was, must have made a deep impression upon Senator Nelson. Twelve years later, when I myself became a Senator, he was still representing Minnesota, although he had aged greatly and seemed infirm. When as a new Senator I was presented to him he at once asked if I was related to the lawyer of my name who had appeared in the Ballinger case. I told him that I was the man and he thereupon, almost with emotion, apologized for what he deemed an act of rudeness but which I could truthfully say I had forgotten.

Everybody was so busy talking about the case and about the prominent people whom it involved that few took the trouble to analyze the proceeding on its constitutional side and to consider what the function of the Committee really was. In January of 1911, when neither the majority nor minority report had been disposed of by Senate or House, Senator Purcell, a friend of Pinchot's, asked my opinion upon these points. I felt bound to tell him that neither the Senate nor the House has, in my judgment, the right to pass resolutions condemning the conduct of executive officials. As I see the situation, it is impeachment, executive discipline or nothing.

I am certain that this view is sound although unpopular. I adhered to it when later in the Senate it became fashionable to introduce resolutions condemning the action of cabinet officers. Later still the utterances of President Franklin Roosevelt and some of his cabinet about the Justices of the Supreme Court were perfect illustrations of indecent comment by one of the three branches of government upon another. Our federal game is a good game as long as it is played according to the rules. As soon, however, as one of the players begins to slug everything gets into a mess. There is then no referee who can send the slugger to the showers or award a heavy penalty against his side. If the people could be made to understand such a situation they would deal with a slugger summarily because American public opinion is almost always sportsmanlike. Unfortunately, however, public understanding in such cases is impossible; and if the high official lacks self-control he can readily do lasting harm to our constitutional system.

Following the Ballinger-Pinchot case it became the habit of newspaper correspondents to mention me as a possible incumbent of various official positions. Some of these, such as the Circuit Court judgeship tendered me by President Taft early in his administration, were actually offered me but others never were. Thus on December 7, 1910, there appeared in a morning paper a news despatch from Washington which ran as follows:

"From an official source it was learned today that the President has under consideration the name of George Wharton Pepper as a possible appointee to the United States Supreme Court. Mr. Pepper has been strongly recommended to the President and meets all of the requirements. The fact that Mr. Pepper appeared before the Ballinger-Pinchot Investigating Committee as attorney for Mr. Pinchot will not in any way affect his decision in considering the nomination of the Philadelphia attorney. The President has made it plain that he will select men of the highest type . . . and that politics and partisanship are secondary matters. Mr. Pepper made a remarkably good impression in Washington by the manner in which he conducted Mr. Pinchot's case. All that can be said now in regard to the possibility of Mr. Pepper's appointment is that he is under consideration by the President. This much the President has himself told to those who have discussed judicial affairs with him."

There had been no previous intimation that my name was under consideration and no official communication on the subject was ever received. Sometime afterward I learned from a reliable source that the offer would have been made if it had not been for the determined opposition of Senator Penrose. He never forgave me for my appearance before the Senate Committee in opposition to Quay's claim to a seat in the Senate.

Already in 1910 and 1911 there were premonitions of a restless movement in the Republican Party which afterward resulted in the revolt of Theodore Roosevelt and his followers and the formation by them of a third party. Some of his doctrines seemed to me destructive of representative government and inimical to our judicial system. In an address delivered at this time my views were expressed at length upon the Initiative, the Referendum and the Recall. The same address favored a continuance of the system by which United States Senators were elected by the several legislatures.

In another speech delivered at the City Club in Philadelphia I supported the movement then under way to create a Public Service Commission in Pennsylvania. Penrose no doubt would have endorsed my views upon the Roosevelt policies but he probably never really favored the establishment of the commission. The regulatory commissions of that era bore no recognizable resemblance to the dominating and sometimes arrogant administrative bodies which, in the name of efficiency, are tending to substitute government control for private management. If such gradual assumption of power is inevitable and if these agencies become drunk with power the ultimate result may prove that the cure is worse than the disease.

In 1911 a group of independent Republican citizens of Philadelphia, numbering between fifty and a hundred prominent men, asked me to enter the September primary that year as a candidate for the Republican nomination for Mayor. This did not tempt me. I had no political ambitions; and anyhow I have always thought that I would be a poor picker of men—almost the worst deficiency an executive can have.

In the meantime the political insurgency of Beveridge and other able men was making trouble for the Republican Party on the national scene. Senator Robert M. LaFollette of Wisconsin got the presidential bee in his bonnet and for a while seemed to be the standard-bearer of the Progressives. Later, when Theodore Roosevelt declared his candidacy, LaFollette was cast aside and almost forgotten. His indignation knew no bounds and he did not hesitate to declare that Pinchot and the other Roosevelt men had double-crossed him.

By merest accident I was given a backstage glimpse of the Progressive drama. One afternoon in February of 1912, having missed my Philadelphia train, I boarded in New York a through train for the West, expecting to leave it at North Philadelphia. It was a long train but singularly empty. Walking through to find my place whom should I encounter but the Colonel—all alone and evidently looking for somebody to talk at. In default of a better he seized upon me. "Come in here, Pepper," he said, "I have something I want you to hear." In his drawing room he motioned me to a seat on the sofa and with something like suppressed excitement "opened up." "I'm on my way to Columbus," said he, "and I'm going to announce my willingness to be a presidential candidate." With that he launched out into the deep and gave me what I then realized was an "advance" of what was destined to be an historic speech. Now and then he would pause for a purely rhetorical question, "What do you think of that?"—but stayed not for an answer. When he touched upon his proposal for the Recall of Judicial Decisions I insisted on being heard and managed to register my protest.

"Bless my soul," he rejoined, "you ought to hear what they wanted me to say!" "Don't forget," he added, "the different types I have to deal with."

When later in that year the Colonel became a third-party candidate I did not cast in my lot with the Bull Moose but supported the regular organization which had renominated Mr. Taft. This decision was due to four reasons. First and foremost, Roosevelt's constitutional doctrines spelled not progress but retrogression. They seemed to me to substitute the democracy of the rabble for representative government. In the second place, his policy of attacking and belittling the courts impressed me as something more than unwise. Third, he had too many wild men around him to make it possible for him to retain his poise. Finally, it seemed clear that the third party movement could be at most only short-lived and that meanwhile it would subtract a vital element from the Republican Party and make the election of a Democrat a practical certainty. Holding these views, I considered it a political duty to vote the regular ticket. This conclusion was reached with plenty of regret, for the Colonel had a virility and a vitality that powerfully appealed to me. Friendly relations with him in later years led me to think that I was one of the few of his opponents in that Bull Moose campaign against whom he afterward bore no grudge. I was not important enough to be reckoned an effective adversary.

The breach between the two defeated candidates had long been widening. Roosevelt was less generous in defeat than such a sportsman should have been and those who were friends of both looked on helplessly at what appeared to be a permanent estrangement. Three years later a surface reconciliation took place. The occasion was the funeral in New Haven of Professor Thomas Lounsbury, at which both ex-Presidents were pallbearers. Lounsbury and my father-in-law had been warm friends, and my wife, who at the time of Lounsbury's death was visiting in New Haven, attended the funeral for old-time's sake. The year was 1915. She gives the following exact account of what took place:

"At the open grave, only ten or twelve feet in front of me, stood Mr. Taft and Colonel Roosevelt with only one other pallbearer between them. I was interested in noticing the backs of their frock coats, as they seemed to show so plainly the difference in their characters. Mr. Taft's seemed very 'roomy' and was hanging loosely—perhaps because it was not buttoned; while Colonel Roosevelt's was very tightly drawn— so much so that there were horizontal creases across the back. When the service was over and after a moment of silence, they started to move

away. At this moment Mr. Taft stretched out his arm in front of the
intervening pallbearer and held out his hand saying, 'How are you,
Theodore?' Colonel Roosevelt, with apparent reluctance, took the out-
stretched hand. It was over in a twinkling but to me it was a moment
of tense interest, because I knew of their long estrangement. They
walked away, but not side by side."

After this incident there was some show of irritation by the Roosevelt
family because the Colonel (it was charged) had been brought without warning into such close contact with Taft. Fortunately, Anson
Phelps Stokes, then secretary of Yale University, had had charge of
the funeral arrangements and, with his usual foresight, had named all
the pallbearers in his telegram of invitation to Roosevelt. The fact that
Taft was on the list had evidently failed to register; but when Stokes
produced a copy of his telegram it became clear that if there had been
any fault it was at the Roosevelt end of the line.

During this period issues in Pennsylvania loomed large. In 1914 there
was the choice of a Governor to be made and also of a United States
Senator. Doctor Brumbaugh, a schoolman, who for the first time
aroused political interest among the Amish people of the Commonwealth, was the Republican candidate for governor. My friend William
Draper Lewis had aspired to a gubernatorial nomination and for a time
conducted an active campaign. I was caught in a crossfire between my
reluctance to support an advocate of Roosevelt's constitutional ideas and
my unwillingness to oppose a warm personal friend. The final way of
escape was to sign up with a nonpartisan committee advocating Lewis's
nomination. Later he withdrew and thus left me free to support Brumbaugh who was elected by a big majority. He was a good citizen but his
administration was not notable. The World War was making local
issues seem unimportant.

In the same year, for the first time, a United States Senator was to be
elected by popular vote instead of by the legislature. A good deal of
friendly pressure was brought upon me to come out as a candidate for
the nomination. Had I done so I should merely have made myself
ridiculous. When, however, Pinchot decided to oppose Penrose another
choice had to be made. Pinchot's constitutional views, if he had any,
were presumably like those of his former chief. On the other hand I
thought that Penrose's cynical political philosophy meant ultimate Republican disaster. At least that is the way I now rationalize my attitude. Probably the true explanation is that I sensed Penrose's dislike
of me and therefore dignified an emotion of resentment by treating it

as a reasoned judgment. I think, too, I had a feeling of loyalty to the man who had once been my client. At all events, I came out for Pinchot. He was unable to secure the support for which he had hoped and Penrose was triumphantly nominated and elected. My impression is that in Pinchot's inability to induce Andrew W. Mellon to support him at this time is to be found the explanation of his subsequent persistent hostility to the man whom he would gladly have welcomed to his corner.

Reviewing the period between 1890 and 1914, I conclude that my dabbling in politics was of small use to me or to anybody else. I did nothing effective and learned surprisingly little about political organization. If I had enlisted as a regular party worker instead of serving as an amateurish volunteer I should have been far better prepared than I was when later the senatorship came my way. I find myself wishing that all young Americans would early develop a serious sense of party responsibility. Especially in the postwar period will there be desperate need for collective action deliberately taken rather than for impulsive outbursts of individual activity.

Twentieth-Century Optimism

"When the sea is calm the careless sailor relaxes."
—OVID: *Ars Amatoria;* Bk. III, l. 259

THE LAW SCHOOL

MY more serious activities included a law practice, which at the turn of the century was growing more and more active, and a heavy teaching assignment at the Law School. In February of 1901 came the long-expected dedication of the new Law School Building. I had opposed so earnestly those who wished the School to be housed in the midst of the city that the final selection by Provost Harrison and the Trustees of a site near the University gave me a feeling of almost personal triumph. I had worked hard in seconding the Provost's money-raising efforts. To see our dream converted into reality seemed almost too good to be true.

The dedication banquet brought together a notable group of people. There were representatives of the historic universities of England, of sixteen American law schools, of the State Judiciary from Massachusetts to Minnesota, of the Federal Judiciary, as well as a number of men distinguished in public life. Among the latter was Wu Ting Fang, the Chinese Minister to the United States, who proved himself a witty and delightful speaker. I had prepared myself to respond to the toast "The University of Pennsylvania" and, when called upon, I got away to a good start. However, I must have overstrained my vocal cords, in an effort to be heard all over the great hall, for suddenly I completely lost my voice. After a few ineffectual efforts at articulation I had to give up and sit down, much to my own discomfiture—and possibly to the satisfaction of diners who were already surfeited. The building went into commission unaffected by my vocal breakdown and in it the Law School entered forthwith upon a new era of development. For the nine ensuing years I met my classes there and spent that large part of my time and effort which was devoted to the teaching of law. In 1903 I was elected Solicitor to the Commissioners of Fairmount Park, a position which I still hold. The same year I was appointed Receiver of the Bay State Gas Company by the District Court of the United States for the District of Delaware.

FRENZIED FINANCE

The dramatic story of the Bay State Gas Company is too long to tell here in all of its myriad details. The leading man in the cast was a daring and picturesque promoter, J. Edward Addicks. I had first heard of him when he was striving to get himself elected to the United States Senate from Delaware. There were all sorts of rumors respecting the means he employed to accomplish his purpose. Whatever they were, they were unsuccessful and he thereafter devoted all of his energies to the spectacular promotion of various corporate enterprises.

Another notable person of the Bay State drama was Thomas W. Lawson. His headquarters were in Boston where he became a disturbing figure in the financial world and at one time was supposed to be wealthy. Brilliant and unstable, he had a genius for effective publicity of all sorts. The only seven-masted schooner I ever saw was named after him. Some magazine articles of his entitled "Frenzied Finance" were widely read and caused a good many headaches among the big capitalists whom it was his "line" to treat with scant respect. Addicks's specialty was outwitting persons of distinction. Lawson's was to subject them to sensational attacks which stopped just short of actionable defamation. Addicks by some bold financing had gained control of the stock of four Boston gas companies and had vested that control in the Bay State Gas Company of Delaware. This remarkable concern was organized under a special charter which Addicks had secured from the Delaware Legislature. After a meteoric career, during which he cut a great figure as a multimillionaire, the day of reckoning came. Creditors and stockholders woke up and began to assert their rights. It was in a bondholder's suit that I was appointed receiver. This was followed by my appointment as ancillary receiver by the Federal Court in Massachusetts and later in New York.

In all three jurisdictions I found complicated financial situations and it at once became my duty to begin a series of litigations of which the three most notable were suits in Massachusetts against Kidder, Peabody & Company, Tom Lawson and Henry H. Rogers.

As in these suits I was attacking some of the most powerful people in New England, whose lawyers included most of the men of eminence at the Boston Bar, I was led to retain as my counsel Sherman L. Whipple who, at the time, had a great reputation as a daring and courageous fighter and was both hated and feared by those against whom I was asserting claims. We lost the Kidder, Peabody suit, effected an advantageous settlement with Lawson and secured a decree against Rogers for an accounting which later yielded a million and a half dollars in settlement. The theory of this last recovery was that Rogers had made a profit on the sale of certain securities by using to his own advantage his position as voting trustee.

STRANGE INTERLUDE

After the United States District Court had entered against Rogers a decree directing him to account, but before the accounting had begun, I was one day called by telephone from New York by Miss Kate Harrison, Mr. Rogers's efficient secretary. He wished to know, she said, whether I could call upon him in the near future at 26 Broadway. "At once," I replied, and took the first train. Entering a paneled reception room on an upper floor, my presence was barely tolerated by two huge Negro doormen in livery. Presently through a doorway in the paneling Miss Harrison entered and explained that Mr. Rogers could not come to his office because the building was surrounded by writ-servers. He accordingly invited me to join him at another place. Those were the days when suits against the Standard Oil Company and its magnates were being pressed in many jurisdictions and by various attorneys general; and powerful defendants had not yet learned that subpoena dodging is a losing game.

"Go down in the elevator," said Miss Harrison. "Speak to nobody. Enter an electric brougham which will be waiting at the curb. Give no instructions to the driver. He knows what to do." He certainly did. As I entered the cab several men sprang into action from observation posts up and down the street; but the chauffeur was too quick for them. We were off on a wilder ride than I had ever known. There were no traffic lights in those days and we swung from one narrow street into another, scattering pedestrians like poultry, the writ-servers left hopelessly behind. Suddenly we stopped at a side door of a large building. I entered. An elevator attendant asked if I were Mr. Pepper. He took me to an upper floor, led me along a corridor, threw open an office door —and ushered me into the great man's presence. He received me affably and for about an hour entertained me with most interesting conversation on general topics but never a word about the lawsuit. He had lately been cruising on his yacht and told a number of anecdotes about Mark Twain, whom he had had aboard as a guest. He showed me photographs and autographs and talked about the events of the day. Finally I rose to go. We shook hands and just before I left he said, "I believe you have some sort of a lawsuit against me." "Yes," I answered, "up in Boston." "Well," he rejoined, "I guess we'll not have any trouble about that." "I hope not," I replied—and the visit was over.

A great deal mystified, I decided to wait for the next move. I did not wait long. In a few days Randal Morgan, an officer of the United Gas Improvement Company of Philadelphia, came to see me and offered to buy some shares of stock in the Buffalo Gas Company which, while listed as assets of my receivership, were actually without market value. He said that if I would "throw in" an assignment of the judgment and claim against Mr. Rogers, he, Morgan, would pay one and a half million dollars for the shares. This sum equaled my estimate of the probable ultimate recovery in the Rogers suit. Of course I asked no questions and promptly accepted the offer. Necessary court approval was obtained and settlement was duly made. Just what relation my interview with Mr. Rogers bore to this adjustment, I do not know. Men of his mold had their own way of doing things. At all events, without making any concessions and without seeming to settle, the suit was actually disposed of —and on terms that were fair to both sides.

For Addicks I conceived the sort of regard that Robin Hood no doubt inspired. Although I had to play the part of Nemesis in his drama he never showed the slightest personal resentment. He wore the same smile in adversity as he had worn when he was on the crest of the wave —and likewise the same priceless fur coat. During five years of this arduous receivership I was ably guided and represented by William B. Bodine and Francis B. Bracken, both of the Philadelphia Bar, whom I had retained as receiver's counsel. Without their wisdom and diligence the remarkable results obtained would have been impossible.

JAMESTOWN RECALLED

With 1907 came a reminder that three centuries had passed since the settlement at Jamestown[1] gave English Christianity a foothold on the Western Hemisphere. It was to commemorate the achievement of these settlers in bringing English Christianity to America and to celebrate the tercentenary of their landing at nearby Jamestown that the General Convention of the Episcopal Church met at Richmond in 1907.[2]

A year in advance of the Convention the Board of Missions had proposed a thank offering by the men of the Episcopal Church for three hundred years of English Christianity. A central committee of three was appointed to carry out the plan. Bishop Greer of New York was chairman, George C. Thomas was treasurer and I was secretary. I threw myself into the enterprise with zeal, conducted an extensive correspondence, made addresses in various parts of the country and attended the Richmond Convention as a deputy.

It was a real experience. The "M.T.O." (Missionary Thank Offering) was presented at a big meeting held in a vast building noted for defective acoustics. Several of the speakers were quite inaudible. Just before it came my turn to speak a man in the crowd did me a great service. He mounted the platform steps and whispered to me that William Jennings Bryan had discovered the secret of how to make himself heard

---

[1] I have asked a good many people who it was that commanded the expedition which effected that historic settlement. The answer usually is "Captain John Smith." He was in fact the captain of one of the ships but the commander of the little fleet was Captain Christopher Newport, the man who had once repaired the shattered fortunes of Sir Walter Raleigh by capturing for him a Spanish treasure ship. This adventurous skipper, in spite of violent storms, brought the *Discovery,* the *Godspeed* and the *Sarah Constant* safely across the Atlantic. They at last dropped anchor in Hampton Roads. The name "Old Point Comfort" gives a hint of the state of mind of Captain Newport himself, of Captain John Smith and of the rest of the storm-tossed settlers. There is a tradition that Newport News was the point at which Captain Newport received the news of the availability of Jamestown as a landing place. I understand, however, that "News" is a corruption of "Newse," the name of the captain of one of the ships in Newport's little fleet.

[2] The habit of reckoning anniversaries once formed is hard to curb. 1907 was not only the tercentenary of the landing at Jamestown but also the bicentenary of that union of England and Scotland which gave Great Britain to the world. It was, moreover, the centenary of the abolition of slavery by the British Parliament. Principally because of Jamestown, however, 1907 was a notable date and the General Convention of that year had a distinctive flavor of its own.

in that particular building. Indicating a certain iron column among the many that carried the roof, my unknown benefactor told me to speak to that column and all would be well. I did so and, as I afterward learned, was heard perfectly by everybody. Why this was so is just another of those mysteries which appear to baffle even the experts.

ACADEMIC EXPERIENCES

In my own life 1907 marked an anniversary of importance. At the commencement exercises my Alma Mater made me a Doctor of Laws. I was immensely gratified but fortunately had sense enough to realize that I was not nearly so big a man as the citation implied.

The next year brought more academic experiences. I shared with Woodrow Wilson the speakers' platform at the seventy-fifth anniversary of the founding of Haverford College. He impressed me as being conscious of intellectual superiority and as having a trace of arrogance. His elocution was admirable and his speech was English at its best.

Later, as commencement orator at the University of the South, I was given the degree of Doctor of the Civil Law.

FEES AND A FARM

From the time of our marriage I was always able to make a comfortable living out of my practice although there were many anxious days. The immense amount of time and effort spent on Church and University no doubt kept my professional income from growing faster than it did. Moreover the freedom with which I have contributed out of earnings to all the causes that were near my heart has always made it impossible for me to accumulate an appreciable estate. In spite of these factors, however, my earnings during this period were steadily increasing and I began to lay something by. Two large fees were received in 1907, one for my services in the Bay State Gas case and the other for the successful handling for several clients of protracted litigation over the will of Henry Norris.

Having suddenly become relatively affluent my wife and I decided to acquire a country place. We were not sending the children away to boarding schools. It was therefore important to provide, if possible, some wholesome attraction which would make their leisure hours less of a problem than when spent in town. A place in the country seemed to be the solution. The choice lay between a small tract of high-priced land near a railroad station and a large tract in the more remote farming area. We decided in favor of a farm and in August of 1907 bought in Easttown Township, Chester County, a beautiful tract of farmland and woodland. The tract comprised 177 acres. The property had once belonged to the sisters of General Anthony Wayne and we were glad to find his signature as an attesting witness to one of the old deeds. Upon the land there stood a stone farmhouse somewhat more than a hundred years old. There was a stream running through the property; and as foxes—as well as other small game—were plentiful, we named the stream Fox Creek and to the place itself we gave the name of Fox Creek Farm. We enlarged the house, being careful to preserve its most distinctive features which included a fireplace about five feet high and eight feet wide.

As the place was more than four miles from Devon, the nearest railroad station, an automobile became a necessity. Both before and after we moved into the remodeled farmhouse we used the place as we had hoped to do. I made up my mind to devote week ends to my son and for several years the office did not see me from Friday evening until Monday morning. My son and I, sometimes with and sometimes without some of his friends, used to camp in the woods or in one of the farm buildings and give ourselves up to the pleasures that are to be found out of doors. We dammed the stream and made a big swimming pool and we also had a tennis court that was really first-class even though homemade. Altogether the acquisition of the farm was an unqualified success and it became the happiest of happy homes. A large part of the third (or attic) story of the house was kept free from subdividing partitions. Equipped with cots after the manner of a dormitory it became known as the "Violent Ward." Here my son or my daughters could accommodate groups of their friends and so make the house a sort of gathering place for the young. My wife took over the management of the farm and soon became a practical farmer. A herd of over thirty cows, a drove of Berkshire pigs, a flock of chickens, butter-making and a milk route would have daunted a less courageous spirit. Her responsibilities in addition to the housekeeping were made heavier by acting as train-dispatcher for the automobile. In those days not so many households had cars of their own and the task of collecting, transporting and discharging both the children's guests and our own and doing the same for all the members of the family was not a light one. All this she managed with extraordinary efficiency and no apparent strain, although actually it must have made an enormous demand upon her vitality.

TEACHING AND WRITING

While I had declined to go on the federal bench in favor of an active advocacy, I still carried on my Law School work. As a sort of by-product of it, I did a great deal of Bible-class and mission-study teaching. Some of this was done in St. Mark's Parish, where my son was in my class; some with groups of young people in other parishes, and some among law students. For several years we held a daily chapel service in the Law School, attended chiefly by students who were in my evening Bible class. Every now and then I meet in different parts of the country former students who recall with satisfaction their share in these activities. In connection with the teaching of my son and other boys I developed a devotional manual which was later published under the title *The Way.* I had intended to prepare two companion volumes, *The Truth* and *The Life,* but absorption in other tasks prevented. Even *The Way* was prepared under difficulties. My habit was to go daily to the 7:45 A.M. service at St. Mark's. This enabled me to reach the office at 8:20 and so gave me every day a forty-minute interval for work on the book before business began at nine.

The little volume was quite widely used. A copy of it some years later came into the hands of Maurice F. C. Honoré, a Roman Catholic layman who, though living in England, had many connections in his native France. He had the book translated by a French priest for the use of soldiers in the trenches during the World War. By an arrangement between us the proceeds of sale, added to some funds which I supplied, were to be used to facilitate the work of Roman Catholic military chaplains in carrying the Communion to soldiers in hospitals and at the front. Mr. Honoré also translated into French and published an essay of mine entitled *Vision of Unity.* The proceeds of the sale of this were to be used for the support of French priests at the front. For a number of years, without ever having seen one another, Honoré and I corresponded. Our correspondence, however, in the postwar period came to an abrupt and unhappy end.

GATHERING SHADOWS

1909 brought sadness into our lives. In August of that year, after a long and lingering illness, my brother-in-law, J. Alison Scott, died. We had brought him to Northeast Harbor in the vain hope that the air of Maine would restore his strength. He had contracted a streptococcal infection during his service at the Pennsylvania Hospital and this gradually wore him down. He and I had been warm friends long before he met my sister and there was no one among my contemporaries who meant as much to me as he did. He had demonstrated his capacity as a physician and was moving forward to a place of leadership in the profession. He had hosts of friends and I never heard anyone speak of him except in terms of praise.

In the following December my father-in-law, Professor George Park Fisher, died in his eighty-third year. For some time his health had been seriously impaired and to him death came as a blessed release. To my wife and me, who could think of him only as he was in his prime, his passing was a poignant grief. He was one of those rare men whom to know was to love and with whom to associate was a liberal education.

THE WAYS PART

In 1910, after having been for twenty-one years a member of the teaching force, I regretfully resigned my professorship in the Law School. Although only forty-three years old I was then the senior member of the faculty in point of active service. For two or three years I had been compelled to reduce my teaching load to a single course on account of the inexorable demands of growing practice. The intensity of the struggle to combine teaching and practice is indicated by the fact that all through the Ballinger-Pinchot case I had to commute between Washington and Philadelphia and meet my classes at hours specially arranged to dovetail with sessions of the Committee.

Sometime after my resignation from the Law School Faculty the Trustees of the University elected me a member of the Board.

JOY AND SORROW

When the summer of 1912 rolled around I took my wife and three children on a European trip. This was to be for the children their first experience of European travel, and for the parents it was a welcome opportunity for uninterrupted companionship with the children. Our idea was to cover a good deal of ground and thus give the children a bird's-eye view of the Old World which later they might explore more thoroughly. We engaged our east-bound passage on the *Titanic*. When that ill-fated ship went down on a west-bound voyage we shifted to the *Kronprincessin Cecilie,* a vessel destined to figure in the World War. Our trip was an unqualified success. Not the least delightful feature of it was our reunion with my brother-in-law, William Forbes Fisher, then a bachelor living in London. He had gone abroad years before to establish the London branch of the banking house of William P. Bonbright and Company and had made for himself a host of friends. Some of his friends, eager to have him a member of a well-known London Club, had proposed to repeal for a day the club bylaw making it a condition of eligibility that a man should be a British subject. All depended upon the attitude of the president of the club, a dignified peer to whom, with some trepidation on the part of his friends, Billy was introduced. "During your London sojourn," inquired the old gentleman, "what, Mr. Fisher, has impressed you most?" Billy's reply was instant and unhesitating. "The way," said he, "in which members of this Club hold their liquor." His backers were horrified. The peer was enchanted. The bylaw was repealed, Billy was elected and the regulation immediately reimposed. Of all the men I have ever known Billy Fisher was the most entertaining and lovable. His humor was irresistible and his kindness overpowering, while his freedom from every sort of affectation was a constant delight. Not long after this he met and fell in love with Mary Putnam, an American woman of a charm not unlike his own. Their marriage was followed by a life of perfect happiness which ended only when, in 1937, Billy died.

On our outward voyage I had read with conviction Norman Angell's book *The Great Illusion*. I gladly accepted his demonstration of the futility of war and made the common mistake of supposing that because a thing can be proved futile its nonrecurrence is assured. As I saw everywhere on the Continent signs of military preparedness I developed a smug conviction of superior intelligence and thought patronizingly that these were merely constant rehearsals for a performance which could never take place.

IRREPARABLE LOSS

When we reached home after a happy journey we were grieved to find my mother far from well. During the winter she gradually failed. She was able in the early spring of 1913 to move out to the Garth, her summer home at Strafford. There were the garden which she had developed and the flowers that she loved. Her last days were spent among them. Then she became acutely ill and on Ascension Day, April 30th, she entered into rest. She had done so much good to so many and she possessed such individuality and charm that to this day, some thirty years later, people often speak of her to me and tell me that they miss her.

BLIND OPTIMISM

Absorption in home affairs and in our own political feuds had made me, during this period, anything but a penetrating observer of world affairs. It was obvious, however, that a good many storm clouds were bursting in the first decade of the twentieth century and that much world history was being made.

Looking backward, I find it almost unbelievable that the spirit of optimism could have been as strong as it was in the years leading up to 1914.

Idealism and Disillusionment

1. REAL WAR

"Know you are *bound to help* all who are wronged—
Bound to constrain all who destroy the law.
What else holds state to state but this alone,
That each one honors the great laws of right."

—EURIPIDES: *The Suppliants*

THE fateful year of 1914 opened (as far as I was concerned) without any warning of mines in the channel. Early in the year I was urged to accept an appointment from the Carnegie Endowment for International Peace to deliver a course of lectures in Japan. Among those who pressed me to accept were President Nicholas Murray Butler, Dr. Hamilton W. Mabie and Charlemagne Tower. I could not, however, afford a six-month absence, involving separation from my family and a dislocation of my practice. It was an unusual opportunity and I passed it by with regret. In line with assertions that there would have been no World War had the United States joined the League of Nations, I suppose I may modestly suggest that if only I had delivered those lectures we should now be at peace with Japan.

Our own relations with Mexico were at this time strained to the breaking point. I was still enjoying the sense of false security which a reading of Angell's book had given me. President Wilson had taken the position that since Huerta had waded through slaughter to a throne he and his government could not be recognized by the United States. This is a type of international policy which almost always ends in trouble. The arrest of some American sailors in Mexico led Admiral

Mayo to demand a salute to the flag to which demand Huerta of course refused to accede. Thereupon Wilson ordered what he called a "pacific blockade" and directed the fleet to seize the customs house at Vera Cruz and occupy the city. I was asked to write, and did write for the Philadelphia *Evening Bulletin,* an editorial on the subject. In it I expressed the view that we were witnessing a hazardous experiment in international law. In the event of civil war in Mexico and the recognition of both parties as belligerents it would be the duty of the United States to respect any effective blockade by either belligerent of the ports of the other. But I pointed out that as we had refused to extend diplomatic recognition to the offending contestant, we could not possibly justify forcible entry upon Mexican territory to take vengeance for what in that event was not a governmental act at all. I concluded that we were trying to cover up a diplomatic blunder by making new law. Fortunately for us it was an unequal contest. Huerta had not the power or resources to maintain his position; and although the salute to the flag was never given, his subsequent resignation was followed by the recognition of Caranza's *de facto* government, and so diplomatic relations were restored. To those who like to have the international game played according to the rules it is exasperating to see our government so often violating them and yet escaping the consequences because of superior force. It is a fair question today whether our State Department would have needled Japan as consistently as for years we have done if we had realized the military and naval strength of the Island Empire.

THE LIGHTNING FLASH

In 1914, when my wife and I arrived at Northeast Harbor, Bishop Brewster of Connecticut, who was about to go abroad as a member of a commission to make some sort of a missionary survey, asked me on July 31st whether there would be a general European war. In sublime ignorance of the true situation I pooh-poohed the idea. The very next day Germany declared war on Russia. I was aghast. The terrible truth dawned upon me. To prove to me that war is futile had been as easy as to demonstrate that the wages of sin is death; but to infer that a thing proved futile cannot happen, I now realized, was as grievous a mistake as to suppose that mere knowledge of consequences prevents sin.

After the lapse of thirty years I can make a fairly objective appraisement of myself as I was in 1914. I had inherited the idea that when the other fellow picked a quarrel the thing to do was to "accommodate" him. I had always assumed that this should be the code of nations as well as of individuals. When Germany violated Belgian neutrality it accordingly seemed obvious that Germany must be punished for such an offense and that it was the manifest duty of the United States to help do the punishing. I did not stop to consider what "punishment" involved or what was likely to happen after it had been inflicted. I had had no occasion to study the tragic history of the peace treaties of the past and I had little or no conception of the degree to which national self-interest could be disguised as unselfish philanthropy. I was convinced that the time to fight had come. France was threatened. England needed help. I was quite ready to see my country involved in a war which seemed all the more honorable because it was not of our own making. I easily satisfied myself that for the United States to remain passive would be as discreditable as for an able-bodied man to stand idly by when a woman or a child was being menaced by a ruffian. Thus the course of my psychological development was almost precisely the reverse of President Wilson's. He began by proclaiming neutrality in thought and ended by trying, through a League of Nations, so to organize the force of the world as to make sure that no nation would ever again dare to take up arms. I began as a violent partisan of the Allies and ended with the conviction that instead of imposing a ruthless treaty upon a prostrate nation magnanimity to a fallen foe is the only effective guaranty of lasting peace.

In the late summer of 1914, however, I could see only one major objective—and that was to defeat the Kaiser. Foch's great victory at the Marne in early September gave new hope to the Western world and quickened the impulse to lend a hand. For the first time I was led seriously to consider the military unpreparedness of the United States. This unpreparedness was, of course, the result of the widespread delusion which had distorted my own outlook. War was futile. It simply could not happen. Why not, as Mr. Bryan suggested, rest comfortably in the assurance that overnight a million men would leap to arms? Heedless of the lessons of the Spanish War, we had persisted in this view. I determined to co-operate actively with General Wood and others who were already laying emergency plans to relieve the situation in which we suddenly found ourselves.

October brought a letter from Sir Gilbert Parker who wrote from London to me and to a number of other men in the United States. He enclosed copies of the three "white papers" issued by the British Government and urged upon those capable of influencing public opinion to promote a clear understanding of the true history of the tragic conflict.

WAR AND PEACE

All the while, although the war was much in my thoughts, I was going about my daily business as usual. In November President Hadley offered me the Deanship of the Yale Law School and earnestly pressed me to accept. His offer compelled me to consider anew the question which I thought I had settled forever when I resigned from the law faculty at Pennsylvania. I did consider it—but reached the same conclusion as before and decided to remain in active practice. If the "Liberals" who now dominate the Yale School read this they may well shiver at their narrow escape.

During the winter of 1914-1915 I devoted all the time I could spare from practice to preparing for delivery at Yale the Lyman Beecher Lectures on Preaching. Lectures on this subject had been delivered periodically on a foundation created in 1871, the lectureship to be filled "by a minister of the Gospel, of any evangelical denomination, who has been markedly successful in the special work of the Christian ministry." Under a very liberal interpretation of this provision the Corporation of Yale College invited me to deliver the lectures for 1915. I was, I believe, the first layman so honored. The lectures, six in number, were afterward published in a volume entitled *A Voice from the Crowd*. The book went through several editions. My aim was constructive criticism of preaching not only from the point of view of the man in the pew but of the greater crowd outside the door of the church.

In the year 1915 I saw no inconsistency between lectures on the preaching of the Gospel and exhortations to take up arms. I am not now, and never have been, a pacifist. I hold now and have always held that the use of physical force so organized and applied as to constitute war is not only often justifiable but is sometimes an inescapable duty. I have never supposed that wars could be classified as offensive or defensive. This is to substitute a mere difference in strategy for a distinction between the aims of the belligerents. The test of a justifiable war is the expected use to be made of victory. In 1915 I had a vision of victory to be followed by a just and righteous peace.

TEAPOT TEMPEST

While both a World War and I were raging, a teapot tempest was brewing in the University. One of my duties as a trustee was to unite with my colleagues in deciding each year whether assistant professors with limited tenure should at the end of their term have their appointments renewed. An assistant professor in the Wharton School, Scott Nearing, seemed to me to be more concerned with advertising himself by sensational utterances in the press than with the responsible discharge of his duties as a teacher. It was one of those cases in which a responsible elector has to decide whether a teacher is doing the institution more harm than good. I thought that he was and accordingly voted with a majority of the trustees against his reappointment. Immediately an effort was made by some uninformed individuals to stir up a widespread protest against what was represented as an attempt to stifle academic freedom. This is the easiest sort of a campaign to conduct. There are always plenty of people who like to write letters of protest. Pretty soon we received a flood of communications characterized by insolent cocksureness, unworthy suspicion and unbelievable narrowness. Some of them were appallingly illiterate. Apart from these there were half a dozen polite letters of inquiry, written spontaneously. In every case the writers of this latter sort appeared satisfied when they learned the facts. The American Association of University Professors also interested themselves in the case and appointed a committee of investigation. My good friend Professor Lightner Witmer wrote a book on the Nearing episode in which I was lampooned as an enemy of free speech or something. Nearing himself, as far as I know, never made any complaint and immediately entered the service of another institution. As to the substance of his expressed views, as distinguished from the manner of utterance, I do not recall any instance in which he had gone beyond the limit of fair comment—except, perhaps, a statement that anybody living on the income of invested wealth is necessarily a social menace. Whether he actually said this I do not know. If so, it was a little rough on some of the people whose money he relied on for the payment of his salary.

Uninformed epistolary attack must be expected by every man in a public or semipublic position who takes a decided stand on a controversial point. This is the reason that cautious men in political office are careful to hedge on public questions. Some, of course, are more honest and have the courage of their convictions. Senator Penrose was of this sort. He spoke out bluntly and took the consequences. He once remarked that he was so used to being kicked on the backside that he never turned around to see who did it. Some of my own experiences of this sort have been very diverting, especially in the case of irate clergymen whom I have found to be among the most irresponsible letter writers. Indeed at one time I gave up reading the church papers because the spirit in which controversies were conducted in their columns seemed to me to be little short of scandalous.

NATIONAL PREPAREDNESS

During the winter and spring of 1915 the movement for national preparedness made great headway. General Leonard Wood was the accepted leader of the movement and Theodore Roosevelt its hearty supporter.

The establishment at Plattsburg in 1915 of a military training camp on a large scale followed successful experiments conducted elsewhere by General Wood during the two preceding years. At first enrollment dragged a bit. Younger men seemed slow to realize the importance of the movement. Like a good many other men of my generation I decided that it was "up to me" to supplement my talk by action. I accordingly made up my mind to seek admission to the camp as a "rookie" in the hope that such a step would influence others to do the like. Although in my forty-ninth year, I was in prime physical condition and accustomed to outdoor life. I knew therefore that I could stand the test. The problem was to get myself accepted. I bethought me of my friend Harry Stimson, former Secretary of War, and on July 21st I sent him the following telegram:

"Have applied for admission to Plattsburg Camp although somewhat over age. Hope you will wire Officer-in-Charge of Military Training Camps, Governor's Island, recommending me as fit for service."

To this came the prompt reply:

"Bully for you! You are a thoroughbred. I have telegraphed General Wood about you and will try to write him today." [1]

Two days later I was notified by wire from Plattsburg that my application had been accepted and when the camp opened I reported for duty. My cousin and partner Franklin Pepper went with me. He was thirty-six years old, of fine physique and in all respects a splendid specimen of American manhood. We were both assigned to a company commanded by a Lieutenant Sutherland. We at once threw ourselves with enthusiasm into the life and work of the camp.

There were many fine men in that camp. One of them was Robert

---

[1] Typical of Stimson's loyal friendship.

Bacon. Several years later, after his death, I wrote at his biographer's request an account of his service at Plattsburg.

At least one incident of camp life at Plattsburg had far-reaching political consequences. It may have had something to do with President Wilson's subsequent refusal to allow Theodore Roosevelt to recruit a regiment for service abroad or to assign General Wood to an overseas command. The incident was a speech to the regiment by Theodore Roosevelt. General Wood had played the game according to the rules and had obtained the official consent of the then Secretary of War to invite the Colonel to address us. Nevertheless the General was subsequently criticized for the Colonel's speech as if the invitation to speak had been unauthorized or as if General Wood or any other power on earth could have controlled the Colonel's utterance. In point of fact, the things that "broke big" in the newspapers of the following day were not said during the speech. I was there and heard all that was said; and I am trained to remember. After the speech the Colonel is said to have talked freely to newspaper men at the railroad station. It was doubtless at this interview, when he was literally "off the reservation," that he made the comments on President Wilson's policy which incurred for General Wood the displeasure of the Chief Executive. All that the Colonel said to us in camp was beyond the reach of fair criticism. He was asked to speak in order to deepen our convictions and to stimulate our morale. He certainly did both. The picture is unforgettable. There stands the Colonel in the open field. Around him, seated on the grass or standing in the background, are the men of the regiment and the Army officers who are our instructors. It is sunset and there is a transfiguring glow upon the speaker's face. It was indeed sunset for him but we had the naïve hope that for the world it was the dawning of a new day.

On the whole the Plattsburg experiment in 1915 was a notable success. I wrote the verse of a song which was sung lustily just before we broke camp:

> "Last night with my head in a puddle—
> Last night as I lay in the rain—
> Last night with my kit in a muddle—
> I swore I'd be coming again!"

We were as good as our word. In 1916 Franklin Pepper and I did go again. Our experiences were much like those of the previous year except that the rookies were more widely representative of American life. Archie Roosevelt, as top sergeant in my company, displayed qualities which compelled esteem. Franklin and I were made rookie sergeants which some wag declared was promotion to the lowest form of animal life. On the hike I had the good luck to share a "pup tent" with William C. Coleman of Baltimore, who later attained distinction as a Federal Judge. Our comradeship ripened into an intimate and enduring friendship.

After the period of training was over I wrote a note to Colonel Roosevelt telling him of the high esteem in which Archie had been held by the rank and file. I have his holographic reply written from Sagamore Hill. It read as follows:

> It was very good and thoughtful of you to write about Archie; naturally Mrs. Roosevelt and I were greatly pleased by what you said, and much touched by your taking the trouble to write. Your presence in the company really impressed Archie and Dick.[2] By the way, I have a pretty nice son-in-law, haven't I? When you are passing through New York, can't Mrs. Pepper and you motor out here for lunch or dinner? Mrs. Roosevelt and I would be glad to see you.
>
> With real thanks, Faithfully yours,
>
> THEODORE ROOSEVELT

CROSSCURRENTS AND ROUGH WATER

Back again at the office in fine physical condition, I found that the camp quickly became a distant memory. In the preceding June the Democrats had renominated Wilson. The Republicans in a determined effort to defeat him had drafted Charles Evans Hughes, then an Associate Justice of the Supreme Court of the United States. I backed Hughes both as the candidate of my Party and also because I was exasperated by what I then regarded as vacillation on Wilson's part. In view of what was to happen a few months later there is an element of grim humor in recalling that the most effective campaign slogan of Wilson's supporters was "He kept us out of war."

The events of 1916 in all theaters of war had been such as to arouse the fighting spirit of everybody who earnestly believed in the Allied cause. The course of the war during that year had filled us with grave misgivings.

President Wilson chose this time for an invitation to the belligerents to announce the terms on which peace might be concluded. The Kaiser promptly took advantage of this invitation and proposed terms that were obviously impossible. He also sought to bring about a round-table discus-

---

[2] Dr. Richard Derby who married the Colonel's daughter, Ethel.

sion with the Allies, without participation in the conference by the United States. The situation seemed fraught with peril because at the moment it looked as if a premature peace would enable Germany to escape the consequences of her ruthlessness. I was one of the multitude who had not yet learned that punishment of the vanquished is merely the prelude to a later war. Accordingly I was strong for decisive chastisement. On the initiative of Dr. William T. Ellis, he and I drafted "A Plea for a Lasting Peace." This was sent to representative men, both clergymen and laymen, in each of the great Christian Communions, Catholic and Protestant. The response was extremely enthusiastic and indicates how easily we Christians can domesticate un-Christian hatred. Dr. Lyman Abbott when appending his signature wrote this:

> "Thank you for allowing me to put my name to the protest against an unjust peace. The dignity of its form is its least value. The spiritual faith and the passion for righteousness which illuminates and animates it make it certainly unsurpassed and, so far as I recall, unequaled by any paper called out by the war. I am very glad to have had the privilege of subscribing my name to it."

The document was published over a great number of important signatures and received commendation from all parts of the country. It also received virulent condemnation. *The Fatherland,* a German-American paper, selected from among the signers a list of eighteen and published it with my name at the head of the list. "Let these names," said the writer of the editorial, "stand written in letters of blood in the Book of Shame." Lord Bryce, on the other hand, later wrote to me from London that this address was "one of the most powerful and impressive documents the war has called forth." He added, "It puts the case against 'a peace without victory' in the clearest and most convincing way."

THE CLOUDBURST

While thus there was intensified warfare abroad and acute dissension at home, I was carrying the usual load of office and court work and also taking every opportunity to promote the cause of preparedness. Of all the meetings at which I spoke two, in retrospect, seem the most notable. Both were in New York—one in Carnegie Hall and the other in Madison Square Garden. Over the former Mr. Joseph Choate presided. It was the last time I ever saw him. He and some other speakers spent their strength in criticizing President Wilson. It seemed to me that what was needed at that particular moment was affirmation and inspiration. I sensed the eagerness of the immense audience for emotional relief. When I spoke it was in this vein. Immediately afterward a woman whom I had never seen came forward and offered to contribute $10,000 to have my speech printed and distributed all over the country. I told her that the occasion and the audience had made the speech; that what I had actually said was in no way remarkable and that if read in print the speech would have little effect. As she persisted, I finally agreed to send her the steno-graphic notes when transcribed so that she could then decide which of us was right. I later sent her the notes and shortly thereafter had from her an extremely interesting letter in which she admitted that the speech when read in the cold gray dawn lacked the compelling power which she had vainly hoped to reproduce.

The second meeting packed Madison Square Garden to the roof—an audience of twelve or fifteen thousand people. I think it was the largest audience which up to that time I had ever addressed. The other speakers were Elihu Root, Mayor Mitchel of New York, Charles S. Fairchild, former Secretary of the Treasury, and President Hibben of Princeton. An organized effort by German sympathizers to break up the meeting was suppressed by members of the Home Defense League who none too gently conducted some hecklers to the fire escapes. Mr. Root was in good form and was loudly applauded. A letter from Theodore Roosevelt was cheered to the echo. I spoke of the importance to the Allied cause of the early appearance of the American flag upon the battle front; and sug-gested the possibility of combing the ranks of the Allies for American volunteers already at the front and assembling them into a single unit under their own flag in readiness for the inevitable declaration of war. From various parts of the United States I received vituperative protests against such an utterance and angry predictions that no American soldier boy would ever cross the sea. Within ten days, however, President Wilson decided that the time had come to act. He made it known that on April 2nd he would address the Congress. At the time appointed for the speech several of us had assembled at the home of my friend Thomas Newhall at Ithan, Pa.[3] These were the days before radio broadcasting had been

[3] Newhall later went overseas as a Lieutenant in the United States Naval Mine Force and was subsequently promoted to be Lieutenant Commander, with head-quarters at Inverness. He rendered (in the language of his commanding officer) "exceptionally able and helpful service in the northern barrage operation." This barrage was characterized by Rear Admiral Clinton-Baker, head of the British mine-laying force, as the "biggest mine-laying stunt in the world's history." It

perfected. It was a matter of adjusting a headgear equipped with "ear muffs" and only one of us could listen in. I was selected as "listener" for the group and I heard every word of the notable speech. I then repeated it to my friends as nearly verbatim as possible. Congress presently, on April 4th, passed a joint resolution declaring a state of war to exist. On the 6th the President signed it—and the United States was at war with Germany.

To Newhall, to me and to others who knew the situation at the Philadelphia Navy Yard the declaration of war was a welcome relief. Two German vessels had been interned there with crews consisting of eight hundred picked men. The vessels had never been searched for arms or explosives and American officers believed they contained both. These men were quartered within a few yards of our dry docks where there were several United States vessels and large stores of essential naval supplies. We had tried without success to impress upon the then Assistant Secretary of the Navy, Franklin D. Roosevelt, the peril of such a situation. It seemed quite impossible to get either him or Secretary Daniels to think realistically or to take the precautions which ordinary common sense would have suggested. The declaration of war, however, happily ended the menace; for the German boats were at once confiscated and the crews removed.

THE COMMITTEE OF SAFETY

As soon as a declaration of war had become inevitable a number of prominent Pennsylvanians urged Governor Brumbaugh to form at once a Committee of Public Safety. I became its chairman, proud to serve in the same capacity as did my great-great-grandfather Thomas Wharton, Jr., during the Revolutionary War. The committee's work was directed by an executive group of twenty which included W. W. Atterbury, president of the Pennsylvania Railroad, who was destined later to be given command in France of transportation of the American Expeditionary Forces, with the rank of Major General, Andrew W. Mellon, Elizabeth Price Martin, a highly efficient organizer of women's activities, and Effingham B. Morris, who as treasurer administered the appropriation of $2,000,000 made by the legislature.

We secured Lewis S. Sadler of Carlisle to be executive manager. He

---

consisted in the laying of a chain of mines from the Orkneys to Norway, thus closing to German submarines the northern exit from the North Sea. All this was at the time unprecedented.

and I worked effectively together. Successive appointments increased the membership of the Committee until it became the largest public organization ever created in Pennsylvania with a roster of some 15,000 representative citizens. As time went on and similar organizations were formed in other states, the name of the Pennsylvania Committee became, for uniformity's sake, the Pennsylvania Council of National Defense and its activities were co-ordinated with those of the National Council. The organization was subdivided into sixteen departments, each with its director.[4] A suite of offices was secured in Philadelphia and there I spent part of each day. The whole organization was soon running as smoothly as the office of any great corporation. Everybody was willing to work. Nobody had to be asked twice. A typical instance of our effective co-operation with cognate national groups was the case of the department of food supply. Organized before the United States Food Administration, our department early assumed its task of awakening the people of the state to the seriousness of the world food situation. Howard Heinz, its director, became the United States Food Administrator for Pennsylvania and our department was, to all intents and purposes, a part of the United States Food Administration when that great organization was set up.

I BECOME A GRANDFATHER

All this time I was eager to get myself accepted for military service. I tried hard to overcome objections based on age and pulled a good many wires; but nothing was offered me except the sort of commission that meant desk-work at Washington. I decided that I could be more effective where I was, although it would have gratified male vanity to wear a military title and to strut about in an immaculate uniform.

I was all the more disappointed not to get into active service because my son George immediately enlisted and was sent to Fort Niagara. He had married Marion T. Myers in June of the preceding year and a son was born to them on May 4, 1917, just three days before the young father joined his regiment. For my part I had the uncomfortable feeling that

---

[4] Some idea of the magnitude of the task can be gained from a mere enumeration of its subdivisions. The departments were these: Military Service, Medicine, Sanitation and Hospitals, Food Supply, Railroads and Related Means of Transportation, Construction and Materials, Plants, Highway Transport, Civilian Service and Labor, Civic Relief, Volunteer Home Defense Police, Finance, Publicity and Education, Legislation, Legal Advice and an exceptionally able Women's Committee headed by Mrs. Martin.

I had done all I could to get America into the war and yet, when the time came, I was left in a place of safety. Franklin Pepper likewise had enlisted. Both boys went overseas and Franklin never came back. My son, after being transferred to the artillery and serving as an instructor at Fortress Monroe, went to France and served there as a lieutenant. After the Armistice he came home—happily unscathed.

PATRIOTISM RAMPANT

From the moment we entered the war, activities of every conceivable sort were proposed by well-meaning patriots. Many of these proposals were preposterous. Some were worth while. By all odds the most effective civilian relief organization I ever saw was the Emergency Aid of Pennsylvania which had been formed in 1914 to help the Allies. Later it ministered also to our own necessities. It was an organization of women, leaders among whom were Mary Brown Warburton and Elizabeth Price Martin. Before its organization my wife had begun relief work for invaded Belgium; but she later agreed to leave that field to a committee of the Emergency Aid and transferred her service to the American Ambulance Hospital (at Neuilly-sur-Seine) and to the supply of artificial limbs to men crippled in action. For these causes she worked ceaselessly and effectively throughout the entire period of the war. Her earlier service for Belgium was later recognized by a Belgian decoration.

Henry P. Davison of the Morgan firm became head of the American Red Cross. In an effort to bring some degree of order out of the chaos caused by the multitude of relief organizations, Davison appointed a small national Co-ordinating Committee and made me a member of it. The first chairman was Judge Lovett who later was succeeded by Charles A. Coffin, president of the General Electric Company. We held innumerable conferences with excited group leaders, not all of whom had been blessed with agreeing minds. In the end, however, we accomplished our purpose.

STEPPING UP THE WAR EFFORT

The Administration could now substitute action for controversy and did so with a will. Newton D. Baker, as Secretary of War, was putting forth immense efforts to recruit military personnel, to organize industry and to provide for hasty military training on an unprecedented scale. Josephus Daniels, at the head of the Navy Department, came in for widespread and severe criticism. I suspect that this was due less to actual inefficiency than to attempts to democratize the service and to a line of unnecessary talk which irritated the old-timers. He was generally referred to as "Inbad the Sailor." It is useless to pretend that a football team, a regiment or a battleship is a democratic institution. War is essentially dictatorship in action and we may as well admit it.

Herbert Hoover at the head of the Food Administration was rendering yeoman service. To make people realize that heatless and wheatless days had a direct relation to the winning of the war, I made numerous addresses in various parts of Pennsylvania and not infrequently I had to respond to urgent calls to speak in New York and in other parts of the country.

TIME REDEEMED

To preserve, if possible, a sense of perspective, I strove, and with some success, to co-ordinate all this war work with my law practice and with normal peacetime activities. Even in May of 1917 I was giving time and thought to the place of classical studies in the college curriculum and in that month expressed my views at length to a trustee of Princeton who had asked my opinion on the subject. This incident seems like a strange interlude; but it serves to show that if among arms laws are silent, letters are not.

By the time the autumn of 1917 had arrived I, like millions of others, was keyed up to a high pitch of nervous excitement. I still strove to retain perspective but there was not much left. I could scarcely recognize myself as a peace-loving Philadelphia lawyer.

During the latter part of 1917 and the first months of 1918 General Allenby was carrying on his remarkable campaign in Arabia and Palestine. Jerusalem had surrendered to the British just before Christmas of 1917 but there still remained an immense amount to be done. On the 1st of March, 1918, Henry P. Davison invited me to join Allenby's expeditionary force and act as representative of the Red Cross. I went to New York to discuss the matter with him but after careful consideration decided not to accept. The opportunity to take even a civilian part in so great an adventure made a powerful appeal. It seemed obvious to me, however, that as long as active military service was out of reach, my place was with my own organization at the home base.

MULDOON'S

By this time I had begun to feel the consequences of months of nervous tension. Looking backward, I marvel that I had not cracked earlier.

Neuritis overtook me and I had to go about my business with my right
arm in a sling. I decided that what I needed was relief from work and
some stiff physical exercise. I applied for admission to Muldoon's establishment at White Plains and soon found myself an inmate of a most extraordinary institution. Muldoon himself had retired from the wrestling
game as undefeated champion of the world. He had then established
this sanitarium and invited the patronage of all who were broken down
nervously, worn out physically or victimized by bad habits. Muldoon got
his satisfaction by playing dictator in this tiny realm. At seventy, or
thereabout, he was a remarkable physical specimen, a fact of which he
was fully conscious. One of the events of our routine day, after strenuous
exercise, was compulsory attendance in the gymnasium to watch the old
man as he posed under the shower bath. He struck successive attitudes,
suggestive of classical models and got away with it in good style.

"Which form of exercise do you prefer—riding or walking?" he snapped
at me when I first reported for duty. I wanted to walk so I said "Riding."
"You walk," he said—and I did—hard, fast and far. My notebook kept
at that time records the statistics of the daily walks. They ranged from
five to eight miles and we were given a limited time in which to cover
the assigned distance. All of life, day and night, was lived under iron
discipline. The dining room was presided over by Mademoiselle, a per-
sonable young French woman who kept a watchful eye on each man's
plate. Nobody was permitted to leave the table until he had disposed
of whatever was put before him. It was good, wholesome food and the
ration was well measured. The society was mixed. Dope fiends, drunks,
victims of overwork, tired businessmen—pretty much every type you can
think of was represented. We were all on friendly terms and several of
the men proved to be agreeable companions. I passed my fifty-first birthday in this environment. Various members of my family tried to reach
me by telephone to give me a birthday greeting. All wires being tapped,
the old man was convinced that I was being relentlessly pursued by
undesirable females and his attitude was appropriately censorious. An
entry in my notebook records that on my birthday I walked five miles
and a quarter in an hour and ten minutes. Part of the daily routine was
passing the medicine ball. This caused me acute pain, as anybody who
has suffered from neuritis will understand. After two weeks the pain had
become so intense that I decided to quit and did so—much to the old
man's disgust. It was a fortunate decision, because it developed that the
source of trouble was a temporary packing in a tooth which a wartime
dentist had forgotten to remove. This had become a center of virulent
infection so that at Muldoon's I had been playing a losing game. Treat-

ment gave immediate relief; but the poison and Muldoon's medicine ball in combination had done something to my right arm from which it never recovered. My forehand stroke in tennis lost both power and accuracy. Notwithstanding this bad luck, my sojourn at Muldoon's was good for my general health and I came back to work as hard as nails and much better for my training season.

INTERLUDES

At about this time came another peaceful interlude. An invitation arrived from Trinity College, Hartford, to deliver the Commencement address. The occasion was made particularly interesting by the presence of Colonel Roosevelt. He, J. P. Morgan and I received honorary degrees. The theme of my address was "Service in a Democracy." In the course of it I voiced contemporary criticism of President Wilson's refusal to assign General Leonard Wood to overseas command. The Colonel was outspoken in his praise, possibly because he himself had smarted under a presidential refusal to let him recruit a division and lead it into battle.

At luncheon at President Luther's I sat next to the Colonel. He was in high spirits and rare form. Archie at that time was in France recovering from a severe wound. "You're a friend of Archie's," said the Colonel, "let me tell you an incident which shows the boy's self-control—a quality," he added with a grin, "that he gets entirely from his mother's side of the family." I wish I felt free to repeat what he thereupon had to say about a comment of Archie's on a certain high government official. It was pungent, to say the least. "You see the boy's self-control," he repeated, "if he had let himself go, you can't tell to what lengths he might have gone." On the train going back to New York the Colonel was instantly recognized by everybody from the Pullman porter up—or down. He talked volubly on all sorts of subjects and in a tone of voice that all the passengers could hear. Of course they were listening intently. What a man! It was the last time I ever saw him. I can almost feel the grasp of his hand as he said good-by.

Back I went to my law office and to my job as Chairman of the Council of Defense. One of the first tasks was to neutralize as far as possible the ceaseless efforts of those who sought to prejudice our foreign-born citizens against the Allied cause. It seemed wise to utilize Independence Day as an occasion for a notable demonstration, in Independence Square, of American unity of purpose. My part was to draft a document conceived in the spirit of the original Declaration of Independence which should

"FAST COMPANY"

President Luther, Theodore Roosevelt and J. P. Morgan.

be signed with appropriate ceremony by representatives of the various national strains included in our population. I drafted it and caused it to be engrossed as nearly as possible in the style of the original Declaration. At the foot of the Declaration space was left for the signatures of five men of each of the following racial strains: Armenian, Assyrian, Belgian, Chinese, Danish, Norwegian, Swedish, Dutch, French, Grecian, German, Hungarian, Italian, Jewish, Lettish, Lithuanian, Bohemian, Moravian, Silesian, Slavish, Carpathia-Russian, Polish, Russian, Serbian, Roumanian and Wexanian.

LIGHTS AND SHADOWS

When, in the summer of 1918, the fortunes of war began to favor the Allies, anxiety about larger issues was relieved but apprehension about our own boys at the front was still acute. When on September 26th the 79th Division launched an attack in the Argonne we waited anxiously for news from the front. When it came many days later we learned that my cousin and partner Franklin Pepper, dear to me as a son, had on September 26th been shot in the head by a German sniper while leading his battalion in an attack on Montfaucon and had died not long after. He had been made a Major in the 313th Infantry. He was a gallant gentleman, beloved and respected by all who knew him. He was later buried in the Romagne cemetery.[5]

After the war Franklin's widow, the lovely Rebecca Willing, went to France to visit his grave. She was alone and oppressed by the feeling that she had not a friend in France. She tarried a day in Paris to gain strength for the ordeal. Happening to pass an attractive-looking hairdressing establishment she stopped for a treatment, thinking that this would rest her. The young Frenchman who was assigned to her spoke English and tried to make conversation. She was absorbed in her own thoughts, however, and answered only in monosyllables. "I saw much of the American officers during the war," he said. Then he added, "They were of the 79th Division." For the first time she gave heed. "Did you know any of the officers of the 313th?" she inquired. "Mais oui!" he responded. "Major Pepper?" she asked, with no expectation of an affirmative answer. "Le plus grand!" he cried excitedly. "He was billeted in our village in my own father's

[5] Benjamin Franklin Pepper, Franklin's elder son, is today (June 1944), as president of the Triumph Corporation, engaged in manufacturing high explosives. George Willing Pepper, the younger son, is a Lieutenant Commander in the Naval Reserve. He was among the survivors when the airplane carrier *Wasp* was sunk by the Japs.

house—and we spent some weeks together when I was recovering from a wound." Her sense of loneliness and desolation left her on the instant. Here was somebody who had known her husband—perhaps the only man still in France of whom this was true; and she had come upon him by a guidance that was obviously providential.

Things began to happen quickly on all fronts. At home congressional elections were approaching and President Wilson unwisely appealed to the country to return a Democratic majority. I say "unwisely," because the people of the several states had enough independence to resent presidential intervention in local elections. On November 5th his appeal was rejected and a Republican majority was assured in both Houses of Congress.[6] I was particularly delighted by the election at this time of my friend William Cameron Sproul as Governor of Pennsylvania. He was chosen by a huge majority. A week later the Armistice was signed at Senlis and, as if with Carlyle's whiff of grapeshot, the World War passed into history.

THE ARMISTICE

It was not until the day after the confused and hilarious day of the Armistice that we began to ask ourselves, "What next?" When we *did* ask, nobody knew the answer. What the terms of peace should be and by whom and when and where they were to be determined, were things about which we could only speculate. I remember walking rather aimlessly to and fro between the office of the Council of National Defense and my own office with numbed sensibilities and a feeling that life had suddenly become purposeless. I was a man without a mission.

While we were demobilizing the Council of Defense I was carrying a heavy load of professional work. I was busy with an important case for the Penn Mutual Life Insurance Company involving questions of taxation on certain life insurance transactions, a litigation in Pittsburgh in which I vainly tried to make some new law in a tangled street-railway situation, and a most interesting stock-purchase case in which George S. Graham and I turned defeat into victory for our client Pierre S. duPont. It was an immense relief to be able to concentrate upon professional work and once more to lead a normal life. I even had time to go to the theater. I remember how good it seemed to laugh over Booth Tarkington's inimitable *Penrod*.

[6] The parallel is striking to the later unsuccessful attempt of Franklin Roosevelt to bring about the defeat in the Democratic primaries of 1939 of Senators who had opposed his Court-packing scheme.

2. SHAM PEACE

"Do not think you are fighting for the simple issue of letting this or that state become free or remain subject to you. . . . Your empire is a tyranny by now, perhaps, as many think, wrongfully acquired, but certainly dangerous to let go."

—PERICLES—as reported by Thucydides

Having for the first time faced the reality of war when nearly fifty; having then worked frantically to effectuate the Allied cause, I was now face to face with the question, "What policy should one advocate as most likely to bring about a durable peace?" What I should have considered before the fight I was now for the first time considering after the fight was over. The more I pondered the clearer it became, that the way to peace was not to grind the vanquished underfoot, and that any attempt to preserve a victorious status by force could mean nothing but the bitterness that ultimately leads to renewed war.

When what was grimly called the Peace Conference was summoned to meet in January and President Wilson announced that *in propria persona* he would represent the United States at the council table, there was plenty of ground for gloomy foreboding. Since he would necessarily be committed to support any treaty he had helped to formulate, the inherent merits or demerits of the settlement would necessarily be obscured by a desire to support or oppose its negotiator. This presaged domestic controversy rather than international peace.

With the turn of the year, and while ominous cloudbanks were gathering over Paris, came the sad news of Theodore Roosevelt's illness and death. Those who had been able to go with him to the end of the political road were heartbroken. They had lost not merely a friend and leader but everything except memory. Those who, like me, had admired him tremendously and had parted political company with him only with deepest regret, felt that the world had lost a vitalizing personality and that our own lives were the poorer for his passing. A meeting in his memory was held in Philadelphia at the Metropolitan Opera House. Every soul in that great gathering was grieving for the Colonel. All had come to the meeting hoping for emotional relief. I made one of the speeches and attempted to supply their need.

THE PEACE CONFERENCE

Meanwhile the news from Paris was most disquieting. The Tiger was justifying his nickname. Lloyd George was playing up to the militant expectations of his constituents. Wilson was battling valiantly but ineffectually for something better than the terrible terms which in spite of him found their way into the Treaty of Versailles. Worst of all was the news that the Covenant of the League of Nations had been so drawn, to use Mr. Wilson's own characterization, as to attempt to enforce peace "by making it so dangerous to break the peace that no other nation will have the audacity to attempt it." This mechanism, intended to bring united force to bear upon future disturbers of world peace, was, as we later learned, to be so embedded in the treaty itself that ratification of the one would involve acceptance of the other.

From my point of view nothing could have been worse than these forecasts of what the perfected covenant would contain. It seemed clear to me that such a settlement was bad enough for Europe but worse for America. For Europe it would mean destructive international controversies. For America it threatened joint responsibility for preserving an impossible status quo. In anticipation of the President's return with the Treaty and the Covenant in his hand, I accordingly set myself to consider what, if anything, could be done to prevent ratification. The President was scheduled to pay an early though brief visit to the United States and did in fact land in Boston on February 24th, bringing with him a draft of the Covenant. On the 26th he gave in the White House a dinner to the Foreign Relations Committee of the Senate and the Committee on Foreign Affairs of the House. After dinner he submitted to questioning by his guests. As far as I could learn, however, nothing significant happened except a statement of his willingness to report to his colleagues in Paris some minor objections that were raised in the course of conversation. Nobody had really thought the thing through. These minor objections were to a considerable extent met in the final draft of the instrument. But the main structure of the League was there in February and it was still there when on July 8th the President returned bearing the interlocked Covenant and Treaty as finally signed at Versailles.

Immediately after the White House conference of February 26th, and before the adjournment of Congress on March 4th, more than a third of the Senators and Senators-elect signed a resolution, drafted by Pennsylvania's Senator Knox, to the effect that the Constitution of the League in the form proposed ought not to be accepted by the United States. This declaration, if adhered to by the signers, would of course have prevented ratification, since that can be accomplished only by a two-thirds vote. But the people of the country, tired of war and eager for rest, were certain to clamor for the prompt acceptance of any measure bearing the peace label. The clergy, in particular, might be counted upon to translate a question of international policy into a moral issue and point the finger of scorn at all who took the other side. Pressure upon the Senate was therefore inevitable and any senatorial signer, without seeming to be inconsistent, could readily escape from his obligation by the acceptance of any reservation, no matter how trivial, with which he might declare himself to be satisfied. It therefore seemed to me essential that an educational campaign on a nationwide scale should be launched at once.

A LEAGUE AGAINST A LEAGUE

The first thing to do was to establish contact with the Senators who had signed the declaration. I sought and secured on March 13th a conference with some of them in Washington. It was most unsatisfactory. Every man had a different idea about the course to pursue and nobody seemed willing to yield to anybody else. I was treated with civility but nothing more. I made up my mind to act along lines suggested by Senator Moses of New Hampshire. Accordingly, with the aid of some kindred spirits who were friends of his and mine, I proceeded to develop, under a corporate charter recently granted,[7] an effective opposition to unconditional ratification. It was not, however, until the 28th of April, after organization had been accomplished and an immense amount of publicity secured, that a plan of co-operation with the Senate group was actually worked out. On the evening of that day at Senator Lodge's Washington house, and the next day at the Capitol, I conferred with him and with Senators Brandegee, Borah, Frelinghuysen, Johnson, Moses, New and McCormick. This time I was received almost as an equal. Medill McCormick of Illinois was more disturbed, emotionally, by the situation than any of the others. Brandegee of Connecticut had the keenest intellect in the group. Mr. Lodge was cautious and resourceful. We discussed the entire situation and reached two decisions: First, that the organization which had been formed should be recognized as an ally of the Senate

[7] The corporate name was The League for the Preservation of American Independence.

group and be used by them for the arrangement of speaking tours and in other ways; and, second, that Senator Brandegee and I should go at once to New York to consult Elihu Root both as to the validity of the objections which we were urging to the Covenant and the wisdom of conducting an educational movement in support of them. From Mr. Lodge's house I called Harry Stimson on the telephone, he being Mr. Root's partner and friend, and through him made an appointment for April 30th. We found Mr. Root at his New York apartment. He received us cordially and at once disclosed definite opposition to the Covenant. He had an amiable habit on such occasions of lecturing the other fellow, the result, I suppose, of being so often consulted as an oracle. He lectured us that day in most interesting fashion, contrasting the efficacy of informal diplomatic conference with the dangers of such highly-organized procedure as was embodied in the Covenant. He heartily approved our effort to make people understand the folly of any commitment to join other nations in using force to preserve a status quo. We came away confirmed in our determination to fight the good fight with all our might.

Anything like a detailed account of my activities in this fight would read like a timetable. I traveled continually on night trains between Philadelphia, New York, Washington and a variety of other points, east, west and south. Our League for the Preservation of American Independence which had been formed with Col. Henry Watterson as president, Stuyvesant Fish as treasurer and Henry A. Wise Wood as secretary, became feverishly active. As chairman of the board I did most of the executive work and became a sort of one-man speaking bureau and the author of most of its literature. We established offices in New York and Washington and organized branches in various cities. At Senator Lodge's request I had spoken at a large dinner-meeting in New York as early as March 6th and met with an enthusiastic response. One of the speakers that evening was Senator "Jim" Reed of Missouri. For a while thereafter he and I worked in friendly harmony. Later a rather trifling misunderstanding arose and our relations became and afterward always remained purely formal. I set about preparing a series of small pamphlets designed to make the controversy comprehensible to the man on the street. Among these the ones that attained the widest circulation were "Deceiving the Sick," "The Old Covenant and the New," "The Battle Above the Clouds," "The Emperor's New Clothes," and "A Primer of the League of Nations." In order to interpret the controversy to English readers I wrote for the *Journal of Comparative Legislation and International Law* an article entitled "America and the League of Nations." This was both published in the magazine itself in 1920 and also widely circulated in reprint form. I take some satisfaction in recalling this effort because I think that everything said in the article has been verified by subsequent experience.

On April 10, 1919, before a Philadelphia audience that packed the Metropolitan Opera House, Senator Gilbert Hitchcock, Democratic floor leader in the Senate, and I debated the League of Nations issue. The debate attracted wide attention. April 16th found me in Indianapolis engaged in a similar joint debate, this time with Senator Atlee Pomerene of Ohio. "To uphold the weaker side," said he, "they have had to import a constitutional lawyer from Philadelphia." "I had rather," I replied, "be a constitutional lawyer from Philadelphia than the most unconstitutional lawyer that ever came out of Ohio." There were other amenities; but at the end we shook hands and, as it turned out, became fast friends for life.

The fact that personal loyalty to President Wilson determined the attitude of many of the advocates of ratification made any honest consideration of the treaty almost an impossibility. Not long after my duels with Hitchcock and Pomerene I had a debate in Witherspoon Hall, Philadelphia, with Congressman McCall of Massachusetts, Vice President Marshall and a third "Big Gun" whose identity at the moment I have forgotten. They all advocated immediate and unconditional ratification and I spoke in earnest opposition. At a dinner preceding the debate I sat next to the Vice President who, in conversation, said many things wholly inconsistent with the speech he subsequently delivered. When called upon at the meeting and introduced as the Vice President of the United States, he walked to the footlights and said, "My name is Marshall." The audience laughed; but he explained that he thus took them into his confidence because of a recent experience in Chicago. There a newspaper reporter had approached him and asked, "Are you the Vice President?" On receiving an affirmative answer, the young man had said, "I want to interview you." "Go ahead," said the Vice President. "What's your name?" queried the reporter. "Since then," said Marshall, "I have made it a rule to play safe." Then he made an eloquent speech in support of the Covenant. As he came back to his chair and sat down, just before I was called to my feet, he put his hand over his mouth and whispered to me, "I haven't read it, but we must stand by the Old Man." Now that more than twenty years have passed this may be told.

THE OLYMPIANS

I suspect that it was the standing which I gained through all these aggressive activities that led the Senators to extend to me a measure of recognition. However, in all my contacts with them, I was made conscious that I was dealing with Olympians whose condescension to a mere mortal was not to be lightly esteemed. It was made clear that I was to do a lot of spade work; but I was led to infer that when the time should come for a grateful public to offer sacrifices, nobody but dwellers on Mount Olympus were to enjoy the sweet-smelling savor. This was all right with me. I was not in public life and never dreamed that I should be. I wanted results, let the credit accrue to whom it might.

Following the activities which I have chronicled and many others of the same sort, we began to get results. You could get the "feel" of a change in public sentiment. A heavily-financed organization aptly entitled "The League to *Enforce* Peace," was making our task easier by emphasizing, as its title indicated, that the Covenant was intended to be made effective by force. Ex-President Taft and former Attorney General Wickersham were active in its organization and their influence was considerable. Our consistent contention, in opposition to theirs, was that the appeal to force was at best futile and at worst dangerous. There were some incidents which served to relieve a situation which tended to be intensely serious. One such incident occurred in early June. The Academy of Political Science, meeting at Columbia University, invited me to present to a great audience my objections to the Covenant. I arrived late at Morningside Heights and took my seat on the platform while Senator Pittman of Nevada was urging ratification in a characteristic speech. His peroration was devoted principally to a personal attack upon opponents of ratification whom he described as "dyspeptic pessimists," with an outlook on life that is "dreary and hopeless." As I was in pretty good fighting trim at the time and appeared neither dreary, hopeless nor pessimistic, and as the Senator's obvious lack of weight might easily have been ascribed to dyspepsia, I got a good laugh out of the audience by suggesting that the pending question be settled by a study of comparative physiques. In the serious part of my address I contrasted the certain futility of an appeal to international force with the possible hopefulness of reliance upon international conference and declared myself favorable to any association of the latter type and unalterably opposed to a league which was based on the former.

THE SENATE FORUM

Following the President's final return from abroad in early June, Senator "Jim" Reed of Missouri went on circuit against the Covenant as did Senator Hiram Johnson of California and the redoubtable Albert Beveridge of Indiana. In the Senate itself able speeches were being made by Borah, Knox and others. These speeches had an authority lacking in unofficial utterances. The Lodge Reservations, designed to mitigate the rigors of the Covenant, were being pressed upon the President. One of the most loyal of his supporters, Senator Swanson of Virginia, went to the President as the latter was about to begin a speaking tour and told him plainly that only an acceptance of these reservations could accomplish a ratification of the Treaty and urged acceptance as earnestly as he could. Years afterward when he and I attended Senator Lodge's funeral in Boston, Swanson described his visit to the White House. He said that the President listened attentively and declined to commit himself but promised to think the matter over. When immediately thereafter, in his Salt Lake City speech, he declared for immediate and unconditional ratification, he, Swanson, knew that the battle was lost and that the rejection of the Treaty was inevitable. This proved to be the case. After all sorts of reservations had been voted up or voted down, Senator Underwood of Alabama, on November 19th, proposed an unconditional resolution of ratification. This brought the Covenant to its acid test. The resolution was defeated by a vote of 38 ayes to 53 nays, seven Democrats voting in the negative along with the forty-six Republicans. The Treaty was again brought before the Senate at the next session and again failed of ratification. The end came when on March 18, 1920, a resolution to return the Treaty to the President was adopted by a vote of 47 to 37. Since that date the Treaty has remained in the hands of the Executive. When the final vote was announced I had a sense of relief comparable to that which followed the Armistice. I cherished the vain hope that the next European War would not involve the United States.

SUNDAY BASEBALL AND PROHIBITION

The foregoing record of intense activity in the League of Nations fight suggests that for the time it had absorbed all my thought and energy. Actually I kept up my professional work, completed the liquidation of the Council of Defense and took a normal part in all community activities.

Baseball on Sunday? This question, in the spring of 1919, perplexed the Commissioners of Fairmount Park. They answered it by a resolution authorizing the orderly playing of outdoor games on Sundays as on other days. Whereupon the Lord's Day Alliance, a local organization of well-meaning but, as I thought, misguided people and other similar groups sprang at once into action. They sought a mandatory injunction to compel the Commissioners to rescind their resolution. It was my duty as Park Solicitor to resist this attack. The legal theory of the plaintiffs was that because of the Blue Laws of 1794 it was a public nuisance to play ball on Sunday. There was, of course, the technical objection that the trifling penalty imposed by the old statute was the measure of the offense and that an injunction was not the proper remedy. But I preferred to press for a decision on the merits. Everybody of the privileged class was enjoying golf or tennis or some other outdoor exercise on Sunday. It seemed to me a shame to deny similar opportunities to the underprivileged. Moreover I felt strongly that the church people were doing a foolish thing in confessing their own impotence and calling on the secular arm for protection. A paragraph in my brief states the case as I saw it.[8] The court refused the injunction. The plaintiffs appealed and a lot of public interest was taken in the argument before the Supreme Court of Pennsylvania. I successfully maintained the position taken in the court below and the decree was affirmed. I then became the target for ministerial attack. The ammunition did not penetrate, however, and no harm was done. Later I debated the question publicly with the Rev. Floyd Tomkins at the Inasmuch Mission and conducted an extensive correspondence with all sorts of people from all parts of the state. All this discussion helped to clear the air. Certainly the action of the Commissioners has been abundantly justified by the way their policy has worked out in practice.

In January of the same year (1919) the Prohibition Amendment to the Constitution had been ratified, to become effective January 16, 1920. At the time of ratification I paid little attention to it. I had always been

[8] "We respectfully suggest to the court that individual citizens who on Sunday desire their rest and quiet in private or the opportunity for undisturbed divine worship in public are entitled to be protected against disturbance by unnecessary or unseemly noise or other form of annoyance; but that the churches as such have no legal right to any other protection than that to which all other organized groups of citizens are entitled; and that in particular they have no right to restrain competition with them of other interests on Sunday or to invoke any form of protection tending to create an ecclesiastical monopoly by compelling people either to go to church or to do nothing."

accustomed to drink when and as I pleased but I expected to be able to adjust myself to the new situation. I never gave a thought to the political and social consequences of what seemed to me to be an interesting, if not a wise, experiment. I could not know then that it was destined to have a devastating effect both upon the lives of individuals and the fortunes of public men.

Late in 1919 labor troubles clamored for adjustment. In Philadelphia a widespread strike of textile workers was threatened. The citizen best qualified to deal wisely with the situation was J. Willis Martin, the universally-esteemed president judge of one of our courts. He appointed a conference committee, naming me as chairman. This gave me a chance to apply to an industrial controversy the conference method which I had been advocating in the international sphere. We met representatives of labor, conferred with the employers, brought about joint conferences and finally reached an agreement acceptable to everybody. I have had a good deal of experience in matters of this sort. Almost always the actual issues lend themselves to peaceful settlement. Where settlement proves impossible, it is usually because of the bitter unreasonableness of a leader on one side or the other, or of the leaders on both sides. More often but by no means always it is the labor leader who is at fault, for the simple reason that his own self-interest is not infrequently best served by a strike. This is seldom the case with the employer who usually has everything to lose and nothing to gain from a strike. The worst thing that can happen is that government should undertake to control the situation in the avowed interest of one or the other of the disputants. The adoption of the Wagner Act in 1935 and the policy of the N.L.R.B. has postponed for a generation the hope of industrial peace. Individual local administrators, like Elinore Herrick, former regional director in New York, have done much to humanize industrial situations. But the Act itself and the Board's conception of its function are, in my judgment, basically unfair.

CONSTITUTIONAL REVISION

Late in the year 1919, Governor Sproul, pursuant to legislative authority, appointed a commission of twenty-five citizens to study proposals for revising or rewriting the Constitution of the Commonwealth. I was named as one of the twenty-five. We met at Harrisburg and organized for work under the chairmanship of William I. Schaffer, at that time Attorney General of Pennsylvania and one of the ablest men at the bar. In January of 1920 and thereafter throughout the year we held frequent

sessions and did an enormous amount of work. I oscillated between
Philadelphia and Harrisburg until our work was done. Pennsylvania had
had four constitutions—1776, 1790, 1838 and 1874. It was our job to study
and compare them and, in the light of experience gained since 1874, to
advise whether necessary changes should be made by amendment or
whether there should be a new constitution. The commission fairly reflected all shades of political, economic and social opinion. It compre-
hended, at one extreme, Judge Reed of Pittsburgh and, at the other,
Gifford Pinchot. Two able women were included, Mrs. Barclay H. Warburton of Philadelphia and Mrs. John O. Miller of Pittsburgh. There
were men with large experience in public life, such as John S. Fisher,
of Indiana County, George E. Alter of Pittsburgh and James Gay Gordon
of Philadelphia. There were others who could qualify as students of constitutional history, such as Hampton L. Carson and Francis Newton
Thorpe.

We sat in the Senate Chamber of the Capitol and week after week
were watched with curiosity by spectators who came and went. Years
afterward I heard from "Charley" Snyder, a politician of an eminently
practical turn of mind, what seems to me an excellent summary of our
activities. "One day," said Charley, "I took one of my workers into the
Chamber to listen while you people chewed the rag. You were debating
some reform proposal which, if adopted, would have cramped our style
in Schuylkill County. 'This is terrible,' said my friend, 'can't we stop it?'
'Let 'em alone,' says I, 'they ain't doin' no harm.'" Neither were we. We
produced after much labor a draft of a new constitution which was submitted to the legislature for consideration. That body, after having received all sorts of protests from all sorts of critics, determined to submit
to the people at the primary election in the fall of 1921, the question,
"Shall There Be a Constitutional Convention?" A huge majority at the
polls said "No." And so the big printed volumes which recorded our
labors were consigned to upper shelves in libraries and the commission
itself passed into history.

ALBERT BEVERIDGE

In anticipation of the annual Commencement in June of 1920, the
University of Pennsylvania tendered an LL.D. to Albert Beveridge. He
accepted and was my guest while in Philadelphia. This was the renewal
of a contact established during the League of Nations fight and proved
to be the beginning of a lasting friendship. Later in the summer when

my wife and I visited the Beveridges at Beverly Farms we found him in the agonies of composition. He had agreed to deliver before the American Bar Association an address on those wartime statutes which, in his opinion, constituted "An Assault on American Fundamentals." With characteristic thoroughness he had at once set about preparing his address, had made a complete draft of it, had then wholly discarded the draft and, when I arrived on the scene, had written another which he submitted to me for criticism. For hours we discussed this second draft, literally word by word. During our talk he made a number of emendations. By the time I left I assumed that he was ready to shoot. Not a bit of it. The second address was discarded like the first and he began all over again. This appears from a letter which he sent me after I had written to thank him for his delightful hospitality. All in all, he was one of the most interesting and agreeable if also one of the most unbalanced men I ever knew. It is not often that one finds in the same individual the readiness of a successful public speaker and the erudition of a painstaking student.

In June of 1921 the University of Pittsburgh gave me an LL.D. My commencement address was an attempt to answer the question, "Why the University?" I described education as self-development in response to stimulus. When an honorarium was offered to me I decided to try an experiment. I returned it for use as a prize to be given to that undergraduate who, in the combined judgment of students and faculty, comes nearest to the ideal of what a man should be. The experiment worked well and I supplied the University with the prize money for several years. I have done the like for Lafayette under similar circumstances and, I believe, with happy results.[9]

A GENTLEMAN OF FRANCE

One of the thrills of a lifetime came in November of 1921, when I was fortunate enough to meet Marshal Foch. He made at least as great an impression upon me as any man I have ever met. During his visit to Philadelphia he and General Pershing were feted and dined. At a big public dinner it was my function to introduce Foch. The influence of his personality upon the audience was electric and helped to give to my introduction a remarkable effect. The people not only rose en masse but each individual fairly leaped to his feet. Here was no conventional greeting. It was an outpouring of spirit which for several minutes surged back

[9] See page 253.

and forth and refused to be stilled. Later the introduction was printed and after Foch had gone home I sent him a copy of it. I had from him the following note:

"Paris, 19 Avril 1922.

Monsieur le Sénateur,

L'envoi que vous me faites, de votre discours de bienvenue à mon passage à Philadelphia me touche profondément et je tiens à vous remercier.

Je garde le souvenir de cette belle journée que vous me rappelez avec tant d'aimabilité et je suis heureux de vous redire le plaisir que j'ai eu de vous serrer la main.

Veuillez croire, Monsieur le Sénateur, à mes bien attachés sentiments.

F. Foch

This happy contact with the outstanding hero of the Great War somehow seemed to mark for me the end of the devastating storm which seven years before had burst upon the world in all its fury. The future was mercifully hidden from Foch's eyes. Perhaps had he lived he could have prevented the collapse of France. Whether, had he lived, the enemy to be vanquished would have been French Facism or French Liberalism no mere onlooker can tell. Possibly both extremes were hopelessly out of line with all that was best in the French tradition. In that event he might have repeated the strategy of the Marne and saved his country by advancing through the center.

PART THREE

7

The Ship of State

"The ship of State is a metaphor re-invented by the bourgeoisie, which felt itself oceanic, omnipotent, pregnant with storms. That ship was, as we said, a very small affair: it had hardly any soldiers, bureaucrats, or money. . . . In our days the State has come to be a formidable machine which works in marvellous fashion; of wonderful efficiency by reason of the quantity and precision of its means. Once it is set up in the midst of society, it is enough to touch a button for its enormous levers to start working and exercise their overwhelming power on any portion whatever of the social framework."

—ORTEGA: *The Revolt of the Masses*, pages 129, 131

1. I GET ABOARD

As in December 1921 I steered my canoe downstream I did not know that for me there was dangerously quick water just around the turn of the year.

I had so far escaped any serious adventure in politics. I had served at Will Hays's request on the advisory committee which assembled material and formulated recommendations for a party platform prior to the Republican Convention held in Chicago in 1920. I had even agreed to be a

135

delegate when Governor Sproul had suggested that I represent the Third District. But in that case I held aloof from electioneering and was quite properly defeated in the election of delegates. I was to have been a machine-made choice and a cog had slipped somewhere.[1]

At the convention in Chicago I was very much a fifth wheel since the recommendations on which Ogden Mills and others of us had manfully labored, received no more attention from the Platform Committee than hundreds of proposals from other unofficial sources. I had expected to see Wood or Lowden nominated but soon realized that the politicians of the Senate were in control of the convention. As a result of the League of Nations fight the Republican senators were feeling their oats. Admitted to some of their conferences, I gathered that their idea was to choose a President satisfactory to the Senate on the theory that what was good enough for the Senate was good enough for America. They would have not merely a senator for President but a senator for Vice President. Pennsylvania's Senator Penrose, though ill at home, kept in constant touch by telephone with the leaders on the ground. The choice, we learned, was to be Harding and Lenroot. When the smoke of battle had cleared away Harding had been nominated as the senators had planned but their omnipotence had been challenged on the vice-presidential issue. Some humble delegates had defied the Olympian thunder and stampeded the Convention for Coolidge.

A FRIENDLY NOMINEE

After the nomination Senator Watson, who cherished no resentment because I had supported Mills for the chairmanship of the Committee on Resolutions, invited me to go with him to call on Senator Harding. I had held no brief for Harding and was disappointed over the Convention's failure to nominate Wood or our own Governor Sproul. However, I was glad to make the call and despite myself I was impressed by the party's nominee. No backslapping but no pomposity. An unaffected cordiality and a certain gravity of demeanor which seemed to fit the part. "I hope to see you often," Mr. Harding said as we shook hands before leaving, "and I want you to think of yourself as one of us." Flattering, of course, but not overdone. What he said I accepted at face value.

[1] I suspect that what afterward developed into an open breach between the Governor and the local Philadelphia leaders had already grown wider than he himself was aware of and that they took satisfaction in knifing his protégé.

I took a citizen's part in the campaign and after Harding's victory was surprised to have a desire to hold public office mistakenly attributed to me. The rumor, late in November 1920, that I was under consideration for the office of Attorney General did not excite me. The simple fact is that never in my life have I felt the itch for public office, impossible as it may be to make people believe this. So far, indeed, were my thoughts from office-seeking that I failed to take the next train to Washington when I had this note from President Harding shortly after his inauguration:

> "The first day that you find yourself traveling toward Washington I wish you would run in and give me the satisfaction of a brief interview. The matter is not urgent, but I would like to see you sometime within the next couple of weeks. The appointment can be arranged any day most convenient to you."

I had not the least idea what was in his mind and when I got around to complying with his request I found that something had intervened which made the interview unnecessary. I learned afterward from George Christian, the President's secretary, that Harding of his own volition had intended to offer me the office of Solicitor General but that Senator Penrose had objected. Penrose had never forgiven me for the part I had played in keeping Quay out of the Senate. Yet in a book of reminiscences published some years later, Attorney General Daugherty [2] took personal credit for this rejection of my name and for the appointment of James M. Beck to be Solicitor General. The simple truth was that I was much gratified when Beck was named. If, for political reasons, the President had to make Daugherty Attorney General, it was all the more important to have a capable and well-qualified advocate in the office of Solicitor General.

In the year 1921, Pennsylvania's senatorial representation was in eclipse. In October Senator Philander Knox had died and William E. Crow had been appointed to succeed him. Crow was taken seriously ill the day after his induction and died nine months later.

Pennsylvania's senior senator, Boies Penrose, had been very ill for more than a year. His illness, like Senator Crow's, was destined to be fatal. With regret I read of Penrose's death on December 31, 1921. While we had little in common I realized to some extent that he had been of

[2] He, Daugherty, mistakenly thought that I harbored resentment against him for this incident and that this accounted for some unwelcome advice I gave him after Mr. Harding's death. *Infra,* page 198.

service to the Commonwealth and to the Nation. I had, however, no sense of personal loss and the question of succession did not concern me. There was talk of the possibility of Governor Sproul's resignation to be followed by his appointment to the Senate at the hands of his successor, the Lieutenant Governor.

On the fourth of January 1922 I was in Trenton trying to solve some problems for clients of mine who lived there. I returned to Philadelphia by an afternoon train. I was not giving so much as a thought to politics. If, en route, a fortuneteller had predicted that within a week I would be either a guide in the Maine woods or a United States Senator, I should have said that the former was the lesser of two impossibilities— and by far the more agreeable. When, on arrival at my office late in the day, I learned that the Governor had been trying to reach me my mind jumped to his rumored intention of making himself senator. As I walked that evening to meet him at the Philadelphia Club I turned over in my thoughts the most tactful way of advising him against such a course. His greeting confirmed my "hunch." "George," he said, "how would you like to go to the United States Senate?" I supposed it was an oblique question meaning, "If you were I, how would *you* like to be a senator?"

"That," I parried, "depends on your title to the office."

"Well, if I were to appoint you, what would be the matter with your clear title?" asked the Governor.

"But," I protested, "we're talking about you, not me."

"Not at all," the Governor said, "I'm quite serious in what I say. I have no intention of taking that place myself and I want to offer it to you."

I was as much taken by surprise as any man could be who had never thought of himself in such a connection. After a moment's silence I asked if this was in the nature of an interim appointment, made to keep the seat warm until a popular election should determine Penrose's successor.

"Certainly not," the Governor assured me. "I should expect you to enter the primaries and, if nominated and elected, to serve out the term."

I asked for a little time and agreed to give him my decision the following afternoon at four o'clock.

There were many factors to weigh. Mrs. Pepper, for her part, did not want to leave our home and family circle but said she would concur cheerfully in any decision I made. My law partners generously agreed to carry on the office organization and enable me to maintain a modified relationship to it, notwithstanding the added load of work this would mean for them. During my term of office the firm would not be able to accept retainers from clients whose claims were adverse to those of the Federal Government, and there was also the strong probability that certain important clients, accustomed to depend on my personal service, would slip away. All this could mean loss of income to the firm. In my own case the pecuniary consequences promised to be serious, since my family and I were dependent on my earnings. With a handsome professional income cut down, I would have to maintain a home in Washington as well as Philadelphia on a salary which was not only small in itself but might be more than eaten up, as afterward turned out to be the case, by the clerical and administrative expenses of my Senate office.

Uncertain what course I should take, I sought the advice of a few intimate friends whose judgment I trusted. Among them were Justice William I. Schaffer and Chief Justice Robert von Moschzisker, both of the Supreme Court of Pennsylvania.

Some years later I learned the "inside story" of my appointment from Bill Schaffer. As set down by him in a letter, it fits in with my own recollection.

"I had been Governor Sproul's attorney from the time he left college and entered business. He had appointed me his Attorney General and, when my term was about half over, he appointed me to the Bench of the Supreme Court. He was my most intimate friend and had been such from late boyhood. It had been customary with us for years to put our heads together and to confer and advise on matters of importance to each of us. We had found that men, like dogs, hunt together best in couples. He came home from Harrisburg over a week-end. We met and discussed the senatorial situation. He told me he had no intention of yielding to the pressure of those who wanted him to resign the governorship to enable the Lieutenant Governor to appoint him to the Senate. I agreed with this determination. I told him of the senatorial ambition of Lewis Sadler but we both concluded that, able as Sadler was in many lines, he could not be the figure in the United States Senate which the needs of Pennsylvania required. Sproul returned to Harrisburg and called me from there. He asked me to come to Harrisburg and meet him at the station, saying that if I should come to the Capitol or to the Executive Mansion newspaper men would draw embarrassing inferences from my visit. He said that he would have a drawing room on the train back to Philadelphia. I did as he asked. We got on the train without, as we thought, being observed and after settling down he said, 'I think the time

has come when I should make a statement about the senatorship.' He
added, 'I am thinking of appointing George Wharton Pepper.' I replied
'Wonderful! That makes me hit the top of the car; you could not make
a better selection.' I had not seen Pepper's name suggested by any of the
newspapers. The Governor then produced a paper from his pocket, in
his own handwriting. He said no one had seen it and asked me what I
thought of it as the statement he should make. After reading it I told
him I approved it and would not change a word. We then discussed
how he should make the offer to Pepper. He suggested that we leave
the train together and go to Pepper's office and that he would offer the
appointment to him. I told him I thought this would be a mistake, that
he should go alone, that the suggestion of Pepper's name had come
from him and not from me and that I believed it more fitting that he
alone should make the proffer. After some demur he agreed to this.
When we got out of the train we realized that our elaborate policy for
privacy had failed. The newspaper men rushed up to us to get a statement but Sproul waved them aside. He asked me to stay in my office
until he could telephone me and inform me of what transpired. In a
little while he called me, told me that Pepper was not in his office, that
he was in Trenton trying a case and that he had arranged to meet him
at the Philadelphia Club that night at 9 o'clock. He asked me to go to
the Union League and wait until he communicated with me. About
10 o'clock or later he called me, told me he had made the offer and that
Pepper was holding it under advisement until he could have an opportunity to talk to his wife, that he had said to him, among other things,
that he did not know whether he could afford to go to the Senate. He
asked me if I would go to Pepper's office early in the morning and urge
him to accept, saying to him, among other things, that it would solve
many political difficulties if he would. I went to Pepper's office at 8
o'clock the next morning, reached there before he did, saw him as soon
as he came in, talked the situation over with him, urged him to agree
to serve and told him all that had transpired. He then said to me that
he would call the Governor and say 'yes' to him."

Bob von Moschzisker threw a challenge at me. "You have made," he
said in effect, "many addresses concerning the responsibility of all citizens to perform their share of public service and civic duty. Your statements, I am sure, were quite sincere. It seems to me now that the significant question is whether or not you will make those declarations good."

When I called the Governor to give him my answer he said that he
had in the meantime sounded out men of political importance through-

out the State and had gotten a favorable reaction. So the matter was settled.

On the following Monday, January 9th, the Governor in his Philadelphia office presented me formally with my commission to serve. He had invited two mutual friends to be present—Chief Justice von Moschzisker and General Atterbury, president of the Pennsylvania Railroad. At the conclusion of the ceremony newspaper men photographed the four of us. In a typical political maneuver this ceremony was utilized to my disadvantage in the primary campaign held a few months later. My opponents broadcast copies of the photograph with the object of proving that I was a tool of the Pennsylvania Railroad and of "the vested interests." The circumstance that I had never, in my entire professional career, represented this railroad but had on the contrary opposed it in two cases, was ignored. Agreeing to Atterbury's presence and having the photographs taken was of course a political blunder on my part. As for the Governor, he not infrequently acted on the impulse to gather his friends around him without considering how the incident might be misinterpreted, a habit which was one of his most attractive characteristics.

A POLITICAL NEOPHYTE

I was, by every test, a rank political neophyte. Though my appointment was praised in a good many quarters, it was viewed with something approaching disgust by many of the men in control of the Republican organization—men who had worked their way up through ward, city and state committee. In the light of the experience which I now have behind me, I can fully appreciate the point of view of those stalwarts. There was, in fact, even more to be said for their attitude than there is for the opposition of the West Pointer to the commissioning of a civilian whose military training has been scant. In the opinion of the party leaders I had given no service for the great reward I was receiving. My leadership in the fight outside the Senate against unconditional acceptance of the League of Nations, my service on the State Commission on Constitutional Amendment and Revision, my efforts in 1915 and 1916 for national preparedness, my activities as chairman of the Pennsylvania Council of National Defense, meant nothing to them.

Had I come up the hard way I should have avoided many errors in political strategy which I was later accused, with more or less justice, of committing—errors which reacted to my disadvantage. Editorials in the newspapers which stressed my lack of political background as a point in my favor served only to accentuate the distrust felt by regular organization workers. They looked on me as an enemy within the ranks.

This became evident when, a few days after my appointment, I received a visit from State Senator Edwin H. Vare, leader of the Philadelphia organization, and his brother William S. Vare, then representative in Congress, the man who was to defeat me in the primaries four years later. I assured them of my loyalty to Republican principles, but this was hardly enough. Patronage was uppermost in their minds.

I explained my position to them. While I made it clear I would not surrender my independence of action on matters affecting either votes or appointments, I said it would be my policy to consult the organization leader in any county from which an appointment to federal office was contemplated.

To this, however, I made one specific exception and that was the appointment of federal judges. It has always been my settled conviction that judicial office must be entirely free of politics. I bluntly told my callers that I intended to support Charles L. McKeehan, who had no organization backing, for the federal bench in the Eastern District of Pennsylvania.

Realizing that I meant what I said, the Vare Brothers dropped the subject and Edwin Vare offered me a cigar—the political equivalent of the tender of the pipe of peace. But at the doorway he paused.

"Senator," he said to me—somewhat ominously, I felt—"this isn't a personal matter. But we are organization men first and last, and there's something I think you should know. It is that with our power over the organization we can send anybody we want to the United States Senate —anybody." He was not boasting. He was stating what he believed to be at that time a simple incontrovertible fact. And I cannot say that he was wrong.

THE OATH OF OFFICE

Since my colleague Senator Crow was ill, Governor Sproul had asked Senator Walter E. Edge to act as my sponsor when I took the oath of office on January 10th, 1922. At the last minute the majority floor leader, the late Henry Cabot Lodge, volunteered to escort me to the bar of the Senate. Later in the day the President pro tem of the Senate, Senator Cummins of Iowa, invited me to take the chair in order that I might have the experience of presiding over the Senate.

Somebody (Lord Rosebery, I think) has said that there are only two happy days in the life of a public man—one, the day he takes office and the other, the day he leaves it. In my case the first day, if not exactly happy, was at least exciting not only for me, but for my wife, my children and their spouses.

Among the congratulatory notes I received, I valued a holographic letter from Chief Justice Taft [3] who, I suspect, was more interested in getting support for his bill to regulate appellate procedure than in the new senator from Pennsylvania.

Senators who are given heavy responsibilities under the Constitution have always taken themselves rather seriously. They still do, but the public takes them less seriously than in Daniel Webster's day. The direct election of senators and the open primaries which prevail in so many states, have obliged candidates for the Senate to go on the hustings for their mandates. This enforced contact with the electorate as well as the unlimited debates in which the Senate had come to indulge, wisely or unwisely, had by the time I reached it, accelerated a popular tendency to deflate senators.

"Senator," said an old Capitol employee with whom I was chatting, "it's strange how customs have changed around this place. You and I are talking like friends; yet when I first came to the Capitol any employee who spoke to a senator without being spoken to would have been laid off for a month without pay." "In those days," he added, "the leaders of the Senate were very choosy as to which of their colleagues they would ride with in an elevator."

2. IN THE ENGINE ROOM

To a lawyer fresh from the courtroom nothing could have been more amazing than the absence of any compelling rule of relevancy or of any felt obligation to stick to the point before the Senate. I shall never forget

[3] Dear Senator Pepper,

I write to congratulate you and Mrs. Pepper, Pennsylvania and the country on your becoming a member of the Senate. It is most fitting, and measures up to the highest standard. I am particularly pleased because we are at a juncture when judicial reforms are necessary in our Federal system and it is most satisfactory that in the Senate such a notable accession to the number, all too small in that body, of leaders of the Bar whose practice fits them to originate or consider properly the needs of our courts and practice. I sincerely hope that you will be given a place on the Judiciary Committee.

Please present my warm felicitations and good wishes to Mrs. Pepper.

Sincerely yours,

WM. H. TAFT

the bewilderment with which I first listened to hours of talk on subjects not related to any matter on which the Senate was about to act, the speaker being obviously eager to gain applause from the galleries, to figure in a possible headline or to pose in the pages of the Congressional Record as the champion of some cause which he thought would be popular at home. Before very long I learned to distinguish between senators who went about their legislative labors as if no spectators were present and those who seemed to derive their greatest satisfaction from the presence of a listening throng. Some members of the latter class, on entering the chamber, immediately raised their eyes to the gallery, likely to be occupied by a number of the most attractive women in Washington, and appeared to be either elated or depressed by the result of their searching scrutiny. The habit invariably recalled my rowing days and the coach's injunction, "Eyes in the boat!" addressed to those of the crew who were fond of casting glances at feminine figures along the bank.

A CAUSE CÉLÈBRE

The big question before the Senate when I took the oath of office was whether or not to unseat Senator Truman H. Newberry of Michigan. He had been nominated in an open state-wide primary in the course of which his friends had raised and spent about $195,000. Immediately thereafter he and 134 others had been charged with conspiracy to violate the Corrupt Practices Act of Congress. A jury had been permitted by a federal judge to regard it a crime for a candidate to acquiesce in the expenditure of more than his own permissible contribution of $3750. Under this preposterous interpretation of the statute Newberry and others had been convicted. On appeal the Supreme Court set aside the conviction, the majority being of opinion that the Act of Congress did not extend to primary elections. Of course no Justice approved the interpretation given to the statute by the lower court. Meanwhile, in a hotly-contested campaign in which the expenditure in the primary was the principal argument against Newberry, the people of Michigan voted him into office, thus expressing the judgment that there had been nothing unreasonable in the expenditure. There never was any evidence of fraudulent use of money. Senator Newberry having thus been fairly elected by the people, the question was whether the Senate should deny him a seat.

The Senate debate proceeded with fire and fury. As I listened with all the rapt attention of a new member I became convinced of two things: first that in the absence of fraud it was not the Senate's business to set aside the deliberate judgment of the people of Michigan; and, second, that the talk of a majority of the senators who were attacking Newberry was hollow and unreal. A few of the attackers sounded fanatical and seemed quite unfit to discharge a delicate judicial duty. This was particularly true of Senator Kenyon of Iowa who clothed himself with self-righteousness as with a garment. Senator Walsh of Montana seemed to me to forget the big outlines of the case and to lose himself in details. "Joe" Robinson, "Jim" Reed and a lot of others talked too good and looked too wise. "Tom" Heflin seemed more impressed by the fact that Newberry had been silent under accusation than by anything else in the case. It was fairly obvious why silence was incomprehensible to him.

It was on the whole a disillusioning debate but was like many I was to hear later. Newspaper correspondents, sitting day after day in the press gallery, develop a cynicism about senators which on the whole is justifiable. These trained observers know perfectly well that a large percentage of noble utterances have no real relation either to the merits of the case or to the moral standards of the speaker.

The resolution to unseat Senator Newberry was lost. I voted against it. Nothing was thereby settled; for the prosecutors kept threatening to renew the attack at a later session and under this sort of pressure Senator Newberry finally resigned. The whole proceeding shocked me at the time and I get angry whenever I think of it. Four years later campaign expenditures were to become an issue in a Pennsylvania primary and I personally was to suffer from the use of funds ostensibly expended in my behalf.[4]

POLITICAL INEPTITUDE

Looking back over my term in the Senate I do not find a case in which I ever cast a vote because of what I thought would be its political consequences. My vote in the Newberry case was typical. Because of it I incurred an immense amount of vitriolic criticism and gained no compensating political advantage. The same thing is true of the votes I subsequently cast against the soldier's bonus and in favor of submitting a Child Labor Amendment to the people. Still later, on the Prohibition issue, I could have gained much political strength either by pretending to be a militant Dry or by supporting that hollow sham, a "light wine and beer" proposal.[5] There was one measure which, had it come to a vote, would have received my support for a purely political reason. That

[4] *Infra*, page 217.   [5] *Infra*, page 211.

was the Dyer Anti-Lynching Bill which would have substituted federal for state law enforcement in the local administration of criminal justice. Terrible as is the crime of lynching, I believe it will have to be prevented by raising the moral standards of the state concerned and not by federal bayonets. The supposed analogy of the suppression of slavery is a false one. The Fourteenth Amendment merely declares the law for the Nation. A federal Anti-Lynching Bill proposes federal enforcement within a state of a law which the state is able to enforce for itself. Central guarantees of the efficiency of local self-government are the first steps toward its ultimate destruction. If no political consequences had been involved I should have voted against the measure but because of the Negro vote back home I had pledged myself to support it.

During 1924 Senator McCormick introduced a resolution proposing an amendment to the Constitution which, if it prevailed, would give to Congress power to regulate child labor. I favored the resolution. This was consistent with my support of the Anti-Lynching Bill but really inconsistent with my theoretical objections to that measure. If the federal government is to exercise a special guardianship over children in industry there is no good reason why it should not extend protection to our Negro fellow-citizens in the South. I co-operated with Senator McCormick and a few others in drafting his resolution and I voted for the submission of the amendment to the states. I think Congress might safely be trusted with power to legislate on this subject and to take account of all the factors which intelligent regulation involves. My advocacy of the amendment was nevertheless to prove a political handicap to me when I ran for re-election, since it found no favor with Pennsylvania industrialists.

My own voting record was to prove that if you exercise judicial judgment when you are leading the legislative life you are pretty nearly certain to lose out in the next election. While you are in, you may render a far better grade of service: but unless you "rise above principle" (as Senator Swanson once jestingly expressed it) you will accumulate enough enemies to make your defeat a certainty. While constituents pay lip service to the senator "who has the courage of his convictions," what most of them really want is the man who is able to adopt *their* convictions as his own. The elder LaFollette, who was in the Senate in my day, had a rule of action which was as effective as it was simple. "I make it a rule," he explained blandly to my informant, E. A. Van Valkenburg, "never to vote for any tax measure or against any appropriation."

NATIONAL FIGURES

One of the interesting experiences of a new senator was to meet men in public life who had made national reputations. Among men of this sort when I entered the Senate was "Uncle" Joe Cannon, of Illinois. He was a member of the House of Representatives and a privileged character although he no longer held that body in his iron grip. Congressman Vare gave me a dinner soon after I went to Washington and Uncle Joe was one of the guests. His talk was a combination of wit and wisdom with an admixture of coarseness which, however, never became offensive. He said what he meant—and said it with brutal frankness. General Dawes told me that once in the course of a campaign in Illinois he had seen Mr. Cannon squelch unmercifully an objectionable constituent. "How are you, Uncle Joe?" the man had asked somewhat officiously. "How are you yourself and all the folks?" Mr. Cannon had replied. "You don't remember me, Uncle Joe?" The man persisted: "What's my name?" "If," answered Uncle Joe, "Saint Peter doesn't remember your name any better than I do, you'll go back to hell where you belong."

The body of which I found myself a member contained more diverse types than any group of comparable size that I have ever known. No two of the ninety-six senators resembled each other, even remotely. Senator Lodge, justly entitled to be known as the Scholar in Politics, was a reservoir of exact information on subjects relating to senatorial precedents and traditions as well as on English and American history and the intricate workings of the machinery of government. In the restaurant, where there is an inner room reserved for senators, Senator Lodge presided over one of the tables. In spite of the frequent interruptions of quorum calls and summonses to vote on pending measures, his conversation on literary and historical topics never ceased to delight me. I recall referring once to an impressive utterance by a Speaker of the House of Commons during the reign of Charles I, that I had come across in a book. I had forgotten the Speaker's name. Senator Lodge immediately supplied it and commented most interestingly on his life and work. On another occasion when Margot Asquith, during her tour of the United States, was entertained at a luncheon given by Senator McCormick in his offices, Senator Lodge and I sat on either side of her. She spoke of a Kentucky feud and of incidental shooting reported in the newspapers and seemed both amazed and shocked that such affairs could occur. I ventured to suggest that, as a woman of Scotch descent, she might recall similar feuds among the clansmen of her native land, and quoted a couple of lines from Aytoun's *Execution of Montrose,* a ballad I had learned in childhood. The reference was unfamiliar to her, but Senator Lodge not only capped the quotation but carried it on through many lines with verbal accuracy and great appreciation. On the floor Senator Lodge always spoke to the point, and often with force. Yet I do not remember him on the whole as a great debater.

No member of the Senate in my time approached in eloquence John Sharp Williams of Mississippi, who declined re-election on the expiration of his term in 1923. When conditions were to his liking Senator Williams occasionally burst into speech which for clarity of thought, purity of diction and cogency of presentation entitled him to high rank among American orators. His sarcasm, when roused, could be devastating, as many senators who crossed him well recall.

Medill McCormick was politically experienced, mentally brilliant, and thoroughly equipped for the work of the Senate. His friendship became to me a cherished possession. His untimely death, following upon his defeat in the Illinois primaries in 1924, added one more to the long list of United States senators who during my time went to their deaths with hearts broken by political reverses.

Frank B. Brandegee of Connecticut impressed me as one of the keenest minds in the Senate, at his best in the committee room or in conference. These men and many other valuable public servants like James W. Wadsworth, of New York, Carter Glass of Virginia, and David A. Reed, later my colleague from Pennsylvania, never lost sight of the issue before the Senate or suffered themselves to make voluble speeches for the sake of impressing constituents at home.

Being a new Republican senator, I was assigned to the Cherokee Strip, which was the grim designation for those seats in the Senate, on the Democratic side of the aisle, not filled by the minority party. From this point of vantage I surveyed my colleagues of both parties. The most conspicuous figure in my immediate neighborhood at that time was Thomas E. Watson, of Georgia, a curious combination of the cold practicality of the politician and the warm emotionalism of the poet. In contrast to some of his brilliant and sometimes ruthless political maneuvers and attacks on Republican leaders, I remember hearing him deliver in the Senate an exquisite and touching two-minute eulogy of a child from his State who had accidentally been burned to death in Washington.

"HARRISON STANDS PAT"

Senators Copeland and Ralston and the Senate Pages stand by.

On a line between me and the chair of the presiding officer sat Senator Pat Harrison of Mississippi. He had a wicked tongue and was called the "party scold." One of his favorite indoor sports was to rise and comment, with sarcasm tinctured with good humor, upon some reported act or utterance of Vice President Coolidge who at the time was presiding over the Senate. As I recall it, an act more frequently than an utterance furnished the basis for the Harrison thrusts. The habit of saying nothing superfluous was one which Mr. Coolidge did not acquire for the first time upon his elevation to the presidency.

Senator Harrison and I were both baseball fans. After a heated session in the Senate it was a refreshing experience to go with him to a ball game and root for the Washington team. We both took a keen interest in the baseball nines organized by the Senate pages and I recall at least one game in which he and I were selected to choose and lead the opposing teams.

Other Democratic neighbors were Senators James A. Reed of Missouri and T. H. Caraway of Arkansas. Both these brilliant and able senators seemed to derive the keenest satisfaction from the discomfort of those whom they singled out for attack. Reed's destructive method of verbal onslaught might be described as chemical: it was as if he had thrown acid upon his victim. Caraway's method might be compared to the use, with unerring aim, of a long-lashed whip. He could sting any part of his victim's person which was exposed. Both men were as likely to launch their attacks on members of their own party with whom they happened to disagree on a pending measure as on one of the opposition. I recall one case in which, replying to a speech made by a Democratic senator in opposition to the confirmation of a presidential appointment, Senator Caraway made a most bitter attack, but later, on the request of the victim, consented to expunge his remarks from the pages of the Congressional Record.

The floor leader of the minority party during a part of my term in office was Senator Oscar W. Underwood of Alabama. A new senator could not do better than note with care both his bearing toward colleagues in the course of debate and his intelligent method of approach to the question under consideration. His retirement from the Senate meant the loss of one of its most effective members and his subsequent death seemed to me a national misfortune.

TARIFF MAKING

In the domestic field, when I took office, the business of the moment was tariff making. Pennsylvania had as large a stake in this great indoor sport as any other industrial state. As the solitary Senator from Pennsylvania, and a green hand at that, I had to work early and late to familiarize myself with the myriad schedules which the pending bill contained and to see that the claims of my constituents were properly presented and pressed before the Finance Committee and in the Senate. My son-in-law, Fitz Eugene Newbold, took leave of absence from his banking office, sojourned for weeks in Washington and gave himself up to an intensive study of the most important problems. Without his help it would have been impossible for me to secure the highly-satisfactory results which finally rewarded our efforts.

When a tariff bill is under consideration a senator's day is a busy one, particularly if he represents a large industrial state. He finds in his office executive officers of industrial corporations, Washington representatives of trade groups, and all sorts of individuals who pretend to be profound economists. Frequently a caller exudes mystery and gives the senator to understand that he has a subtle influence over the votes of enough members of House and Senate to accomplish his purpose and that out of bounteous good-nature he is simply offering the senator a chance to get aboard the bandwagon. This type of visitor usually refers casually to senators, cabinet members and other officials by their first names.

It is natural enough that the comprehensive term "lobbyist" should be popularly applied to all these visitors. In point of fact, however, the nature of their several activities is diverse. From the man who intelligently presents the facts in regard to his industrial problems the senator gets invaluable help, while he soon learns to distrust the political economy of the visitor with the professorial air.

It would be a great mistake to suppose that there is anything like party unanimity in regard to raising or lowering duties, even among those who are popularly regarded as representatives of the industries with a common interest in tariff protection. In Pennsylvania, for example, immense quantities of tobacco are grown. This tobacco is for the most part of the quality used in the filler in the manufacture of cigars, whereas the leaf used as a wrapper is imported, in times of peace, from Sumatra or elsewhere. In Connecticut the shade-grown tobacco makes acceptable wrappers. It follows that the Republican tobacco growers in Pennsylvania would like to see the foreign wrappers on the free list while the Republican tobacco growers in Connecticut would not object to a prohibitory rate.

There is also the inevitable struggle between eastern seaboard manufacturers who use a raw material produced abroad and the producers of that same raw material which happens to be found, let us say, on the Pacific coast. The eastern man would like to see that particular material on the free list, so as to save the increased cost resulting from the transcontinental freight rate, while the western producer wants a high duty on the imported article in order to compel the eastern manufacturer to buy his product.

It was not long before I perceived that in the fight over the tariff bill the real struggle is not between two parties, but one between sections of the country. Senators from the western states are desirous of overcoming the advantage of position of long-established industries, by bringing about, when possible, some constructive advantage for the West or by dealing destructive body blows at eastern industry when they find they cannot serve their constituents in any other way.

A mere statement of these issues makes it easy to see how confused the discussion of them is bound to be. The rhetorical advantage is always on the side of those who want to keep duties down because they can make inflammatory speeches against individuals who have grown rich when duties were high. In 1922, for example, Andrew Carnegie was the favorite illustration of the evils of high protection. Anyone who attempts a fair adjustment of the rate on any particular import can do no more than present a statistical analysis which is as dull as dishwater. A really intelligent consideration of the items in a tariff schedule involves enough debatable figures to make one's head dizzy. That general satisfaction should result from the enactment of any tariff bill is too much to expect. The easiest part of the whole transaction is to make dire predictions of the widespread national disaster which will follow the enactment of the bill. Another easy matter for a senator with the gift of caricature is to pick out particular items in the schedule and by humorous comment make the whole bill seem ridiculous. Thus (to anticipate a little) when on September 19, 1922, the final vote was about to be taken, Pat Harrison made a most amusing speech on "jointed dolls," "silk chemises," "cuckoo clocks," "roulette wheels," "bird cages," and "hot water bottles." When, immediately after this illuminating utterance, I was called to vote upon the conference report which had settled the differences between the two Houses, I was one of 43 who voted aye. The nays were 28; 25 senators did not vote.

Most anything that anybody can say in criticism of the American method of tariff making is abundantly justified. And yet the criticism is hardly worth-while because nobody, as far as I know, can suggest a better way. Compromise, bargaining, trading, double-crossing and log-rolling in all its forms—all seem to have a place in the game.[6]

Senator Smoot ("Republican:Ut" as Ogden Nash designated him) was chairman of the Finance Committee. He was a storehouse of accurate information and an indefatigable worker. He treated me with friendly consideration and helped me to feel at home in my new surroundings. Smoot had weathered many storms. At one time some estimable women had attacked him because of his relation to the Mormon Church and his supposed belief in polygamy. The brilliant wife of my friend William Romaine Newbold was asked to sign a petition for his expulsion from the Senate. "How many wives has he?" she asked. "One," was the reply, "but he believes it right to have many." "I do not think I shall sign," said she. "I prefer a polyg that monogs to a monog that polygs."

FACING THE VOTERS

Senators, I very soon learned, may be classified in three ways: first, those who understand how to get the office and keep it; second, those who can discharge the duties of the office when they have it; and third, the rare men who can do both these widely different tasks. It did not take me long to discover how difficult it is to learn the technique of keeping an office, once attained. Before my ears had ceased to ring with the predictions of optimistic friends that a Republican senator from Pennsylvania could, if he wished, remain in the Senate all his life, I detected the sound of a coming storm. I was not to be permitted, I heard, to receive at the May primary the Republican nomination. I was to be pictured by some of the organization leaders as the "representative of special interests" and the enemy of the working man.

My friends advised me to give the county leaders and the voters a chance to meet me and draw their own conclusions. Overnight the map of Pennsylvania took on, for me, an entirely new significance. I had been

---

[6] A flexible tariff and a bipartisan Tariff Commission are only a partial solution. The real tariff makers are the administrative officials who write the regulations and manipulate the schedules at will.

accustomed to think of the State in terms of judicial districts and court-houses. Now I was to learn, as must every newcomer in politics, how little I really knew about the people who controlled the vote in the State's sixty-seven counties; I was to discover that I was unknown, even by name —despite my statewide activities on the Council of National Defense during the war—to many of those who were effectively engaged in plying locally the trade of king-maker.

With a colleague on his deathbed, and with Senate technique to learn, it was out of the question that I should take the time to visit every county in the State. Wise advisers indicated the strategic centers and put me in touch with upstate leaders, of whom I knew as little as they knew of me. Then began a series of night journeys from Washington to distant points in Pennsylvania; meetings, on arrival, with local committees hastily organized to greet me; solemn conferences in the offices of men higher up; maiden political speeches to groups gathered in courthouse squares or in available halls, and endless handshaking in the lobbies of local hotels. I felt like a kind of rare museum piece presented for inspection. One chairman at a political meeting introduced me as "George Washington Pepper," and others merely mumbled my name. However, I gradually made myself known, chiefly through the effective aid of W. Harry Baker, whose association with Penrose had given him an unmatched knowledge of the entire Commonwealth.

I was at the time a member of the Committees on Banking and Currency, Military Affairs and the Library of Congress. These assignments required frequent attendance at meetings and long hours of study over bills. I was trying to guard the interests of Pennsylvania as well as of the country as a whole in the complex tariff-making situation. I was profoundly concerned with the problem presented by the limitation-of-armaments treaties; and was deeply involved in discussions of the proposed bonus for veterans of the World War, the Dyer Anti-Lynching Bill and a host of both public and private measures which called for careful consideration. In the midst of all this I spent, at intervals, twenty-five days in twenty-five of the sixty-seven counties in Pennsylvania making an average of five speeches a day.

My chief opponent in the 1922 primary was an experienced office-holder who had served acceptably as congressman-at-large and had had the experience of actually polling a heavy statewide vote. Carrying a union card and proclaiming himself as a fellow toiler with the working-men, he was able to appeal to a wide audience. With a sagacity born of experience, he listed various public questions on which I had declared myself and by taking the opposite side on each, found a ready-made constituency whose friendliness to him was, in fact, less dynamic than its opposition to me. I had, for example, come out definitely against a bonus measure granting an outright sum of money to all veterans of the World War. Advocacy of the grant became one of the strongest planks in my opponent's platform.

As my campaign progressed I became aware that the senatorial contest was being deprived of much of its usual significance by the circumstance that a great political battle was being staged in connection with the struggle for the governorship. The able administration of Governor Sproul was drawing to a close. A caucus of state Republican leaders had proposed as a candidate George E. Alter, of Pittsburgh, who was eminently qualified but most reluctant to run. Gifford Pinchot saw his opportunity and was quick to seize it. Although he had himself been rescued from political eclipse by being made a member of the Governor's cabinet and owed both gratitude and loyalty to Sproul, he campaigned under the unjustified but effective slogan, "Clean up the mess at Harrisburg." In this way he won the nomination by the slender margin of 9,259 votes. This gave him less than a majority but his was the highest name on the list. In the resulting astonishment at what had happened, the fact that I had won the Senate nomination by a majority of 241,159 votes passed almost unnoticed by the Pennsylvania public.

The campaigning I was obliged to do at the very beginning of my term impaired my ability to serve the State with undivided energy, but it had its advantages in bringing me into closer contact with constituents and in increasing my capacity to understand and properly represent my Commonwealth.

An important factor in Pennsylvania politics at this time was Joseph R. Grundy, who later sat for a while in the Senate by appointment of Governor Fisher. He always managed adroitly to hold a balance of power in factional fights within the Party. His theory was that political control, at one time exercised by the railroads and later by the liquor interests, could be more beneficently exercised in the name of business. This was plausible enough; but I never was able to perceive that it meant an appreciable rise in ethical or governmental standards. He was an old-line conservative and regarded with unconcealed dismay my views on various governmental questions. During my preprimary campaign he was not unfriendly to me although he was principally concerned in securing the gubernatorial nomination of Gifford Pinchot, to whom he had thrown his support because he had parted company with

POSING AT PITTSBURGH

Campaign Reception Committee.

My Manager, Ira Jewell Williams, Esq., looks anxiously over my shoulder.

the regular Republican Organization in the selection of a slated candidate.

A little later, when I gave my support to Baker as Chairman of the State Republican Committee instead of to Grundy's candidate, believing as I did that this was the only way to preserve the state organization, a political breach was created between Mr. Grundy and me which was never afterward bridged although our personal relations were unaffected and remain cordial to this day. I had been made National Committeeman from Pennsylvania, to succeed Penrose, not because I had the necessary political sagacity but because, having no political background, I had few enemies and my selection would not reopen the factional fight which alone had made Pinchot's nomination possible.

Looking back on the ructions that I have seen and experienced in the open primary, I should say that the system intensifies factionalism, confuses issues, calls for unwholesome expense and imposes a back-breaking strain upon candidates who thus have to wage two successive campaigns, one in the primary and one shortly thereafter for the general election. When there has been a long and bitter preprimary fight between two qualified candidates, the danger is that the friends of the loser will either not work for the winner in the general election or will even bolt and vote for the candidate of the other party. This difficulty is of course not absent from the convention system but it is much more acute in the open primary. A candidate defeated in a statewide primary is popularly regarded as having been as effectively thrown into the political discard as if he had been beaten in a general election. Defeat in a general election usually results, as in Jim Wadsworth's case, in losing to the Senate the continued activity and service of a man the Party can ill afford to lose.

The difficulties which have arisen in attempts to regulate primary expenses by law are born of the fact that the primary system is by its nature an expensive one. The process of disseminating political information is costly and varies in different states. In Pennsylvania a single well-written form letter, addressed and mailed to each Republican voter, could cost $150,000 or more. While much of the criticism of primary expenditures in large states is uninformed and, at times, malicious, it serves a good purpose because it is a deterrent to waste and tends to make campaign managers careful instead of prodigal. At best, however, the primary system is an expensive luxury and in the long run it may prove dear at any price. As in Senator Newberry's case, it is the system itself which merits criticism and not its inevitable consequences.

3. LEARNING THE MACHINERY

My majority of a quarter of a million in the primary, though un-noticed at home, sent up my stock in Washington. I was now regarded as a political factor of importance. This view I myself shared, not then realizing the extent to which the result was a machine-made product. While the Vares in Philadelphia had not actively advocated my nomina-tion, they had tolerated it and their organization had given me half-hearted support. I remembered, of course, that the Vares had warned me that what the machine could give the machine could take away. But I had a comfortable feeling that I might surprise them and that my big majority in the primary could be retained as long as I wanted to retain it, provided I worked hard and rendered intelligent service to the people of the Commonwealth. From this naïve impression I at the time derived considerable satisfaction.

Two months after the primaries Senator Crow died and Governor Sproul appointed David A. Reed to fill his place. No appointment could possibly have been more agreeable to me. I gained a colleague with whom to work was stimulating and with whom to associate was an intellectual delight. We campaigned together before the November election, Pinchot heading the ticket. The campaign meant more meet-ings and speeches, more absences from Washington. We and most of the other Republican candidates were elected with substantial majori-ties. My self-confidence was considerably increased by the fact that I led my Democratic opponent by 351,159 votes.

Pennsylvania was no longer in eclipse in the Senate. I had gained in prestige at the election, while Dave Reed's solid ability and lightning-like wit served the Republicans well. As floor leader Senator Lodge was diligent in the discharge of his duties and quick to lock horns with the Democrats on any issue which seemed to him of major importance. He was, however, inclined to ignore, with something like intellectual con-tempt, the thrusts of debaters who attempted to make political capital out of the discussion. I rejoiced in the increasing confidence with which, after his induction, Dave Reed not merely repulsed attacks of this sort but carried the war into the enemy's country and effectively exploded bombs on the Democratic side of the aisle.

Dave's mind is, I think, the most alert I have ever seen in action and his is a lively wit. On one occasion he and I paid a visit to Harrisburg for a conference with Governor Pinchot on some subject not ripe for

"A KNOTTY PROBLEM"
Pennsylvania's Senators Try to Solve It.

public discussion. The legislature not being in session, we expected that our visit to the Capitol would attract no attention. "What are you two United States Senators doing here?" shouted the members of a legislative committee whom we came upon unexpectedly in the rotunda. While I fumbled for an answer Dave looked up quickly at some vacant mural niches. "We've come to be fitted for our statues," said he. Before the laughter had subsided we had made our getaway.

THE DAILY ROUND

After election my work pyramided. I was told by the superintendent of the Senate post office that my daily mail, both going and coming, was the heaviest in the Senate. While Congress was in session, my incoming mail ranged from three hundred and fifty to five hundred letters daily and on occasion mounted to a thousand or more. These letters called for some form of reply—information to be supplied or service rendered. I worked incessantly, early and late, and took far less time than I should have taken for exercise and social diversion. This condition of things was due to the size of my State and its proximity to Washington. Nearly ten million constituents is a big group to serve and a surprisingly large number of them wanted service—or jobs. Anybody with a bright idea could leave home and reach my office with little effort. The contrast is great between the population statistics of Pennsylvania and those of some other states. I figured there were seventeen states with a representation of thirty-four senators whose aggregate population was less than Pennsylvania's. Or, to put it differently, if Senator Reed and I had represented, say, Allentown, we should have had as many constituents as a senator from Nevada.

Mrs. Pepper took her social responsibilities as seriously as I took my senatorial duties. The Capital's social life in the twenties was highly organized. There was nothing haphazard about it: the code, though unwritten, was definite and exacting. The wife of a new senator was expected to leave cards at the White House within the first twenty-four hours of her Washington sojourn and in quick succession to do the like at the homes of the Vice President and the Speaker of the House. Monday was the day for calling upon the Justices of the Supreme Court, Tuesday for calls on Representatives, Wednesday for the Cabinet, Thursday for Senators and Friday for the Diplomats. Mrs. Pepper, with the aid of a competent secretary, carefully systematized her social life. It interested me greatly to see how thoroughly it was done. A card catalogue was made, with the cards of one color for the Supreme Court, of another color for the Senate—and so on. Itineraries were worked out so that in any given neighborhood as many calls could be paid as were in order on that day. The maximum number of calls she succeeded in paying in a single day was seventy-five. This, I should think, was "an all-time high," made possible by the fact that individual cards prepared in advance could be left in batches at neighboring hotels and apartment houses.

Dinner invitations were supposed to be answered within twenty-four hours and it was good form to send both communications by hand.

Little metal clips on the cards which Mrs. Pepper kept indicated invitations to luncheon or dinner. Precedence at social functions was in accordance with inexorable law. A hostess arranged her table in strict conformity with it. Only a few questions were unsettled. One was whether the Chief Justice or the Speaker should sit on the right of the hostess. This weighty problem was solved by following the advice of Mr. Cook of the State Department never to invite both those functionaries to the same party. The wives of the senators lunched together in the Senate Office Building once a week, half a dozen of them acting as hostesses. In addition to duties such as these Mrs. Pepper, from the gallery reserved for senator's wives, closely followed debates and votes and greatly helped me by taking in tow visiting constituents who wished to "see" Washington. She took them to the Executive Offices, at prearranged hours, to be greeted by the President, secured for them seats in the Senate gallery, sometimes introduced them to various senators and often took them to lunch in the Senate restaurant. All this made busy weeks for her which were always ended by our return to Philadelphia on Saturdays to spend Sundays at home and thus maintain contact with the children and the enlarging circle of grandchildren.

Social life meant, for me, occasional dinners of a formal sort. One evening, at a dinner given by Mr. and Mrs. Henry P. Fletcher, Mr. Justice Holmes and his wife were the bright particular stars. After dinner I joined Mrs. Holmes, whose society was altogether delightful. After a while I said, "Mrs. Holmes, I am not holding your interest. You are thinking about something else." "I am the ranking woman here tonight," she replied. "It is time to go home. Nobody can go till I do and I can't go till I catch the Justice's eye. Look at him." I looked across the room and saw the Justice devoting himself to Mrs. Gifford Pinchot, who was looking particularly well in her evening gown. He was evidently in no hurry to leave. "There is a horrid little animal called the Wart Hog out at the Zoo," said Mrs. Holmes. "He gives you a baleful glare out of the corner of his eye. The Justice has just given me that Wart Hog eye."

THE L'ENFANT PLAN AND THE LIBRARY OF CONGRESS

Occasionally there was a dinner with a serious purpose. My wife and I gave such a dinner for the discussion of plans for beautifying Washington. As Chairman of the Committee on the Library of Congress I had a more extensive jurisdiction than the name would indicate. I conceived the idea of assembling informally various influential people each of whom was pressing some special interest in a way that antagonized the others. To preserve the integrity of the l'Enfant Plan was the consistent objective of Charles Moore, head of the Fine Arts Commission, as it was of Senator Fernald, of Maine, Chairman of the Senate Committee on Buildings and Grounds. Fernald was anxious to construct the Memorial Bridge over the Potomac and to remove some wartime shacks which defaced the Park between the Union Station and the Capitol. The Director of the Botanical Gardens for his part wanted for his greenhouses a permanent location on their existing site, thus encroaching upon the space reserved for the Mall. Some Army men wished to retain for stable use land to which the Botanical Gardens might have been removed. Representatives of each special interest were lobbying to prevent the accomplishment of any project other than their own. Each group had enough influence to obstruct but not enough to achieve. All interests were in fact reconcilable. My idea was to get the warring factions together and agree upon a combination program which all could support. This was done. Team play resulted and the way was opened for what ultimately came to pass. The shacks and other eyesores were in due time removed. The Botanical Gardens were transferred to a suitable location. The Mall was preserved and the Memorial Bridge was built. At that dinner, after we had been sitting around the table for hours, Mrs. Pepper had suggested to Senator Fernald that we might adjourn to a neighboring room and sit in greater comfort. He whispered, as she later told me, "Don't you do it; we'll never get this crowd together again."

Part of my work on this same committee was to sponsor legislation providing for the development of a great national Arboretum, for which the latitude of Washington is ideal. The valley of the Anacostia River, which flows through the District of Columbia and empties into the Potomac, possesses a soil particularly favorable for such a development. If this valley had not been taken over by the Nation, it soon would have become the scene of a building operation. One of the most earnest proponents of this civic enterprise was Mrs. Frank Noyes, of Washington. When after all sorts of opposition the bill for the acquisition of the land was finally passed there came a rumor that, for reasons of economy, President Coolidge intended to veto it. Mrs. Noyes thereupon hastened to the White House to plead for approval. She later gave me an account of the interview. In the midst of her presentation she suddenly and to her own astonishment burst into a flood of tears. The President, completely taken aback, was as much embarrassed as it was possible for a man to be. "Why, Mrs. Noyes," he stammered, "I had no idea that you felt so deeply about this matter." Still in tears she assured him that her heart would break if he vetoed the bill. Whereupon he signed it; and so the great Arboretum project was made secure.

It was a providential circumstance that Andrew Mellon was throughout this period Secretary of the Treasury. His eagerness to beautify Washington was illuminated by good taste and his official jurisdiction was broad enough to enable him to apply effective pressure. His subsequent munificent gift of his priceless pictures and of a gallery to contain them was only one of his contributions to the development of the capital city.

With the building up of the Library of Congress itself, the committee was equally concerned. Senator Fess of Ohio, Congressman Moore of Virginia, and I encouraged the compilation and publication by the Government of *Documents Relating to the Formation of the Union*. Dr. Herbert Putnam, then the librarian, had been for years developing plans to make this great institution not merely a storehouse of books but a radiating center of culture. Individual donors, in increasing numbers, were tendering endowments for various related activities. A conspicuous instance was the generous offer of Mrs. Elizabeth Sprague Coolidge to build an auditorium for chamber music and to provide for the rendering there of the best that the world has to offer. The problem before my committee was to provide a legal way to accept such gifts and to administer them effectively when made. We evolved the idea of the Library of Congress Trust Fund and I embodied it in a carefully drafted bill. It was passed and the machinery thus set up has since worked as intended.

THE COMMITTEE ROOM

I had not been in the Senate long before I realized that, for all the fire of debate on the floor, the Committee room is the real battleground in which the struggle over legislation takes place. The measure of a senator's greatest usefulness must be taken when he is in committee, although the popular verdict is apt to be determined by his performance in the open Senate. During my term I served at various times on the following Committees: Military Affairs, Naval Affairs, Banking and Currency, the Steering Committee, Revision of the Laws, Foreign Relations, Printing, Rules and the Library of Congress. A new Senator is asked by the Committee on Committees to indicate his preferences. If he is wise he will not at once press for a place on a major committee but will attain his ambition by hard work. I was anxious to serve on Banking and Currency but hesitated to declare myself. I was, therefore, much flattered when its Chairman, Senator McLean of Connecticut, himself asked that I be appointed. "Not a personal matter," he explained when I thanked him. "I like to be chairman but I hate to work. You have a reputation as a hard worker; so I shall keep the chairmanship and expect you to do the rest." This suited me and we made an effective team. He was a man of great ability and of genuine charm. My association with him was an unmixed pleasure. When public hearings were to be conducted he appointed me chairman of a subcommittee to conduct them. Of particular importance were the hearings at which war raged between those who favored and those who opposed branch banking.[7] These hearings were conducted with due regard to dignity but with enough informality to insure dispatch. There was plenty of scope for the examination of witnesses but there was no browbeating and no rudeness.

I doubt whether I should have been appointed, after only two years of Senate service, to the powerful Committee on Foreign Relations had it not been for Dave Reed's effective insistence that I should be assigned to this position at the same time that he became a member of the important Finance Committee. I had a reluctance, amounting to weakness, about pressing myself for consideration. Some indication of what must have preceded the decision to allot me a place on the Committee on Foreign Relations was disclosed by Senator Brandegee when I ex-

[7] *Infra,* page 220.

pressed to him my satisfaction at having become a colleague of his on this committee.

"We'll be glad to have you with us, Senator," he replied, "if you'll remember always, while on the Committee, to rely on your brains instead of your emotions."

Pending before the Committee when I joined it was the complicated question of this country's adherence to the World Court.[8] Also the question of a treaty with Turkey which omitted such guarantees to Armenia as the Allied Powers had exacted in the Lausanne Treaty.[9] And there was the long-standing controversy with Cuba over the Isle of Pines.[10]

Much of the work of the Senate Naval Affairs Committee had an international significance. The great appropriation bills, of which the Naval Appropriations Bill is one, sometimes gave rise to acute differences between Senate and House. When the House bill has been radically amended in the Senate and conferees meet to consider the problem thus presented, heated discussion often ensues, and the Senate conferees and the House conferees eye one another across the table like French and German delegates at Versailles. An acute difference of this sort arose in my time in connection with the cruiser-building program. President Coolidge and the House were opposed to beginning work on certain 10,000-ton cruisers, the building of which had previously been authorized. The Senate, feeling sure that whatever limitation of armaments might be agreed upon these ships would be well within our quota, inserted by amendment the necessary appropriation item. Senator Hale of Maine, the diligent and able chairman of the Senate Committee, Senator Swanson[11] of Virginia and I were the Senate conferees. We had the hard task of maintaining our position against both the President and the House; but the soundness of the Senate's view was finally recognized. Some of the public comment on my position convinced me that it is often necessary in times of peace to be charged with bloodthirstiness and a militaristic spirit to secure even the minimum requisites of national defense. Now that in wartime a realistic view is being taken of our naval requirements I find nothing to regret in the stand I took more than twenty years ago.

The Joint Committee on Printing, while it gets very little publicity, handles an immense volume of business. For a period I was chairman of this committee as well as of the Library of Congress Committee.

[8] Infra, page 174.
[9] Infra, page 176.
[10] Infra, page 183.
[11] Subsequently Secretary of the Navy.

Among its other functions, the Committee on Printing supervises contracts for the purchase of paper and supplies for the Government Printing Office, the largest establishment of its kind in the world. Today the output of government printed matter is stupendous but even in my time the office turned out yearly 200,000,000 money order application blanks, 32,000,000 books and pamphlets (in one year for the Department of Agriculture alone) 92,000,000 income tax blanks, and a vast number of post cards which, as some of its statistically minded officials boasted, would attain a height of two hundred miles if stacked in a single pile.

THE UNITED STATES CODE

"Revision of the Laws" sounds a bit dull. Actually, however, the term recalls one of my most interesting senatorial experiences. The project of assembling the widely-scattered federal statutes and arranging them, code-fashion, in a single volume had long been contemplated. A diligent Representative had actually prepared such a code. The House enacted it on his assurance of accuracy. When the House bill reached the Senate, Senator Ernst, Senator Bruce and I, as members of a special committee, soon found that the work was full of dangerous errors. We declined to recommend Senate approval. Then ensued an unpleasant controversy. Speaker Gillette and other friends of the author came over to the Senate and urged concurrence. The House Committee insisted that the work was accurate. An impasse was the result. Senator Ernst, Chairman of the Senate Committee, relied on me to settle the matter. I suggested that the deadlock be broken by referring the bill to Professor Chamberlain of Columbia and to Professor Mikell of Pennsylvania, both experts in statute law. This was done and the report of the umpires fully sustained the Senate contention. This was tragic for the author, who had spent years of effort on the work. Nevertheless, facts had to be faced; and the question was what to do next. I suggested that we invite two great publishing houses to co-operate, under our supervision, in the preparation of an adequate code, using their experts for the gigantic task. I was given a free hand. The president of the West Publishing Company, Mr. Homer P. Clark, and of the Edward Thompson Company, Mr. Blair Wailes, accepted an invitation to become my house guests at Devon. The project was unfolded to them and, in fine co-operative spirit, they agreed to undertake the work jointly. So the project was launched. Progress was enormously facilitated when Congressman Roy G. Fitzgerald of Ohio became chairman of the House

Committee. He was as enthusiastic as I over the possibilities of our enterprise. Finally the code was completed and was embodied in a single bill. As it contained all the congressional legislation from 1789 to date that was still in force, the bill was perhaps the most voluminous that had ever come before Congress.

How to get it passed by the Senate was the next question. At this juncture I sought the co-operation of Senator Walsh of Montana who in such matters was the Solon on the Democratic side. After much discussion we agreed upon a legislative formula. The bill, when enacted, was not at once to repeal all existing laws but was to be evidence of their content, thus driving one who asserted inaccuracy to prove it. Repeal of existing laws and the substantive enactment of the code were to follow after the work had withstood the test of use. When introduced in the form of a bill, it was a formidable document. Since, under the rules, any member can demand that a pending measure be read from beginning to end,[12] a single senator could have prevented a vote upon the bill by resorting to such tactics. Fortunately the senators on both sides of the aisle agreed to let the measure pass. Pass it did; and the Government Printing Office in a miraculously short time produced a splendidly printed volume of 1,718 pages. The House concurred in the action of the Senate by passing the bill without change. Few had realized that all effective federal legislation could be assembled within such narrow compass. Yet there it was—an accomplished fact—and our labors had been crowned with success.

The publishers promptly brought out an elaborately annotated edition of the code in fifty volumes. Fitzgerald, for the House, wrote a preface and I, for the Senate, a foreword. We both paid well-deserved tribute to the public service rendered by the publishers. Each of us was glad to have his name associated with an epoch-making work.

THE VETO AND PARLIAMENTARY STRATEGY

A senator is in something of a dilemma when his commitment to a certain piece of legislation comes in conflict with his feeling that he should support the President as the responsible executive and the leader of his Party. Early in my term of office a bill came up to increase the pay of postal employees. I had given them my word that I would vote

[12] In 1925 Senator Howell of Nebraska, by exercising or threatening to exercise this right, succeeded in preventing action upon a voluminous bill for the payment to American claimants of the old French Spoliation Claims.

for the bill and I did. President Coolidge vetoed it on the ground that
it failed to make provision for the raising of postal rates to meet the
increased expenditure. I felt it my duty to support the President when
an unsuccessful attempt was made to override his veto. I redeemed my
pledge to the men, however, by helping at once to formulate and enact
a substitute measure containing the requisite revenue features. Such a
measure was finally passed and received presidential approval.

No matter what was the legislation at issue, I soon learned that the
senator was most effective who both understood his subject and re-
frained from wounding the susceptibilities of colleagues who differed
from him. A bitter attack by a well-informed partisan might delight
constituents but it was likely to alienate the votes by which alone he
could attain the result that he and they desired.

The effort to pass a bill against determined opposition often brings
on a battle of wits. One such conflict occurred when I had charge in the
Senate of a House bill for the payment to Bethlehem Steel workers of
the wartime pay which had been awarded to them by the War Labor
Board just after World War I. The condition of Senate business was
such that the bill could not be considered except by unanimous consent.
Senator Dial of South Carolina objected every time the calendar was
called. Finally he agreed to allow the bill to be considered provided an
amendment was added which really defeated the whole purpose of the
bill. I agreed and the bill was passed as amended. It then went to a
conference committee of the two Houses. The conferees rejected the
destructive amendment and the bill was reported back to both Houses
in its original form. Since a conference report is privileged and its consideration cannot be blocked by a single objection, the report was considered, the bill was passed in 1925 and the workers at long last got
their pay.

RUEFUL RECOLLECTION

During my Senate term, Chief Justice Taft was urging further limits
upon the right to invoke appellate jurisdiction of the Supreme Court.
This was the measure about which he wrote to me when I first took
my seat in the Senate. We talked the matter over one day in President
Coolidge's office and later the Chief Justice wrote me as follows:

November 14, 1924

My dear Senator Pepper:

I am availing myself of the conversation I had with you the other day
at the White House to emphasize the importance of putting through at
the present Congress the bill to help the Supreme Court in reducing its

docket by an enlarged power of certiorari, and by the simplification of the statutes which govern the jurisdiction of the Court, so that they shall not continue to be, as they now are, a trap for the unwary. I enclose a short description of the bill which I prepared, and a much longer discussion and elaboration of the effect of the bill upon existing legislation. The bill was prepared two years ago by a committee consisting of Judge Day, Judge Van Devanter and Judge McReynolds and myself, as ex-officio member, and was then submitted to the entire Court, which unanimously recommended its passage. As I told you, Senator Walsh and Senator Shields are both opposed to giving to the Court any additional power of certiorari. In this respect they are quite at odds with the practice as granted by the Legislature of the various States to the Supreme Courts of the States. I think there must certainly be a dozen States in which some such method of winnowing out the unimportant cases is given to the Supreme Court. It is the only method by which the business can be properly kept up. I hope that you will give your attention to this matter and that you will aid us in securing what is badly needed.

Sincerely yours,

WM. H. TAFT

There was acute difference of opinion respecting the Chief Justice's proposal among members of the bar. Some of the opposition came from those claiming an inalienable right to weep on the shoulder of the august tribunal for no better reason than that the lower court had decided against them. Others were hesitant about giving more power to the powerful, fearing that discretion might be abused. If I could have foreseen certain cases of mine in which the learned Justices later erred and strayed from the way like lost sheep, I might have lined up with the opposition. As it was, I took the side advocated by the "Chief" and this finally prevailed. I accordingly have only myself to blame if, in the matter of granting or refusing certiorari, the Justices have occasionally left undone the things that they ought to have done and done those things that they ought not to have done.

TO PHILADELPHIA AND RETURN

While Senate work had the right of way, occasionally I could go home for a day or two and thus maintain contact with my law office. Now and then I found it possible to try a case. While I expected to be drafted for a second term by an enthusiastic and grateful constituency I thought it the part of wisdom to keep the home fires burning so that there would be some place to go in case I were finally left out in the cold.

Throughout my Senate term Mrs. Pepper and I made it a practice to spend Sundays in Philadelphia. We left Washington on each Saturday afternoon and returned early Monday morning. Until 1923 we continued to make 1730 Pine Street our headquarters. After that we built a much smaller house in a recently "reclaimed" street, called Panama Street, and lived there over week-ends during winter months. On one occasion when Magnus Johnson, Farmer-Labor Senator from Minnesota, was coming to speak in Philadelphia, I invited him to spend the night at my house. On the train from Washington he remarked, "I suppose, Senator, you live in a palace." Then he added meditatively, "I don't know how to behave in a palace." I told him not to worry and that when he saw my palace it would be revealed to him how he ought to behave. When the motor that met us at the station turned into Panama Street I said, "Here we are!" "Is *this* where you live, Senator?" he asked in astonishment. Then, after a moment's pause, he exclaimed, "My God, Senator, you live in an alley!" "I'll wager," I said, "that you have made speeches at the crossroads in Minnesota boasting of your simple life among disgustingly rich senators living in palaces; and now when you face the facts you find me living in a street too unfashionable to suit you and Mrs. Johnson." He grinned sheepishly for he knew it was true. We frequently gibed one another about our political and economic differences. On one occasion I put my jest into a rhyme:

> It's funny how we've floundered on
> Thru weary, wasted years.
> It's funny how we've thrived upon
> Our mingled sweat and tears.
> We never found the formula—
> We always went astray
> Till Minnesota gave the world
> The Man Who Found the Way.
>
> It's so simple—when you know it:
> Just reverse your common sense
> And assume you're rich in wisdom
> When your ignorance is dense:
> When a man has special training
> You remove him from his place;
> Incapacity is fitness;
> Experience disgrace.

When other nations tremble
We are saved from War's alarms—
For our farmers do our banking
And our bankers run the farms.
Our lawyers mend the plumbing,
And our doctors run the trains,
While our nurses use the pick-axe
And our lunatics their brains.

When plumbers play the violin
And carpenters the flute—
When ev'rybody's out of tune
And harmony is mute;
When the teamster toots the trombone
We are sure that all is well;
And that Magnus Johnson's orchestra
Is outside raising hell.

It's just the same in everything
No matter where you turn—
What you do not know already
It is better not to learn.
Let's glorify damfoolishness
And tell the country how
Mrs. Magnus milks the motor
While her old man cranks the cow.

THE SENATE AT ITS WORST

Everybody was "out of tune" and harmony was "mute" in the Senate
following the inauguration of Coolidge and Dawes. The bitterness
aroused by the Teapot Dome incident,[13] exploited by the Democrats as a
major campaign issue, had put the Senate on edge. This became evident
when the President sent to the Senate the nomination of Charles Beecher
Warren, of Michigan, to be Attorney General. He was in my judgment
eminently qualified for the office both as respects character and capacity.
I testified to my belief in a speech in the Senate. How confirmation
failed by the margin of a single vote and how the name was submitted
a second time and was again rejected are familiar episodes in Senate history. If the men who, wallowing in self-righteousness, attacked Warren
for having in private practice represented the Sugar Trust some years

[13] *Infra*, page 196.

before had themselves been of his intellectual and moral caliber the
senatorial level would have been considerably higher than it was.

A similar element of smugness characterized the attacks on Harding
and Coolidge in the course of the Teapot Dome debate.[14] Senator
Walsh of Montana, who had been the leader of the prosecution, was
able and relentless. He nevertheless lacked a sense of perspective and
would have been the better for a vein of humor. "Joe" Robinson of
Arkansas was also active on the Democratic side. In debate he showed
less of the judicial quality than almost any man I ever knew. He had a
violent and explosive temper and occasionally made an exhibition of
himself by threatening personal violence to a colleague.

Unpleasant as were such outbursts, they were mild compared to some
which had stirred the Senate in the days before the Civil War. I was
told by Mrs. Eugene Hale, the mother of my friend and colleague, Senator
Frederick Hale of Maine, that in those days southern senators were wont
to say things in debate which northern senators, because of the strong
northern sentiment against the duel, were unable to answer by a challenge to fight. Mrs. Hale's father, Senator Zach Chandler of Michigan,
Senator Ben Wade of Ohio and Senator Simon Cameron of Pennsylvania,
had thereupon signed a compact to go armed in the Senate and to shoot
the first southerner who should insult either of them or their states.
Mrs. Hale treasured the original of this compact and the belt with
pendant revolver and bowie knife which her father had carried in pur-
suance of it. She added that from the time the existence of this compact
became known there was not a peep from any of the former tormentors.
In contrast to such senatorial turbulence was the Olympian calm of the
Supreme Court of the United States. This was impressed upon me when
I had accepted the Court's invitation to act as *amicus curiae* and to make
an argument in support of the power of Congress in a case then pending before it.[15]

THE NAVAL ACADEMY

There were other pleasant extracurricular duties which now and then
broke the Senate routine for me. One was a brief sojourn at the Naval
Academy at Annapolis as a member of the Board of Visitors periodically
appointed by the President. Another was my service as a member of
the Board of Regents of the Smithsonian Institution.

[14] *Infra,* page 197.
[15] *Myers v. United States,* 272 U.S. 52 (1926). For a discussion of this case, see
page 361, *infra.*

At the Academy I found the Commandant, Admiral Wilson, a little nettled by a recent display of bad manners by a distinguished visitor, the English Admiral, Lord Beatty. It seems that the midshipmen, when reviewed for his delectation, had done their stuff perfectly and all plans for the visitor's entertainment had worked smoothly. Not a word of commendation had, however, escaped his lips. Finally, in the crypt of the chapel, he was shown the tomb of John Paul Jones. "Very fine tomb," said the Britisher, "but I don't know what he did to deserve it." Whereupon Admiral Wilson exploded. "It is a tradition in our navy," he said, "to give such a tomb to any officer who with all the odds against him sinks an English man-of-war." At which Lady Beatty, standing near-by, exclaimed, "I'm so glad you said it to him."

On our official visit to the Academy I was assigned by our Chairman, President Angell of Yale, to inspect the English Department. Its head, Professor Smith, described the course of study. I asked whether he trained the midshipmen in verbal memory. He replied that he did, by requiring them to memorize the opening sentences of The Declaration of Independence, The Preamble to the Constitution, The Star-Spangled Banner and Lincoln's Gettysburg Address. "Why not add a character-making poem?" I asked. "For instance—what?" said he. "Kipling's 'If,' " I suggested. "But *that*," he objected, "was not written by an American." "Neither were the Sacred Scriptures," I answered, "but they are generally approved." "Besides," I added, "that poem is Kipling's estimate of the character of George Washington." "Prove that," he said, "and I'll make every midshipman learn it."

I thought the required proof would be easy to get. My friend the late William A. Law had spent a week-end with Kipling at Burwash. Law had there asked the poet to confirm a statement previously made by him (Kipling) to Law's daughter Margaret when she interviewed him during his visit to Philadelphia. The statement was to the effect that the poem had been inspired by Washington's character. "That is true," Kipling had replied and added, "Anybody who reads that poem without thinking of Washington takes the saddle and leaves the horse." All this Law had repeated to me on his return to Philadelphia. It gave special significance to the position of the poem which is printed immediately before the story of "Brother Square Toes" in the volume *Rewards and Fairies*. I thought it would be simple to get a confirmation direct from Kipling himself and made a request through our then Ambassador at the Court of St. James, Colonel Harvey. I had, however, reckoned without my host. Kipling at the time was having a brainstorm at the expense

THE SMITHSONIAN INSTITUTION

The Centenary of Alexander Graham Bell's birth was marked with appropriate ceremonies. Front row (left to right): Senator George W. Pepper,* Vice President Charles G. Dawes,* Chief Justice William H. Taft,* Senator Reed Smoot,* Senator Woodbridge N. Ferris,* Hon. Henry White.* Back row (left to right): Rep. Walter H. Newton,* Mr. Irwin B. Laughlin,* Rep. Albert Johnson,* Rep. R. Walton Moore,* Mr. Robert S. Brookings,* Secretary Charles D. Walcott, Mrs. Gilbert H. Grosvenor (daughter of Dr. Bell), Mr. Walter S. Gifford (President American Telephone and Telegraph Co.),-Mr. Victor Salvatore (Sculptor); Mr. Frederick A. Delano,* Mr. Dwight W. Morrow,* Mr. Charles F. Choate, Jr.,* and Mr. Gilbert H. Grosvenor.   (* Regents)

of all Americans because of our tardiness in entering the war. He therefore angrily contradicted to Harvey what with clarity and emphasis
he had previously told both Miss Law and her father. The proof that
I was seeking being unobtainable, the poet's anger lost for his poem a
status of which he might well have been proud.

THE SMITHSONIAN INSTITUTION

At the meetings of the Regents of the Smithsonian, Chief Justice
Taft always presided. On one occasion, when elaborate plans had been
laid for arousing interest in the Institution, President Coolidge threw
cold water on them by declining an invitation to attend. "Cheer up,
gentlemen," said Taft, "nothing is so bad but that it might be worse";
and then, with a chuckle, added:

> "On the F. Street Bridge a Russian stood
> Gnawing his beard for lack of food.
> Not nearly so good as bread and meat—
> But a d—d-sight better than shredded wheat!"

The only trouble with my Smithsonian service was, like so much Senate
work, its brevity. At about the time I had familiarized myself thoroughly
with the operations of the Institution my term came to an end. The
work was quite fascinating while it lasted.

THE FILIBUSTER

While I was in the Senate Vice President Dawes threw the spotlight
of national publicity on the filibuster. It had become a favorite indoor
sport of senators who on occasion, finding themselves in the minority
on a question, resorted to this obstructive strategy to prevent the question from coming to a vote.

The filibuster, it should be understood, may be used to thwart a vote
either on a Presidential appointment, on the confirmation of a treaty, or
on the enactment of a piece of legislation. In the case of a Presidential
appointment, the filibuster seldom becomes a serious problem, since there
are almost always some members of the minority party who are reluctant
to embarrass the President in the matter of appointments. Such action
sets a precedent for which they themselves might suffer when political
fortunes have changed.

In the case of a treaty, ratification requires the concurrence of two-thirds of the senators present. If this proportion of senators are eager to put a treaty through, they can, under present Senate rules, vote for cloture after sixteen members of the Chamber have signed a motion to bring the debate to a close. The difference between the Senate and the House rule on terminating debate is that a two-thirds majority in the Senate is required for a cloture vote. This is reasonable and in my opinion advisable where a treaty is concerned. Where a two-thirds majority are clearly in favor of passage—as was the case when I brought up the Isle of Pines Treaty [16]—the cloture motion may be held in reserve as a threat to force a vote. So I see no need to reform the rule of cloture as regards treaties.

What outraged General Dawes was the type of irresponsible filibuster which held up purely legislative business for long periods of time. As a result of this practice, he held, the Senate fell so far behind with its calendar that at the end of the session it frequently rushed through important business, such as appropriation bills, without giving them adequate consideration. In an analysis of bills passed during the previous five Congresses, he showed that the House had enacted only three and one-half per cent of the heterogeneous mass of bills and resolutions introduced, while the Senate had passed ten and a half per cent. "These outbursts of speed," he argued, "are a dangerous reaction from the cumulative reaction preceding them." As a remedy he proposed that the Senate amend its rules to permit, when legislation is pending, the passage of a cloture motion by fifty-one per cent of the senators instead of a two-thirds majority. Opposing this reform, Senator Norris of Nebraska argued that the filibuster was a threat only in those short sessions of the Senate which expired on the fourth of March every second year following the November election. He believed the remedy lay in a constitutional amendment directing the newly elected members of Congress to take their seats on the first of January following. Such an amendment, also setting forward the date of the Presidential inauguration, has since become part of the Constitution. But General Dawes's argument still has force and I favor his view. Filibusters are from time to time attempted by stubborn minorities. The practical effect is the same as if the Constitution provided that a thirty-four per cent majority in the Senate had the right to defeat a bill. Whether such a reform as General Dawes urged can be put through, is another question. There is bound to be strong opposition to it on the part of those southern men

[16] *Infra,* page 183.

who fear the enactment of an anti-lynching bill or some other measure deemed by their minority to be unconstitutional or a threat against their established social system. The filibuster successfully conducted in the autumn of 1942 against the abolition of state poll tax laws as applied to federal elections is a case in point.

SENATORIAL SELF-IMPORTANCE

The Senate, when all is said and done, is a stratified body. On the surface there is friendliness of intercourse. Just below the surface there is cleavage between the Republican and Democrat. One layer further down there is the vein of mutual suspicion and distrust between radicals and conservatives. Still deeper lie a very considerable number of personal animosities. Deepest of all is the secretly-cherished ambition of individuals whose words and votes are unintelligible until you learn where they are trying to land. In the closing days of a session the fighting takes place on the lower levels. Surface friendliness disappears, party lines cease to hold. Even the line-up between radicals and conservatives cannot be counted on. As each senator starts down the road, seeking last-minute action on an important measure, a band of secret enemies gathers to wait for him at the crossroads. The people back home never understand why their most excellent measure died with the session.

Somebody with a flair for psychoanalysis ought to turn a senator inside out and demonstrate him to interested onlookers. Probably his most distinguishing characteristic is lack of perspective. Whether ringing the elevator bell three times to command instant attention, or exacting immediate service from a page, or sailing grandly past obsequious door-keepers into any private office in Washington, or outranking members of the House at social entertainments—your Senator feels himself one with the Sun, Moon and Stars. Another manifestation of the same failing is a delusion of grandeur respecting the importance of the Senate. The Senate *is* an important body. But even so, it is not by any means the whole congressional show; and there are places on the map even outside of Washington where things important to America and the world take place.

Perhaps the most unpleasant manifestation of senatorial self-importance is cowardice. This is the only term that fits the badgering of defenseless witnesses before committees and the making of defamatory utterances on the floor of the Senate for which the person defamed can never get adequate redress. Until the Senate can develop a tradition of good manners and fair play critics will be justified in denying to it the pre-eminent position which senators like to claim for themselves.

4. INTERNATIONAL UNDERTOW

When I took my seat in the Senate in 1922 the Conference on Limitation of Armaments was then being held in Washington. At the very outset the United States made a dramatic gesture by an immense sacrifice of tonnage under construction. This probably made possible the adoption of the 5-5-3 ratio which emerged as a definite result of the conference. I supposed at the time that we had acted wisely. If in appraising international relations I had relied upon my brains instead of my emotions I should have viewed the sacrifice as a tragic mistake.

The outcome of the present titanic struggle is as I write [17] uncertain and the history of the next peace conference is still to be written. But on the basis of our past experience Will Rogers, I believe, was right when he said that the United States had never lost a war or won a conference.

The best I can say in retrospect about the sessions of the Washington Conference is that they were marked by two remarkable performances. One was the masterly way in which the then Secretary of State, Mr. Hughes, presided. The other was the amazing feat of memory performed by the official interpreter. It is some evidence of the unreality of the whole performance that my attention was riveted upon the mechanics of the conference rather than its product.

THE WORLD COURT

Of equal importance with limitation of armaments was the question of this country's adherence to the so-called World Court. The issue was still before the Senate Committee on Foreign Relations when I became a member of that body in 1924. On February 24, 1923, President Harding had sent a message to the Senate proposing that we "adhere" to the World Court. Secretary of State Hughes had also recommended adherence, subject to four minor conditions.

While I was wholly sympathetic with the conception of a permanent international court, I did not believe that the Secretary's conditions met the most serious objection to the Protocol. The Senate had, it should

[17] May, 1944.

be recalled, refused to join the League of Nations on the terms proposed by President Wilson and public opinion had supported the Senate's view that this country must not commit itself in advance to coercive action designed to implement the League's decisions. Now we were asked to join a World Court which, by its constitution, was obliged to give an "advisory opinion" on any dispute between League members whenever requested to do so by the League. This semipolitical function of the Court in effect made it "the advisory organ of the League of Nations," as it was styled by Judge de Bustamante of Cuba, one of the Court's strong advocates.

This link between the Court and the League clearly destroyed the Court's judicial character. Under such conditions it could not be an impersonal tribunal but rather a political instrumentality. The instant you impose on any court the duty of advising a political body you inject the germ of disaster.[18] So it seemed to me most dangerous and unwise to combine a strictly judicial function to be performed for litigant nations with an advisory function to be performed at the behest of the League. This fatal weakness in the Protocol was admitted by that distinguished American jurist, John Bassett Moore, who was at the time one of the judges of the Court. He conceded that its advisory function was "admittedly inconsistent with and potentially destructive of the judicial character with which the Court has undoubtedly been invested."

Unwilling to have this country adhere to a Court which was obviously to be made the political tool of the League, I advocated in the Committee on Foreign Relations and on the floor of the Senate the separation of the Permanent World Court from its organic relationship to the League. When it became evident that this could not be accomplished, I sought Judge Moore's advice in drafting a proviso which would have made it

[18] In England an ancient usage gave the King and the House of Lords the right to demand an opinion of the King's judges upon legal or legislative questions. The attempt of the political arm of the government to assert supremacy over the judicial wrote many unhappy chapters in English history. The effort to transfer the practice of advisory opinions to the American judicial system has fortunately failed. In only seven states did the practice gain a foothold, and even in them the governors have never had such a call upon the courts as that to which the World Court was subjected by the Fourteenth Article of the League Covenant. Recently, in August 1942, President Roosevelt (according to press reports) broke a wholesome precedent by consulting a Justice of the Supreme Court, Mr. Justice Byrnes, on the Executive's powers in wartime.

possible for the United States to protect itself against political action by Court or League. My draft read as follows:

V. That the Court shall not . . . without the consent of the United States, entertain any request for an advisory opinion touching any dispute or question in which the United States has or claims an interest.

With this condition attached, the resolution authorizing our adherence to the World Court was passed by the Senate on January 27, 1926, by a vote of 76 to 17.

Had the little group of Powers which dominated the League so desired, the universal acceptance of this proviso would have quickly followed and the United States would have taken its place as an adherent of the World Court. Instead, Geneva became a center of influence adverse to acceptance and our conditions were in fact never assented to. Later with considerable adroitness, amendments to the Protocol and Court Statute [19] were made which in my opinion professed one thing and meant another. Purporting to accept the Senate conditions, a "joker" was inserted in both amendments which effectively nullified the Senate's intent. This last phase developed in 1930 after I had left the Senate, when the Protocol, this time with the joker attached, again came up for consideration. I appeared with others before the Committee on Foreign Relations in opposition to the substitute, which happily was not accepted by the Senate. I also debated the substitute in Chicago with Salmon O. Levinson, the dreamer who later claimed to be father of the Kellogg peace plan. This was the only public debate in my experience in which my adversary forgot his manners and lapsed into angry personalities. I came back at him harder than he expected and the audience expressed emphatic disapproval of his poor sportsmanship.

TURKISH TREATY

Another aspect of the international court problem involved our relations with Turkey and came before the Committee on Foreign Relations. This question was whether or not we should join the Geneva Powers in a policy of enforcing peace by coercion. In the old days, when Turkey's judicial system gave no guarantee of justice to litigants, the great Powers stipulated that charges against their nationals in Turkey should

[19] The "protocol" was, in effect, the constitution of the Court while the "statute" supplied its bylaws.

be tried only in the consular court of the nation to which the accused belonged. After the Great War, Turkey, at Lausanne, forced the European Powers to surrender these so-called capitulatory rights. The United States was not a party to that European treaty; but our State Department negotiated and the President signed a separate Lausanne Treaty with Turkey in which we made the same concessions as had been made by the Allied Powers, but we did not exact from Turkey a promise of fair treatment of the Armenians. The omission, in my opinion, was a wise one. If Armenia were ill treated, it would be the business of the European Allies to protect her and we could co-operate with them or not, as we might decide. Had we, however, exacted a separate promise, and had that promise been broken by Turkey, we should have had to acquiesce ingloriously or else resort to arms. A foreign war to protect even the most deserving minority seemed to me unthinkable. Unfortunately the Democratic Convention of 1924 declared against ratification, thus making the treaty a party issue. Still more unfortunately, a large body of Protestant clergymen fell an easy prey to propaganda hostile to the treaty and, as too often happens, succeeded in so disguising a question of international policy as to make it appear a moral issue. As a consequence of this combined opposition, we never were able to muster the necessary two-thirds majority for ratification. Since the old treaty of 1839 had been abrogated, we were thus left without normal diplomatic relationship with Turkey, to the great disadvantage of American business men and of our missionaries in the Near East. This disadvantage was mitigated by Turkey's willingness to give us temporarily the rights of the most favored nation.[20]

THE LEAGUE OF NATIONS AGAIN

The League of Nations issue had been mildly revived in 1923 by the visit of Lord Robert Cecil. This delightful gentleman came to influence sentiment in favor of American membership. Thomas W. Lamont, whose house guest he was, suggested that I call on Lord Robert for conference. We had a long and earnest talk. I told him that renewed pressure for unconditional and unreserved League membership was hurtful to his cause. When asked to state my objections I specified several of the consequences which the provisions of the Covenant unmistakably entailed.

[20] In 1933 a Treaty of Establishment and Sojourn was proclaimed by President Hoover. A Treaty of Commerce and Navigation had been made three years earlier.

"Oh, but it would not work in that way," he replied. "If such a situation developed, you simply would not consider yourself bound." I reminded him that he as an Englishman had been trained under an unwritten constitution, the prescriptions of which are formless and vague, whereas Americans are accustomed to think in terms of a written instrument and to take seriously its exact provisions. Asked for constructive suggestions, I proposed such an amendment to the Covenant as would either eliminate its appeal to force or provide for a Western Hemisphere membership on terms suited to the conditions peculiar to the North and South American republics. He expressed great interest and said that we might confer again when he visited Philadelphia. At that time he requested me to put the two suggested amendments in legislative form for consideration by his colleagues. I did as he requested.

A few days later he and I were among the speakers at the dinner in New York of the Newspaper Publishers Association. He made an eloquent plea for unconditional League membership but hopefully intimated a possible agreement on terms. Speaking on the Press as "The Tongue of the World" I emphasized the importance of a foreign policy that unifies rather than divides domestic sentiment and urged the newspaper men to concentrate upon the great underlying principles of international cooperation rather than upon mechanical details. If we were to agree upon the substance of what we want, I contended, it would be easy enough to determine what modifications of League Covenant and World Court Protocol were necessary to conform them to our will. Lord Robert heartily commended the speech, which was of course intended to encourage him to consider the proposed amendments. Unhappily when he returned to England he lapsed back into a Wilsonlike determination that we must sign on the dotted line or not at all. He decided that nothing could be done to meet the objections to American membership and preferred to luxuriate in the hope of unconditional adherence.

The amendments which I had drafted were explained in the following letter dated April 4, 1923, in which I submitted them for his consideration:

My dear Lord Robert:
I have set down on paper and herewith enclose alternative suggestions respecting possible modifications in the Covenant of the League.
If 'A' were ever to be adopted it seems to me that the structure of the League would thereby be conformed more closely than at present to the ideal of the League as you present it. I apprehend that the United States would then desire admission to membership, although of course there would be at first an acute difference of opinion among public men.

If 'B' were accepted, I believe that the United States would apply for Associate Membership; and I suspect that many present Members would transfer themselves to the roll of Associates. If, for example, all the American Republics were to do this, the aspiration for a League of New World nations would be at once realized—without weakening the structure of the existing organization.

If, after consideration, you were to be of opinion that either of these proposals would receive favorable consideration, I should be glad to discuss with some of my colleagues whether a 'next step' could be taken and, if so, how.

Yours sincerely
GEORGE WHARTON PEPPER

A few days later I received from him a letter of acknowledgment written from Ottawa under date of April 9, 1923. The letter follows:

My dear Senator:

I am very grateful to you for your kind letter of April 4th, and for the suggestions as to the possibility of an amendment to the Covenant which you make. It is really very good of you to have given so much time and thought to the matter since our talk.

As I was able to say to you in Philadelphia in the very brief conversation we had on the subject I see some difficulty in extensive modifications of the Covenant. There are several of the smaller continental nations who would, I think, be alarmed at such a proposal. On the other hand the suggestion of associate membership seems much more hopeful. I cannot, of course, say what the other delegates to the Assembly would think, but at first sight my impression is that some such plan could be worked out. In any case it is well worth investigation. But before I begin to discuss it with any of the more influential people in League circles I should be very glad if you would add one more item to my debt of gratitude to you, by telling me what support you think such a plan would receive from your colleagues in the Senate? Obviously there are two quarters from which opposition might come. There are the irreconcilables who would regard it merely as a first step towards the League, and there are the old Wilsonian democrats who might object to any modification of the Covenant. I could perhaps make discreet enquiries about the latter class, if you would tell me what in the first place the irreconcilables would think, and in the second place what support your proposals might get from moderate republicans. I cannot tell you how anxious I am that the United States should join in international co-operation, which I honestly believe is as necessary for her as for the rest of the world, but if possible her policy in that respect should be national, and not party policy. We want 100% of United States feeling, and not merely 51%.

With very many thanks for what you have done, and assurances that I will not be wanting in anything I can do to promote the settlement of this question.

Believe me,

Yours sincerely

ROBERT CECIL

The following was my reply, dated April 19, 1923:

My dear Lord Robert:

I thank you for your letter of April 9th written from Ottawa.

I appreciate the force of your observations in regard to amendments.

I agree that the idea underlying the associate membership proposal is the more serviceable of the two. I have tried to find out how it would be received by resolute opponents of the League. I submit the following summary of my conclusions:

1. The proposal would be generally recognized as really meeting all valid American objections except the final objection that any and every possible relation to the League is dangerous and undesirable. The proposal would therefore receive widespread popular approval.

2. The serious opposition would come from those who, upon the merits, would be satisfied with the associate membership plan but who would fear its political weakness as being a half-way proposal and would therefore feel bound to fight it in order to guard against a swing of sentiment in favor of unconditional membership.

3. The number and strength of such opponents would depend upon the seriousness with which League advocates might press the 'immediate and unconditional' membership proposal. If such pressure were to be seriously and generally attempted, there would be a prompt line-up of all the old League opponents and the whole League proposition, lock, stock and barrel, would thereupon be buried under tons of granite. The United States as a whole is unalterably opposed to the League as it is.

4. Encouraged by your visit and the sentiment which you have aroused there is a real and growing danger that League advocates will unwisely force the issue just specified. If they do, and if at the next session of the Senate in December the associate membership idea were proposed it would probably be rejected by a combination of extremists on both sides.

Upon such a state of facts I have the following suggestions to make to you:

1. That as a result of your American visit you should yourself upon your return to Europe, advocate a membership distinction within the League.

2. That this distinction should be based upon the essential difference between conditions in the Old World and in the New, and that it should correspond in substance, and, possibly, in name, to the development of Eastern and Western Departments of the League; the statute of the States of the West to be substantially as outlined in memorandum B recently submitted to you.

3. That a clean-cut proposal along these lines be submitted by you, or at your instance, at the meeting of the League to be held next Autumn; to the end that when Congress later convenes the Western membership idea will actually have been launched and a focal point for everybody's thought and action will thus have been presented to the world in general and to the American public in particular.

With reference to the foregoing suggestions, I venture the following observations:

1. That they involve no general revision of the Covenant but only a single clear and definite amendment.

2. That the self-consciousness of Western nations recently stimulated at Santiago would make the suggested Western membership a proposal highly acceptable to the States of South America.

3. That the actual creation of such a membership by the League itself would work out so clear a course for the United States that a resolution to enter would prove irresistible. In the face of it, advocates of unconditional membership would no longer continue to butt their heads against a wall and the opponents of such membership would no longer have anything to fear.

4. That there is no other feasible way in which to capitalize the efforts which you have put forth in the course of your journey.

I earnestly commend these suggestions to your serious consideration. I shall hope for an opportunity to talk with you about them when we meet at Mr. White's dinner.

My proposals are printed in full elsewhere in this volume.[21] The significant amendments contained in draft A were those which eliminated commitments to resort to war except in the exercise of a nation's free will formed in the presence of an actual emergency. Other amendments provided ways in which world opinion might quickly be expressed and

[21] See Appendix, page 393.

focused upon any covenant-breaking nation, implemented by concerted pressure of a financial and economic sort. One of the proposed amendments is not without interest in that it anticipated by many years the substantive declarations of the so-called Kellogg-Briand Pact.

The amendment in question read as follows:

> The Members of the League recognize that war between any two or more States not only entails social and economic loss upon the combatants but is likely to disturb the peace of the world, to undermine universal standards of morality and to impair respect for the sanctity of human life. They, therefore, declare war in general to be an evil so great that severally and collectively they are ready to use all efforts and to make all sacrifices consistent with national honor and self-preservation, to make its recurrence unlikely or impossible.

The proposal "B," providing for associate membership in the League, contemplated what would be in effect a western division of that body although the language was broad enough to cover the case of a state wherever situated. The provision on this subject was as follows:

> Any such fully self-governing State, Dominion or Colony may become an Associate Member of the League if its admission is agreed to by two-thirds of the Assembly and any Member of the League may at any time terminate its membership and become an Associate Member by depositing with the Secretariat a declaration of intention to that effect. Associate Members shall have such rights and be subject to such obligations as are defined in Article 10.

Another proposed article was as follows:

> Associate Members shall have the rights and privileges of other Members but shall not be subject to the obligations resulting from any of the following Articles in the Covenant.

The articles last referred to included all those which contained commitments for specific action made in advance of the actual emergencies for which they were intended to provide.

At the time of my conferences with Lord Robert I had high hopes that he would make a serious effort so to modify the controversial provisions of the Covenant as to make American membership a practical possibility. Anybody who studies the amendments which I proposed will perceive that under the Covenant, so amended, all voluntary collective action could effectively be taken and that the only eliminations were provisions for compulsory action which Lord Robert himself admitted would be ineffectual if found by any state to be inconsistent with its self-interest.

THE ISLE OF PINES

Our Senate Committee had also to tackle a problem affecting international relations in the Western Hemisphere. It involved an acute controversy with Cuba over title to the Isle of Pines. After the Spanish War a considerable number of American citizens had settled in the Isle of Pines, south of Cuba, in the hope that under the terms of the treaty of peace with Spain this territory would be appropriated by the United States and that farm products could thus be imported into this country free of duty. Cuba deeply resented this effort to deprive her of a valuable island which had been governed for years from Havana and was regarded as Cuban territory. Two treaties were negotiated between Cuba and the United States, one ceding to us a coaling station at Guantánamo, the other surrendering to Cuba our claim to the Isle of Pines. The former treaty was promptly ratified by the Senate. The latter, as a result of the urgency of the American settlers and investors and largely because Senator Penrose had espoused their cause, had remained unratified for more than twenty years. This situation had caused deep resentment against the United States throughout Latin America. I believed our conduct to be indefensible. We had fought the Spanish War to end Spanish oppression and to free Cuba. To substitute American spoliation would have been a tragic outcome. I therefore urged that the treaty be brought out of committee and ratified. After it had been favorably reported Senator Borah, chairman of the committee, with characteristic fairness, delegated to me the duty of handling the treaty on the floor, as he himself was opposed to ratification. A parliamentary struggle along party lines ensued. A filibuster organized by Senator Copeland of New York was finally worn down and the treaty was ratified. By way of expressing gratitude for what I had been able to do the Cuban ambassador, Señor Torriente, invited me to Havana, with the promise that, if I accepted, a national holiday would be declared in my honor. I was never able to put this hospitable offer to the test.

THE RUSSIAN PROBLEM

In the Committee on Foreign Relations we had in 1925 lengthy discussions over recognition of Russia. In retrospect this episode has special interest as a reminder that not so long ago a present ally was generally regarded as a public enemy. Senator Borah introduced and had referred to the committee a resolution advising the President to extend recognition to the Russian Soviet Republic as distinct from the Union of Social Soviet Republics. In committee he urged that public hearings be held on his resolution. I opposed such hearings on the ground that nothing was likely to be developed which would change the attitude of our Government and that only embarrassment to the Administration would result. Everybody else favored the hearings and they were ordered held. It was, I suspect, a method of shelving the proposition with decent regard for Borah's feelings.

Doubtless as a mild measure of discipline for my opposition, Senator Lodge, then chairman of the committee, made me a member of the subcommittee to conduct the hearings. Senator Borah presided. Witnesses from the State Department presented an admirably prepared documentary case, establishing to my satisfaction that at that time disturbing and dangerous propaganda was inseparable from the governmental activities of the Soviet. While the hearings were still in progress, Lenin's death was announced in the papers. At the next hearing Borah as chairman announced that Lenin's death had introduced a factor of such uncertainty into the Soviet situation that it would be unnecessary, for the time being, to take further testimony. Hearings were suspended and during my term in the Senate nothing more was heard of the matter. In point of fact the only governmental organization that could by any possibility have been recognized was the "Union of Socialist Soviet Republics." [22]

OUR MERCHANT MARINE

From time to time treaties came up for consideration which would have tremendous influence on our internal policies as well as on our international relations. There was the acute problem of our merchant marine, so important to our defense and trade. At that time, the American Merchant Marine, despite its mushroom growth during the World War, was bottled up and there were only four ways of escape. One was by modifying the LaFollette Act which imposed on American shipowners and operators an obligation to pay higher wages and provide better living conditions for the crews than were offered by foreign cargo

[22] In May, 1943, Stalin announced the discontinuance of the Third Internationale and of aggressive efforts to affect the governmental policies of other nations. Max Eastman, however, in a powerful article in *The Reader's Digest* (July, 1943) contends that the Stalin announcement is without practical value.

carriers. While American shipowners felt themselves unfairly handicapped, it was perfectly clear to me that there could and should be no relaxation of the standards set by the LaFollette Act. That way out was closed. A subsidy would have helped the Merchant Marine; but the farmers in the West and Middle West would not consent and their senators held the balance of power. A possible third way out was to regulate rail rates to the seaboard so that a differential should be given to goods intended for export in American ships. The opposition of the rail carriers obstructed this channel. There seemed to me to be only one other way to enable the Merchant Marine to put to sea—and that was a preferential tariff in favor of goods brought into this country in American bottoms. My study of the history of American shipping convinced me that it was this very system which, within a short space of years following the winning of our independence, had built up our shipping industry and later made possible our naval successes in the War of 1812.

In the course of considering the Merchant Marine problem, our Committee discovered that the State Department, intent upon establishing cordial relations with other countries, had approved for general use a form of treaty that would bar the United States from laying such a preferential tariff and had, in fact, negotiated a treaty of this sort with Germany. In Committee I was one of those who strongly maintained that the point should be safeguarded before the treaty became operative. After the difficulty was made clear to our State Department, we did succeed in having Germany accept the principle of a preferential tariff to the extent of an agreement not to protest should the United States at any future time discriminate in favor of goods brought in on American ships. Thus a way was kept open for the development of our Merchant Marine, but as far as I know our Government never followed up the advantage thus preserved for it. Until the present war broke out our Merchant Marine had been even more neglected than the Navy. As I write (in 1943) we are feverishly attempting to make up for lost time. The staggering naval losses at Pearl Harbor are being repaired and an adequate program of new construction is being pressed.

At this point, as the reader will perceive, I am merely chronicling what happened while I was in the Senate. I enjoyed my work on the Committee on Foreign Relations more than any other department of Senate activity. While I contributed comparatively little I learned much. In particular I learned the importance of testing hopeful proposals by asking myself—"But will they work?" And I became convinced of the futility of attempting to treat problems of international policy and political science as if they were questions of moral philosophy.

5. THE ADMIRALS ON THE BRIDGE

I was first exposed to the charm of Warren G. Harding's personality when I met him in Chicago immediately after his nomination.[23] As I grew to know him better I became convinced that his warmth of manner was not assumed—as the politician's so often is—but that it reflected a genuine interest in his fellow men.

Soon after I had taken my oath of office in the Senate I called on the President to pay my respects. By way of welcome he invited me to join a number of my colleagues in the Senate who were accustomed to gather at the White House on occasional evenings for a game of cards. I had to explain that I had no card sense and had never learned to play. He laughingly put the matter by and offered me for my pipe some of his favorite tobacco. We sat and smoked for some time while he talked in a most interesting way about some of the measures then pending in the Congress in which he took a special interest.

More clearly than ever before, I was beginning to understand the immensity of the postwar problems of government. These looked formidable enough when seen at a distance but they loomed larger as one approached the seat of government. I also realized (for the first time adequately) the network of political obligations spread in the way of a President nominated under the conditions which existed in the Republican National Convention of 1920.

Five of the men in Mr. Harding's cabinet were already my friends—the Secretary of State, Mr. Hughes; the Secretary of the Treasury, Mr. Mellon; the Secretary of Commerce, Mr. Hoover; the Postmaster General, Mr. Hays; and the Secretary of Labor, Mr. Davis. With the Secretary of War, Mr. Weeks, I later formed a lasting friendship. The others I had never met. The Secretary of the Navy, Mr. Denby, was later a target for Congressional attack. The Secretary of the Interior, Mr. Fall, and the Attorney General, Mr. Daugherty, were the only two cabinet officers with whom I never had more than a formal acquaintance.

As all Presidents do, Harding needed trustworthy lieutenants to advise him wisely and to act with loyalty in the execution of his plans. I believe now, as I did while he was in office, that the majority of his appointees

[23] *Supra,* page 136.

responded in fine spirit and with admirable efficiency. In a few instances, we were later to learn, his confidence had been misplaced. The unhappy events which ensued were to cast a shadow over much of his administration. But at the time of which I am writing the President was attacking his problems with wisdom and vigor and he seemed fired by no other ambition than abundantly to justify the popular verdict which gave him his title to office.

CONSTRUCTIVE ACHIEVEMENT

So much has been written to the discredit of the Harding administration that the constructive achievements have been overlooked. To take one example, the enactment of legislation on behalf of the ex-service men and their dependents was begun at a special session of the Sixty-seventh Congress summoned by President Harding. The original act and its amendments have created a system of hospitalization and insurance unrivaled, as far as I know, in any other country. It was later that Congress yielded to the pressure of lobbies and extended benefits to veterans and their families whose disabilities were not service-connected.

Perhaps the most important act that President Harding signed and put into operation was the national budget law. The budget system is now so much a matter of course and until recently was considered so necessary a part of our government structure that we forget the immense amount of executive self-control required in the first instance to accept and enforce legislation which in so many respects subordinated the President to the Congress. President Wilson had vetoed a similar act because he wanted the executive department to maintain its supremacy. President Harding not only signed the bill, but overcame seemingly insurmountable obstacles and made the system work.

By persuading General Dawes to become the first Director of the Budget, President Harding won the first victory. But even the general of "Hell 'n Maria" fame could not have made the machine work without steady and firm executive support. Officials in the executive departments who had been accustomed to have a free hand in seeking appropriations and expending them, openly resented what they considered dictation by the Director of the Budget and by the Comptroller General. One day the new Director called on the President and said, "I am not getting far with your heads of departments."

"Why not?" asked the President.

"Because I can't afford to cool my heels in their waiting rooms and they won't come to see me," the Director answered.

Having learned which Cabinet officer was the latest recalcitrant, the President at once called him by telephone and requested him to come to the Executive Office. On his arrival Mr. Harding said, "The General and I are talking over some items in the appropriation to your department and we want you to advise with us." The Cabinet officer sat down and the discussion began. Presently the President said, "I have no more time now to give you fellows. Just step into the other room and talk this out." They did so. The contact was established and the difficulty did not recur. This is typical of the method employed by Harding in bringing together minds which seemed far apart. There is something in such a method that leads one to recall the wisdom and tact of President Mc-Kinley.

WHITE HOUSE HOSPITALITY

During the long summer session of 1922, when the day's senatorial work began at nine in the morning and lasted until midnight, it was a lifesaver for me to be invited by the President to use the White House tennis court. At seven o'clock on three mornings each week, spirited contests there took place in which Senator Hale of Maine, Theodore Roosevelt, Jr., and I were regular participants, while either Senator Wadsworth of New York or my colleague, Senator Reed, made a fourth. While we were playing tennis the President was often practicing golf strokes on the lawn and the relative merits of the two sports became the subject of good-natured banter. A shower and some breakfast made everybody fit for the day's work.

Mrs. Harding, though always hospitable and kind, was seldom carefree. She not only took seriously the responsibilities of her position but was as much concerned with the details of her husband's work as she had been with the events leading up to his nomination. She was a shrewd politician and, except where her personal likes and dislikes were involved, a keen judge of men. On one occasion she told me that she had kept for years a little book in which she entered the names of people whom her husband ought not to trust and the names of those in whom he might safely confide. I have often wondered what the book would disclose in regard to some of those who later shamefully abused Mr. Harding's confidence.

Her highly nervous organization gave Mrs. Harding a liking for fast driving which sometimes made an automobile ride with her a thrilling experience. Once when Mrs. Pepper and I were motoring from Baltimore to Washington in the White House car with the President and Mrs. Harding, we had as narrow an escape from a serious collision as I ever hope to experience. We were making not less than fifty miles an hour on a highway intersected by crossroads. A driver approaching at right angles paused to allow the motorcycle outriders to pass and then, not realizing that they were the advance guards of the approaching car, started to cross the road, only to find us bearing down upon him at lightning speed. He stopped his car at right angles to our approach. There was no room behind him and only the narrowest possible channel between his headlights and a telegraph pole. Through the passage the presidential chauffeur piloted his car, just escaping the pole and the other automobile.

"Close call," said Mrs. Harding in a matter-of-fact tone.

On another occasion when a caravan of cars was following the President and Mrs. Harding from Washington to Gettysburg, such a pace was maintained by the presidential car that all who tried to keep up were in peril. Just ahead of me was General Pershing's car and just ahead of his was that of General Dawes. When the procession halted for a few minutes in front of the house that had been Admiral Schley's, the occupants of most of the cars dismounted, happy to be again on terra firma. I can still see General Dawes, his eyes flaming, walking up to the President's car and shaking his finger at Mrs. Harding while he took her seriously to task for permitting her own and other precious lives to be jeopardized.

THE COAL STRIKE OF 1922

President Harding, like the rest of us, may have had his failings but he was not the irresponsible executive that popular legend has made him. During the spring and summer of 1922 a serious anthracite coal strike darkened the sky for workers, operators and consumers alike. By midsummer all parties had reached what appeared to be a hopeless deadlock. The then Secretary of Commerce, Mr. Hoover, suggested to President Harding that I, as Senator from the "Anthracite State," might be of use as a mediator between miners and operators. I had previously told Mr. Hoover, when he broached the idea, that as a new senator I felt I had no standing to volunteer but that I would do what I could if the President asked me. On August 12 I received from him the following letter:

"I am told that Mr. Lewis has indicated willingness to confer at once with the anthracite operators in case they invite him to do so. I suggest to you as the Senator from the state most directly concerned that the operators will be acting in the public interest if they promptly send him a cordial invitation to attend a conference to be called by them at such time and place as they may choose, with a view to the immediate resumption of production in the anthracite field. I feel justified in making this suggestion, because these operators have manifested throughout a spirit of co-operation with the Administration in seeking a fair basis upon which to adjust the anthracite strike.

I understand that as a basis of conference Mr. Lewis stipulates for a return of the men at the old wage-scale and the acceptance by the operators of the so-called Shamokin proposals. In extending their invitation I hope the operators will indicate a willingness to take the men back at the old scale till a commission or other agency has had an opportunity to examine into the whole situation. As to the Shamokin proposals, I am hopeful that Mr. Lewis will regard them as proper for consideration at the conference rather than as subjects of commitment in advance. I am hopeful of this because I credit both operators and miners with a sincere desire to resume anthracite production and I am sure that neither will place any unnecessary obstacle in the way of fair adjustment.

As to the time, I hope that the conference will take place in the immediate future.

No time is to be lost. Even if production is resumed at once, the future consequences of past delays must necessarily be serious, but, if there is any further delay, we shall be in danger of nothing short of nationwide disaster.

As to place, I suppose that there may be advantages in meeting somewhere in the anthracite region rather than in Washington. The Mayors of several of the important cities in that region have assured me of an intense public sentiment among their people in favor of prompt settlement. It may be that in such an atmosphere the prospect of quickly reaching a fair adjustment would be bright. This, of course, is a point to be determined by those who issue the invitation."

I at once established contact with Governor Sproul, and with him I called upon the late William A. Glasgow, Jr., a friend of many years. He was at the time counsel for the United Mine Workers and had the confidence of their president, John L. Lewis. Lewis was at the moment in Indianapolis, where Mr. Glasgow called him on the long-distance telephone, told him of my mission, advised him to consider my proposal sympathetically and ended by putting me on the telephone in his place. As a result, Lewis came to Philadelphia where we conferred. With his approval, the Governor and I established contact with a committee repre-

senting the operators. There ensued a long series of conferences in which
Lewis and his lieutenants on one side and the committee of the operators
on the other argued backward and forward for hours at a time. When it
looked as if an agreement was in sight I took advantage of a short Senate
recess and hastened to Northeast Harbor. Mrs. Pepper was keeping a
diary at this time and under date of August 23rd, two days after arrival
there, I find the following entry:

> "Long telegrams from Lewis, the Miners' representative, and Mr.
> Warriner,[24] saying that the week's meeting (which G.W.P. had been
> instrumental in getting them to have) was breaking up with nothing
> accomplished unless he could come down. Of course he left next day.
> Poor thing! He gets no rest."

I hurried back, missed the midnight train out of Philadelphia for Washington, took the 3:50 A.M. and on arrival at once arranged another conference. We sat from ten in the morning till two o'clock the next morning, subsisting on sandwiches which were brought in to us. The only
gleam of humor came when, a trifle impatiently, I asked Philip Murray,
one of Lewis's lieutenants, what he meant by "collective bargaining."
After a moment's reflection he answered, "It's a bargaining where you
collect something." Finally, an agreement was reached, the conferees
signed it and departed to secure the approval of their constituents. It then
developed that the operators were reluctant to ratify and I was urged to
go to Philadelphia, meet them one by one and persuade them to approve.
I felt that I should not leave Washington because a vote was about to be
reached on the Soldiers' Bonus of which I was a determined opponent.
However, I succeeded in catching a train for Philadelphia and did what
I could to satisfy the operators of the fairness of the settlement. They
then went into conference, and from 10 A.M. till 7 P.M. I awaited their
decision. At that hour I telephoned them that President Harding had just
sent word that, if no settlement was reached, he would order out federal
troops to seize the mines. This brought the operators to terms. At 9 P.M.
they met in my Philadelphia law office. Our stenographers were standing
by and over every telephone in our suite a newspaper man was yelling
excitedly to his editor. Finally at midnight on August 27th the last signature was affixed. I called up the White House and reported to President
Harding that the great coal strike was over.

[24] Then President of the Lehigh Coal & Navigation Co. and one of the representatives of the operators.

Throughout the negotiation I had the indispensable assistance of my new colleague, Senator Reed. He played an important part in bringing the minds of the disputants together. Even though we were in the thick of an election campaign, he and I sought to make no political capital out of the settlement and we avoided rather than courted publicity. The terms reached proved satisfactory to both sides, a basis was laid for the appointment of the United States Coal Commission, a year's agreement was signed, the men resumed work, and the public got its coal.

Postwar industrial unrest was prevalent in 1922 and 1923. The contrast between Mr. Harding's attitude toward labor problems and Mr. Coolidge's subsequent method of dealing with them was as striking as were the other differences between these two men. Harding's approach was that of a warmhearted, impulsive man who was ready to throw himself into the breach and to use the power of his personality to bring the warring elements together. Coolidge kept whatever feelings he had under stern control and played the part of an impersonal executive.

THE RAILROAD SHOPMEN'S STRIKE

Another serious labor controversy into which President Harding injected himself was the strike of the railroad shopmen. In the summer of 1922 this strike was creating a serious situation in the transportation field. I foresaw trouble for the President if he became involved in an acute controversy over which the Railroad Labor Board had already taken jurisdiction. I wrote him a personal letter intended to suggest, tactfully, that sound administrative policy required him merely to enforce the decisions of the Board and not himself to perform its functions. I received in reply the following letter, dated July 31, 1922, which shows clearly that his aim was true and that he was not to be diverted from his purpose:

"I had your autographed note of July 27th. Frankly, I do not agree with the proposition that the President, in a great emergency, cannot act as mediator in the settlement of any difficult problem. The difficulty with the railroad executives' position is that they expect me, as the responsible head of the government, to enforce to the letter the decisions of the Railroad Labor Board as such decisions relate to the employees, while the railroads have again and again ignored the decisions of the Board where the fulfillment was encumbent on railway managers. This is the very thing which necessitates mediation in order to bring about a settlement of the pending strike. I have already declared my support of the Labor Board. Any settlement which is negotiated through mediation will be based upon both managers and working men agreeing to accept the decisions of the Labor Board and complying therewith as contemplated by the law.

I am always grateful for your interest, and am very glad to have your suggestions."

This letter of Harding's, together with his insistence that the coal operators accept the settlement reached through mediation, is proof that he considered it his duty to act in the interest of all the people, not of the "interests" of which he was supposed to be the tool.

As time went on, however, it became increasingly clear to President Harding that he had undertaken an impossible task in seeking to settle the railroad shopmen's strike. He therefore asked me to attempt, through mediation, to allay some of the bitterness of feeling that had been engendered during the strike. I established friendly relations with the striking shopmen and held many conferences with the representatives of the carriers. It may be that these efforts did good. At all events they relieved the President of a burden which had weighed heavily upon him. He wrote me on March 5, 1923, an appreciative letter which in his own hand he marked "personal and confidential." After this lapse of time there can be no objection to publishing it. It read as follows:

"From various parts of the country, especially from Pennsylvania, come reports of the continuing seriousness of conditions growing out of the Shop Crafts strike, which remains unsettled on a considerable minority of the country's railroads. Feeling strongly that this condition demands that every facility be afforded for promoting adjustment as soon as possible, I am asking you if you will continue, in such manner as your own good judgment may dictate, your most tactful and helpful efforts in behalf of such adjustments. Appeals have constantly come to me, for some employment of the government's influence to this end, but as you know the full measure of the government's authority, as now fixed, has been futile thus far, I shall feel grateful if I may be assured of your readiness to continue the efforts you have been putting forth heretofore, and you will be confident of my support in every possible way.

Most sincerely yours,

WARREN G. HARDING"

Of course he received the assurance for which he asked, for I was anxious at all times to do what little I could to effectuate his policies and to support his administration.

POLITICAL PRISONERS

Another instance of President Harding's willingness to meet an issue and to face it with courage was the case of the so-called "political prisoners." These were a score of men, still in federal prison, who during the war period had been convicted and sentenced for violation of the Sedition laws. When their situation was brought to my attention, I said that, as a Senator, I was not under any duty to intervene in their behalf, but that as an American lawyer I felt bound to take cognizance of their plight. With the volunteered aid of a young member of the Philadelphia Bar, Ira Jewell Williams, Jr., I examined critically the record in each case and reached the conclusion that practically all the prisoners had either been unjustly convicted or had already suffered quite enough. I thereupon appealed to President Harding for pardons. He heeded the appeal, and, after taking such advice as he thought proper, pardoned all the prisoners and set them at liberty in time for Christmas Day 1922. I admired the President's courage. There was enough of the war spirit left to inflame many people against him. My own part in the transaction was bitterly criticized. I had acted in conformity with the principle which Beveridge and I had agreed upon long before, namely, that wartime injustice will go unredressed unless the Bar fearlessly champions the helpless victims.

PRESIDENTIAL APPOINTMENTS

While my relations with President Harding were friendly I did not ask him for many political favors. Recommending men for appointment to federal office is considered a senatorial prerogative, except for the appointment of postmasters which is regarded as the privilege of representatives. At the outset I had the impression that I was free to commend to the President any friend of mine who combined persistent ambition with honesty and ability to fill the office in question. I soon found, however, that for every vacancy which my social friends aspired to fill, my political friends had perfectly good candidates who could point to a record of party service. As between two men of equal qualifications I could not, as a party man, justify the choice of a friend without such a record in preference to a stranger who had it. Thus I unexpectedly found my freedom of choice greatly limited and I actually made very few recommendations on the basis of mere personal friendship.

I did, however, approach President Harding when a vacancy in the

Supreme Court occurred. The resignation of Mr. Justice Pitney in the latter part of 1922 led Senator Reed and me to urge the President to name a Pennsylvanian as his successor. Our State had not been represented since the resignation of Mr. Justice Shiras in 1903. The then Chief Justice of Pennsylvania, Robert von Moschzisker, was well qualified for the place by learning, character and judicial experience. The President, however, intimated to us that within the Court there was unfriendliness to this suggestion and that he, the President, did not wish to make an unwelcome appointment. While no name was mentioned I inferred that the objector was Chief Justice Taft. My final talk with the President on this subject was interesting. After I had again commended von Moschzisker and urged the recognition of Pennsylvania, Mr. Harding turned in his chair, leaned forward and said with earnestness, "If *you* will accept an appointment I will send your name to the Senate today." I reminded him that I was there on behalf of a friend and therefore could not honorably consider a tender to myself. I added that, so soon after a popular election, my duty to serve as a senator seemed paramount. He put his hand on my shoulder and said, "Perhaps you are right: but I should like to appoint you." Not long afterward he sent in the name of Edward T. Sanford of Tennessee, who was confirmed and took his seat.

President Harding's unexpected death on August 2, 1923, came as a great shock. Mrs. Pepper and I were at the time at Northeast Harbor. I made at the Sunday morning service in St. Mary's-by-the-Sea an address in his memory and then hurried to Washington to the funeral. Following it Senator Hale and I called on Mrs. Harding and had a long and intimate talk with her. While she bore herself with restraint and dignity, it was evident to both of us that in her husband's death she had received her own death-wound.

COOLIDGE TAKES OVER

The King being dead, it was time for the traditional cry "Long Live the King!" but Calvin Coolidge had little about him that was regal. He unostentatiously took the presidential chair and devoted himself to business. Much later Charles Hopkinson, the artist, painted his portrait. During a sitting he asked Mr. Coolidge what thought entered his mind when he heard of Harding's death and realized that he was President of the United States. "I thought I could swing it," was Mr. Coolidge's characteristic reply.

Following the death of President Harding and Mr. Coolidge's succession to the Presidency the stream of national life was for a brief time placid. Secretary Mellon gave me an account of a visit paid to the new President. Mellon called on him with a written resignation in his pocket, as is customary among cabinet officers when a new Chief Executive assumes office. He is thus assured of complete freedom of choice in the selection of his official family. After greeting the Secretary of the Treasury cordially, Mr. Coolidge plunged into a discussion of the entire financial system of the government and displayed an accuracy and breadth of knowledge which took Mr. Mellon by surprise. The interview was so interesting that not until he reached the anteroom after its conclusion did Mr. Mellon remember that he had not offered his resignation. Re-entering Mr. Coolidge's office he said: "Mr. President, I neglected to tell you that I had come to resign." "Forget it," said the President. And, fortunately for the country, Mr. Mellon did. It is hard to keep one's temper when from time to time some sniper undertakes to minimize Mr. Mellon's masterly Treasury operations by describing them as sums in simple arithmetic.

After his succession to the Presidency Mr. Coolidge asked President Harding's secretary, George Christian, to carry on for a while until the new administration had established itself. Nobody could have been more impressed than Christian by the difference between his two chiefs. "If I stayed much longer with the new President I should come to love him for the way he handles problems," he said to me after a few weeks of contact.

"One day," Christian added (this was late in August 1923, when the coal settlement we had made was about to expire), "I responded to the President's bell and found Mr. Coolidge looking out of a window opening on the White House grounds while he smoked a big cigar. 'Mr. Christian,' said he, 'it is about time for many people to begin to come to the White House to discuss different phases of the coal strike. When anybody comes, if his special problem concerns the State, refer him to the Governor of Pennsylvania. If his problem has a national phase, refer him to the United States Coal Commission. In no event bring him to me.'" Mr. Coolidge resumed his cigar. As far as he was concerned the impending strike was over.

TEAPOT DOME

The biggest political rumpus following Coolidge's induction was the Teapot Dome incident. I had first heard of Teapot Dome only a few days after my election to the Senate. Senator Tom Walsh of Montana had then proposed an inquiry by the Public Land Committee into certain leases of government oil reserves in the tract bearing that name. The resolution was adopted, the inquiry proceeded and I thought no more about it. After Mr. Coolidge became President it began to be whispered about the Senate that a scandal had been uncovered by the Committee and that shortly Teapot Dome would become a political issue. Faithlessness to their public trust began to be charged informally against Fall, Secretary of the Interior, Denby, Secretary of the Navy, and other officials in the government service. Misconduct of this sort was peculiarly hateful to a man of the Coolidge type and he promptly took notice of the evidence produced before the Committee, announced that prompt action would be taken to punish wrongdoers and proceeded to choose special counsel to represent the United States. It immediately became evident that Senator Walsh and his Democratic associates were going to be suspicious of anybody whom the President proposed. They wanted action but they also wanted the political prestige to be gained from directing it. They turned thumbs down on several names informally suggested. "Mr. President," I said at an interview which I had sought for the purpose, "the Administration needs the best available man for this job. I know one who combines character, ability, fearlessness and wide experience and against whom no disqualifying insinuations can be made." "Who is it?" he asked—and I named Owen J. Roberts, now a member of the Supreme Court. After hearing what I had to say about him the President became interested. At his request I asked Roberts to come to Washington and introduced him to Mr. Coolidge. Coolidge, in spite of his matter-of-factness, was powerfully affected by an impressive personality. I can see him now as he looked the tall and handsome Roberts over from head to foot with evident admiration. He asked Roberts some searching questions. One of them I thought was not clear and ventured to restate it. The President instantly snubbed me. "He knows what I mean," he snapped. Roberts did and answered it and all the others to the President's evident satisfaction. The President turned to me and said, "I don't see any reason why I shouldn't appoint this man." And in due course he did.

In the interval the President asked me to sound out Walsh and his group to find out whether a fight over the nomination would be made. I went to Walsh's apartment and stated the case with entire frankness. I found him peevish and unresponsive. It quickly developed that he had been offended because in a Senate debate that day I had referred to some argument of his (on another subject) as "ridiculous." I apologized and offered to instruct the official stenographer to substitute "unsound" in

the permanent record. This mollified him and the outcome of the interview was on the whole favorable. A meeting between him and Roberts
took place and I suspect that Walsh was as much impressed as the President had been. Walsh reserved his right to oppose the nomination but
his opposition was evidently "for the record." The President in due course
sent Roberts's name to the Senate, joining with it, for reasons of political
prudence, the name of a highly respected Democrat—ex-Senator Atlee
Pomerene of Ohio. Pomerene's nomination was promptly confirmed but
a special executive session was ordered to consider the case of Roberts.
At this session I reviewed his qualifications in detail and made an earnest
plea for confirmation. On the roll call there were 68 ayes and 8 nays.
Walsh of Montana was one of 20 who abstained from voting.

The net result of the work done by special counsel was a complete
justification of their selection. The oil reserves were repossessed by the
Government. Secretary of the Interior Fall was disclosed as the recipient
of large sums of money from the beneficiaries of the deal. Denby, although untainted by personal corruption, was found to have been asleep
at the switch. The record of President Harding was smirched, as is always
the case when a too-trusting executive is betrayed by a subordinate; but
I have yet to see the slightest bit of evidence that he knew or suspected
what was going on. Taken in connection with the unhappy record of
Forbes in the Veterans' Bureau and the unwholesome atmosphere which
surrounded Daugherty in the Department of Justice, the actual facts
about Teapot Dome gave plenty of political ammunition to the Democrats. I was in favor of a frank admission of these party liabilities in the
sure confidence that an operation is the effective way to stop the spread
of infection. I so expressed myself in a speech made before a Republican
State Convention in Maine. This, however, was considered bad politics
by those whose unbending formula is "admit nothing: claim everything."
Coolidge was alarmed by my frankness and let it be known that he was
not responsible for my utterance. I suppose I made too little allowance
for the fact that it is always easy for an opponent to misrepresent by
exaggeration the slightest admission of party mistakes. It is therefore
considered wiser and safer to give him no opening whatever. The incident
accordingly led the "regulars" to question my political sagacity and,
judged by their rules of political conduct, they were undoubtedly right.

At one stage of the Senate investigation of Teapot Dome, when the
pot had begun to boil, Attorney General Daugherty invited a few senators
on the Republican side to meet him in conference at his apartment that
evening. When six or eight of us had assembled he brought up the matter

of requests for his resignation, stated that he did not propose to resign under fire and said that he would assume the approval of all present unless somebody had something to say on the other side. There was a dead silence. As it was evident that nobody else was going to say anything, I spoke up and told him bluntly that I thought he ought to resign because the situation had become embarrassing to President Coolidge who was in the delicate position of having inherited his Attorney General from the preceding Administration. The air at once grew pretty chilly. Mr. Daugherty, obviously angry, nevertheless kept his self-control. The others folded their tents like the Arabs and silently stole away. Immediately thereafter I took the trouble to write him as decent a note as I knew how to write, telling him how unpleasant it had been to give him unwelcome advice but that as he had asked for my opinion I had to give it honestly. His code was such that he felt justified in weaving extracts from this personal note into a letter of defiance which he proceeded to publish, charging that my advice had been dictated by personal resentment against him for having blocked my appointment as Solicitor General. As I had never wanted that office and never for a moment felt any resentment against him or anybody else in that connection, I attributed the outburst to bitterness of spirit over the collapse of a career and never took any notice of it. At any rate Daugherty's resignation followed soon after my outspoken advice and the President was left free to choose a successor. His choice fell upon the present Chief Justice of the United States— Harlan F. Stone—who at that time was Dean of the Columbia Law School.

THE CAMPAIGN OF 1924

Almost before we knew it 1924 had come and everybody's attention was focused upon the election. I stood for election as delegate-at-large to the Republican Convention at Cleveland. The size of my statewide vote was reassuring.[25] The nomination of Coolidge was a foregone conclusion and the choice of a Vice President was the only problem. Various people were thought of as vice-presidential possibilities, including ex-Governor Lowden and Senator Borah. I was commissioned to "sound out" the latter. I telephoned to my friend Charles G. Reinhardt, at that time acting as my legislative secretary, asking him to interview Borah in Washington. He promptly reported a midnight interview at which the Senator emphatically refused to allow the use of his name. There was a current

[25] 560,133.

rumor that Mr. Coolidge had previously suggested to Borah a place on the ticket and that Borah had parried by asking, "Which place?" Some effort was made by the friends of Senator Curtis of Kansas to secure the nomination for him. The choice finally fell upon Charles Gates Dawes who in President Harding's time had rendered yeoman service as Director of the Budget.

The Convention was uneventful. The only disturbers of the peace were delegates from Wisconsin who found some satisfaction in making unanimity impossible. I was called to the chair at one stage of the proceedings to preside over the Convention and from that point of vantage saw the sights characteristic of those great gatherings. Alternately docile and turbulent, listless and enthusiastic, convention delegates are not unlike the mass of people whom, at least in theory, they represent. Up in the gallery at this Convention sat a little group of male spectators whose politically minded wives were seated as delegates on the floor below. These men adopted for themselves the slogan, "We are sorry that we have only one wife to give to our country."

A few days later Madison Square Garden housed a different kind of convention. It took 103 ballots for the Democrats to nominate John W. Davis and Charles W. Bryan, the brother of the "Great Commoner."

It was in the platform adopted at this Convention that the Democrats, by ridiculous exaggeration, lost whatever political value there was in the Teapot Dome incident and the other betrayals of Harding's trust. The following extract from that platform illustrates my meaning:

> "We urge the American people to compare the record of eight unsullied years of Democratic Administration with that of the Republican Administration. In the former there was no corruption. Party pledges were faithfully fulfilled and a Democratic Congress enacted an extraordinary number of constructive and remedial laws. . . .
>
> "Never before in our history has the Government been so tainted by corruption and never has an Administration so utterly failed. The Nation has been appalled by the revelations of political depravity which have characterized the conduct of public affairs."

This was followed by highly misleading statements about Teapot Dome coupled with an attempt to smear Coolidge with unspecified guilt. That this type of denunciation is politically ineffective should have been made clear to Democratic strategists by the overwhelming support given by the voters to the Republican nominee. Nevertheless the same kind of exaggerated statement was again adopted by the Democrats four years later at the Convention which nominated Al Smith. Indeed, the language used in the 1928 platform was even more vitriolic—the intensity of denunciation being inversely as the weight of the evidence. Not until 1932 did wiser counsels prevail. In that year the platform was characterized by moderate statement and constructive proposal. That it proved to have no relation to President Roosevelt's policy does not detract from its excellence or its effectiveness with the electorate. Since a platform originates with a committee composed of one delegate from each State, the work of composition being assigned to a sub-committee, since pressure groups noisily urge the incorporation of favored declarations and since the resulting hodge-podge is adopted by the Convention without debate, one wonders that party platforms are not worse than they are.

After a brief vacation I plunged into the presidential campaign in which the principal contestants were Coolidge, Davis and LaFollette. For the *Yale Review* [26] I wrote an article entitled "Why Not Calvin Coolidge?" I also spoke in many states. At one stage of the campaign there was anxiety in the Coolidge camp lest LaFollette should split the Republican vote and by preventing any candidate from receiving a majority of electoral votes should throw the election into the House. As election day drew near, however, it became clear that Coolidge had gained popular confidence. The public were evidently not to be deceived by palpable exaggeration. They properly localized the responsibility for Teapot Dome. They realized that everything possible was being done by him to vindicate the rights of the public. When the electoral votes were counted he had received 382 to 136 for Davis and 13 for LaFollette. The country, as usual, accepted the result with calmness and we in the Senate were again able to give undivided attention to current business.

This vote of confidence was in no small measure due to the high character and marked ability of the lawyers whom President Coolidge had chosen to conduct the Teapot Dome prosecution. By the end of the term to which the people elected him the results attained by Roberts and his colleague fully justified the popular verdict.

THE REAL COOLIDGE

Many attempts have been made to analyze Mr. Coolidge's character. He has been depicted, more often than not, as a man devoid of feeling. The truth is, I think, that this Yankee President belonged to the breed of men who believe that feeling is a thing to be hidden and that to manifest it is a weakness. One Sunday Mrs. Pepper and I had been to church with

[26] October, 1924.

the President and Mrs. Coolidge. Afterwards, at the lunch table, he asked what we thought of the sermon. Its theme was gratitude and the text was, "Were there not ten cleansed? but where are the nine? There are not found that returned to give glory to God, save this stranger." I commended the sermon but the President said, "I'm not at all sure that the man who came back and prostrated himself was a bit more grateful than the nine who went about their business. When I appoint a man to office I don't want him to thank me. I want him to go and make good." There was much self-revelation in this remark but no basis for inferring insensibility. If Mr. Coolidge never thanked those who had served him faithfully he was merely doing as he would that others should do to him.

On another occasion Mrs. Pepper and I were among eighteen or twenty guests at a dinner on the presidential yacht, *The Mayflower*. When we had all taken our places the President looked across the table at me and said, "Senator, will you ask a blessing?" I was a trifle disconcerted but of course did as he asked. It seems that he had learned from my wife who sat next to him that at home we had the habit of saying grace before meals. He had been trained in that way and he liked it but his reserve was so great that he could not in public ask the blessing himself.

When Calvin Coolidge was alone with people whom he trusted he talked as freely as anybody. He always had something interesting to say and his dry humor was much in evidence. He often entertained me with accounts of his experiences. While he was Vice President he and Mrs. Coolidge lived at the Willard Hotel. One evening a fire alarm brought all the guests to the lobby, many of them in much less than full dress. When the trifling fire was under control, Mr. Coolidge started upstairs but was halted by the fire marshal. "Who are you?" asked that functionary. "I'm the Vice President," Coolidge replied. "All right—go ahead," said the marshal. Coolidge had gone only a step or two when he was halted a second time. "What are you Vice President of?" the marshal inquired suspiciously. "I am the Vice President of the United States." "Come right down," said the fire chief. "I thought you were the Vice President of the hotel."

Before they took up residence in the White House Mr. and Mrs. Coolidge spent a week-end with us at Fox Creek Farm. The men on my farm could never get over talking of the interest Mr. Coolidge had shown in them. Two years later, when Coolidge was President, Mrs. Pepper was giving to our farm manager his first glimpse of Washington. As they stood in the line of visitors in the Executive Office, before Mrs. Pepper could do more than say a word of reminder, Mr. Coolidge delighted our friend by offering him his hand and asking, "How is everything back on the farm?"

I LIKED THEM BOTH

Reviewing the administrations of these two Presidents I distrust my capacity to make a convincing appraisement of either Harding or Coolidge. I liked them both; and I am so constituted that it is hard for me to believe evil of a friend.

I liked Harding because he always tried in the presence of a controversy to generate an atmosphere which would make agreement possible. He was a firm believer in the value of conference. This, fundamentally, was because he liked people and trusted them. Indeed it was this virtue—or fault—that was his undoing. After his death Mrs. Harding spoke to me of this characteristic and said that she had long ago made it a habit to check whenever possible his impulsive response to personal appeals. She did not say in so many words that my name was on her short list of men whom her husband could trust, but I encouraged myself to hope that it was. She admitted that often her husband had disregarded her warnings and had trusted somebody whom she thought he ought not to depend upon.

I liked Harding, too, because he showed a lively and unselfish interest in the political welfare of his friends. He knew how dangerous it was for the President to intervene in political controversies within a state. Yet I am quite sure that had he been alive during my preprimary campaign in 1926 he would have contrived to throw into my scale some of the weight of presidential influence. In this respect Coolidge was as different a type as it is possible to conceive. I have reason to think that my return to the Senate would have gratified him. But as between Vare and me he observed an icy neutrality and during the campaign did nothing whatever to influence the course of events one way or the other. Far from declaring his political preferences in local contests, he was even sphinxlike in regard to his own personal program—as witness the public uncertainty as to whether he would again be a candidate after his first full term.

Somebody may be stuffy enough to say that I liked Harding for his weaknesses. I prefer to express it by saying that I liked him because he was a warmhearted human being—and in spite of the weaknesses often found in such people. If I was drawn toward Harding by qualities with which I was sympathetic I liked Coolidge primarily because he was so different. His homely directness, his economy of words, his utter absence of affectation, his lack of respect for personages and his capacity to appreciate the point of view of plain people all were qualities for which I developed an admiration not unmixed with amusement. The critics who charged him with a sort of negative responsibility for the Teapot Dome scandal based the charge upon his failure to utter scathing denunciations of official misconduct. Such critics wholly fail to understand the Coolidge type. I believe he had as profound a contempt for the sort of thing that Fall did as any honest man could have. But when he had appointed the ablest and most irreproachable counsel he could find to protect the public interest, to see the thing through to the bitter end and to mete out punishment to those found guilty he had done all that he could effectively do —and he shrank instinctively from doing anything ineffective. To adopt the role of a denouncer—such a role as Theodore Roosevelt could play so admirably—would have been out of character to such an extent that he would thereby have made himself ridiculous. The only time he ever suffered himself to pose was when, to gratify his western hosts, he donned a ten-gallon hat. Coolidge as a cowboy would have been all of a piece with Coolidge as the violent denouncer of other people's sins.

As to the relative capacities of Harding and Coolidge to handle executive business there is no doubt in my mind that Coolidge was by all odds the more effective of the two. Harding was a poor judge of men. Coolidge had the insight of a credit man in a conservative bank. Harding interested himself in the items of presidential business to such a degree that he lost his sense of perspective and wore himself out with details. Coolidge set definite limits to his official activity and attended personally only to those major matters which had a rightful claim on his attention. Instead of attempting, like Franklin Roosevelt, to be the whole show he preferred to limit himself to the discharge of his constitutional duties. In determining what these duties were he was a strict constructionist. It never would have occurred to him to dictate or even to supervise appointments to subordinate offices in the executive department or to control the business of the State Department or to deduce from his titular office as Commander in Chief the duty to take over the running of the Army and Navy. It is too soon to determine which of two types of President the American people will finally prefer. It may be, however, that the sheer impossibility of doing well all that an ambitious and forthputting President is moved to attempt will prove a convincing reason for choosing the type of man who undertakes only what a normal human being may do with success.

The actual governmental achievements of the Harding-Coolidge administrations will be differently appraised by those who are predisposed to be hostile and by those who, like me, are predisposed to be appreciative. A student who is neither hostile nor friendly will find that a vast amount of public business was successfully transacted during the Harding-Coolidge period. I have already referred [27] to the setting up of the national budget system by President Harding and to the tactful way in which he secured for it the support of reluctant heads of departments. This was made possible only by the entire absence on the President's part of anything like greed for executive control over the expenditure of appropriations made by Congress. It was not a spectacular achievement but it was of immense importance to the country. It may be that the executive manipulation of the budget which has characterized the last ten years of federal financing will result in discrediting the whole system. My judgment is that this will not happen and that when we get back to normal financing the budget system as approved by Harding will be recognized as indispensable to national economy.

I have also referred to legislation for ex-service men and their dependents sponsored by President Harding.[28] In the field of agricultural relief there were over a score of acts of major importance passed under the two administrations. Some of these were in the form of amendments and amplifications of existing laws. Many inaugurated new policies and were steps in advance of anything previously undertaken. The financial record was even more significant. To reduce the interest-bearing public debt by nearly seven billions of dollars and to refund, at a reduced interest rate, over four billions of the remainder was in itself a stupendous achievement. Nor must it be forgotten that four federal tax reduction laws were enacted, aggregating an annual saving of one billion eight hundred million dollars to taxpayers; that annual interest charges were reduced by three hundred and twenty-six million; that the tariff legislation of 1922 produced an annual revenue in excess of half a billion of dollars and that the refunding of more than eleven billions of foreign loans yielded an annual payment to us of interest and principal of more than ninety millions.

At a time when economy has become a lost art and a war makes debt reduction a forgotten experience a record such as this may, to some, seem old-fashioned and unconvincing. But when the emergency has passed

[27] Page 187, *supra*.   [28] Page 187, *supra*.

it is possible that presidents who have advocated such policies and actually brought them to pass will be regarded as public servants whose example deserves imitation.

THE TARIFF AGAIN

In referring to the so-called McComber-Fordney Tariff Act of 1922, I am on debatable ground. It used to be assumed that the Republican Party was the party of protection and that the Democratic Party was the party of free trade. Of course the historical fact is that the protective system, for good or for ill, was accepted by both parties as an integral part of our economic life long before the Harding-Coolidge era. The tariff controversy at any particular time is not a controversy between economic theories but is narrowed down to two issues: first, what imports from abroad shall be admitted free of duty; and, second, in the case of dutiable imports, what the rate of duty on each shall be.

I voted for the final draft of the McComber-Fordney Bill because I accepted the tariff as an economic necessity and believed that the schedule of duties was about as fair as it could be made. I was aware, of course, of the impasse which results when high duties on imports from abroad are accompanied by our insistent demand for the payment of debts by debtor nations whose exports, constituting their medium of payment, are thus all but excluded from our home market. I reflected, however, that when foreign nations propose to borrow from us, both borrower and lender know just what are to be the obstacles in the way of repayment. If, under the pressure of necessity, the loan is made and later the debtor is forced to default, it is actually easier for us to charge off a bad debt than to dislocate our whole industrial system in order to enable the debtor to pay. In any event it would be more honest for the debtor to plead poverty than to contend that the loan was to be regarded as a contribution motivated by the self-interest of the contributor. As to the charge which has often since been made that the tariff of 1922 was responsible for the panic of 1929 I lack the economic equipment to trace the relation of cause to effect if indeed any such relation existed. I am certain, however, that if neither Harding nor Coolidge foresaw the future catastrophe they were no more shortsighted than most of the people who claim to be experts in economic analysis.

That debating the issue of protection versus free trade is only shadow-boxing is made clear by tariff history. In the presidential election of 1912 the Democrats declared for a "tariff for revenue only"; but the Under-wood Tariff Bill which they enacted in 1913 was not framed on any such basis. The underlying theory was what its sponsor termed a "competitive" principle, i.e., the policy of permitting enough importation of foreign goods to bring about active competition with home products. In practice this merely meant increasing the free list and reducing the rate on dutiable imports. The outbreak of war in 1914 immediately followed the enactment of this measure and, by reducing imports, made the legislation for five years largely a dead letter. Following the Armistice, however, the flood of imports permitted by the Underwood Act created a nationwide demand for an upward revision of rates. It was the aim of the tariff of 1922 to satisfy this demand.[29]

EFFECTIVE INVECTIVE

There is one difficulty in the way of a just appraisement of the contributions of Harding and Coolidge not generally recognized but nevertheless in my judgment highly significant. Few people realize how a clear vision of past events can be obscured by deliberate and persistent misrepresentation so timed as to have maximum effect. I am not referring to crude overstatements such as the platform diatribe quoted above but to more subtle methods of character assassination. During my time in the Senate there were senators on the Democratic side of the aisle who were past masters of the art of invective. Jim Reed, Caraway, Robinson

[29] When changing industrial conditions required a further revision this took place under President Hoover. The net result of the tariff of 1930 was some change in the free list and much modification of rates of duty. In the Democratic platform of 1932 there was a pledge of return to a competitive tariff for revenue; but when that party gained control of Congress this pledge was not redeemed. Instead an act was passed giving the President carte blanche authority to make binding tariff agreements with foreign countries. The theory underlying this measure is that we in the United States should not produce any article which can be more efficiently or economically produced abroad. When the emergency of war compels us to face realities, any policy which so definitely limits our national self-sufficiency is seen in its true light. The sooner we realize that future self-preservation requires us to make the most of our own productive resources the better able we shall be to defend ourselves against foreign aggression. Just as the advent of war in 1914 protected the country against the evils of the Underwood tariff so the present war may prove to most thoughtful people that these reciprocal trade agreements are fatal to our own self-sufficiency. I have learned my lesson about limitation of armaments and I hope that in a related field we are not going to impair our capacity for effective and all-round national defense.

and Harrison had in this respect talents of a high order. Save for David Reed there was nobody on the Republican side who at a moment's notice could successfully cross swords with them. It is not easy for anybody who was not in the Senate at the time to realize the extent to which air superiority was on the side of the Democratic minority. Republican infantry massed for an approach to some important question were suddenly and destructively attacked from the air. One of the opposition would rise and deliver a carefully-prepared philippic directed against the President or members of his Cabinet or against the Republican Party in general. This would be so timed as to end as the newspaper deadline or the hour pre-arranged for adjournment was about to be reached. It was easy, after adjournment, to get the facts and to prepare an answering statement. But the sensational charges had been flashed nationwide and had had their effect. The answering statement, made at a later date and only when an opportunity came, was apt to be a dry-as-dust presentation of the facts which had no news value and seldom registered. Persistent attacks of this sort gradually created a widespread public opinion that President Harding was guilty of official conduct far more reprehensible than the appointment of unfit officials. A similar impression was created about Secretary Mellon who was even accused of corporate manipulation and income tax frauds—all with a view to private gain. The dishonest and disgraceful conduct of a few men was imputed to those against whom there was no scintilla of evidence; and to a very considerable extent history has been colored to their disadvantage. It is true that a similar attempt to discredit President Coolidge signally failed but this was because there were no half-truths which could be plausibly exaggerated to his disadvantage. Being neither impulsive nor rich he was not so good a target as his predecessor or as Secretary Mellon. On the general principle that the party in power is properly held responsible for the conduct of its representatives the student will find, I think, that there was material enough out of which to create a political issue. But this he will differentiate from insinuations against innocent individuals of conduct to which they were actually strangers.

The suggestions which I here advance are made for the consideration of the future historian. He, better than I, will judge what weight should be given to them. My guess is that, as time passes, the attack on a single phase of Harding's private life and the default of those who betrayed his trust will cease to color estimates of his actual achievements. As to Calvin Coolidge's administration of his office, I always found myself admiring the practical wisdom with which domestic policies were fashioned and carried out, although sometimes irritated by the lack of that scientific imagination which is indispensable in dealing with foreign affairs. He will, of course, be denied by posterity the rank of Pitt, but he may in time be recognized as the Palmerston of our political history.

6. I AM PUT ASHORE

In the fall of 1925 I was confidently anticipating re-election upon the expiration of my Senate term. There was the consciousness of having worked diligently and the feeling that there was nothing to apologize for. If re-elected I wanted to wear no political collar but to be as free in my second term as in my first. With no apprehensions about the future I began in September the work of organizing to secure the renomination in the ensuing May. This was earlier than is customary but I wanted to get as much campaigning as possible out of the way before Congress began its session early in December. I made my formal announcement, stating that the support of the entire State organization would be sought but that I did not want to be regarded as the particular candidate of any one county organization.

STICKING OUT MY NECK

"I am convinced," I said in my statement, "that the best interests of the Republican Party require the Senatorship to be treated as a mark of confidence by people of all the counties and not as an office to be bargained for with powerful groups in some of the counties.

"I do not say this in hostility to any group. On the contrary I advocate political organization in each county according to the temperament and character of its people.

"But I do not believe it to be wholesome for any of the counties to be overweighed by the influence and power of others. This is a Commonwealth. The senatorial office is the concern of the whole State. The senator ought to be the free choice of all the people."

Had I been willing to ask the Vare organization to sponsor my candidacy overwhelming victory could have been mine. But I was convinced that to seek the support of the Vare machine would have involved so great a sacrifice of independence that a Senate seat thus acquired would not be worth having. So I determined to proceed under my own power. To the above announcement I added later a reiteration of earlier statements emphasizing determination to keep the judicial office out of politics.

I realized that sooner or later there must come a test of strength and that in taking an unequivocal stand I was necessarily inviting the test. As I had expected, my statements were received unfavorably by a number of powerful political leaders. They sensed in what I said a double affront: first, my declaration of independence of the Vare-controlled Philadelphia organization; and second, my pronouncement against what seems to me to be the vicious doctrine of "regularity" in the primary.

Even though I had stuck my neck out, my guess is that William S. Vare would have hesitated to accept the issue and risk single combat. He preferred to reckon on the intervention of Pinchot which at that time was probable but not certain. Vare's advisers did all they could to amplify the call of the people to which Pinchot's ear is sensitive. It will, I suppose, never be known just how much of the demand for his (Pinchot's) candidacy was actually inspired by men acting as *agents provocateurs*. After their victory in the primary the Vare camp with pardonable pride reckoned the building of Pinchot's candidacy as their most astute move; and undoubtedly it was.

A THREE-CORNERED CONTEST

In due course Pinchot announced his candidacy for the nomination, a step which assured a split in the vote which would normally come to me. Vare lost no time in seizing the opportunity thus afforded and announced his candidacy on an antiprohibition platform. The situation presented an interesting triangle. Whatever advantage may be credited to incumbency in the office which we three sought was mine, although I had built no political organization in my own interest. Pinchot, as governor of the State, capitalized the support which four years in that important office had put at his disposal. Vare, as leader of the Philadelphia organization, could count on tremendous strength in his home city. His strength was further increased not only by the appeal of his wet platform but by the fact that Pinchot and I were certain to split the Prohibition vote. There were multitudes of prohibitionists who took delight in Pinchot's militant utterances as contrasted with my acceptance of the milder declarations of the Republican platform. With both Pinchot and Vare the prohibition question was a political issue, while to me it presented itself as a social and economic problem which could not be solved by violent advocacy of either extreme. My position on this issue was therefore, from the political angle, weak and vulnerable.

All my life I had been accustomed to the use of alcohol. I had been brought up to believe that the moral significance of conduct depends upon whether it is the result of compulsion or of an exercise of free will. I, however, realized that we as a nation had, in the matter of drink, used our freedom foolishly and that the Eighteenth Amendment was a reaction against abuse. I felt bound to accept it as such. I saw nothing in the contention that my rights had thereby been violated. A legal right is merely a legally protected interest. If, by constitutional processes, protection of any interest of mine is denied or withdrawn, that is the end of my "right." If I am displeased I may agitate for constitutional change or start a revolution or leave the country—or obey the law. I regarded agitation for repeal of the Eighteenth Amendment as at least premature because the Prohibition experiment had not been tried to a conclusion. Neither revolution nor exile appealed to me. I had accordingly accepted law observance as an ordinary civic duty and had lived up to it.

My position, of course, had no political value. No position has political value if it can be readily misrepresented by an unscrupulous enemy. Indeed it had no other merit than common sense. It therefore pleased neither the fanatic Drys nor the angry Wets. But it represented my honest opinion and I declared it.

The results were interesting. An important political leader in Philadelphia called to tell me that my declaration was "bad politics." An influential county "boss" gave notice that his promise of support was withdrawn. A prominent physician, a member of one of my committees, wrote me an angry letter of resignation. Organization hostile to me was begun among those who were socially my friends. On the Dry side, Pinchot and his kind spoke of my stand in characteristic fashion. Vare, counting on Pinchot's candidacy to cut down my vote, had announced his own candidacy for the Senate on a "light wine and beer" platform. Frantic friends begged me to make an utterance that would satisfy those Wets who, for other reasons, wanted to vote for me. My refusal to modify what I had said was ascribed in many quarters to a lack of political acumen. "Too bad," said a citizen of average political knowledge to a friend of mine, "that Pepper hasn't sense enough to take a different position." "But the position he takes is an honest expression of his views," observed my friend. "Would you have him be dishonest about it?" "I never thought of it that way," said the citizen.

THE PLOT THICKENS

Meanwhile a bigger and more bitter fight was being waged for the nomination of Pinchot's successor in the governorship. Linked with this nomination were many other candidates, including those for the office of Lieutenant Governor and of Secretary of Internal Affairs. In addition to these, approximately thirty-six candidates for Congress, twenty-five candidates for the State Senate, two hundred and eight candidates for the State House of Representatives and a multitude of State and local committeemen were to be chosen.

AN UNWELCOME ALLIANCE

My own preference, reinforced by wise advice from experienced friends in the Senate, was to make my own fight and avoid all connection with the gubernatorial contest which was being waged by two candidates both of whom were my friends. At this time W. L. Mellon had become a power in Pennsylvania politics and he decided that there must be in the primary a "ticket" made up of the names of selected candidates for various offices, including both the governorship and the senatorship. He had had no political experience comparable with that of some of my senatorial advisers. His uncle, Secretary Mellon, sent for me and offered me the senatorial position on such a ticket, John S. Fisher being already the slated candidate for governor. I explained that I had formed my own committee, was proposing to raise and spend a very modest campaign fund and that I hoped he would agree to let things take their course along these lines. He insisted, however, upon the ticket plan and remarked, "Of course I can get along very well with Mr. Vare." Had my political experience been greater I should have told him that he could take Vare and that I would fight independently against his ticket. Had this been done I should have had a clean-cut issue on which to go before the people and mine would have been the popular side. However, having to decide on the instant, I agreed to join forces with him but told him that this probably meant defeat for me. He disagreed; but the result was what my advisers had predicted. From that moment I realized that the outcome was in doubt, with the probabilities against me. The universal experience of senators is that they dare not get their candidacies mixed with the candidacies of state office seekers. If they do they thereby multiply their political liabilities and divide their political assets.

As far as possible, the distinctiveness of my campaign was preserved. I retained my central organization, my chairman, the chairman of my own finance committee and my treasurer. The only campaign fund over which we had any control was devoted to the single pursuit of the senatorial nomination. The campaign for the entire ticket headed by Fisher and me was in hands over which we had no control and represented an effort in the interest of all the men on the ticket. While my own little campaign fund was raised and expended by my friends, the dominating influences in the collection and disbursement of the "ticket fund" were men who owed me no personal loyalty and to whom I was *persona non grata* for a number of reasons. I had offended many Republican industrialists by publicly deploring the increasing use by federal judges of the injunction in labor disputes,[30] and I had in the Senate advocated submission to the states of the proposed Child Labor Amendment, believing that agitation for this reform would persist until the states had had a chance to express themselves.

My attitude on these two questions undoubtedly did me serious harm in some quarters while it gained me no appreciable number of votes. So far as there was anything that could be described as a labor vote, Pinchot had it. In the coal regions he was particularly strong because he had acquired the support of the United Mine Workers by his shrewd political manipulation of the anthracite strike situation in 1923.[31] The supporters of the child-labor proposal, for their part, had little political strength and the stand of many of them in the campaign was determined by other considerations.

The Soldiers' Bonus question created another issue which had to be faced or evaded. It seemed clear to me that the proposal to make cash payments to men who had served in the World War and had emerged unhurt was from every point of view an unsound proposal. In the individual case the payment was not large enough to have business value. In the aggregate the amount involved was sufficient to impair our ability to do justice to the disabled men. Sentimentally, the payment of money to those who had earned the country's lasting gratitude seemed to me like offering a tip to the man who had saved your life at the expense of

[30] When in July of 1924 members of the American Bar Association made an English pilgrimage I was invited to address them before they sailed. In view of the interesting English legislation on injunctions in labor disputes, I suggested the pilgrims study the English solution of this serious problem.

[31] *Supra,* page 191.

his own. Newspaper men asked me to express my views and I did so. I thus incurred the opposition of the American Legion and some of this opposition was incredibly bitter. It took various forms. Some legion posts passed fiery resolutions. Individuals wrote threatening letters. A soldier who had lost a leg was employed in the interest of one of my adversaries to appear at political meetings and declare that he had sought an interview with me in Washington and that I had told him "to get the h—l out of here."

BATTLE ROYAL

Like all primary campaigns in which serious issues and warring ambitions are involved, this developed into a vigorous and expensive one. Personally, I made two hundred and thirty-five campaign speeches. Thousands of letters were mailed by all the separate candidates, huge advertisements were inserted in periodicals and in newspapers printed in English and in those printed in foreign languages, posters appeared on billboards and fences throughout the State, men and women were hired as organizers, speakers, publicity directors, watchers at the polls [32] and to perform the various other duties for which political workers expect and receive compensation. The sums of money contributed and spent for the support of opposing tickets in the Pennsylvania primary of 1926 were thus expended to further the nomination of a host of candidates whose appeals were addressed to an aggregate population representing about one-twelfth of the entire population of the United States. At its conclusion, the overwhelming support given to Vare by his Philadelphia organization won him the election with a count of 596,000 votes as against my total of 515,000. As against Vare, I carried sixty-two out of the sixty-seven counties of Pennsylvania and came to Philadelphia with a plurality of more than 140,000, which the support of his local organization converted into a decisive plurality for him. In the gubernatorial campaign, John S. Fisher defeated Edward E. Beidleman. Thus a complete victory was gained by neither faction.

[32] In the political campaigns of today almost everyone wants to capitalize his or her party activity for money. When I was young, service at the polls on election day was freely rendered by men who never thought of asking pay for the time thus spent. Today our national absorption in the pursuit of wealth has changed all this. Service to a party appears to be regarded as a legitimate basis for compensation. This economic fact, which, however deplorable, is nevertheless a fact, is lost sight of by many earnest reformers.

An illustration of the power at that time of the Philadelphia machine was seen in the way in which an extraordinary public demonstration in my favor occurring only a few days before the election was completely neutralized by unemotional "regulars." I had seen a good many enthusiastic meetings in my life but never anything quite like this one. The crowd that filled the Philadelphia Academy of Music was a tiny fraction of the crowd in the street. A long procession in ranks of thirty with bands and noisy demonstrations of all sorts, were among the features. An unforgettable reception was accorded me when I spoke from the stage of the Academy where in *The Acharnians* my first public appearance had been made forty years before. I was not deceived, however, because by that time I realized that ruthless submarine warfare is as effective in politics as in international strife.

The smoothness with which the Vare machine worked was extraordinary. In many city wards where a considerable vote was cast for me the official returns indicated that literally every vote cast had been for Vare. These were called "zero wards." A mild-mannered friend of mine, attempting to vote in one of them, was told to stand aside. "You have voted already," the election officers shouted. "No, I haven't, gentlemen," said the astonished citizen. Nevertheless he was crowded to one side while the regulars cast their ballots. A big wicked-looking negro sidled up to him and whispered hoarsely, "You get the hell out of here." My friend promptly complied. "Did you let them get away with that?" his two-fisted brother later asked contemptuously. "Sure I did," was the reply. "I was willing to vote for Senator Pepper but I wasn't willing to die for him."

There were, of course, many ways of intimidating voters other than by physical violence. Vare's campaign manager was skillful in the use of all types of weapons. On the eve of the election masses of handbills were distributed among ignorant voters so worded as to make the individual believe that for some mysterious reason he would be committing a criminal offense if he went to the polls. I print two specimens of these intimidating circulars:

HEADQUARTERS OF
THE GOOD GOVERNMENT SOCIETY

1510 Chestnut Street
Philadelphia, Penna.

Dear Sir or Madam:
    In looking over the assessors list of the City of Philadelphia, Penn., we failed to find your name upon any of the said lists, and therefore the

issuing of a tax receipt to you without your name being assessed is a violation of Election Laws of our City and punishable by fine of one thousand dollars, and a sentence to prison, so if you vote upon the tax receipt issued to you by the registrars, you will be arrested and punished.

Yours respectfully

THOMAS THOMPSON, Sec.
Committee of Good Government

J. Alfred Jones,
Hampton L. Miles
Johnston Sherwin, Jonathan Stoewir.

Of course this was altogether false. There was no such "Society," all the names given were bogus and the circular was sent to people lawfully entitled to vote. The address given was that of the Corn Exchange National Bank.

The second circular was used to arouse against me the antagonism of Roman Catholics. It ran as follows:

THE TRUTH

Senator Pepper is for the Smith-Towner Educational Bill in Washington, and this bill will place all authority in the hands of Congress.

There will be a Bureau in Washington with full charge to govern every school in this Country. There are eight Western States who have declared in favor of it. This means they will amend the Constitution again, and the Catholics will lose all their schools.

CONGRESSMAN VARE IS AGAINST THIS. The bill was first introduced as the Smith-Towner Bill. It is now called the Sterling Bill, and as sure as you live this will come to pass unless Catholics are awake.

I was in fact opposed to the measures referred to and to all other attempts to take the public schools out of local control. It was proclaimed to last-minute gatherings of negroes that I was against the Dyer Anti-Lynching Bill, although I had not only supported it but had attempted to defeat the filibuster staged against its passage. There could be no opportunity for the effective denial of such misrepresentations as all were timed with devilish ingenuity.

There were vitriolic broadsides, too, from the Pinchot camp. After I had run in the primaries and lost, I attended a luncheon given by the city of Philadelphia on July 4, 1925, on the occasion of the Sesqui-Centennial of the Declaration of Independence. Some mastermind in charge of the seating arrangements assigned Governor Pinchot to take Mrs.

Pepper out to luncheon and accorded me the honor of escorting Mrs. Pinchot. As we sat down Mrs. Pinchot said, "Senator Pepper, I have understood that you were offended by letters published over my signature during the recent campaign." I suggested that we had been thrown together only by a social accident—that we owed it to our hosts not to talk politics—and proposed that instead we discuss the "Day We Celebrate." "I insist upon an answer," said she. "Very well," I said, "the fact is that letters bearing your signature several times reached me after first appearing in the papers; that my secretary would say, 'We have another nasty letter from Mrs. Pinchot; what shall we do with it?' 'Put it in the file,' I would reply—and into the file it would go." "I should like you to know that I did not write or sign those letters," she said. "Gifford and I think they were written by some enemy of ours to get us in bad with you." My only comment was to express regret that, when published over her name during the campaign, she had not immediately repudiated them. So that was that.

CAMPAIGN EXPENDITURES

The campaign expenditures made in my behalf by the only committee of which I had control were small. While I knew nothing about it until after the election, the expenditures made in the interest of the "ticket" were lavish. These expenditures, from which I derived no benefit, were publicly referred to as if made only in my interest. While of course the sting of defeat was for a short time painful, the insinuation that I had benefited by large expenditures of money hurt much more. A senatorial committee "investigated" the campaign. I appeared before them and explained to their satisfaction my relation to the whole matter. My unfortunate but victorious adversary, Bill Vare, did not fare so well. His pre-primary campaign had been heavily financed and although he had won in the general election, the Senate refused to seat him.

There was talk of trading and of election booth irregularities. While I had suffered from some of them myself, I saw no definite proof that these charges were true to any such extent as to change the result of the primary. I accordingly followed the maxim familiar to lawyers, that your first duty is to take your licking like a gentleman. Pinchot, however, brought the charges prominently into the light when, in his official communication as Governor, certifying to the Senate Vare's election following his victory in the primaries, he made the assertion that the nomination was "partly bought and partly stolen."

The Vare case, it seemed to me, was the Newberry case all over again, except that here the sums involved were vastly greater. In that case my contention had been that the people of a state, voting in the general election with full knowledge of preprimary expenditures, are the final judges of what is reasonable. I adhered to this view in the Vare case, although of course I held no brief for him and did not regard him as qualified for senatorial work. He was an interesting character with a definite conviction that he was a man of destiny. He himself told me, at a dinner given to President Coolidge by Secretary Davis a few days before my term expired, that he (Vare) could not but believe his friends were right when they declared him a superman. This was said with evident seriousness and with no trace of humor. In the end the Senate refused to seat him and he died not long thereafter, a sadly disappointed man.

After Senator Harry S. New had been defeated in Indiana in a primary contest not wholly unlike mine, he was walking one day down the stairs in the Capitol to the long tunnel that leads to the Senate Office Building. A woman visitor to the Capitol had become bewildered by the network of passageways. Accosting Senator New, she said, "I am trying to get out of the Senate. Can you tell me how to do it?" Bowing low, he replied, "Madam, I advise you to run in an Indiana primary." My only criticism of this advice is that it limits unduly the geography of escape.

One of the incidents of my defeat in the primary had been a lot of laudatory editorial comment and an avalanche of friendly letters. They came literally from all parts of the world and from all sorts of people—colleagues, friends, strangers, persons of importance, and admirers of whom I had not even heard. In so many of them the note of sincerity was evident that I felt well repaid for the immense amount of effort which I had put into my work. Every now and then, however, I had to submit to being mourned over as if I had lost a remunerative job. It seems almost impossible for the American people to measure an office except in terms of salary or to realize the pecuniary sacrifice which some men make in accepting public office. If a lawyer of distinction is appointed to an important position either judicial or otherwise, the headlines of the news item will probably read "John Doe Gets Ten Thousand Dollar Job." As I could earn in practice ten times my senatorial salary and as I had in fact turned back the salary and, in addition, an equal sum out of my own earnings in an effort to maintain an efficient office, it was a bit galling to have my defeat treated as if an unemployable had been dropped from the relief roll.

LAME BUT NOT LIMPING

The sting of my defeat lasted about as long as my disappointment over the outcome of a football game or a boat race. Such defeats actually killed many of my contemporaries in the Senate—McCormick, Townsend, Cummins, McKinley and others. But with them the Senate was their all. There was nothing left. With me it was merely an incident—albeit an important one. My law office was yawning for me and the thought of private life was refreshing. So with a light heart I went back to Washington immediately after the primary in May of 1926 and resolved to do my work there for the remaining months of my term just as if nothing had happened. Although classified as a "lame duck" I was determined not to limp. And I did not. In fact I think I rendered more effective service during these months than I ever had done before.

When on July 3rd Congress adjourned my pleasure in returning to my office was dimmed by anxiety for my dear friend Bayard Henry who was in poor health. He and I had been happily associated for thirty-six years. One younger man after another had been added to our group of partners until in 1926 there were eight of us altogether. We all joined in wishing Bayard "Godspeed" when he and Mrs. Henry started for Honolulu in quest of health. It was, however, ordained otherwise. On the homeward journey they got no farther east than San Francisco. There he died in September of 1926 and left behind him an untarnished name and a great circle of devoted and sorrowing friends.

The summer of 1926 was Philadelphia's ill-fated celebration of the Sesqui-Centennial of the Declaration of Independence. When it was first projected I had been called upon to secure federal co-operation, both in the form of government participation and an appropriation. Unfortunately the whole enterprise was given from the outset a political character and was from every point of view a lamentable failure. Philadelphia has unrivaled advantages for staging a good show. I had tried hard to induce the leaders in the movement to "feature" those aspects of Philadelphia life and those places of great historic interest which everybody wants to see. To attract attention to the celebration and to arouse discussion I had outlined publicly a plan to make Philadelphia, for the period of the celebration, the most conspicuously interesting spot in the country. This, however, had been received with ridicule by politicians eager for building contracts and for concessions of various sorts. The contrast between the Centennial Exhibition of 1876 and this one was accordingly rather painful. The former restored Philadelphia to an honored place on the map. The latter blacked it out with an ink spot.

November found me back in Washington. Before the adjournment in July, an extra session of the Senate had been scheduled for the trial of the impeachment of a federal judge. In the interval, however, the judge had resigned and the President had accepted his resignation. The managers on the part of the House accordingly notified the Senate of their intention to recommend to the House the dismissal of the impeachment proceedings and requested an adjournment until the House should have opportunity to act. An adjournment of the Senate sitting for the trial of the impeachment was then taken until December 13th and the extra session was adjourned sine die. Thereafter the regular session of Congress began and the House accepted the recommendation of the managers. On December 13th the Senate, having been reconvened as a court, was asked to make an order dismissing the impeachment proceedings. An order was accordingly submitted and agreed to by a vote of 70 to 9. I voted with the majority because I thought it futile to proceed to the trial of a question which had become moot by the resignation of the accused. Being out, he could not be put out; and the possibility that he might thereafter be appointed to an office of trust or profit seemed too remote to require consideration.

THE PEPPER-McFADDEN BILL

Once the impeachment proceedings were out of the way and the regular session had convened I turned to the business of breaking the deadlock on the banking bill. The purpose of this measure was to liberalize the charters of national banks, to deal with the head-on collision between the advocates and opponents of branch banking and to extend the charters of federal reserve banks which were about to expire by limitation. I had introduced the bill in the Senate and Congressman McFadden had sponsored it in the House. This vitally-important measure had had hard going between the two Houses. When conferences were resumed, Senators Glass, Edge and I, conferees on the part of the Senate, worked hard to reach an agreement with the conferees on the part of the House. The House had receded from its objections to most of the important provisions and I was prepared to advise the Senate to yield on the few remaining points of difference. The problem now was to get the matter up for consideration and to bring it to a vote. Beginning in January, I took advantage of every parliamentary opportunity but again and again action was prevented by the obstruction of the Senate group led by Bob LaFollette and others who were backing the so-called McNary-Haugen Bill, famous for its highly controversial scheme of farm relief. Finally, after almost a month's delay, it seemed as if cloture must be resorted to. I accordingly secured the signatures of a sufficient number of senators to a petition to close debate under the Senate rule. Before it was presented Vice President Dawes, perceiving the deadlock, sent for representatives of the opposing groups. We met one evening in his room. By the sheer force of his personality he forced an agreement that both measures should be voted upon. This agreement was carried out. Both bills passed. The McNary-Haugen Bill was vetoed by President Coolidge while the Pepper-McFadden Bill became law. To General Dawes more than to any other one man credit is due for the extension of the Federal Reserve charters. Significant as the Pepper-McFadden Bill seemed at the time, its vital importance became evident much later during the banking crisis following the inauguration of Franklin Roosevelt. During that period, when ill-considered financial and economic experiments shook the very foundations of industry, the Federal Reserve System, while it worked no miracles, proved to be a stabilizing factor of highest value.

LAST DAYS

During the short time that remained before the end of the session I was ceaselessly busy with all varieties of Senate work. In the closing days my interest centered upon a judicial vacancy in the District Court for the Eastern District of Pennsylvania. After anxiously weighing the relative merits of two first-class men I decided to recommend one of them, William H. Kirkpatrick, for appointment. My successor-elect, Mr. Vare, had another candidate who in my judgment was not in Kirkpatrick's class. It was therefore essential to bring about a nomination by the President and to secure a confirmation before adjournment. With the co-operation of the Attorney General progress was made and the nomination finally came up from the White House on March 3rd, but this was on the eve of adjournment. In regular course a reference to the Judiciary Committee followed. That body, unfortunately, was to have no other meeting. I, however, secured the consent of its chairman, Senator Norris of Nebraska, to poll the Committee. All members signed their approval. In closed executive session Senator Norris gained recognition by the Vice President and asked and secured immediate consideration. The question was put, there was a unanimous affirmative, and the federal judiciary gained a fine recruit.

As the hands of the clock approached noon on March 4th, Pat Harrison of Mississippi got the floor and, untrue to his reputation for sportsmanship, commented in vitriolic fashion upon the recent Pennsylvania senatorial election at a moment when there could be no opportunity for a reply. He thus brought the session to a close in the same atmosphere of ill-feeling which for the last two years had made the Senate a mighty unpleasant place in which to live. At 11:58 the Vice President cut him short and in a sentence or two recorded his view that the laxity of Senate Rules had been responsible for an unsatisfactory session. At twelve he brought down his gavel and declared the Senate adjourned sine die. I was then and there automatically promoted to be an ex-Senator of the United States.

SENATORIAL SELF-RIGHTEOUSNESS
For God and Gallery

PART FOUR

The Ship Storm-Tossed

"They that go down to the sea in ships, and occupy their business in great waters;

These men see the works of the Lord, and his wonders in the deep.

For at his word the stormy wind ariseth, which lifteth up the waves thereof.

They are carried up to the heaven, and down again to the deep; their soul melteth away because of the trouble.

They reel to and fro, stagger like a drunken man and are at their wit's end."

—PSALM 107: V. 23-27

1. I EMBARK AGAIN AT SIXTY

As soon as the Vice President's gavel brought the 69th Congress to an end everybody hurried out of the Senate Chamber. I said good-by to my particular friends and among them to Vice President Dawes to whom I had become much attached. I then went to my office in the Senate Office Building to arrange for the removal of personal effects. Among them were the two silk flags, the National Colors and the State Flag, which the Commonwealth had given to me at the beginning of my term. My office force and some of those whom I had recommended to federal offices later purchased from the Government the desk and chair of which I had had the use and presented them to me for use in my Philadelphia law office.

HOMEWORK

My immediate task upon quitting the Senate was to readjust myself to the methodical practice of law. This made a heavy demand on will power. After all, most of the work of a senator is necessarily superficial. Its volume and extent forbid thoroughness. Transition to the careful preparation of cases was a good deal like returning to the teaching of mathematics after being for five years an automobile salesman. The effort was worth while, however. I think I have since done better legal work than I had ever done before. In a sense life began for me at sixty.

In connection with the estate of a Pennsylvania resident named Frank H. Buhl, I had rendered to both Belgium and France at the request of their respective ambassadors a large amount of professional service. Buhl had bequeathed several millions of dollars for the relief of sufferers in the devastated areas in those countries. There was much to be done in the gradual liquidation of the estate, the collection and remittance of installments of the legacy and in arranging for the organization in both countries of responsible agencies for the distribution of the benefaction. Both governments expected that a large fee would be charged but I declined to accept compensation. The Belgian authorities were profuse in expressions of gratitude. I was made by the King of the Belgians a Knight of the Order of Leopold, the decoration being conferred by the Baron de Cartier, at that time Belgian Ambassador at Washington. As a mark of personal friendship the Baron himself gave me a most interesting bronze statuette of Benjamin Franklin which years before the Baron's father had given him in Paris. Except for an informal and personal expression of appreciation from the late M. Jusserand, sometime French Ambassador, I never received as much as a "thank you" from France. The enthusiasm which the French used to arouse in wartime was, I fancy, rather quickly dispelled when one had financial dealings with them in times of peace. The Three Musketeers were magnificent swordsmen but as debtors they were an unsatisfactory lot.

"PEPPER FOR PRESIDENT"

In advance of the Republican Convention of 1927 there was the usual amount of irresponsible talk about possible presidential candidates. I was strong for Hoover. William S. Vare, who by defeating me had solidified his position as a leader, offered me a place on the Pennsylvania delegation. I accepted. After being elected I found it impossible to attend. Being still a member of the National Committee I gave my proxy to Senator Moses of New Hampshire so that he might serve in my place on the Committee on Contested Claims of delegates to seats. Talk about any candidate but Hoover would have meant nothing in my life but for the receipt one day of a letter which is one of my cherished possessions. It was written by a little girl who, with her mother and small brother, had called on me when I was in the Senate. They had apparently appreciated my efforts to make their visit to the Capitol a happy one. The letter follows:

> "My dear Senator Pepper,
> I saw a little article in the morning paper about you that Secty. Mellon thought he would have you run for a dark horse. What do they mean by a dark horse? I surely would like to have you President, there is no one in this whole country that could half come up to you in that or any other position, but this dark horse business I didn't quite like the name of it; and I have never had it in my civil government. I wish if you could, you would run for President and we will all vote for you again down at school. Of course, it doesn't count but it is a lot of fun. Do you think if I wrote to Mr. Mellon to please not have you for that, but just plain president he would do it? My! wouldn't it be great to have you President. I still remember how lovely you were to Mother and Jimmy and me when we were in Washington.
>
> Constance Ryder"

Although thus assured of support, if not of votes, I remained true to Hoover. I did some campaigning for the ticket and was made happy by his sweeping victory in November.

SUNLIGHT AND SHADOW

At a time when I expected re-election to the Senate my wife and I reluctantly decided that we ought to part with Fox Creek Farm. Fortunately our daughter Eleanor and her husband, Fitz-Eugene Newbold, were eager to acquire the place and make it their home in order to bring up their boys in the country. We worked out a plan by which the Newbolds took over the farm while we reserved a twenty-acre house site for ourselves. For this our son George Jr. designed a most attractive house built of local stone. We gave it the name of "Hillhouse" because this was both descriptive of its location and reminiscent of Hillhouse Avenue in New Haven where my wife was born.

In the spring of 1928 Eleanor, young, beautiful, accomplished and the picture of perfect health, developed what was diagnosed as appendicitis. We were encouraged to believe that the resulting operation had been successful. Thereupon, with an immense sense of relief, my wife and I decided upon a European trip. Sailing from Quebec we paid a happy visit to my brother-in-law and his wife at Tufton Place in Sussex and took a delightful motor trip in northwestern France. Mont St. Michel and Chartres were its high spots. During our brief sojourn in Paris the Kellogg-Briand Pact was signed at the French Foreign Office in an atmosphere of optimism. Mrs. Pepper and I attended at the Embassy a brilliant dinner given by Ambassador Herrick to Secretary Kellogg. My incurable lack of faith in international promises made me less enthusiastic than the rest of the company. They felt, or pretended to feel, that war had at last received its death-wound.

Returning home we found to our dismay that we had been cherishing false hopes. Eleanor was gravely ill. A second operation disclosed a hopeless condition. Yet during eighteen months of prolonged suffering she never failed to greet us with a smile. To be near her we made Hillhouse our all-year-round home. After her death we continued to live there and carried on as best we could.

THE *I'M ALONE*

In the spring of 1929, my old friend Harry Stimson, whom President Hoover had made Secretary of State, asked me to represent the United States in the *I'm Alone* case. This was a controversy with Canada arising out of the sinking by United States revenue cutters of the Schooner *I'm Alone*. The vessel, enjoying Canadian registry and flying the British flag, was in fact a notorious rumrunner. She was accustomed to operate on the Atlantic seaboard between St. Pierre de Miquelon and Belize, in British Honduras. She usually landed her cargoes on the Louisiana coast by means of swift "contact boats" which, by prearrangement between the schooner and confederates on shore, would put out to meet her when she came to anchor. The skipper was always provided in advance with half of a dollar bill. When the navigator of the contact boat was able to produce the other half, identification was complete. On her last voyage she was sighted by the United States Revenue Cutter *Wolcott* as she was lying off the coast of Louisiana near Trinity Shoals. Having "power aboard" (i.e., engines as well as sails) the rumrunner got under way but was ordered to stop and permit boarding and search. She disregarded the order and with the cutter in hot pursuit she made for the open sea. The pursuing vessel was joined by another cutter, the *Dexter,* and at first the two and afterward the *Dexter* alone kept the fugitive within range until she reached a point some two hundred miles offshore. Here the pursuer decided that the time had come for a showdown. After firing some warning shots the *Dexter* notified the schooner that if she did not stop she would be sunk. Her skipper, a rather self-conscious hero of the movie type, declined to stop and assembled his crew aft in a place of safety. A shot near the bow gave the schooner her death-wound. She sank. The skipper and his crew were rescued by the crew of the pursuer, one man dying as the result of exposure. They were taken to New Orleans and placed under arrest but after a brief confinement were liberated and repatriated.

On the face of the record this was a grave international incident. Notes were accordingly exchanged between Canada and the United States, the applicable provisions of the Convention between the two governments were invoked, and two Commissioners were duly appointed, Mr. Justice Van Devanter, for the United States, and the Chief Justice of Canada, the Right Honorable Lyman Poore Duff. I look back with keenest pleasure to association both with the Commissioners, men of the highest rectitude, and with my Canadian adversary, John E. Read.

The questions at issue were interesting and important. Under the international Convention the schooner was bound to permit boarding and search if hailed within a specific distance from the shore. If, after being hailed within the three-mile limit, she were to make for the open sea, the pursuing vessel would be entitled by well-settled international usage to stage a hot pursuit. The *I'm Alone,* however, had been hailed outside the three-mile limit, although (as claimed by the United States) inside the limit fixed by the Convention, one hour's sailing distance from shore. What in fact was the schooner's speed capacity? Could she or could she not have reached within an hour the position in which she was hailed? Upon the answer to this question depended the decision whether she was within or without the conventional limit when summoned to haul to. If within it, did the right of "hot pursuit" arise in favor of the pursuing vessel, as admittedly it would have arisen if the flight had begun within the three mile zone? The United States said "yes." Canada said "no." Assuming that the United States was right on this point, did the right of hot pursuit include the privilege deliberately to sink the escaping vessel upon her refusal to haul to? Finally, if the deliberate sinking was unjustifiable, was it a material circumstance (if true) that the actual beneficial interest in the schooner was vested in certain American bootleggers who were using Canadian registry as a mere device to facilitate violations of federal law?

After a preliminary argument at Ottawa the Commissioners united in deciding that (even if the right of hot pursuit attached) the deliberate sinking of the vessel was unjustifiable and that therefore there had been at least a technical affront to the British flag. In so deciding they rejected my contention that the right of pursuit was really no right at all if the privilege to sink was denied. Next came the battle over proof of beneficial ownership and this was fought at Washington. The collection of the evidence to prove undercover ownership by American bootleggers was a difficult process, as every effort had been made to conceal the true facts. Two lucky chances worked in my favor. Captain Randall, in the long interval between the sinking and the trial, broke into print in a magazine article styled *A Skipper of the Seven Seas*. In this he boastfully admitted a lot of facts which otherwise it would have been hard to prove. The other chance happening was quite remarkable. The smugglers had caused a freight car (ostensibly loaded with rice) to be placed on a certain railroad siding near the point where the contact boat had secretly landed. The smuggler selected by his pals to get the bill of lading from the local freight agent was a novice. He became entangled in his talk and, overcome with nervousness, fell over in a dead faint. The agent forthwith made a careful examination of the car, found the liquor containers hidden in the rice and thus discovered that the consignee of the cargo (a chicken farm in Northern New Jersey) was involved in the conspiracy and was in fact the missing link in the chain of distribution. After hearing the skipper, members of his crew and a long string of witnesses, and after both sides had pressed their arguments, the Commissioners again found themselves in agreement. They found in my favor that the real owners and operators of the schooner were a bunch of American bootleggers and that therefore heavy damage claims for loss of vessel and cargo must be disallowed. The deliberate sinking having been, however, unjustifiable, they assessed a small sum by way of damages for the loss of the crew's belongings and recommended that the United States apologize for the affront to the British flag. The report of the Commissioners was approved by both governments, the award was paid, and the apology tendered and accepted. Thus ended a controversy which, at an earlier day or if handled less tactfully by the Commissioners, might have been followed by grave consequences.

LAW AND OTHER THINGS

While I was busy practicing law throughout 1928 and 1929 the service of the Cathedral and a good many other outside interests made claims upon me. I again took up work for the University under the inspiring leadership of President Gates. I made the dedicatory address [1] at the opening of the new building of the Free Library of Philadelphia on the Benjamin Franklin Parkway. As a gesture of friendship President Hoover asked me to serve as a commissioner under the treaty of amity and commerce with Finland. I concluded, however, that I might decline this honor without precipitating another World War, little dreaming how soon Finland would be sucked into an international whirlpool. I also declined, with real regret, to become a trustee of the Library Trust Fund of the Library of Congress—a trust which while in the Senate I had helped to establish. Among the speeches made during this period was one before the American Bar Association at Memphis. It was an after-dinner affair, and a long list of preceding speakers had bored the audience to distraction. It was after midnight when I was called upon. The situation was fairly desperate. I discarded a prepared speech, spoke in lighter vein and told a story the point of which required the use of a few cuss words. The listeners were grateful for the relief and there was much laughter and prolonged applause. One hearer undertook some weeks later to repeat the story during a speech in Boston. The atmosphere there being chillier and the occasion wholly different, somebody in the audience rose in protest and even suggested censure. "Why, I heard Senator Pepper tell that story," exclaimed the dismayed speaker; whereupon a Boston newspaper the next day carried a conspicuous headline: "Senator Pepper Accused of Blasphemy."

THE FRANKLIN MEMORIAL

As I had when a young lawyer attempted unsuccessfully to break Franklin's will [2] it was no more than fair that in maturer life I should

---

[1] June 2, 1927. This fine building was the outcome of years of effort by my friend and classmate, John Ashhurst, 3rd, who as librarian finished the work which Dr. Pepper had begun years before.

[2] *Infra,* page 350.

help preserve his memory. In the winter of '29-30 a long-discussed project
to create an adequate memorial to Franklin actually took form and substance when the Poor Richard Club, led by Morton Gibbons-Neff, and
the Franklin Institute proposed a united effort to raise the necessary
millions. The energizing spirit in the enterprise was that fine citizen
Cyrus H. K. Curtis. He had lately been studying anew the life of the
great American and was filled with zeal to make Franklin's influence
live. Munich had shown the way by creating a museum which had about
it none of the qualities of a mausoleum but was a living and breathing
presentation of all that is most significant in the field of science and
invention. I agreed to be Mr. Curtis's right-hand man and to lead what
some, because of the financial depression, considered a forlorn hope. In
an amazingly short time a great army of volunteers was enlisted and a
campaign organization effected. At a dinner given by Mr. Curtis in December 1929 the project was launched. In my speech entitled "An Evening with Doctor Franklin" Franklin was represented as alive and as
actually entering the room. I undertook to repeat the conversation which
he was supposed to have with our distinguished guests as each was introduced to him.

THE VALLEY OF THE SHADOW

I think I worked all the more desperately because Eleanor's illness had
at last reached its final stage and her release was only a question of days.
At the frequent campaign meetings I did my best to keep everybody at
a high pitch of enthusiasm. Just as our campaign ended successfully
Eleanor, on June 6, 1930, entered into rest. She left to us and to a great
circle of devoted friends a shining example of calm courage and simple
faith. Some of the members of her Garden Club erected a touching
memorial to her in an appropriate part of the Cathedral Garden at Washington. An ancient stone bas-relief representing a woman kneeling in
prayer, set in the north wall of the garden, forms a background for a
bed of flowers.

I suspect that the giving of my name to the great library room in the
projected Franklin Memorial in recognition of my services during the
campaign was inspired as much by sympathy as by appreciation. Be this
as it may, the millions had been raised, the contracts were let and on the
18th of July, 1930, ground was broken for the building. Although the
architect lost an opportunity to do a great piece of work he at any rate
did a good one.

At one of the luncheon meetings during the campaign Mr. Curtis suddenly turned to me and said, "I am under great obligation to you." "Not the slightest," I answered. "I have merely done what I could in a worthy cause and under the inspiration of your leadership." "Nevertheless," he rejoined, "I am going to do something for the interest nearest your heart —which I fancy is Washington Cathedral." The next morning I received a note from him enclosing a check for $100,000 for the Cathedral Building Fund. Other men might have said, "Some day I want to do something for you." With Mr. Curtis, however, a generous intention was always translated promptly into action. He was a great citizen and a loyal friend.

MR. JUSTICE ROBERTS

By 1930 I had become Chancellor of the Philadelphia Bar Association. In June of that year Mr. Justice Sanford died. David Reed was in London as a member of the Conference on Limitation of Naval Armaments. We exchanged cables and again [3] brought forward the name of Chief Justice von Moschzisker. We found that the prejudice against him within the Court still persisted, whereas there was widespread demand for the appointment of Owen J. Roberts whose able and fearless conduct of the oil prosecutions had made him a national figure. Roberts did not want the appointment. He was happy at the Bar. He begged his friends not to press for the consideration of his name. Nevertheless public sentiment was so strong and his qualifications so obvious that the position was offered to him and with secret reluctance he felt bound to accept. This simple statement of fact ought to dispel the mistaken impression that Roberts's influential friends were instrumental in bringing about his appointment.

MR. HOOVER'S GOOD WILL

In 1931 another Disarmament Conference was called in Geneva for the following February and General Dawes was named as chairman of the American delegation. When later some pressing business compelled him to remain in this country President Hoover, who never gave up working for limitation of armaments, urged me to take his place as chairman. I appreciated this mark of his confidence but decided that the chance of being able to accomplish anything useful was not sufficient to justify acceptance. The results of the Washington conference of 1921 had made me look on such conferences as mere gestures—or worse. There were

[3] *Supra*, page 195.

other signs of Mr. Hoover's good will, such as my appointment, together
with James Sheffield and others, as a commissioner for the United States
under the treaty of amity and commerce with Switzerland. This was so
definitely a mere "token appointment" that by the time Franklin Roosevelt's administration had begun I had forgotten that I had been named
in the treaty. One day while Roosevelt was looking around for jobs
which could be tendered to his supporters, we commissioners received
letters from Secretary Hull asking for our resignations in order that the
President might reconstitute the Commission. To take such a step in
the case of an unpaid sinecure seemed to be the *reductio ad absurdum* of
the spoils system. Of course we resigned, expressing the hope that our
successors would suceed as well as we had done in keeping the peace
between the two Republics.

AN ARTIST PRINCE

In 1931 I accepted an invitation to deliver before the law school of the
University of Virginia three lectures upon the White Foundation. I
chose as my subject historic controversies between Presidents and Congresses respecting treaties, nominations and investigations. The lectures
were afterward published under the title *Family Quarrels*. Among the
delightful people I met in Charlottesville were Prince Pierre Troubetzkoy
and his wife, the former Amélie Rives. Their home at Castle Hill was
one of the most charming of Virginia country places. The Princess, although an invalid, still retained the beauty for which years before she was
noted when she won fame by writing *The Quick and the Dead*. I have
seldom met a man who charmed me as greatly as did the Prince. He too
was strikingly handsome and possessed in eminent degree "that nameless
finer leaven, lent of blood and courtly race." He told me many interesting stories of Mr. Gladstone and of other distinguished people who had
sat to him for their portraits. Gladstone was, he thought, a bit "stuffy."
When the Prince told Gladstone that he would need one sitting more than
had been anticipated, Gladstone with much pomposity replied, "Young
man, you are impinging upon the time of the Empire."

COUNSEL FOR A KING

Not long after the decision in the *I'm Alone* case I was retained by
His Majesty's Government in Canada in a controversy that had arisen
concerning the waters of the Lake of the Woods. People who live in

Minnesota or elsewhere in the Northwest know all about this lake. People in the East, however, are apt not to know what a disturbing factor this vast body of water has been in the attempt to draw the boundary line between Canada and the United States.

In point of fact, the Treaty of 1783, which ended the Revolutionary War, failed to specify the location of the Canadian boundary line between the Lake and the Mississippi River; and after the Louisiana Purchase there was similar uncertainty about the dividing line between the British and French possessions. Repeated efforts at settlement failed. In 1818, however, the problem was solved by taking the extreme northwestern point of the Lake of the Woods as a starting point, thence running a North-and-South line to intersect the 49° parallel of latitude, and from the point of intersection following that parallel westward to the Rocky Mountains, a distance of some 887 miles. In the international convention of 1818 the Rocky Mountains are styled the "Stoney Mountains." [4]

The Lake has as its outlet the Winnipeg River which is eccentric enough to flow north. Power dams built in the river under Canadian authority had raised the level of the Lake and thus flooded great areas of land both in Canada and on the United States shore. The two governments had by treaty created an international Joint Commission, whose report led to another treaty, making provision for the determination of the rights of land owners. One of the treaty provisions was that each government on its own side of the boundary should assume responsibility for damage; that Canada should pay to the United States $275,000, and that should this sum prove insufficient to cover such damages as might be awarded to landowners, the excess should be borne fifty-fifty by the two governments. To determine the damages on the American

[4] Speaking of the Canadian boundary line, I recall a litigation in Canada in which objection to the validity of a deportation statute was based upon the theory that for Canada to force an "undesirable" across the international boundary would be an act unfriendly to the United States. The Canadian Courts having made short work of the objection, a persistent advocate carried the case overseas to the Privy Council. "How long *is* the boundary line?" asked one of the law-lords. He was given the figures. "Does not the line pass in some places over precipitous mountain slopes?" was his next query. "It does, my Lord," said the advocate. "Then would it not be practicable," asked his lordship, "to place the undesirable at a selected point on the Canadian side and let nature take its course?"

side of the line, proceedings to condemn the flowage easement were begun in the Federal District Court for Minnesota.

The substantial question was whether in determining the value of the flooded lands, the actual use and special adaptability of those lands for the flowage and storage of water available for the generation of power might be taken into consideration or whether the land which was in fact nothing but farm land was to be valued as such. The difference in dollars was enormous. To take as an illustration a single tract out of the many that were involved, the valuation on the farm land basis was $900, as contrasted with a claim on the power site basis of $46,000. Two of the judges in the Circuit Court of Appeals took the view of the trial judge that the jury should properly be confined to estimating farm land value. One of the judges dissented and favored the other basis of valuation. The Canadian landowners were, I believe, satisfied, but the American farmers were promptly "organized" to present a united front before the Supreme Court. Had the larger payment been approved, Canada's contribution to the resulting damage fund would have been heavy. It therefore became my duty to uphold in the Supreme Court the view taken by the majority in the Circuit Court of Appeals. There was an element of novelty in prefacing my oral argument with the statement that I was appearing as counsel for His Britannic Majesty. Later, in an opinion by Mr. Justice Butler, 292 U.S. 246 (1933), the Supreme Court affirmed the judgment of the lower court and so the case was won.

THE HOOVER ADMINISTRATION

During the Harding and Coolidge Administrations I was a member of the cast. During Hoover's term [5] I was merely a spectator in the audience. But I closely followed the course of events and applauded from my seat in the auditorium. My appraisal of his Administration has as its factual basis two authoritative books [6] and, on the personal side, a background of official and friendly contacts continued through a period of twenty-five years. If my facts can be successfully disputed my objective appraisal is of course without value; but I do not think I can be mistaken in my first-hand impressions of the man.

[5] Hoover was inaugurated March 4, 1929.

[6] *The Hoover Administration; a Documented Narrative,* by Myers and Newton, Charles Scribner's Sons, New York, 1936. *The Hoover Policies,* by Wilbur and Hyde, Charles Scribner's Sons, New York, 1937.

When elected in November of 1928 Herbert Hoover was generally recognized as the man who had rendered to people everywhere as great a social service as had ever been known. The scope of that service at home and abroad satisfied me that for him there could be no such thing as a "forgotten man." He was intimately acquainted with the social, economic and political structure of all nations, including his own, and his attitude toward all his fellow beings at home and abroad was that which we rightly think of as characterizing the Society of Friends. With such a background it is not surprising that he was the first President of the United States to offer federal leadership through the utilization of economic resources and by stimulating individual initiative, for the solution of the problems of depression.[7]

In his inaugural address on the 4th of March, 1929, he made a statement of his objectives and immediately thereafter addressed himself to their attainment.[8] In the field of relief he sought to place primary responsibility upon local communities, with the federal government ready to take over only when local resources were exhausted. To achieve social security and the protection of mothers and children, to safeguard public health and to conserve natural resources he recommended to Congress action along lines approved by the most authoritative thinkers in each field.[9] He addressed himself to tariff revision, urging difference between cost of production at home and abroad as the measure of duty. He strove to strengthen the Federal Reserve System, launched the Home Loan Bank experiment and advocated the timing of public improvements to coincide with cyclical periods of depression. When, soon after he took office, the stock market crash occurred [10] he immediately appraised its true signifi-

[7] All previous Presidents had either doubted the constitutionality of federal relief measures or had treated relief as the exclusive function of the several states.

[8] "The preservation of self-government and its full foundations in local government; the perfection of justice whether in economic or in social fields; the maintenance of ordered liberty; the denial of domination by any group or class; the building up and preservation of equality of opportunity; the stimulation of initiative and individuality; absolute integrity in public affairs; the choice of officials for fitness to office; the direction of economic progress toward prosperity and the further lessening of poverty; the freedom of public opinion; the sustaining of education and of the advancement of knowledge; the growth of religious spirit and the tolerance of all faiths; the strengthening of the home; the advancement of peace."

[9] In support of these statements of fact I refer to Wilbur and Hyde, *supra*, page 234 (footnote).

[10] October, 1929.

cance [11] and began on a score of fronts a battle to defeat the resulting depression. Commenting on the notable industrial conference which he promptly summoned the *Journal* of the American Federation of Labor said, "The President's conference has given industrial leaders a new sense of their responsibilities. . . . Never before have they been called upon to act together . . . in earlier recessions they have acted individually to protect their own interests and . . . have intensified depression." [12] He organized the Reconstruction Finance Corporation, by all odds the most useful of the measures for which credit is popularly given to his successor. These and many other forward-looking measures [13] were carefully developed and earnestly pressed. Hoover's struggle to balance the budget and to protect the gold standard adds much to the credit of his administration.

Otto T. Mallery [14] was one of the first to appreciate the importance of a legislative timing of public improvements to coincide with cyclical periods of depression. Hoover, then Secretary of Commerce, had initiated this proposal through the Conference on Unemployment as far back as 1921. Of this Mallery was a member and he and Mr. Hoover worked persistently to gain support for such legislation. Just after my senatorial term was over I appeared, at Mallery's suggestion, before a Senate committee and urged the inclusion of the principle in the then pending Public Buildings Bill. Finally the Federal Employment Stabilization Act was passed and was signed by President Hoover in 1931. For this the President gave public credit to Mallery. I have the permission of the latter to quote from him the following statement which has never been made publicly:

> "President Hoover was blamed for not having sponsored the Employment Stabilization Act which he signed in 1931. It was said that he had not assisted its passage in any way. The contrary was the fact. The bill originally introduced by Senator Wagner had been dead in House and Senate Committees for many months when President Hoover intervened and through his representative proposed to the Chairman of the House Committee, Graham of Pennsylvania, certain amendments, including the idea of a six-year program of planned public works rather than an

[11] An illuminating report of Hoover's accurate diagnosis will be found on page 129 of Wilbur and Hyde. *Supra.*

[12] January 1, 1930.

[13] For a detailed account of all these measures see Wilbur and Hyde. *Supra.*

[14] Author of *Economic Union and Durable Peace,* Harper and Brothers, New York and London, 1943.

indefinite period. President Hoover told me personally at that time that if it were known that he favored the bill it would never come out of the committee because certain senators were ready to oppose anything that he favored. Therefore, no one in Congress, so far as I know, with the exception of Congressman Graham of Pennsylvania, knew the source of these amendments which I had assisted in preparing; in fact, I had a good laugh on Congressman Graham when I went to see him and congratulated him on the wisdom of the amendments he had proposed, whereas he had had nothing to do with them and I had had a great deal. The original draft of the bill with the amendments in my handwriting is in my possession and this statement can therefore be proved by document."

The simple truth is that everything President Hoover attempted was met in the Senate by a passionate opposition led by Senator Robinson, the Democratic floor leader, and was successfully misrepresented to the public by the propaganda department of the Democratic National Committee.[15] In spite of all obstacles the President persevered in his efforts to liquidate the stock boom and to alleviate the depression. By midsummer of 1932 he saw with immense relief the turn of the tide and the definite beginning of the movement back to a normal economic condition. "Historians," wrote Walter Lippmann in November 1933, "will . . . see that President Hoover, Secretary Mills and Governor Meyer had hold of the essence of the matter in the spring of 1932 when . . . they arrested the depression."[16] The upswing continued until Roosevelt's election in November, after which the situation changed for the worse. The determined refusal of the President-elect to declare himself on fundamentals, his persistent rejection of Hoover's urgent request for co-operation and the continuance of obstruction in the Senate threw the vast machinery of confidence and credit out of gear and prepared the way for the Panic of March 1933.[17] The spectacle, unhappily familiar during the winter of 1932-33, of men and women thrown out of work through no fault of their own, standing in breadlines, selling apples on the street, homeless and despairing, was more than enough to cause heartaches to every-

[15] For a vivid description by Frank Kent of this campaign of abuse, see *Scribner's Magazine,* September 1930, Vol. LXXX, No. 3, page 290.

[16] Quoted from Myers and Newton, *supra.* An impressive array of authorities (including a reference to the League of Nations charts) supporting the statement respecting the turning of the tide in the summer of 1932, are collected by Wilbur and Hyde, *supra* at page 524 *et seq.*

[17] Wilbur and Hyde, *supra,* page 527.

body more fortunately situated. It was also a spectacle which suggested dramatic possibilities of immense political significance. Of these the incoming President was not slow to take advantage.[18]

While I was able to applaud all of Hoover's domestic policies I felt differently about his handling of foreign relations. In particular I deplored the attitude of his Administration toward Japan and I opposed the attempt to commit the United States to the World Court enterprise with no safeguards other than the equivocal Root amendments to protocol and statute. If, as I devoutly hope, an International Court is accepted as part of any postwar program of reconstruction, I trust that it will be a detached tribunal, independent of any League or other governmental institution, existing solely to adjudicate legal controversies between nation and nation and relieved of the destructive function of uttering "advisory opinions."[19]

As to Hoover the man, I suppose my friendly admiration disqualifies me as an impartial appraiser. Moreover, I have a suspicion that his attitude toward public questions is so much like my own that in estimating him I am passing judgment on myself. He, in a big way, and I, in miniature, represent a sort of middle-of-the-road liberalism displeasing both to reactionaries and radicals. Here, however, the analogy between us ends. While my knowledge is far from profound, Hoover knows more than any public man I ever met. Unfortunately he lacks the capacity to dramatize his ideas for popular consumption. The coldness of his manner is often regarded (I believe mistakenly) as indicating lack of human sympathy. I am tempted to say that if to Hoover's knowledge and power of thought there were added Roosevelt's dramatic gift of interpretation the result would be the greatest man of our time. But in such a statement there lurks a fallacy; for there is something fundamentally inconsistent between sound doctrine and play-acting. Hoover might have Roosevelt's gift and yet be restrained from exercising it effectively. Hoover, for example, carefully considered the closing of the banks and recognized that such a coup would have dramatic value. He decided, however, that the step was not justifiable; so he and Ogden Mills laid the proposal aside.[20]

[18] See page 241, *infra*.

[19] *Supra*, page 175.

[20] In *Carter Glass, a Biography*, by Smith and Beasley, Longmans, Green and Company, New York, 1939, there is on page 340 an account of a telephone conversation between President Hoover and President-elect Roosevelt, Glass sitting with the latter. To President Hoover, Roosevelt said, "My own opinion is the

Hoover's advance toward an objective is step by step. Roosevelt proclaims his objective as already attained. The step-by-step progress makes people impatient. The confident announcement arouses popular enthusiasm. For political purposes it is the announcement that counts.

2. BIG WIND AND HIGH WATER

Mr. Hoover had done a good administrative job but had lacked political imagination. People were eager for a change. They longed for somebody to stir things up and, as it soon appeared, Roosevelt was the man for the moment.

If I criticize in the pages that follow his approach to the problems which confronted him I do so not because I fail to recognize the right of "the common man" to work and enjoy the fruits of his labor but because of my settled conviction that the policies pursued by the New Dealers will be found, when the books are balanced, to have robbed both the working people and the propertied class of all opportunity to live "a more abundant life." To me "the New Deal state of mind" seems to be the state of mind of people who, no matter how good their impulses are, have no idea of financial responsibility and who, if unrestrained, will land this country in a bankruptcy just as devastating as that which overtook Germany and France.[21] I may add that, as expressed in legislation or in the talks of Mrs. Roosevelt, the New Deal seems to me to have done (and to be doing) more harm than good by arousing expectations that cannot possibly be gratified and by creating a sentiment of hostility to the industrialists of America who are as necessary as the working people to the winning of the war. The New Deal, as a living force, is dead; but its dead hand rests heavily upon American life.

THE NEW DEAL

After Roosevelt's term had begun there was plenty for lawyers to think about. What seemed to most of us to be altogether impracticable

---

governors of the various states can take care of the bank closings wherever it is necessary . . . No, I prefer that you issue no proclamations of this nature." After Roosevelt had hung up Glass asked him, "What are you planning to do?" "Planning to close them, of course," replied Roosevelt.

[21] A prospective National Debt of $300,000,000,000 combined with the padding of the federal payroll and the waste justly chargeable against Army, Navy and all government departments should arouse much more apprehension than it does.

schemes were forthwith launched by the new President with bewildering rapidity. The voters were getting what they wanted and what the Republicans had failed to give them. The new President's idea appeared to be to put forth every few days a new scheme before the public had had time to evaluate its predecessor. Like everybody else I was kept busy studying the legislative curiosities which, under orders from the White House, a subservient Congress was daily enacting. If we had been at war and if American business had been the enemy, the New Deal strategy might have been described in the words in which General Grant is said to have defined his own: "Find out where the enemy is; hit him as hard as you can and as often as you can and keep moving."

At that time outsiders could do no more than guess at what was going on in conferences between members of the Brain Trust and the subsequent interviews at which the members of that motley group competed with one another for the ear of their chief. The publication [22] by Professor Moley of his story of the rise, progress and collapse of the New Deal has substituted certainty for speculation—whatever one may think of the good taste of these revelations. His narrative confirms the contemporary impression that measures announced with the finality of divine revelation were really undigested proposals made at frenzied eleventh-hour conferences and were in most instances compromises between people seldom in wholehearted agreement.

All this was done under the trademark of "liberalism," a term which has now lost all specific meaning except as indicating a readiness to conceive and attempt experiments which to the conservative seem reckless. Without liberalism there would be little effort to solve new problems. Without conservative opposition liberalism would end in chaos. The resultant force drives onward and upward—but too slowly to please the liberal and fast enough to alarm the conservative.[23]

[22] *After Seven Years,* by Raymond Moley, Harper and Brothers, New York, 1939.

[23] The New Deal boys are fond of invoking Mr. Justice Holmes as if he could be counted as sympathetic with their philosophy of government. At 84, after a life spent in evaluating social experiment, he had this to say: "I believe that Malthus was right in his fundamental notion and that is as far as we have got or are likely to get in my day. Every society is founded on the death of men. In one way or another some are always and inevitably pushed down the dead line. I think it a manifest humbug to suppose that even relative universal bliss is to be reached by tinkering with property or changing forms of government so long as

After the spectacular "banking holiday" came the Agricultural Adjustment Act, the so-called "Beer Bill," the several inflationary measures, an offhand suggestion to fifty-four nations to abolish offensive weapons and reduce armaments and the bill setting up the stormy T.V.A. Then followed the now defunct Industrial Recovery Act, of which Mr. Roosevelt observed that history will probably record it as "the most important and far-reaching legislation ever enacted by the American Congress." After careful study of this measure I advised a number of clients that the code-making authority which it attempted to confer upon the President was a palpably unconstitutional delegation and that the making of interstate commerce coextensive with all commerce was, if valid, a long step toward industrial despotism. Upon this advice several clients protested at code conferences in Washington against price-fixing proposals which were then being pressed. I also warned that notwithstanding apparent legislative waiver of antitrust laws there were grave possibilities of criminal liability if prohibitions upon conspiracy in restraint of trade were violated. I was retained by a large number of processors injuriously affected by the so-called "tax" levied under the A.A.A. which was intended to provide a fund with which to bribe farmers to limit production. I advised them that the exaction in question was a mere device to enable Congress to regulate purely domestic production and that, as such, it should be declared unconstitutional. The President in my opinion lacked sound legal advisers (which means advisers who were wise enough to agree with me) and was at any rate in no mood to accept unwelcome advice, no matter how sound.

It was possible to gain at this time some interesting side lights on the way in which farmers had been persuaded to vote for the repeal of Prohibition. In the interest of one client, a large producer of alcohol made from sugar, I went to Washington to protest against the code regulation requiring that only grain alcohol should be used for beverage purposes. There was no suggestion that my client's product was not as fit for potable use as the others. The lawyer, at that time counsel for the Agricultural Administration, explained with engaging frankness that Mr.

every social improvement is expended in increased and unchecked propagation. I shall think socialism begins to be entitled to serious treatment when and not before it takes life in hand and prevents the continuance of the unfit." *Oliver Wendell Holmes, His Book Notices and Uncollected Letters and Papers,* Central Book Co., New York, 1936, at page 181. I myself should be unwilling to subscribe to any such program as is here outlined but I echo the Justice's appraisement of what he describes as "manifest humbug."

Roosevelt had promised the farmers an alcohol monopoly if they would vote to repeal the Eighteenth Amendment and that the Administration was merely trying to keep its pledge. As a Republican, I was glad to see the excellent policy of pledge-keeping adopted by Democrats but not at the expense of the constitutional rights of my client. The impossible restriction was removed.

On behalf of another client, a highly skilled manufacturer of lace, I lodged a protest against an N.R.A. code regulation devised by his less skillful competitors and designed to put him out of business. I was promised that there should be an immediate investigation by a competent member of the N.R.A. staff. Shortly thereafter I was called on the telephone by a woman lawyer, a subordinate who had been assigned to the case, and asked for information on various matters of fact. This was supplied; but before action was taken I went abroad on a summer vacation. In my absence, as I learned upon return, my client had been sent for and informed that he was handicapped because he was represented by a Republican ex-senator and that it would be to his advantage to retain a young Democratic attorney whom the lady would be glad to name. Being an irascible American of German descent he asked, "Do you mean I should dismiss my good friend Mr. Pepper?" On receiving an answer which he interpreted as "yes," he exclaimed with more loyalty than gallantry, "Please go to hell." In spite of his handicap he was not further molested.

Trivial incidents like this are worth recording because of a fact sometimes overlooked, namely, that administrative schemes that appear well on paper are often failures because of what actually happens in the bureaus charged with their execution and even in spite of the efforts of the men higher up.

THE BLUE EAGLE TURNS BLUER

Early in 1935 the Supreme Court decided the suit [24] which had been brought to test the validity of the N.R.A. and adjudged with unanimity that the statute was unconstitutional. Shortly thereafter, when Eugene Meyer of the *Washington Post* asked me to write a comment upon the decision, I discussed both the facts and the law in simple and untechnical fashion. I wanted to show how unwise it is to permit Congress either to hand over any of its law-making power to the President or to take out of

[24] *Schechter v. U.S.,* 295 U.S. 495 (1935).

the hands of local legislatures the control of commerce internal to the state. I took as a text Benjamin Franklin's answer to the woman who, when the Constitutional Convention had adjourned, asked him whether we were to have a republic or a monarchy. "A republic," replied the Doctor, "if we can keep it." After I had gone over the draft of the article with my friend W. W. Montgomery and improved it in the light of his criticism, I published it under the title *Page Doctor Franklin*. It appeared in a number of papers in addition to the *Post*. From editorial comment and from a large number of commendatory letters I concluded that my effort at popular education had been worth while. I suppose that an immense body of Americans are ready to read the writings of any man who can interpret to them in simple terms great constitutional issues of which otherwise they have a hopelessly imperfect understanding. This particular decision was represented by the New Dealers as an unwarranted destruction by the judiciary of a wise and beneficent reform. In point of fact, the N.R.A. scheme always had in it the seeds of its own dissolution. It would have died a lingering death if the Court had not quickly put it out of its misery. It was not unnatural, however, that the President should blame the judges for the failure of his pet experiment rather than concede that death resulted from congenital complications.

"TRIPLE A"

Of comparable importance with the N.R.A. case was the litigation instituted to test the validity of the Agricultural Adjustment Act. Although it was obviously to public advantage to bring its constitutionality to an early test, the government resolutely interposed to the many suits which my colleagues and I had brought for that purpose every procedural objection that ingenuity could suggest. However, we pressed the fight on many fronts and succeeded in getting a number of cases heard upon their merits. After the argument of one of these the attorney for the Agricultural Administration naïvely said to me, "Senator, you may not think much of our law but you must admire the skill with which we have kept cases from coming to trial."

In various federal courts decisions adverse to the Act were rendered. Had any of these cases come before the Supreme Court the great constitutional questions which they raised would have been complicated by the government's procedural objections. Fortunately in Massachusetts there arose a case in which no such technical objections could be made. In the receivership of the Hoosac Mills the federal government itself, presumably in a moment of forgetfulness, went into the United States District Court as a complainant, seeking an order to compel the receivers to pay the processing tax which the Act imposed. The receivers asserted the unconstitutionality of the Act, the Circuit Court of Appeals for the First Circuit sustained their position, and the government was thus forced to apply to the Supreme Court for a certiorari. This was granted and the case took its place on the list for argument. My old friend and sometime senatorial colleague, William M. Butler, was one of the receivers and their counsel were Messrs. Hale, Sanderson, Byrnes and Morton, of Boston. These gentlemen invited me to co-operate with them in preparing the briefs and to take part with them in the oral argument.

The case came on to be heard on the 5th and 6th of December, 1935. The courtroom in the new Supreme Court building was crowded with spectators, among whom were many diplomats and other distinguished visitors, including the Archbishop of York.[25] There were also many lawyers from various parts of the country who had cases pending which would be ruled by the decision of the Hoosac case. Because of political implications the press too was keenly interested. Long lines of people were waiting to gain admission to the courtroom. The government's side of the case was presented by the then Solicitor General, Mr. Reed.[26] I had had the advantage of long study, careful preparation and the experience gained in the argument of the same questions in the lower courts. Nevertheless the professional responsibility was a heavy one. Although I was not conscious of nerve strain I did in fact lose eight pounds in weight during the week before the case was reached. I had given a great deal of thought not only to the substance of the argument but to the form of it and to the method of approach to each of the questions involved. After the lapse of a month the Court on January 6, 1936, decided the case in our favor by a vote of 6 to 3.[27]

A LAST APPEARANCE

All these controversies arising out of New Deal legislation naturally aroused much popular interest in everything relating to the Constitution.

[25] The Rt. Rev. Dr. William Temple, the present Archbishop of Canterbury, who at the time was the guest of the Bishop of Washington, the Rt. Rev. James E. Freeman.

[26] Now Mr. Justice Reed.

[27] The case is reported in 297 U.S. 1 (1936). The official reporter did me the unusual honor of publishing in his report the stenographic record of the argument.

IN WASHINGTON'S CHAIR

"The Convention Will be in Order"

They even stirred up such histrionic talent as members of the bar may have and stimulated lawyers in California and elsewhere to attempt the dramatic reproduction of the proceedings in the Convention of 1787. The Philadelphia Bar decided to follow the California example. A cast was selected, lines were memorized and the proceedings diligently rehearsed. Franklin Spencer Edmonds as Benjamin Franklin and Robert T. McCracken as Alexander Hamilton did their parts particularly well. I attempted to impersonate the Father of his Country and, in order to "make up," shaved off my mustache. This was big news for the papers. Prominent men, given to facial landscape gardening, were interviewed and with mock solemnity gravely discussed my "sacrifice." I announced my regret that I had only one mustache to give for my country. This and similar pleasantries put everybody in good humor. A large part of the credit for the performance given in Convention Hall before a huge audience was due to Anthony Boch, the theatrical wigmaker, who did wonders with our unpromising countenances. A half century earlier he had made me up for the part of Dikaiopolis in *The Acharnians*. To this extent he was, as respects my theatrical career, responsible for both entrance and exit.

DIVERSITIES OF OPERATIONS

In spite of good resolutions to do less public speaking, pressure of various sorts kept me continually on tap throughout 1936. Such resolutions are easy to make but hard to keep when you are almost tearfully appealed to in the interest of causes near your heart. At home I made several addresses on political subjects, a speech at the opening of the campaign for the Community Fund, an Easter Chapel Service address at the University and various missionary addresses in churches in and around Philadelphia. At Lafayette College, at the invitation of my old friend President William Mather Lewis, I addressed a conference of the Trustees of Colleges and Universities. I also delivered the Prize Day Address at Kent School and the Commencement address at Williams College. A grandson bearing my name was in the graduating class at Kent and two other grandsons were in lower classes. In New York Town Hall I made an address on James Madison at the centenary meeting held in his memory. In Washington, before the Men's Club of St. John's Parish, I delivered a carefully prepared address on "The Evolution of the Book of Common Prayer." Having in 1938 become president of the American Law Institute after George Wickersham's death, I did

my part at the annual meeting in May. In late September I journeyed
to California and there delivered the Morrison lecture before the State
Bar Association assembled at Coronado Beach. The address itself was,
I thought, a mediocre performance before a generous audience. The
trip though hurried gave me my first glimpse of the Pacific and of the
wonders of the Grand Canyon and of many places that I had visited
only in imagination.

NO PLACE LIKE HOME

In bygone days the place of a man's domicile was not a matter of
much public importance and there was little disposition to question his
own statement that he was domiciled in such-and-such a place. When,
however, enormous inheritance taxes began to be imposed by the several
states there was apt to arise a lively controversy between them as to which
should appropriate a generous slice of the estate of some deceased million-
aire. His own declarations respecting his domicile began to count for
little. The facts of his life came to be regarded as more significant than his
words.

What was "home" for the late Colonel Green? This was a question
with which, in the course of practice, I was called upon to grapple. His
declarations pointed to Texas. His mother, Hetty, the "Witch of Wall
Street," had had her domicile in Vermont. Her son was born in England, spent much of his life in Texas, some of it in New York, where he
maintained a costly apartment, and some of it in Florida and Massachusetts in both of which states he had palatial residences. He finally died
in Essex County, New York. He left behind him, no doubt reluctantly,
collections of stamps, of coins and of jewels to which fabulous values were
ascribed. A full-rigged whaling vessel moored upon his lawn at South
Dartmouth was only one of the curiosities in which he took delight. By
his will he undertook to give all his property to his sister, who already
had her half of her mother's millions. Before the existence of his will
was known my firm was retained by his widow to protect her interests,
it being at that time supposed that he had died intestate. Years before,
on the eve of her marriage to the Colonel, she had signed a release of
all her rights in his estate in return for a small annuity.

When after a time the sister produced the will, the question arose
whether the widow was bound by her release or whether she could set
it aside and claim a widow's share of the Colonel's property. The answer
to this question depended to some extent upon the determination of

domicile, because state laws differ respecting the efficacy of premarital releases, the validity of wills made before marriage and the extent of a widow's statutory interest in her deceased husband's estate. The Colonel having died in Essex County, New York, the county courthouse at Elizabethtown became the main battleground in the ensuing warfare, with hotly contested engagements in New York City, Texas, Massachusetts and Florida. The tax commissioners of the interested states circled over the battlefields like expectant birds of prey. Mrs. Sylvia H. Wilks, the Colonel's sister, made it reasonably clear that she intended neither to ask nor to give quarter and that whatever her sister-in-law was to get she must win. After a vast amount of time and effort had been expended by all concerned we became convinced that our elderly client could not afford longer to wage a doubtful war, the outcome of which might not be determined in her lifetime. Through the good offices of the Surrogate, Judge Owen, a settlement was finally made which assured to the widow an ample income for the rest of her life while leaving to Mrs. Wilks millions enough to keep her from the bread line. It also left her plenty of occupation in the way of carrying on the tax controversies with hungry states. The Supreme Court ultimately took jurisdiction of the domicile controversy on the theory that insufficiency of assets to pay all state claims in full made this, in effect, a controversy between the competing states. The final decision was that the dead man's domicile had in fact been Massachusetts which was as near the truth as a human tribunal was likely to get. The uncertainties with which such cases abound exhibit our federal union at its worst. If contemporary predictions are justified that within a decade most of us will be living and dying in trailers, bankrupt states may have to engage not merely in a controversy over domicile but in a ghoulish scramble for the remains of the deceased.

REFORMING THE JUDICIARY

Roosevelt's second term was only a few weeks old when he announced his plan to pack the Supreme Court. The bill prepared under his direction and sent to Congress for enactment purported to seek reform of the federal judiciary in general. This mask, however, was quickly torn off and the true nature of the proposal was disclosed. It was then seen to be a measure conceived in hate, drafted with cunning and projected with reckless disregard of consequences. Many people are of the opinion that the draftsman was the then Attorney General, Mr. Cummings. There is some evidence to support this theory. I suspect, however, that the scheme was really a Cohen and Corcoran plan, "sold" to the President at a psychological moment and then dressed in decent habiliments to make it look respectable.

The immediate public reaction must have taken the President by surprise. From every source except the federal payroll came prompt and bitter disapproval. Popular confidence in the Supreme Court was evidently something that not even a super-popular President could destroy overnight. The *Journal* of the American Bar Association promptly constituted itself a forum for presentation of pros and cons. The negative testimony was overwhelming. The title of the article which I contributed was "Plain Speaking." My contention was that the Constitution and the Court as its interpreter, are the real guardians of minority rights and that executive control of the Court meant the destruction of civil and religious liberty. Desperate efforts were made to find somebody of standing to take the President's side. One qualified person after another declined. Finally Thurman Arnold, then an assistant in the Department of Justice, was drafted to support the Administration.[28] He wisely decided to substitute ridicule for argument and produced a readable but unconvincing answer to the views of the bar.

When the Court-packing measure was first introduced it was generally assumed that the Administration could easily force it through both Houses. The critical struggle took place in the Senate and in that body some Democratic Senators who placed country above party made a fight which history will not soon forget. The Democratic floor leader, "Joe" Robinson of Arkansas, stifled what must have been his convictions and strove valiantly to gain approval of a measure which was daily arousing more and more popular opposition. There were well-authenticated rumors that one of the judgeships which would be created by the passage of the pending measure was to be Robinson's reward for putting it through. Mr. Justice Van Devanter's resignation gave the President a chance to give Robinson his reward. Roosevelt, however, failed him. The adverse current grew stronger and stronger. One day Robinson fell dead, having succumbed to the strain to which he had been remorselessly subjected. The bill shared the same fate. As in the A.A.A. Case the Supreme Court had for the time being protected the people against executive tyranny in industry and agriculture, so now the Senate had halted an executive

---

[28] Later Mr. Arnold was put in charge of the antitrust division of the Department and did much notable work. He is now a judge of the Court of Appeals of the District of Columbia.

assault upon the Court. Two of the organs of American government had proved equal to the emergency. The judicial compass was still something safe to steer by when sailing the open sea.

A REBUKE FROM THE HOUSE

After the Senate had disposed of the Court-packing bill it remained for the House to do its part in preserving constitutional balance. The opportunity came when the so-called Reorganization Bill was pushed through the Senate and was pressed for prompt approval by the House. This measure, as in the case of so much New Deal legislation, professed one purpose and had another. That reorganization of many governmental agencies is badly needed is a fact long recognized. President Hoover attempted some reforms but his proposals met a frigid reception by those whose jobs would have been affected. But Mr. Hoover, an earnest advocate of civil service reform and of a sound budgetary system, never dreamed of substituting executive domination for the civil service board and for an independent controller-general. Roosevelt not only conceived such a substitution but caused a bill to be drawn to effectuate it and carried the measure through the Senate. In that body a more adroit and tactful floor leader, Senator Barkley of Kentucky, had succeeded the irascible Robinson. Although of very moderate ability he did a clever bit of parliamentary maneuvering and effectively directed the personal political pressure upon which the President was relying to secure the much-needed support. When this was forthcoming by a slender margin the scene shifted to the House. As in the case of the Court-packing scheme the country then began to realize the significance of what was going on and citizens everywhere became alarmed at the dictatorial drift. Telegrams came pouring in upon the Representatives and made them aware that the "folks back home" were up and doing. The result was that, in spite of intense organization pressure, enough Democrats joined with the Republican members to send the bill back to committee and thus complete the demonstration of the value of our governmental system. Supreme Court, Senate and the House had each in turn defeated an executive aggression.

From a political point of view the action of the House on the Reorganization Bill was more significant than that of the Senate on the Court-packing scheme. The former was a rebuff to the President not merely in form but in substance. The latter was on the face of the record a presidential defeat; but much of Mr. Roosevelt's purpose, as he himself later boasted, was nevertheless actually accomplished. Resignations, possibly precipitated by the attack, gave him a chance to make important judicial appointments and there was a general impression that the mental attitude of the Court toward problems of constitutional interpretation was much affected by his persistent criticism. Still later, when Mr. Justice Cardozo and Mr. Justice Butler died, other opportunities for judicial appointments came to him so that during his first two terms five out of nine Justices received their commissions from his hand. Later, in his third term, he was able to appoint two more Justices and to commission the Chief Justice.

If after this record of achievement Mr. Roosevelt is able to keep his head and appraise himself justly, the attainment of such poise will be the greatest achievement of them all. Perhaps no other man has had such opportunities as he to serve the best interests of his country. Whether he shall have succeeded when finally he steps down from Washington's chair only future historians can determine.

3. RIDING THE WAVES AFTER SEVENTY

After all, the seventy-year line is a purely imaginary thing. Once you have crossed it, the watery waste is either rough or calm just as it was a moment before. In my case, life after seventy has gone on as before—if anything with greater intensity. My daily legal work has continued without abatement and I have had some unusually interesting cases to argue. The only definite change which I have noticed is a tendency on the part of younger people, especially younger lawyers, to treat me with mingled curiosity and respect—as if they were in the presence of Confucius or Methuselah. I have found, too, that I am available on alumni programs and for speeches of various sorts where it is desired to hear a Voice from the Past and to listen to an account of life in the Stone Age.

An incident of old age is, I have observed, the availability of my bosom for the display of medals. Various worthy organizations are wont each year to bestow a gold medal on somebody in recognition of a real or imaginary achievement. The dignity of the presentation ceremony is greatly enhanced if the recipient can be referred to in delicate but unmistakable terms as having ended his career and as having planted at least one foot in the grave. This gives those present the comfortable feeling that they are anointing the guest of honor for his burial. Thus in 1939 the National Institute of Social Sciences, at a dinner in New York, awarded me their medal of gold for what they were pleased to regard as my services to humanity. The funeral note was softly present but other notes were happily louder. This award was all the more gratifying to me because at about the same time somebody had published a magazine article asserting that lawyers spend their entire time in promoting fraud and chicane. It was comforting to know that the writer's opinion was not universally accepted. Herbert Hoover came across the continent to act as presenter at the ceremony and, presumably, to take a last look at his old friend.

Later in the year the Pennsylvania Society of New York honored me in similar fashion—this time for "Achievement." I was deeply touched by the loyalty of my fellow-members of the Farmers' Club [29] who, at the invitation of one of our number, Martin W. Clement, the President of the Pennsylvania Railroad, had come over in a body to witness the doing of honor to their bucolic comrade. Tom Dewey, whose presidential boom had then lately been launched, was the principal speaker. Both his boom and my bosom were much in evidence. I returned thanks for my decoration in a speech in which I intimated that I myself might make a strong presidential candidate since I was in a position to pledge myself not to outlive a second term and could even hold out hope that I would not survive the first.

FRANKLIN AT HOME

Medals are not the only mark of advancing age. All sorts of memorial celebrations are suitable occasions on which to "feature" venerable men. Possibly this is why I was selected to make the dedicatory address when in Philadelphia, in the spring of 1938, an heroic statue of Benjamin Franklin was to be unveiled with appropriate ceremony. The Benjamin Franklin Memorial,[30] looking out upon the Parkway which bears his name, was so designed as to provide a suitable setting for a statue of the sage himself. Dedication of the Memorial was postponed until the statue should be brought to life by the sculptor, James Earle Fraser. In anticipation of this new birth three days in May of 1938 had been set apart for the formal dedication of the building and the unveiling of the statue. At an early stage of the preparations I suggested that the occasion would be appropriate for emphasizing the homely virtues of which Franklin's life was a manifestation. The suggestion was approved by the president of the Franklin Institute, Nathan Hayward, by his successor, Philip Staples, and by the Board of Managers. Henry Butler Allen, our able and genial Director, secured the necessary financial backing. He also enlisted the interest of Dr. Nathan Goodman, a student of Franklin's life and work, who prepared nine little pamphlets on as many distinct topics, each pamphlet embodying Franklin's own words on the subject in hand. Each carried a foreword by a man thought to be qualified to speak on its subject-matter.[31] The publication and wide distribution of these pamphlets are part of a concerted effort to reawaken in American youth an interest in Franklin and the Homely Virtues. Our theory is that nothing but a reincarnation of the man himself will bring about the popular acceptance of teachings which, as pure abstractions, are likely to be unconvincing. The Museum and the Fels Planetarium lend themselves to a program of this sort for everything in them speaks of motion and life. If Franklin were actually to return and see with penetrating eye all that has been accomplished in his favorite fields since 1790 he would find it hard to preserve the outward calm which philosophers affect.

We of the Institute were determined to make it easy for Doctor Franklin to keep open house in the Philadelphia home which we had provided for him. A series of fortnightly conferences each dealing with a single phase of Franklin's life and work, was accordingly arranged to begin in the autumn of 1939 and to continue till the following spring.[32] The caption of the series was "Meet Doctor Franklin." Carl Van Doren, author of the most authoritative biography so far written, began the series in October and closed it in April. Each of the intervening meetings was conducted by a leader selected for his familiarity with the subject assigned to him. I agreed to speak on "Molding the Constitution" and discussed Franklin's influence in the Constitutional Convention of 1787. I had prepared a chart intended to present graphically Franklin's eighteenth-century world. Copies of this were distributed to the audience in advance of the lecture to supply a sort of background for the discussion. My thesis was that Franklin made his colleagues make the Constitution; and that his dominating influence was due to the combination of homely virtues of which he was a conspicuous embodiment.

[31] *Biography in Outline:* Nicholas Murray Butler; *Religion:* John R. Mott; *Art of Virtue:* Douglass Freeman; *Industry, Frugality and Thrift:* William Allen White; *Good Citizenship:* Roland S. Morris; *Honesty:* Thomas S. Gates; *The Practical Franklin:* Charles F. Kettering; *The Way to Wealth:* Carter Glass; *Peace:* George W. Pepper, Franklin Institute, Philadelphia, 1938.

[32] The sponsors of the Conferences were the Franklin Institute, the American Philosophical Society and the Historical Society of Pennsylvania.

As my life has spanned half the space that separates us from Franklin's century it was appropriate enough that on these various occasions I should figure as a sort of liaison man between the ancient and modern world.

COLLEGIATE AWARD AND TRIBUTES OF FRIENDSHIP

Another mark of respect for my years came in the form of an invitation to make an address at Rutgers University and to receive an honorary degree from that venerable institution.[33] I should like to make one really adequate address of this sort before the curtain is rung down. So far I have never succeeded in doing so—and did not on this occasion. It must be a soul-satisfying experience to do what Kipling and Barrie did in the rectorial addresses at St. Andrew's, when they gave "Independence" and "Courage" to the world.

At Lafayette College I had a most stimulating experience. The graduates who in their day had won the Pepper Prize[34] had journeyed back to Easton and united in tendering me a dinner.[35] Of the seventeen winners all were present except two—and the absence of these was unavoidable. Each man present gave an informal and most interesting account of his experiences since graduation. Their accounts covered a wide range and presented a vivid picture of America as the young college graduate finds it. I was gratified by their assurances that the prize had been a factor of real importance in stimulating them to play up and play the game.

Two opportunities to give some sort of expression to pent-up feelings of deep friendship came to me in the winter of 1939-1940. The first was a chance to bear my witness to the saintly character and the spiritual achievements of Bishop Brent.[36] A meeting had been arranged in New York to mark the tenth anniversary of the Bishop's death and to secure needed support for the educational work begun by him among the Mohammedan Moros in Zamboanga. The sacrificial service rendered in that faraway land by Mrs. Lorillard Spencer is itself a testimony to the Bishop's capacity to inspire everybody to do his best. The loyal support given at home by Mrs. Nathaniel Bowditch Potter during a long course of years is another illustration of the same sort. Cameron Forbes, that

[33] April, 1940.

[34] For an account of this prize see page 133, *supra*.

[35] June, 1939.

[36] Charles Henry Brent, first (Episcopal) Missionary Bishop of the Philippines, elected in 1901.

fine public servant, was on hand at the meeting and so was General Frank McCoy, gallant soldier and wise administrator. The presence of Mrs. Leonard Wood and of Mrs. Robert Bacon awakened many memories. Dr. William Adams Brown testified to the Bishop's fruitful labors in the cause of Christian Unity. Katherine Mayo spoke of phases of his work in the Philippines and President Ogilby of Trinity College paid high tribute to the influence of the Bishop's personality upon all who came within its range. As presiding officer I had opportunity to record my own personal obligation to a great and good friend.

My other opportunity came when on January 2, 1940, William Irwin Schaffer took his seat as Chief Justice of the Supreme Court of Pennsylvania. He had asked me to represent the Bar of the Commonwealth and to deliver the address of greeting which is customary on such occasions. I took satisfaction in welcoming him to the chair which it had been the highest ambition of his life to occupy, a chair which he filled with distinction and probity to the end of his judicial term.[37]

From time to time have come opportunities to express one's feelings about friends who have died. After the death of Mr. Justice Cardozo in 1938, the customary bar meeting was held in due time in the Supreme Court room at the call of the then Solicitor General, Mr. (now Mr. Justice) Jackson. He invited me to be one of the speakers. I was glad to accept, for Mr. Justice Cardozo was, as Mr. Justice Holmes once observed, "a beautiful spirit." As a common law judge I had for him a great admiration. In the field of constitutional law I found it difficult to follow him. I surmise that men of his type never would themselves have evolved any constitution whatever.

Later Mr. Justice Butler died and was sincerely mourned by the Bar and by an unusually large circle of friends. Francis Biddle had become Solicitor General when the Bar meeting in his honor was held. I was made Chairman of the Committee on Resolutions and so with my colleagues had opportunity to express our affectionate regard for a just judge, a faithful public servant and a loyal friend.

SURVIVORS CELEBRATE

Neither my weight of years nor any amount of rough water in the channel of national life could interfere with the celebration by the Class of '87 of our fiftieth anniversary of graduation. By a coincidence, just

[37] December 31, 1942.

" 'TWIXT CHURCH AND STATE"

Bishop Taitt and Chief Justice Schaffer attend the dedication of the Municipal Court Building.

fifty of the surviving classmates came from far and near and we had two happy June days together. The first was spent at the Fish House, where we were the guests of Somers Smith. The quaint old house with its beautiful lawn on the bank of the Delaware was looking its best. In spite of our half century we felt young when our span was measured against the life of what is reputed to be the world's oldest social organization with a continuous existence.[38] In spite of Fish House punch (which according to tradition led General Washington "the day after" to leave a blank page in his diary) four of us in the late afternoon repaired to a boathouse on the Schuylkill and rowed together in a four-oared gig. Alan Whittaker had come from Atlanta. Frank Green had recently returned from Honolulu. Frank Gummey and I completed the four. We had not rowed together for more than fifty years and we got a great "kick" out of the adventure. My youngest grandson, Billy Newbold, acted as coxswain and guided his crew with skill. Next day's proceedings were more formal— a memorial service at the Ivy Stone, the reading of an Ode by Oliver Huckel, the presentation of $50,000 to the University as '87's Class Fund, and the deposit in the University Library of great volumes of class records diligently compiled through the years by our permanent secretary Witmer Stone. In the Alumni parade we had the right of the line and at the baseball game with Princeton on Franklin Field we sat together in the stand and cheered our team to final victory.

Even before attaining three score years and ten I was occasionally reminded that '87 is no longer the freshman class. A college senior whom I did not know wrote me a letter explaining that he was about to get his A.B. and that he would like my help in securing a scholarship in the Law School. Then, evidently wishing to add a human touch, he asked whether I was the Mr. Pepper of whom he had often heard who, with Fanny Kemble and other well-known people, used to summer at his great-grandfather's country place in Chester County in the early fifties. I wrote promising help in his scholarship application but explained that I could not speak confidently about the house party because my memory was growing dim as to events preceding the assassination of President Lincoln. Later I had the pleasure of telling my contemporary Owen Wister that I had been mistaken for his grandmother's boy friend.

[38] "The State in Schuylkill" (its corporate title) is a quaint and unique organization incorporated in colonial times. By the terms of its charter, it is required to deliver annually to the Proprietors one sunfish as consideration for the grant. The delightful home of the organization is on the banks of the Delaware, a dozen miles above Philadelphia.

THE CONSTITUTION AMONG FRIENDS

The year of our Class Reunion I accepted an invitation from the Mayor of Philadelphia to make the principal address to be broadcast at a big public meeting at Independence Hall on September 17th, thus commemorating the hundred and fiftieth anniversary of the signing of the Constitution. The affair was colorful, although marred somewhat by a heavy rainfall. To speak in that historic building is always a thrilling experience and I hope that I transmitted some of the inspiration which I felt. One never knows what fraction of the effort made by the speaker on such an occasion is converted into communicable heat or how much of it is altogether wasted. This particular occasion had for me many incidental elements of interest. I was within a stone's throw of the spot where just fifty years before I had begun the study of law. In the wings of the building itself, during the sojourn there of the Law School, I had for several years met my classes; and in the long-since abandoned courtrooms I had first tasted the sweets of victory and the bitterness of defeat.

THE INS ARE OUT

There was a touch of melancholy in the contrast between the idealism of Independence Hall and the crass realities of Pennsylvania politics in the years between 1934 and 1938. Details are out of place here. Suffice it to say that by the end of that period the affairs of the Commonwealth had been brought to a deplorable condition. But the day of reckoning had come. Governor Earle seeking election to the United States Senate, was decisively defeated by James J. Davis. Senator Guffey, as Earle's principal backer, faced political eclipse. The Republican candidate for the governorship, Arthur H. James, proved to be a formidable campaigner and was by a large margin elected over his Democratic opponent. One of my contributions to this result was a radio speech commending James to my friends throughout Pennsylvania. As an evidence of earnestness I paid out of my own pocket the bill for my radio time. A fifteen-minute broadcast cost me $2,750, a sum which helps to explain why legitimate campaign expenditures necessarily run into such big figures.

In Philadelphia in the ensuing year there developed an acute controversy over the proposal to secure a new city charter. This proposal was endorsed by a very considerable number of good citizens who saw in the "city manager" plan and in the principle of proportional representation a hopeful chance for better municipal government. I thought the project should be sponsored by the local Republican organization and did my best to bring this about. Unwisely, as it seemed to me, the Republican leaders refused to accept this view and in the legislature prevented the passage of the measure which would have submitted the charter issue to popular vote. When the general election came around in the fall of 1939 some Republicans, embittered by the fate of the charter, announced their intention to support the Democratic candidates for the mayoralty and other local offices. This insurgency had been adroitly stimulated by the Democratic leaders who, although no more in favor of the charter than the Republican "regulars," had given it lip service and in so doing had gained an important strategic advantage. While sharing the disappointment of all true friends of the charter, I thought it a political absurdity, under the circumstances, to risk the surrender of municipal control to the Democrats in a presidential year. The Republican nominee for the mayoralty, Robert M. Lamberton, was in all respects worthy of support and I heartily gave him mine. Two campaign speeches, one of them over the radio, and much publicity subsequently given to my statement were regarded by many as effective contributions to the Republican victory which in due course followed.

NEVER AGAIN?

The Republican upswing in 1939 and thereafter made the approaching election of a United States Senator in 1940 a matter of more than usual importance. Some influential party leaders throughout the Commonwealth expressed the friendly opinion that I could be nominated and elected in something like triumphant fashion. It was suggested that Republican voters, especially in Philadelphia, were anxious to wipe out what they were pleased to regard as an organization "mistake" made when I was defeated in the Republican Primary of 1926. This, of course, was music to my ears but it was not martial music: it failed to awaken any desire for a return to public life. I could not bear the thought of again leaving my law work and all my community interests. To cut off professional receipts and to incur Washington expenses was simply an impossibility in the light of my responsibility to other people. So, treating the friendly suggestion as seriously intended, I gave a definite and final negative and breathed a sigh of relief when the decision was irrevocably made. It would have made me happy if my former colleague Dave Reed had been selected to carry the flag. Since the expiration of his term of service in the Senate he had, however, been out of touch with current politics and (largely because of severe illness) had had no opportunity to serve the party. As an excellent alternative Jay Cooke became the "slated" Republican candidate and in the April primaries easily won the nomination. We Republicans confidently expected his election. It did not seem possible that the people of Pennsylvania would a second time send to the Senate as vulnerable a candidate as Joe Guffey, whose capture of the Democratic nomination appeared to have split the party wide open. Certainly we did not foresee the political upheaval which was destined to result from Roosevelt's quest of a third term.

A GENERAL UTILITY MAN

Service in the ranks suits me better than officeholding. A chance to do a turn as an enlisted man came to me in November of 1939. John Hamilton, at that time Chairman of the Republican National Committee, asked me to head a group of six[39] charged with what some thought an impossible task. A debt of $660,000, a hangover from the 1936 presidential campaign, was a millstone around the neck of the National Committee. To get rid of this handicap before the 1940 campaign was essential. Our little group was asked to do the trick—and we did. Early in January, just as the Democrats were planning to eat their way out of debt at a Jackson Day dinner costing $100 per plate, we were able to announce that six hundred and sixty loyal Republicans had each put up $1,000 for the honor of the Party and that the debt was a thing of the past.

There was a serio-comic sequel to this. A ranking official of the National Committee wrote me an exuberant letter of thanks for what my colleagues had done. This letter was addressed to the Senate Office Building at Washington. There, in due course, it was received and opened by Senator Claude Pepper, of Florida, perhaps the most uncompromising New Dealer and Third Term advocate in the Senate. With an apology he forwarded the opened letter to me. I replied by inviting him to seize this favorable opportunity to come over into the fold where all good little Peppers belong. From his friendly response it appeared that he was appreciative but reluctant—in view of Republican inability to agree upon a leader. I came back with an expression of confidence in the wisdom

[39] The other five were Ernest T. Weir of Pittsburgh, Jeremiah Milbank of New York, Silas H. Strawn of Chicago, Edgar M. Queeny of St. Louis and Sewell L. Avery of Chicago.

"FAMILY FOURSOME"

Three generations take part in the University's Bicentennial Regatta: 1940.

of a multitude of counselors and confessed surprise that anybody accustomed to the rich variety of the tropics should be content with a Party which could do no better than trot out the same old candidate term after term. By way of reply he sent me his photograph under which was written—"To one of the greatest of the Country and no doubt the greatest of the Peppers—George Wharton Pepper—this is enviously subscribed by just one of the Peppers." In response to his request for an exchange I sent him mine, upon which I wrote: "To the Pepper that Is from the Pepper that Has Been."

THE CAMPAIGN OF 1940

After the turn of the year all thoughts were focused upon the approaching Party Conventions. Jockeying for position kept the leaders busy. Being in power the Democrats might have been expected to hold their Convention first. Wisely, however, they maneuvered the Republicans into first place and by meeting later assumed the attitude of an opposition party. I say "wisely" because temperamentally the Democrats are best fitted for attack. Give them a target and bang go their guns. They clearly outrank us Republicans as shrewd and resourceful politicians, although when it comes to administration I think we have the better of the argument.

Speculation about candidates began early. Roosevelt resolutely maintained a crafty silence about his own plans and thus discouraged any other aspirants from throwing their hats into the ring.

In the Republican fold there was no dearth of aspirants. Tom Dewey, New York's able and spectacular District Attorney, was the first to suffer himself to be announced as a candidate for the nomination. Senator Bob Taft was early in the running, commended to popular consideration by his character, ability and experience. Wendell Willkie, the most dynamic personality of the lot, was widely supposed to have the qualifications for the presidency but was at first left out of serious consideration for the double reason that he had but recently become even a nominal Republican and that as a "utility magnate" he might be expected to be vulnerable to partisan mudslinging.

I had not expected to take an active part in the campaign, either before or after the nominations, but I grew eager to get into the fight when it became clear that Roosevelt was arranging to get himself drafted for a third term. At first it seemed as if my usefulness would not go beyond some more money raising, an unpleasant but highly-important job. It was well enough to have wiped out the Republican deficit of 1936 but who was to raise the campaign fund for 1940? The easy answer was to penalize success by drafting the same old crowd, and this was promptly done. All agreed that of the resuscitated committee Ernest T. Weir should be the chairman. He divided the States into zones and asked me to be his vice chairman for New York, New Jersey, Pennsylvania, Delaware, Maryland and the District of Columbia. My responsibility was to supervise the activities of the chairman in each of those jurisdictions and to unite with the rest of the group in approving a national campaign budget and in setting up an organization to make sure that the budget allowances would be adhered to.

The difficulty of our job was increased by the passage during the campaign of a supplement to federal legislation regulating political receipts and disbursements. The act (styled the Hatch Act) no doubt had a laudable purpose, but was so obscurely worded that nobody could be absolutely certain of its precise meaning. However, we tried to conform both to its letter and spirit and did so, I think, successfully.

Meanwhile it began to look as if I would have to take on some other and more exacting assignments. My friend Joseph N. Pew, whose influence in party counsels was great, suggested that I should stand for election as one of the two delegates to the Republican Convention from my congressional district which includes Chester and Lancaster Counties. The local leaders approving I was elected without opposition. Also at Pew's instance I was nominated by the Pennsylvania Delegation to be their representative on the Resolutions Committee of the Convention, a major responsibility. Although both my election and selection were due to Pew's influence he never once sought my vote for any presidential candidate or asked me to support any particular platform plank. He has been widely attacked as a ruthless political boss; but if he be a boss at all he is of a different type from all the others I have met. He neither wants public office himself nor is he interested in patronage. He seems to have only one objective and that is the upbuilding of a strong Republican Party patterned after the major political parties in England. With this end in view, he has for seven or eight years made lavish expenditures of time, effort and money. In 1938 he had the intelligence to see that Pennsylvania might be returned to the Republican column if an aggressive candidate were chosen and loyally supported. In spite of defeatism and factional opposition he put his program through and received as recompense little but criticism and abuse. If (as he and his family have done) you make your money out of oil, it is easy for any expert in defamation

"PUTTING PEP INTO IT"

Republican National Convention of 1940.

to spread the impression that you must be a slippery customer. Thus Secretary Ickes in a platform address or over the radio can so enunciate the name "Pew" as to give it a highly unpleasant implication; and of course he and his sort have no hesitation in adopting this form of attack. However, recollection of service is apt to remain long after defamation is forgotten and my guess is that in retrospect Pew's political service will be gratefully recognized.

The Pennsylvania delegation caucused long in advance of the Convention and voted to unite in supporting, so long as he was in the running, the candidacy of Governor James. As time passed the "We Want Willkie" movement developed momentum and it began to look as if he would be a serious contender. At an earlier time I had established a friendly relation with him following the appearance of his brilliant review of Cecil's "The Young Melbourne." Contacts with him after he emerged as a candidate ended in an undeclared determination on my part to support him if James proved unavailable.

PLATFORM MAKING

Meanwhile the Resolutions Committee, under the chairmanship of Herbert Hyde, was summoned a week in advance to consider a set of proposals drawn up by a large and representative group headed by Glenn Frank. When it was publicly announced that I had been made chairman of the platform-drafting committee, the then Secretary of Agriculture, Wallace, gave out an ill-tempered statement to the effect that because some years before I had argued the A.A.A. case, my appointment was "an insult to the American farmer." Apparently the American farmer did not share the view thus urbanely expressed; for later, as a candidate for the Vice Presidency, the Secretary failed to carry those agricultural states the capture of which was, as far as I can see, the only excuse for his nomination.

The Resolutions Committee made much greater use of the Frank document than had been made of that other advisory report which twenty years earlier I had had a hand in preparing for the Chicago Convention. The hardest nut we had to crack was the formulation of the National Defense plank, which necessarily involved foreign relations and brought about a head-on collision between those who favored maximum aid to the Allies and those who advocated an unqualified pronouncement against foreign war supported by a declaration that under no circumstances should American soldiers ever be sent abroad.[40] I personally was still hoping that American involvement could be avoided but I thought that a party platform should recognize the differences of opinion that actually existed and should not limit the geographical use of our armed forces if the worst happened. At long last everybody's patience was rewarded and both a Defense Plank and an entire Platform were unanimously accepted by the special subcommittee, by the Drafting Committee and by the entire Resolutions Committee. This happened late on the second day of the Convention after I had spent nine days and nights in intensive effort. I thereupon asked for and received an overnight leave of absence in order to get a good night's sleep. On the previous day, in addition to the platform grind, I had had the responsibility of making at a special outdoor session of the Convention a patriotic address in Independence Square. All these efforts meant nervous strain and a big demand upon vitality; but the toughest experience of all came the morning after my night off when upon arriving early I found in my absence, and after the Resolutions Committee had approved our final draft, a night session had been persuaded to reconsider the Defense Plank and to insert the unconditional declaration against foreign service which had been dropped for the sake of harmony. For once I completely lost my temper, said some unparliamentary things to the man whom I thought responsible, gathered my papers together and walked out of the Committee room. Soon my colleagues, through one of their number, asked me to return. This I did and after further conference the inserted sentence was withdrawn by the man who had been most eager for its inclusion. This was the redoubtable "Curley" [C. Wayland] Brooks of Illinois, a veteran with a brilliant record in the World War, a convinced isolationist and at the time of the Convention a candidate for the United States Senate, an office to which he was elected to complete the term of the late J. Hamilton Lewis and re-elected. He was magnanimous enough to accept my apology for words spoken in anger.

So much for the Platform—which was unanimously adopted by the Convention—but who was to stand upon it? The delegates were in doubt but the galleries were not. The nationwide enthusiasm for Willkie was obviously growing. It was undoubtedly this that made the galleries so effectively vocal. Our delegation voted for James on the first ballot. Several of our delegates left him after the first ballot and went to Willkie.

[40] Moreover I had vivid recollections of the amazing shift of public opinion on this very subject twenty-three years earlier. See *supra*, page 114.

I thought that after the next ballot the situation would be clearer but in the interval did all I could for James. At one stage I jumped upon a chair, took my coat off, swung it around my head and led the cry, "We Want James." After the second ballot I satisfied myself that the Governor was no longer a possibility. On the third and all subsequent ballots Bob McCracken and I voted for Willkie.

After the fifth ballot Willkie's strength had grown to such a point that Pennsylvania's solid vote, if cast for him, would undoubtedly give him the nomination. A conference of our delegation was held and it quickly developed that there were many delegates who, for official or other reasons, were still hesitant about leaving the Governor but who for several ballots had been eager to go to Willkie. At this point the sixth ballot was actually being taken and there we were, losing precious time. I pleaded for immediate action. The Governor thereupon stated that he desired to hold nobody who wanted to leave him. A poll of the delegation was hurriedly begun. As names were called it was evident that all but a handful were for Willkie. Dave Reed, realizing that Pennsylvania was about to be reached, rushed from the conference room to the floor just in time to ask that Pennsylvania be passed. This was all that at that moment he could do; but tragically enough Pennsylvania had lost her strategic position. Her indecision at a critical moment brought boos and groans from all over the vast convention hall. Almost immediately and before most of the Pennsylvania delegates had returned to the floor Willkie's nomination was assured. Thereupon Reed, recognizing that the battle was over, did what he could to relieve the situation by announcing a unanimous Pennsylvania vote for Willkie.

When Mr. and Mrs. Willkie appeared upon the rostrum the whole place went wild. The scene was one I shall never forget. Even those most keenly disappointed over the defeat of favorites joined heartily in the demonstration. Everybody seemed to realize that this was the American system in perfect action; and this realization somehow brought a lump to the throat and something very like tears to the eyes. When presently and without serious contest the Vice Presidential nomination went to my good friend and sometime colleague Charley McNary it seemed as if We the People had already spoken and that the November election could not fail to be a mere confirmation of our choice. What the future actually had in store was mercifully hidden from our sight.

THE DEMOCRATIC STEAM ROLLER

In rather startling contrast to the free-for-all in Philadelphia was the machinelike precision of the Democratic meeting in Chicago. From somewhere in the lower regions of the vast hall an amplified voice cried out for a third term. Thereupon the Roosevelt roller went into action and quickly flattened all opposition. The faithful Farley was humiliated. The veteran Senator Glass who put him in nomination was treated with scant courtesy and his reference to Jefferson was jeered. An effort by the delegates to choose their own Vice President was stopped before it could gain momentum and Henry Wallace was named as running mate for Mr. Roosevelt.

Then came an interval of calm. Willkie retired to Colorado for a much-needed rest which as a matter of fact he never got. He invited me to join him there and help him with the preparation of his acceptance speech. I put my suggestions in writing, assured him that I would respond if really needed but declined to join the crowd who were daily draining his prodigious store of nervous energy. The fact that the speech when delivered was not up to his standard is some evidence that it was prepared amid distractions and that he himself was weary when he should have been at the top of his form. His challenge to Mr. Roosevelt to debate the issues of the campaign was sidestepped by the President who doubtless realized that he is at his best when he has the stage to himself.

Willkie was handicapped from the outset by lack of co-operation between the regular Republican organization, both national and in the several states, and the loosely organized groups of his most enthusiastic supporters. For this he had only himself to blame. Owing his nomination primarily to the rising tide of popular opinion he evidently thought it wise to maintain a degree of aloofness from party leaders. More worldly-wise and with a greater appreciation of the importance of organization, Mr. Roosevelt wholeheartedly accepted the support of the well-oiled political machines which in great centers of population operate with the efficiency of mechanized units in modern warfare.[41] What Willkie gained by thus gratifying the prejudices of his volunteer army he lost through the resulting lack of enthusiasm among the regulars. He was a liberal

[41] The Hague Machine in Jersey City, the Kelly-Nash combine in Chicago and the Pendergast Organization in Kansas City, Mo., became and remained Mr. Roosevelt's principal reliance in these important centers. No word of criticism of them ever escaped him.

carrying the banner for an army composed of conservative regulars and enthusiastic guerillas. He bore it with an energy and enthusiasm which nobody but a born crusader could have mustered. Confronted as he was by serried ranks of federal employees, W.P.A. beneficiaries and people on relief, he never faltered and never seemed to doubt that clouds would break. Indeed his whole campaign seemed to me to be political heroism of a high order. Nothing but a stout heart and an amazing physique could have carried him through. Late in getting under way, he soon developed surprising momentum and eventually drove the President out into the open, forcing him to go upon the stump and make five major political speeches.

Like hundreds of other Willkie supporters I welcomed his idealism and threw myself into the campaign with enthusiasm but bitterly regretted his utter indifference to team play. In addition to intensive money-raising efforts I spent time and energy in helping to co-ordinate the activities of the Republican Organization and the Willkie Clubs. To the extent that they eventually marched shoulder to shoulder it was rather from nervousness than from good will. I made a number of campaign speeches, one of them over the radio. I presided at the great open-air meeting at Shibe Park which the candidate addressed when he visited Philadelphia. For weeks I kept constantly on the move, attending meetings and conferences of all sorts and, in general, seizing every opportunity to promote the cause to which I had dedicated myself. To the very last moment I had high hopes that the Third Term movement would fail and that with Willkie in the White House national unity, national defense and national happiness would be immeasurably promoted. But it was not to be; and when early on November 6th Willkie's defeat was conceded I felt as if I were hearing the death-knell of American liberty.

On Armistice Day I listened to Willkie's fine radio address to the twenty-two million fellow-citizens whose faith in him had been so abundantly justified. I hoped, though falteringly, that the President would at once seize the opportunity to salute a worthy adversary; that he would recognize the importance of a patriotic opposition under a leadership which I then hoped [42] would be intelligent and constructive and that he would thus disclose himself as President of all the people and not merely

[42] I use this form of expression because my enthusiasm for Willkie has been cooled by his apparent ignorance of the first principles of party organization and by utterances on international policies which do more credit to his heart than to his head.

the political leader of his recorded majority. I felt that if this were to happen I might be justified, as far as politics are concerned, in calling it a day. But again I had to face disappointment. Instead of a gesture such as a sportsman would have made, all that Mr. Roosevelt found it possible to say was that he had not listened to the speech and had not had the time to read it; Edward J. Flynn, his campaign manager, adding that he and the President had been gossiping until the hour for the speech had passed, and that then he had exclaimed, "My Lord—we forgot to listen to Willkie."

The incident led me to re-enlist for the rest of my life in a struggle which has evidently only just begun. The struggle, that is, to prevent the permanent surrender to the Executive of powers which the American people would never delegate except in a great emergency and then only for the period of its duration.

HILLHOUSE

9

Cloud Banks and Thunderheads

"I knew all the swift importings
On the wilful face of skies.
I knew how the clouds arise—
Spumèd of the wild sea-snortings."

—FRANCIS THOMPSON: *The
Hound of Heaven*

1. NEUTRALITY FOG

WHILE war clouds over Europe were lowering our own weather was far from clear. The public mind was much perplexed and from 1935 to 1941 each of us was groping for light. In the autumn of 1938 news came of Chamberlain's now violently criticized Munich "appeasement." Christopher Morley has well described [1] the sense of relief that it brought to many Americans and to me among them.

[1] *History of an Autumn*, J. B. Lippincott Company, Philadelphia and New York, 1938. I quote a striking passage: "Really fine poetry few people notice; and really fine music few people can guess how to translate into behavior. What everyone could understand was what Mr. Chamberlain did. That grave and weary voice, speaking when all sounded hopeless, will not be forgotten. Let him who has never stood under such a burden be slow to jibe. That one magnificent stroke of courage—even if it should be apologized for by every historian to come—almost atoned for a generation of weight-shifting and flagpole-sitting in British foreign policy. Men will be arguing about it long after new atlases have been published. But some will like to think of the man who went out into the most threatening sky the world has ever known, with no weapon but a furled umbrella. And Orion rose again, while men were asleep."

Before the war in Europe had actually begun there were among us five groups of equally patriotic Americans. The first included those who from the outset recognized that Hitler's primitive brutalities and vicious doctrine of race hatred constituted a threat to the very existence of any civilization built on Christian or humanistic principles. These people were eager for prompt intervention. The second group was made up of people who, having close personal affiliations with England, were ready at once to go to her aid. A third group had small liking for Britain but attributed to Hitler hostile designs against the United States. Such people favored the use of Britain as a buffer state on the theory that she was fighting our fight and that we should aid her as a measure of self-defense. A fourth group of Americans, rightly or wrongly, did not consider Hitler and his gang a lasting menace to civilization in general or to the United States in particular and hoped that we could be kept out of what was essentially a European War. In this group were many who, like me, had close affiliations and warm sympathy with England but who realized that there were, relatively, so few Americans who felt this kinship that it ought not to be translated into a national policy. A fifth group (and they constituted the immense majority) were without definite opinion respecting the European mess but cherished a hope that we could be kept out of war and, in particular, that our boys would never again be sent overseas to fight. Today all these varieties of opinion have lost everything but historical value. Many of those who in the thirties were most strongly opposed to participation in a foreign war are intensely proud of what their sons are doing in France, in the South Pacific and in various places once deemed remote but now within the zone of our daily thinking.

Until the Japs blasted Pearl Harbor[2] our position, as a nation, was officially neutral. "Neutrality" had two stages and, in the second stage, two distinct meanings. The first stage began in 1935 when a joint resolution was passed by Congress declaring, prospectively, that if and when there was a war, the United States would be neutral. The resolution also imposed an embargo on the sale to any belligerent state of arms, ammunition and implements of war. The President struck a popular note when he declared it to be "the fixed desire of the Government and the people to avoid any action which will involve us in war." This was a good definition of the sort of neutrality contemplated by international law and desired by most Americans. It meant such a course of conduct on our

[2] December 7, 1941.

part as would make it impossible for any belligerent to complain that we were playing favorites. The embargo feature of our policy, however, was something more than traditional neutrality. It meant a surrender of the time-honored right of the citizens of a neutral state to sell contraband goods to a belligerent and to carry them on the high seas in unarmed merchant ships, subject, of course, to the right of the aggrieved belligerent to search and seize the goods. Apparently, therefore, the Administration was so determined to keep out of war that the surrender of some traditional rights was deemed a fair premium to pay for insurance against involvement. This policy was highly controversial and in some quarters evoked bitter denunciation. Nevertheless the President's unqualified and unmistakable declarations of real neutrality were of immense advantage to him in the campaign of 1936. Whatever was actually going on in his own mind, he gained millions of votes from those who took him at his word.

WAR AND POLITICS

Opportunity to take sides while professing neutrality was supplied by the civil war in Spain. This had broken out in July of 1936 when Conservatives, Fascists and Monarchists, under the leadership of General Franco, had combined in a revolt against the "Popular Front" government. The revolutionists (who came to be known as "Nationalists") were actively aided by Hitler and Mussolini and were favored by British Conservatives who thought that, as between Hitler and Communism, the latter was the greater menace. The Nationalists were favored also by a number of American groups, including the Catholic Hierarchy. The Government Party, styled "Loyalists," likewise had many American friends, some of whom were eager to help with shipments of munitions and supplies. The embargo provision of the Neutrality Act of 1935, as amended, applied only to shipments to foreign states engaged in war and not to shipments to a state divided by civil war. The Administration accordingly pressed for Congressional authority to extend the embargo to shipments to Spain but, while professing this to be a neutrality measure, failed to include Germany and Italy in its provisions. The desired authority was given by joint resolution on January 8, 1937. The effect of this was to hurt the Loyalists and help the Nationalists, since shipments in aid of the latter could still go forward by way of Germany and Italy while shipments to the Loyalists were blocked. This action was made the subject of a violent but ineffectual protest to our State Department on the ground that the United States was really taking sides in a foreign civil war.[3]

All this controversy about neutrality had been precipitated by premature and (as I thought) unwise governmental action. Why proclaim neutrality when there was no war? My own attitude was definitely on the side of a clean-cut policy of noninvolvement unless and until the self-interest of America required action. If this be "isolationism" then I was an isolationist. I had certainly learned enough from World War I to restrain me from an impulsive effort to control the international conduct of other nations. I expressed this point of view when invited to appear before the Senate Committee on Foreign Relations[4] and in an article in the *American Legion Magazine*.[5] In my statement to the Committee (made before the outbreak of the war in Europe) I advocated a repeal of all the neutrality legislation and the dispelling of the fog by a return to settled principles. This course the Administration resolutely opposed.

When in September of 1939 the long-expected war between Great Britain, France and Germany was actually declared, our governmental policy entered its second stage. Now there really was a war and the line-up was known. It was therefore the time to declare true neutrality or to propose aid to the favored belligerent. Within forty-eight hours after war was declared President Roosevelt issued a neutrality proclamation in conventional form and followed it up[6] by urging Congress to repeal the Neutrality Act of 1935 and its subsequent amendments. In his message he expressed regret that Congress had ever passed the Act and that he himself had ever signed it. Repeal was the course which four months earlier I had advocated and he had opposed. It was therefore a satisfaction to find that the Administration itself had at long last realized that settled principles of international conduct, worked out through centuries of experience, are preferable to hasty and impulsive statutory experiments. But the satisfaction did not last long; it shortly became evident that the President had no intention that we should be neutral in the normal sense of the word and was merely groping for another formula to reconcile pro-

[3] The protest was made in June of 1937 in a memorial presented by American friends of the Loyalists to Secretary Hull. In his letter of May 12, 1938 (*United States in Foreign Affairs* (1938), page 367) Mr. Hull undertook to justify the Spanish policy of the Administration. His argument would have been less unconvincing if the embargo had included Germany and Italy.

[4] May 6, 1939.

[5] Vol. 27, No. 2, page 8, August 1939.

[6] September 21, 1939.

fessed neutrality with conduct essentially nonneutral. This was accomplished by giving to neutrality a hitherto unfamiliar meaning. As in commercial life you may have a silent partner with limited liability, so now an attempt was made to make the United States a special partner in the partnership between Great Britain and France. We were to contribute capital, take no part in management and (it was hoped) escape liability beyond the amount of our contribution. This was the "short-of-war" policy which the President advocated and commended to the American people. A new legislative measure was accordingly brought forward repealing the embargo, reviving the cash-and-carry project and extending it to embrace goods of such sorts as might be defined by executive order.[7] The argument of the proponents of this new measure was obviously disingenuous. The repeal of the embargo and the revival of cash-and-carry were urged not on the ground that they would facilitate aid to the United Nations but on the theory that otherwise we should somehow or other become involved in war. The contention was so obviously disingenuous that it actually helped to lift the fog; for while the people at large accepted the Administration's protestation of neutrality, there was a growing realization among friends of Great Britain and France that what the President was cleverly doing was easing the country into the war and on their side.

PUBLIC OPINION

The gradual change in public opinion produced by these events could be sensed at the time more easily than it can now be described. When the European war clouds burst almost everybody assumed that Germany was the most important factor in the situation. The probability that an oriental storm would drift in our direction was sensed only by the weather-wise who realized that for six years our policy toward Japan had been shaping toward an ultimate offer to her of the alternative of losing face or fighting. As far as people at large were concerned, the immediate effect of the European cloudburst was to confirm each American group in the opinion which it theretofore held.

In October of 1939 Hitler made what was called a "Peace Move." This

---

[7] This hodgepodge measure was styled by the Council on Foreign Relations "a medley of disharmonies." *United States in Foreign Affairs* (1939), page 187. Just before Pearl Harbor the measure was amended by the repeal of three of its most significant sections.

in substance was a proposal that Germany and Russia should consolidate their conquests and call it a day. Hitler, as conqueror, was proposing a conqueror's terms; Britain and France might purchase peace but only by confessing inability to make good their Polish commitment and by suffering a humiliating loss of prestige. On the other hand, it seemed clear enough that if the terms were rejected and if America were to remain aloof, Germany and Russia must in the end accomplish by conquest what they were proposing to gain by treaty. Thus the policy of the United States appeared to be pivotal; I found myself pulled in one direction by emotion and in another by reason. The idea that the lives of American boys should again be sacrificed to settle conflicts of European interest appeared to me wholly unreasonable. The practical impossibility of vindicating the rights of small European States was, I thought, demonstrable; and even the temporary loss of British prestige did not seem too high a price to pay to avert another World War. But while I was reasoning with myself I was increasingly conscious of some sort of affinity with England which made neutrality seem unworthy and even cowardly. I was also influenced by a growing realization that the existence of civilization was at stake. I think that confident assertions to this effect by many wise people did move me to a considerable degree; but in retrospect it is easy to imagine one's motives to have been nobler than they really were.[8] I cannot honestly say that I ever believed that German romanticism was potent enough to enslave the world or even that Hitler seriously contemplated the subjugation of America. After all, it is to be remembered that not he but his enemies and admirers are the ones who have injected definiteness into his grandiose vagueness.[9] I stood out as long as I could, because I realized that the war would have to be fought by the young and that old men like me who know what war means owe a duty of restraint to those whose imaginations cannot conceive its awfulness. But the sequence of events was too much for me. The Russian invasion of Finland in November made my blood boil—and how could I know that soon I should be welcoming Stalin as a friend and contributing my earnings to Russian relief? All through 1940 the unreasoning call of the blood

[8] In the spring of 1940 my friend Henry L. Stimson made over the radio a powerful speech in favor of immediate military intervention. It was immediately after this speech (and to Stimson's complete surprise) that President Roosevelt tendered him the portfolio of Secretary of War.

[9] Attention is called to this point in *The Making of Tomorrow*, page 266, by Raoul de Roussy de Sales, Reynal & Hitchcock, New York, 1942.

grew stronger as the position of Britain became more perilous. April witnessed the debacle in Norway. May saw the Netherlands overrun. The "Nine Days Wonder" at Dunkerque quickened my admiration. When the collapse of France in June left Britain standing alone I was deeply moved. When the night raids on London began in August and continued thereafter with fierce intensity I began to feel as if my own home were being bombed. Finally, when the British people, after intense suffering and strain, were found to be about equally divided on whether reprisals would be justifiable, I gave myself up to the luxury of unrestrained emotion. I said, "These people deserve to win; and we must help them do it."

This is, I think, a fair summary of the process by which, long before the Japanese attack on Pearl Harbor, I came to favor an offensive and defensive alliance with Great Britain. The possibility that civilization might be engulfed, hatred of Hitler and all his works and contempt for Mussolini were contributing factors. The net result was a spirit of wholehearted co-operation with all forms of Allied relief and something like eagerness for the day when sham neutrality would be replaced by honest belligerency.

2. HURRICANE

On the evening of Saturday, December 6, 1941, my wife and I were dining with our neighbors and friends the John Hamiltons. Mr. and Mrs. Herbert Hoover were the house guests of our hosts and some agreeable people had been invited to meet them. After dinner we discussed the Japanese situation. We did some wishful thinking and managed to conjure up a hope that Hull's ultimatum [10] might not, after all, compel the Japs to fight.

It was a cold clear night: nothing to suggest that a hurricane was brewing. But at the very time we were talking the Japs were on the way. Next morning they struck their devastating blow at Pearl Harbor. In a moment of time they dispelled the myth of American naval preparedness, deflated our superiority complex, gained for the time being a surface control of the Pacific and drew first blood in what threatened to be a long and sanguinary war. They had also accomplished, in the twinkling of an eye, what the President had been unable to achieve through years of foggy diplomacy—a national determination on our part to fight, to fight hard and to keep on fighting until final victory is won. Thus the dra-

[10] This was communicated to the Japanese "peace mission" on November 26th.

matic success of the Japanese attack will in the end be found to have been the undoing of Japan.

THE FACTS SUPPRESSED

Following the Congressional declarations of war against Japan, Germany and Italy,[11] the thing that impressed me most was everybody's calm confidence that victory over our three antagonists was predetermined. Of course we did not know till long afterward the actual extent of the Pearl Harbor massacre. The Administration evidently did not dare to give us the facts.[12] To this day people are divided in opinion as to the wisdom of this policy of suppression. It is always easy to support it on the theory that disclosure would give aid and comfort to the 'enemy. My guess is that the enemy is almost always thoroughly well-informed upon all matters of military and naval importance. In this particular case the Japs could not have realized the extent of our helplessness else they would have immediately occupied Hawaii. In such an exceptional case it is proper enough for the Government to announce that serious damage has been done but that its extent will not presently be revealed. But under no circumstance is it justifiable to tell half-truths. Unhappily this type of falsehood seems to have become the settled policy of our censorship.

While the wreckage caused by the hurricane still strewed the beach there naturally arose a popular demand that those responsible for the disaster should be punished. The ranking general and admiral in the Islands were relieved of their commands and will in due course have to face a court-martial. The President appointed a commission to visit the scene of the disaster with instructions to investigate and report. The naming of Mr. Justice Roberts as Chairman implied a full and fair inquiry. It turned out, however, that the scope of the inquiry did not include the extent of the damage done, and the report, as far as I could judge, had little effect on public opinion. Knowing our Ambassador to Japan, Joseph Grew, I was confident that he might well have had premonitions of a surprise attack and that, if so, he certainly would have warned the State Department. I was not by any means so sure of what the State Department would have done. Its policy for several years has impressed me as alternating between starry-eyed idealism and impotent

[11] December 8, 1941, as to Japan and three days later as to Germany and Italy.
[12] They were finally released by Elmer Davis, Director of the Office of War Information on December 7, 1942.

protest. It has since developed that Grew *did* have premonitions and that he *did* send a warning. It has also appeared that the Secretary of State passed the warning on to the Secretary of the Navy who, in turn, issued a similar warning; and that at least one radio operator at Pearl Harbor actually heard and reported, some time before the attack, that Jap planes were on their way. Were these merely perfunctory interdepartmental memoranda not calculated to warn? If seriously intended, why they were disregarded will have to be explained some day "at God's great Judgment-Seat"—whether or not those responsible for the ensuing massacre shall have been previously brought to trial. I do not join in the popular condemnation of the Japs. We knew in advance that their standards of conduct are not ours. They did just as any savages would do under similar circumstances. If our military and naval authorities thought they had civilized beings to deal with and acted accordingly, the responsibility for the massacre rests upon our own people and not upon the savages who merely ran true to form when they went on the warpath and scalped their defenseless victims.

"TOMMY THIS AND TOMMY THAT"

Having gone to war we witnessed the end not only of unreal neutrality but also of confident talk about our preparedness and self-sufficiency. We were confessedly and dangerously unready. A two-ocean navy and an army of seven or more millions of men at once became recognized necessities; and the production of everything involved in so vast a program of expansion immediately became the objective of American industry. Thereupon the same Administration which had persecuted and pilloried business, large and small, made a rightabout-face and eloquently appealed to American industrialists to come to the rescue of their country. Some day some qualified person will chronicle the response to the appeal of the Administration made by American industrialists and business men of all sorts. My guess is that it will be one of the most amazing chronicles ever penned. There will be inkspots on the record where a few unprincipled profiteers and dollar-a-year men disgraced themselves by their selfishness. But, by and large, the chronicle will record the way in which captains of industry went to work with a will—often under the direction of the New Deal officials who in peacetime had planned their destruction.

THE FOG DISPELLED

During the period of awakening I noticed a curious difference between the popular attitude toward Germany and toward Japan. In spite of all the evidence of popular support given by the Germans to Hitler, millions of Americans cling to the belief that someday the German people will recover from their madness and will again become what we used to believe them to be. In the case of Japan, however, there is no Hitler and no differentiation between the Mikado and the rank and file. Many Americans now hate the Japs individually and collectively with a hatred which sometimes appears terrible in its stark ferocity. If, as I believe, the Japs are more formidable than the Germans this state of the public mind may in the end prove to be an important factor in the winning of the war; but unless passion cools quickly after victory has been won the hope of a wise peace treaty will certainly evaporate.[13]

[13] I quote from a recently published book: *Singapore Is Silent,* by George Weller, Harcourt, Brace, New York, 1943. "Japan is not merely America's enemy for this war alone, as perhaps are Germany and Italy; it is America's enemy for all time. If Japan wins, it will grow even stronger. If Japan loses, it will not forgive. . . . However the war seems to end, it cannot be ended by any single peace. . . . It will go on, failing discovery of an ethical rendezvous, until not only the body but the soul of one power or the other is annihilated, until the land of one is plowed with salt, its men dead, and its women and children divided and lost among another people." Contrasted with this prophecy is the following extract from a sermon by the Rev. Dr. Harry Emerson Fosdick: "Once we get into the center of our minds the question that is really central, 'What shall we do to the children that shall be born?' hatred is shown up for what it is—both ethical and political folly." Reported in the *Herald Tribune,* Monday, March 22, 1943.

Quick Water and Calm

"There were pleasant parties and well-ordered homes and nice lads and jolly hunters in war-wracked Greece. History never takes account of such pleasantries, but they have their importance. The Greek world would have gone insane if Thucydides' picture had been all-inclusive."

—EDITH HAMILTON: *The Great Age of Greek Literature*, page 210

1. WARTIME ANXIETY

MY wife and I avoid war talk as much as possible. We are painfully aware that the news we get from day to day is so incomplete as to be unreliable and that it is accordingly useless to be alternately uplifted and let down. The five grandsons in active service are an overshadowing anxiety but they are where they ought to be and we would not have it otherwise.[1] Their parents [2] are bearing themselves with the

[1] George 3rd, after combat service in the Solomons and elsewhere, was made a lieutenant. His ship is the destroyer *Claxton*. He is now somewhere in the Pacific theater of action. Heyward (also a lieutenant) is communications officer on Admiral Hewitt's flagship. William Sergeant Pepper is a second lieutenant in the Marine Corps somewhere in the Pacific; John Sargent Newbold, an ensign in the Naval Reserve, is with an amphibious unit on the Normandy coast; and William Fisher Newbold, a private in the army, is taking a specialized course at Clemson College in South Carolina.

[2] In World War I George Jr. was a first lieutenant in the Coast Artillery. He was an instructor at Fortress Monroe and later served overseas with his outfit. Eugene Newbold saw overseas service as a first lieutenant of Artillery.

sort of restraint that becomes those who have sons in the service of their country. George Jr. has a responsible position in a war plant. His wife Marion has done her bit at the Kellet plant at Llanerch which is busily engaged in a phase of airplane manufacture. My daughter Adeline Newbold [3] was for a long time on duty in the airplane interceptor service and is now working for the Red Cross. My eldest granddaughter Charlotte [4] and her younger sister Marion Pepper have done hospital duty as Red Cross Nurse's Aides and the latter is now driving motor cars for the Army.

George 3rd and Heyward made an early start. They enlisted in the Naval Reserve in 1940, took their battleship cruise in the summer of that year and went back to the University for the academic year '40-41. They reported at Northwestern University in June of 1941 for some months of training and study and were commissioned ensigns before the Pearl Harbor disaster. My friend Thomas Newhall, with characteristic thoughtfulness, presented to George 3rd an officer's sword. Its value to the boy was not a whit diminished by the fact that within a few days the Navy abolished the wearing of sidearms. Both boys were almost immediately called to active duty.

THE RANGE OF IMAGINATION

I am finding that wartime anxieties are an additional incentive to hard work. The less leisure the smaller the margin for worry. The call of my grandsons to active service emphasized the contrast between the comfort and safety in which I continue to live and the hardships and dangers of all boys in the fighting forces. I find it easier to realize in wartime what they are up against than it was in peacetime to appreciate the anxieties of the so-called "underprivileged." In the past I have repeatedly tried to imagine what it is like to be hungry and cold and harassed by debts but I have always ended by admitting the inadequacy of mere imagination. Rolling along in a comfortable car, spending my days in congenial work, going back at nightfall to a happy home without fear of landlord or sheriff, I simply could not imagine what it is like to be an elevator boy or a taxi driver or a share cropper or a coal miner or a veteran too old

[3] Adeline, to our great delight, married Eugene Newbold January 8, 1937.
[4] Married to Samuel Welsh Madeira and the mother of my second great-granddaughter

MRS. PEPPER

Protected by an airplane engineer and two lieutenants.

to be employable or a man with a sick wife or child and unable to afford medical care or nursing comforts or a white-collar worker conscious of inherent capacity but up against a dead end with no chance of promotion. In the case of the Services, however, it is somehow different. I know enough about the conditions under which the boys do their bit, whether ashore or afloat or in the air, to be able in imagination to live with them and actually share their problems and their perils. But the fact that I can do it only in imagination makes me inwardly uncomfortable. There is only one consideration that lightens this spiritual burden and that is the fact that this time I did nothing to precipitate war but rather did my little best to avert it. During World War I, I cherished the illusion that it was all worth while. But when the disillusioning aftermath developed and the tragic consequences of Versailles became evident I began to experience something like remorse for having done all that I could to get the United States into the fight. Whether my effort had or had not counted in the actual result, at least I had done all I could: and there I was, just beyond war age but quite vigorous enough to be in the line of scrimmage, living in safety and comfort while Franklin Pepper and others of the Nation's best were dying at the front. Today this element of remorse is absent but there is an overhanging sense of unworthiness which no amount of reasoning can dispel.

A WARTIME SORROW

On Memorial Day 1942 my sister Frances Scott entered into rest. She had been ill for a time and thereafter had seemed to recover her strength. But a relapse followed and she fell asleep. She was so near and dear to me that I felt disqualified to write the story of her life. A friend of both of us [5] undertook to do this and there resulted a sketch characterized by insight and charm. It was duly printed for private circulation and was welcomed by the many who craved some memorial of their inspiring friend. Frances's beauty, the aura of culture which surrounded her, her self-effacing devotion to the welfare of others, her extraordinary achievements in the service of her Church—all these things were recorded with sympathy and good taste. I doubt whether any brother and sister ever meant more to one another. Looking backward through the years I cannot recall a single incident that tended to mar

[5] The talented and loyal Miss Sarah Lowrie.

our relation. In my own life she was a powerful influence for good. It seems appropriate that she should have died in wartime. I feel as if a comrade had fallen at my side and I sorely miss her companionship.[6]

HORROR AND HATRED

I think that I feel the horror of the war situation somewhat more keenly because as I have grown older the idea of taking life has become more and more distasteful to me. I am certain that I could no longer—just for sport—kill a deer or even a cock-pheasant or any other beautiful creature—any more than I could bring myself to cut down a fine oak tree just for the fun of swinging an ax. Some such feeling, greatly intensified, fills me with dismay when I read of planes shot down, of vessels sunk and of soldiers and sailors wiped out by gunfire and when I learn that the nerve-strain on combatants in this war is filling the hospitals with victims whose plight is unspeakably terrible. Of course my feeling is most intense when casualties happen to our own boys; but it also haunts me in the case of our Allies and (strange as it may seem) when I read of the death of some young German soldier. I cannot stifle the thought that in every such case somewhere there is a brokenhearted parent or wife or sweetheart. As to the Japs I feel it to be quite different, in spite of the time and money I have spent to lead them to adopt the standards of conduct which we profess. I know that each individual Jap is as much an object of divine care and compassion as I am; but if it became my duty to kill *somebody* I am sure that I should put a Jap at the top of my priority list. It is not exactly hatred. It is rather a feeling that there is not room enough on earth for both of us in view of our opposing conceptions of life and conduct. Of course this feeling will spend itself by and by. We cannot afford to let it dominate us for all time. But at the moment I cannot but confess that I am what I am.[7]

Speaking of the Japanese, I sometimes wonder what has become of my friend Roknichiro Masujima, of Tokyo, who at one time interested me in the project of bringing to Japanese law students some knowledge of American constitutional law. I gave some money and raised more to

[6] She is survived by three children: Frances, the wife of Rev. Albert Lucas, Canon of Washington Cathedral and Headmaster of St. Alban's School; J. Alison Scott, engaged in war work in the S.K.F. plant; and my law partner Ernest Scott.

[7] See footnote to page 276, *supra*.

provide him and his students with a library of books adapted to this end. He had been counselor to the Japanese Embassy in London and had developed deep and intelligent interest in constitutional government. We met seldom, for he came to America only at long intervals; but we corresponded with some regularity and I had for him a sentiment of genuine friendship.

PRIVATE RIGHT AND PUBLIC INTEREST

The American constitutional law which in peacetime this Japanese friend and I wished to commend to his fellow countrymen was a different body of law from that which goes by the same name today. The difference has come about through a change of attitude on the part of the Supreme Court of the United States. This change in the Court is itself the result of the now prevalent doctrine that when private right and public interest appear to be in conflict a strong presumption at once arises that the citizen's right must be overridden. While this presumption that the government is always right is at the peak of its popularity in wartime, the changed relationship between citizen and government which gives rise to it had its origin before the war. Prohibition and the Income Tax were probably responsible for the original substitution of hostility for mutual confidence. When the Eighteenth Amendment was repealed the situation should have become better but it actually became worse. The rapid growth of taxation and the immense extension of New Deal regulations made the property-owning citizen even more rebellious and the official correspondingly more suspicious. Little by little the citizens of this class came to think of the federal government as an avowed enemy and the official began to regard the taxpayer as an undesirable alien.[8] The young gentlemen in subordinate government positions gradually became more formidable than Nature's God ever equipped them to be. They thought and acted as if the whole power of the Government was available to support them in whatever contentions they were pleased to make in any matter under consideration. In so comporting themselves they were merely taking color from some of their superiors who, in their turn, were quick to reflect the rapidly-increasing authority of the Executive which has been so distinguishing a characteristic of the Roosevelt

[8] As long as the federal government was financing itself at the expense of the privileged few, Uncle Sam was regarded as a benefactor and friend by less prosperous citizens. Whether his popularity will survive more inclusive taxation and unwelcome regulations time alone can determine.

regime. This being the drift at Washington it was inevitable that sooner or later the Supreme Court itself would move with the current.

In the pre-Rooseveltian era when I arose to address the Supreme Court on an issue between the federal government and a citizen I felt myself in the presence of judges who were not conscious of being part of the governmental machine. In that respect they were wholly different from the revenue official or the regulatory commission or the executive agency from whose edict I was appealing. Today the atmosphere surrounding the Court is such that the citizen's advocate is conscious of a courteous but definite predisposition on the part of the Justices to find the government in the right unless the facts make it intellectually stultifying so to do; and what we lawyers, whether on or off the bench, can do without consciously stultifying ourselves is indeed "something"! In other words, the advocate who nowadays argues before the Supreme Court is before just another federal agency—manned, indeed, by able and honest men but men whose conception of primary duty is to keep the federal steam roller rolling.

When the proposition is stated abstractly there appears to be every reason why the "public interest" represented by government should outrank "private right." There are, however, two important qualifications to this statement which should hold good even in wartime. One is that the Voice of Government is often only the voice of a petty official in an executive department heard as if through a loud speaker. The other is that there are many private rights which it is greatly to the public interest to protect. When for the moment it suits the purpose of an Administration to disregard contract obligations or to assume control of commerce internal to a state or to give to Presidential vagaries the force of law, there is need for a tribunal sufficiently farsighted to perceive that in such cases the invasion of private right will in the long run be destructive of the public interest. To the extent that the Supreme Court does not today satisfy this need it is merely reflecting the recently-developed hostility between the citizen and the federal government and in the controversies that arise between them is tending to take the government's side. If in the past there has been undue emphasis on private right, certainly the pendulum is swinging far in the other direction. Perhaps the time is not far off when the citizen-litigant will again have a more sympathetic hearing before that great tribunal than he has today. Of course this prediction will be falsified if after the war the United States perpetuates our wartime totalitarian philosophy. If this should happen there will be no American Constitutional law to teach to the

Japs or to anybody else. On the contrary we ourselves will have to become the learners instead of the teachers and may have to go to school in Tokyo; for while we now have most of the evils of totalitarian government we are administering it wastefully and inefficiently.

2. LAW PRACTICE IN WARTIME

These observations on the prevalent deification of government are not a digression from the theme of this chapter, for in wartime the practice of law is concerned principally with problems of government relationship. Government cases in a normal law office bear to the whole volume of the firm's practice a proportion about like that borne by government bonds to the whole list of securities in an investor's portfolio. Business men and lawyers trained under a different conception of the state naturally find it difficult to adjust themselves to an entirely new set of economic and legal teachings. A good deal of my time and energy is spent in reminding myself that times have changed and that I must thoroughly understand the modern point of view even if I cannot accept it.

My own share in the work of my firm has not diminished as I have grown older. In my seventy-eighth year I am not conscious of failing powers, although an important argument takes more out of me than it used to. I can still affirm with perfect sincerity that I am as enthusiastic about my profession as I was a half-century ago.

All through the years my office relationships have been happy. Each of my twelve partners, good fellows all, has his specific contribution to make to the work of the firm. William Budd Bodine, for example, is an expert debunker. He can prick the bubble of fallacious argument more quickly than anybody I ever knew and he is merciless with his needle. He came to me as a student more than forty years ago. We have been fast friends ever since, notwithstanding what he has consistently done to many of my brightest ideas.

Isaac Pennypacker is our conservative partner. When he expresses himself I am apt to think of a toast which Theodore Roosevelt once proposed to my dear friend Mrs. Henry Stimson who, sitting next to him at luncheon, had been laying down the law. "Here's to the health of Mrs. Stimson," said the Colonel, "compared with whom I am a flabby sentimentalist." Thomas Stokes combines with sound learning the courage and poise of an old polo player. Philip Leidy attacks his work with the *élan* that discloses his French extraction. Fred Spotts is at his best when he ridicules some proposition that everybody else has applauded just as Athanasius gained his fame by boldly opposing the rest of the world. Layton Schoch till his sudden death in 1940 used on courts and juries the vigor and tactical experience gained when he played football for Cornell. He was by all odds the best trial lawyer at the Philadelphia Bar. Joe Conwell, in addition to his legal work, serves the community as president of Hahnemann Medical School and Hospital. My nephew Ernest Scott and James Alan Montgomery, Jr., the son of my classmate and lifelong friend, carry heavy loads of office work but have found time to render effective wartime service—one as chairman of a rationing board and the other, first, as a member of a draft board and later in the Office for Strategic Services at Washington. In similar fashion each of the other members of our team plays his part effectively. Many a time the credit for a touchdown has gone to me when the others have done all that was necessary to put me in scoring position. The partners, as well as the younger men in the office, do all they can to lighten my load; and I am sure that no group of lawyers leads a happier community life. This is true even in wartime. We miss the men [9] who have gone into the service but we are proud to have their stars on our flag. In 1941 John D. M. Hamilton became a partner in our firm. Having for several years rendered yeoman service as Chairman of the Republican National Committee, he decided to return to the practice of his profession. He has since resisted all efforts to draft him back into political life. His experience and skill have greatly strengthened our organization and his companionship has contributed much to the pleasure of life in the office. The other congenial accession is that of Thomas E. Comber, Jr., whom we were fortunate enough to secure to do the heavy trial work for which we had depended on Harold Baile before his induction into the service. Frank A. Bedford, Jr., one of my most dependable younger partners, died suddenly in February of 1944. His passing was not only a grievous loss to us but to an unusually large circle of devoted friends.

Through the years we have acted on the theory that, in office management, the only efficiency worth having is the efficiency which results

[9] Harold S. Baile, Lieutenant, U.S.N.R.; Richard Benson, Lieutenant Commander, U.S.N.R.; William C. Bodine, Lieutenant (j.g.), U.S.N.R.; Clement J. Clarke, Lieutenant (j.g.), U.S.N.R.; Walton S. McDougal, Lieutenant, Field Artillery; James A. Moore, Lieutenant (j.g.), U.S.N.R.; John Sailer, Lieutenant, U.S.N.R., and Layton M. Schoch, Major, Air Service.

Joseph S. Conwell, Jr., and William M. Keenan are expecting to be called. In the interval Conwell has enlisted in the Coast Guard Reserve.

from contentment. I do not claim that our small organization is in any respect ideal but I know no other office where through the years people have been happier. Ours is a small group, comprising twelve partners, nine associates [10] and seventeen women. We work on a profit-sharing basis. Two and a half per cent of the firm's net earnings have been for many years set apart for those on the payroll and distributed semiannually as a bonus. At no time, even in the depths of the depression, have salaries been reduced or payment of the bonus omitted. There has grown up in the office a family relationship which, with few exceptions, has tended to loyalty and efficiency. Whenever I enter the office I am conscious of a welcome, spoken or unspoken, by everybody in the place. At intervals some sort of office festivity takes place which discloses that we are all on a level of sociability and good fellowship.[11]

What the future has in store for law offices in general and ours in particular it is idle to speculate. The firm is the outcome of a lifetime of hard work. I take in it a proper pride. I should hate to have the office disintegrate under wartime pressure; but this is the fate of many organizations and we have no claim to immunity.

An unhappy evidence of wartime passion was exhibited in a case (still pending) in which a client of ours is claiming damages for a libel published by the defendant, the Philadelphia *Record*. John O'Donnell, the well-known Washington correspondent, on April 17, 1941, wrote an article in which he stated that there was about to be made in the Senate a charge that American warships were being sent to convoy vessels of other nations carrying Lend-Lease supplies. For this statement of fact he had first-hand evidence from several Senators; but President Roosevelt so far forgot himself as to state publicly that O'Donnell was a liar. The *Record*, whose editor David Stern is a close friend of the President, proceeded to chastise O'Donnell in an editorial captioned "An Outrageous Lie." In this screed the correspondent was accused of being pro-German and of favoring the "liquidation" of the Jews. All the charges being damaging as well as false, a suit for libel was promptly brought in a Philadelphia court and in due course came on for trial before a Common Pleas jury. We have a rule of practice in Philadelphia that in such a case the plaintiff must not state to the jury the

---

[10] Including the men in the Service.

[11] Such a festivity was a party given in June of 1942 by John Hamilton and his wife at their farm near Paoli. For that occasion I wrote and recited some nonsense verses individualizing everybody in the office.

amount of his damage-claim lest the minds of the jurors be affected in a way prejudicial to the defendant. John Hamilton, trying for the plaintiff, scrupulously observed the rule; but on the second day of the trial, when things were going well for the plaintiff, the *Record* (defendant) published of its own accord a headlined statement that in the suit the plaintiff was claiming $50,000. Thereupon the trial judge, with a perversity difficult to understand, of his own motion and against Hamilton's protest, declared a mistrial, withdrew a juror and adjourned the case until a later date, thus giving to the defendant's own statement the effect which would have been given if the plaintiff had violated the rule.

Before the case came up again for trial President Roosevelt, after one of his press conferences, waited until O'Donnell and most of the correspondents present had filed out of the room and then handed to the last of them a package for delivery to O'Donnell which, when opened, was found to contain a German Iron Cross. Wide publicity was at once given to this extraordinary incident which the President sought to justify on the ground that in another and wholly unrelated article O'Donnell had given comfort to the enemy. Whether this was an attempt to bolster the *Record's* case is obviously a matter of inference; but, if it was such an attempt, it signally failed; for at the second trial (this time before Judge Sloane and a jury) Hamilton and Comber so conducted the case that a jury of three men and nine women promptly returned a verdict for the plaintiff and fixed the damages at $50,000. As the trial judge in his charge to the jury had in effect narrowed the issue to a question of veracity between O'Donnell and Stern the result was as gratifying to the one as it was unwelcome to the other.

After long delay the *Record's* motion for a new trial has been granted. Unless on appeal the Supreme Court of Pennsylvania reinstates the verdict, the whole drama will have to be enacted again before another jury. The defendant certainly cannot complain that the way of the defamer is hard.

3. UNDECLARED CIVIL WAR

In spite of all obstacles, both inevitable and unnecessary, our expectation of victory in this war is unshaken. This happy assurance is clouded a little by our seeming inability to keep peace at home. We have become so accustomed to the wrangling of A.F. of L. and C.I.O., to the spectacle of strikes and to the din of labor controversy that we do not always realize how terrible the industrial situation has recently become. Yet if we think realistically we must conclude that a bitter, albeit a bloodless, civil war is being waged continuously (and even in the presence of external enemies) between great groups of American citizens. Not even the winning of the war or the making of a wise peace settlement seems to me more important than the solution of our own American labor problems.

When industry's abuse of the power to hire and fire and of the right to fix wages had led to the formation of labor unions, the labor leader emerged as a necessary incident of the revolution. His aim was ultimately to include all workers within his own organization. With such an aim, his strategy must needs be aggressive. He was as convinced as is the Christian missionary that his message must be made effective everywhere and that it should be accepted by all. Just as the disciple of Confucius or of Buddha regards the coming of the missionary as an impertinent intrusion, so the owners of a plant where there are no labor troubles brand the aggressive labor organizer as a troublemaker and bitterly resent his activity. When after years of struggle the cause of labor organization had made great progress and, like the medieval Church, had begun to feel that universality was almost within reach, inevitable schism marred the integrity of the structure and resulted in two militant labor groups where there had been one before. Thus we have the unlovely spectacle of two groups of citizens more or less united against the employer but at bitter odds with one another. Can America survive this War between the Classes?

When I try to predict an answer to this question I am baffled by discovering inside each great labor group, and to some extent within every local union, a struggle for mastery between two radically different conceptions of labor policy. If I may again use the analogy of religious organization, what is going on today inside the unions is the conflict between the Christian and the Mohammedan conception of how converts should be made. Shall it be by appeal to fair play, to public opinion and to the employer's better self? Or shall the employer be offered the alternative of accepting Allah and his Prophet or of feeling the edge of the scimitar? This conflict of policies is made more significant by the fact that the honest advocates of a policy of force are reinforced by allies whose real aim is not the betterment of labor but is the use of the labor movement as an instrument to subvert the American system of constitutional government. These allies are really the worst enemies the worker has.

I can be hopeful that labor organizations will gradually be purged of this "Fifth Column" element, but I am not at all sure that the spirit of sweet reasonableness will determine the labor policies of the future. Nor am I certain that it would be best for the worker if this were to happen. It is only if a similar spirit were sure to animate the employing class that the prospect of industrial harmony would be bright; and there is something in the virile self-confident make-up of a captain of industry that makes it hard for him to credit the worker with his full contribution to the joint result. Indeed I distrust any solution which does not remove the cause of the trouble, by substituting community of interest for the present deep-rooted conviction that the interests of employer and employee are opposed. "Men and Management" is a good enough phrase; but there is a limit to the extent to which one set of men can be managed by another set. I have not explored the co-operative movement with thoroughness and it may be proved by longer trial to be impracticable; but as I look ahead I find myself hoping that labor and capital, men and management, will gravitate toward the conviction that their interests are identical and that the organization of industry should reflect that identity.[12]

PERSISTENT NIGHTMARE

While our labor troubles thus have the quality of civil war, our domestic differences of opinion about capitalism, communism and socialism are more in the nature of bad dreams. They are disturbing but not fatal. Much contemporary discussion of the merits and demerits of these systems is, as usual, clouded by failure to make basic definitions. For me the term "capitalism" has a definite meaning. It is an economic system in which the individual may acquire wealth through effort and may control the disposition of what he has thus acquired.[13] Communism also presents a clean-cut conception. It is the system under which the increment of individual effort belongs to the community and is to be controlled for the common good. As between capitalism with all its known

[12] A valiant effort to emphasize this identity of interest is being made by the men and women who, collectively, constitute the Oxford Group, now better known as the movement for "Moral Rearmament." Their dramatic "Revue" presented in many industrial plants appears to have demonstrated that both managers and men will respond happily to an appeal to their better selves.

[13] This system, when in motion, is often called "free enterprise." An effective argument in its support is made by Edgar M. Queeny in his recently published *Spirit of Enterprise,* Charles Scribner's Sons, New York, 1943. To combine with it the co-operative principle is not to modify the system but to reappraise the contributions of those who combine to produce a profitable result.

evils and communism with its long record of historic failures I predict
the survival of the former for my own country; because it is possible to
mitigate the abuses of a system that is fundamentally sound but impossible to fit Americans into a mold which, if once accepted, would inevitably stifle the qualities which distinguish them from other people.

It may well be that the regime which began with Trotzky and Lenin
and has reached its climax under Stalin was precisely what was needed
by the Russian people. But why in the name of common sense the surgical treatment for Russian cancer should be commended as a specific for
American indigestion I for one cannot imagine.

While capitalism and communism have for me definite meanings I
find socialism so elusive a conception that it is always just beyond my
grasp. My search for a definition is like a nightmare which I have had
from time to time in which I am frantically chasing a departing train
that I never succeed in overtaking. The only description of socialism
which satisfies me is one which every socialist would angrily repudiate.
But, after all, a believer in the American system must have the right to
poke fun at his tormentors—as they are constantly doing to me. I put it
thus: Socialism is the state of mind of those who, being dissatisfied with
capitalism and afraid of communism, imagine that the advantages of both
can be enjoyed free from the disadvantages of either.

CAPITALISM AND THE CHURCH

I recognize a further contrast between capitalism and communism.
Capitalism is a purely economic system. If it is to promote the well-being
of all it must be supplemented by religion. Communism, on the other
hand, is an integrated, self-sufficient system. It is not only an economic
conception but is intended to be a complete way of life. Church and
State are one, in the sense that the State has swallowed the Church. If it
be true that when religion is put out at the door it comes back through
the window, we may anticipate the resurrection of the Church in Russia,
purged, no doubt, of whatever imperfections it had developed. But, to
the extent that Christianity thus reasserts itself, communism will have
fallen short of its ideal. It will have developed the fatal spiritual weakness
which overtakes all men whose lives are ordered by a rigid system of
imposed discipline. Such a system is at its best in wartime. I can be
enthusiastic over Stalin as a military leader but I should hate to have
him as my employer or section foreman in time of peace. I suspect that

he could become as hard-boiled as a capitalist untouched by the spirit of Christianity. It appears to me that the failure of communism is more obvious in the sphere of ethics than in the domain of economics. Communists have a capacity for domesticating disorder and treachery to a degree that must excite the envy of Hitler.

It is at this point that the contrast between communism and capitalism becomes most vivid. Under the latter system the individual has the responsibility of choice. He may make a generously social use of what he has acquired or else a bitterly selfish use of it. Christianity, as a spiritual dynamic, seeks to arouse in him a sense of stewardship. If he responds favorably, he develops all the qualities of the good citizen and becomes the sort of fellow one covets as a companion. If he rejects the teaching he shrivels spiritually and emerges as a social liability. The Church is not dependent upon capitalism; but a wholesome capitalism desperately needs a dynamic Church. If the Church fails, communism will become inevitable.

Meanwhile the socialist impresses me as a less effective creature than either capitalist or communist. He hampers the initiative of the capitalist but fails to exterminate him, thus substituting continual domestic unrest for the Pax Romana of the Communist.

All these grave domestic issues loom large in the foreground of thought. If one wants to look forward to Victory and to what lies beyond he must overlook them or peer around them. The labor problem bears a definite relation to Victory. Plans for postwar reconstruction are colored by the economic views of their proponents. There is, moreover, a definite cleavage of opinion between those who think that peace and security are objectives to be directly aimed at and those who hold that neither security nor peace can properly be made the object of policy. According to this view, which seems to me to be obviously sound, these are merely the by-products of wholesome and generally satisfactory international relations.[14] To set up, for example, a police force to preserve an unsatisfactory world order is to invite trouble instead of averting it. The League of Nations is the classic example of the futility of a mechanism directed primarily at military security.

With all these thoughts churning about in my mind I can nevertheless look confidently for the day when Victory is achieved and when the big question of the moment will be the terms of the Armistice.

[14] Carr, *Conditions of Peace* (Macmillan), page xxiii, quoting A. G. B. Fisher, *The Clash of Progress and Security*.

"QUALITY"

Sir Norman Birkett, President Lashley and Attorney General Jackson at the American Bar Association Convention, Indianapolis, 1941.

4. FAMILY AND FRIENDS

It is not often that in old age a man makes new friends who really count with him. I have been lucky enough to do this in at least two instances. It was not until 1940 that Lally McCarthy, of Toronto, and I were thrown together, and not until the following year that I met Sir Norman Birkett. McCarthy, an eminent K.C. and a leader of the Canadian Bar, came to the meeting of the American Bar Association in the fall of 1940; and Birkett, then in the front rank of English barristers, attended the Indianapolis meeting a year later. These men already knew one another well and I fell for both as soon as I met them. We three quickly became fast friends and we have since maintained in correspondence the relation which was begun in congenial companionship. On his return to London in late 1941 Birkett found that in his absence he had been appointed by the King to be a Judge of the High Court of Justice. In the spring of 1942 he accepted my invitation to return to Philadelphia by plane to speak at the dinner of the American Law Institute. Everybody who heard him either at Indianapolis or at Philadelphia remembers him as a man of great personal charm and a speaker able to combine serious thought with delightful humor. His mind is stored with all that is best in literature. He has not only a remarkable verbal memory but a certain dramatic gift which enables him to do more than justice to any poem that he recites. In the midst of his Philadelphia speech the sirens sounded a blackout and he finished his remarks by candlelight. The incident merely served to increase the effectiveness of what he said. When he, McCarthy and I get together for a carefree evening we are sure of fellowship at its best.[15] My only regret is that these two friendships have come so late in life's voyage and that it is necessarily doubtful whether Lally and I will ever again see Norman face to face.

[15] Antoine de St. Exupéry, the aviator, has thus apostrophized friendship in *Wind, Sand and Stars* (Reynal and Hitchcock, New York, 1939), page 45: ". . . What constitutes the dignity of a craft is that it binds men together and fashions for them a common language. . . . We forget that there is no hope of joy except in human relations. If I summon up those memories that have left me with an enduring savor, if I draw up the balance sheet of the hours of my life that have truly counted, surely I find only those that no wealth could have procured me."

LAW AND AGRICULTURE

There are two standing social engagements which, war or no war, I always keep if possible. One of these is the dinner of The Legal Club, which comes three times a year. The other is the monthly dinner of the Farmers' Club which falls upon the Thursday nearest the full moon.

The Legal Club brings together a most interesting group of judges and members of the bar, twenty-four in all, over whom John Hampton Barnes for many years presided with rare tact and good judgment. He guided our informal round-table discussions and often brought some distinguished stranger to speak about whatever happened to be on the visitor's mind. When in 1939, greatly to our regret, Barnes felt compelled to resign I was chosen president in his place. At such a gathering you see the bar at its best.

The Farmers' Club is a unique institution with a continuous existence of more than ninety-four years. There are at any one time twelve members, each of whom has a genuine interest in farming, horticulture, cattle-raising or some similar activity. Each member entertains the Club once a year and is privileged to invite as many additional guests as he pleases. Business dress is the custom of the Club. This insures informality and also makes it easy for men to come direct from their offices to the home of the host. The estates of the members are of all sorts—from a small country place like mine to "Longwood" where Pierre duPont's gardens and greenhouses are the delight of all beholders. I doubt if there is any social organization out of which its members get more fun.

HOME LIFE IN WARTIME

In spite of wartime regulations the stream of our domestic life flows on as usual. Having habitually gone to my office by train I am not so much affected by gasoline rationing as many of my friends. With true Yankee prudence my wife anticipated gas and tire shortages and long before they happened bought a little Crosley car in which we can travel more than forty miles on a gallon of gas. The car is so light that the wear and tear on the tires is negligible. In this I drive to and from Devon station on weekdays, often picking up neighbors on the way, and to church on Sundays. Living as we do in the deep country four miles from the station we can see little of our friends; but this bears more hardly upon my wife than upon me because my working day is spent amid crowds of people. What we like best is to have congenial guests over a week-end. Above the door of our living room is an inscription copied years ago from God-Begot House in Winchester: "The glory of the house is the friends who frequent it."

ROUTINE

Perhaps the record of a routine day should have a place in this chronicle.

The alarm clock gets me out of bed at 6:45. After setting-up exercises, shower and a light breakfast I reach Devon station in time for the 7:57. At the newsstand Miss May hands me my paper and makes a few breezy comments on the news of the day. She doubts whether we can win the war unless the Democrats are run out of Washington. While waiting for the train there is always pleasant talk with the other commuters—men, women and school children. There is a sort of camaraderie among people living on the same schedule. In winter these exchanges take place under the electric lights because we are up before the sun. On the train I allow myself two stations for the news summary or headlines. This leaves me a solid half hour for the work which emerges from my brief case; and this is matched on the homebound train at the end of the day. As wartime travel crowds the trains and as I still feel bound by some social customs that are, I fear, outmoded, I occasionally have to give my seat to a woman commuter. When she protests I am tempted to tell her the simple truth— which is that something inside makes me positively uncomfortable if I continue to sit while a woman stands.

As I arrive at the office building there is friendly chatter with the elevator boys and some more comments on sporting events and the war. Somebody with a gift for reporting should write an account of elevator conversations—both those in which you take part and also those overheard between strangers. The world in microcosm is to be seen and heard in elevators and if one keeps eyes and ears open there is never a dull moment.

This is true, too, of travel by taxi. The taxi driver is just as definitely a distinct species as the old-time London bus drivers. In Philadelphia, New York and Washington I have had many an amusing conversation with the philosopher who at the time was guiding me through the traffic. Now and then there has been a touch of pathos. Once in New York I complimented my good-looking young driver on his new suit of clothes. "This is the first anniversary of our wedding," he said, "and I had saved up five dollars to take the wife out to dinner and to the movies; but she made me spend it on these second-hand clothes because she thought I didn't look as neat as I ought to." When I paid the fare I handed him a five dollar bill and told him to take the wife out as he had planned to do. If ever grateful surprise lighted up a face it was when that boy said, "Mister—never has anybody in my whole life done anything like that for me and I guess I'll never get over it." I confess I had something like a lump in my throat as we said good-by.

Some of these taxi conversations have taken place in the early morning en route from the 30th Street Station to the Land Title Building. There Eddy the doorman is waiting to grip my hand and pull me out of the taxi. If my friend Marshall Morgan, president of the Fidelity-Philadelphia Trust Company, has already passed by, Eddy is a trifle downcast; otherwise he says jubilantly, "When he comes along I'll tell him he'll have to get up earlier if he wants to get ahead of the Old Man."

Sometimes I am first to reach the office and let myself in with my key. Sometimes several of the "family" arrive together—usually the girls— as they seem to spring into action earlier than the men—except our faithful accountant, John V. Martin, who is on the job early and late. My secretary Miss Emma Kane and I vie with one another in the race to arrive first. The office day, once begun, moves fast and it is time to hurry for the six o'clock train almost before I know it. Dictation, conferences with partners, interviews with clients, outside meetings of all sorts, briefwriting, an argument in court, the occasional luxury of study in the library—all help me to realize the soundness of Benjamin Franklin's advice: "Rise early or trot all day."

"TAKE IT OR LEAVE IT"

I have never seen good come from volunteered advice, but I suppose that if something of that sort is ever justifiable it is at the end of the story of a long life. I accordingly hazard three bits of advice backed by years of experience. One is to form the habit-habit. Another, to utilize scraps of time. The third to learn the art of sleeping at will.

I have found it well worth-while to cultivate the habit of deliberately forming habits and of assigning to them, when formed, a place of high authority in life. If you form the habit of never laying down your pocketknife and never lending it, you will be able to keep it indefinitely. If you force yourself to put each tool back in its place no matter how soon you expect to use it again, you may make a poor farmer but you will save yourself a vast amount of trouble. If you always throw back the bedclothes on rising and always leave your room in apple-pie order you will find that your briefs become more orderly and your statements more lucid than if each day gets off to a sloppy start. If you form a fixed habit of church-going, of saying your prayers, of morning exercise, of always taking the same train, of voting, of setting aside a liberal percentage of your income for charity and of keeping food and drink habits under control you will find, perhaps to your surprise, that it is really more fun to be a vertebrate than a mollusk.

Utilizing scraps of time is a most rewarding custom. Suburban trains yield a big opportunity for practicing it. Even a ten-minute trolley ride or the same time spent waiting for a train—or for a friend late at the point of meeting—gives you a chance to open your brief case and to make a tiny bit of progress on the matter in hand. Soon you learn never to deceive yourself by thinking that you are going to read a certain book or do this or that "when you have time." You will make up your mind that it is now—or never. Perhaps the only "out" on this advice is the fact that following it has produced this autobiography. It has been written in scraps of time. On reflection, however, it will be seen that I am not advising *how* it is worth-while to spend time that you save: I am merely pointing out a way to avoid a waste of precious minutes which in the aggregate make days and weeks and years.

My final bit of advice has a direct relation to working capacity. I long ago learned the art of sleeping at will. The two unrelenting enemies of sleep are memory and imagination. Place both of them in captivity, grin broadly—and off you go! To shackle memory I always repeat a poem long enough and complicated enough to engross attention but so well memorized as not to require conscious effort. For this purpose I use Francis Thompson's *Hound of Heaven.* To enchain imagination I keep the inward eye fixed on the trunk of an oak tree (not the whole tree— just the trunk) with attention riveted upon the roughness of the bark. The broad grin is to keep the brow from contracting and so to relax head and body muscles. Complicated? Yes—when described; but simple enough to apply if you mean business. It has seldom failed me in forty years. In the middle of a busy day I can tell the telephone operator to protect me, lock my door, stretch out either flat on the floor or on my office couch and out of fifteen minutes of relaxation get ten minutes of sleep. Whether this, or anything like it, was the system used by my uncle, Dr. William Pepper, I do not know. But he, too, could sleep at will; and in this, as in many things, I have tried to emulate him.

Here endeth my volunteered advice—with respect to which the gentle reader has the inalienable option either to take it or leave it.

THE THIRD AND FOURTH GENERATION

In 1943 my wife and I acquired new dignity on the eve [16] of the Feast of the Epiphany when Genie Newbold's wife Marion presented him— and the world—with a daughter. Thus to become great-grandparents means much to my wife and me, especially as the child bears the name of her father's mother, Eleanor Pepper Newbold. Our grand-daughter Charlotte Madeira has since presented us with a second great-grand-daughter. Feeling as vigorous and vital as I do it is hard to realize that the Golden Wedding Anniversary is a thing of the receding past and that the status of great-grandfather has now become a fact of the living present.

I believe that identification with the interests of children and grand-children has helped to keep me fit for the day's work. Association with them on a footing of comradeship brings refreshment of spirit and an infusion of youthful vitality. Adeline and George Jr. have been my com-panions on all sorts of winter and summer expeditions on land and water. Eleanor and I, in the joyful days when she was still with us, had as our Mt. Desert slogan, "A mountain a day keeps the tummy away." My son-in-law Eugene Newbold and I have had, and still have, many happy outdoor hours together. Of course a necessary incident of such relationships is intense concern for the welfare of each of the young people. I say "welfare" rather than "safety"—because "safety first" has always seemed to me to be an ignoble slogan; and if this be true in peacetime it is all the more so in time of war. I am happy in the confi-dence that each of the six grandsons will prove equal to any emergency with which he may be faced, as their fathers showed themselves to be when overseas in 1918. They have all been brought up in the country and have had plenty of rough camping. Several of them have unusual mechanical skill. The grandson who is now making airplane engines built, when fifteen years old, a fast nine-foot gasoline launch and, later, a sea-going motor boat. These were excellent pieces of work. At about the time he was making the smaller boat he and I together made in my carpenter shop a scale model of a destroyer. When he was planning the larger craft he asked me if I would be interested in helping. "Sure," said I. He was evidently pleased and handed me a copy of the *Popular Science Monthly* containing the plans and specifications which he had selected. "Study this for a couple of days," said he, "and then we can talk more intelligently."

[16] January 5.

PART FIVE

The Things That Truly Last

"Heroic daring and the imponderables of high civilization were
the inheritance they (the Athenians) were born to."
—EDITH HAMILTON: *The Great Age of Greek
Literature*, page 116

1. THE CHURCH

THE word "Church" has for me, at seventy-seven, a meaning different
from its meaning when I was twenty-one. Then it was the Protestant Episcopal Church in general and St. Mark's Parish in particular.
Today it is a collective name for all who are willing to be counted in
the company of Our Lord's disciples. Then the Episcopal Church was a
great and satisfying reality and other groups of Christians seemed remote
and unreal. Today all Christian groups seem to me like dwellers in so
many mansions in the Father's House, although often tragically unaware
that spiritually they are neighbors. Accordingly when a serious proposal
is made to translate unrealized neighborliness into an actual working
relationship, I am at once predisposed to accept it. If, on analysis, I am
convinced that the proposal calls for no sacrifice by either group of
inherent elements of spiritual strength, then I make my acceptance definite. The proposal for the Joint Ordination of the clergy of the Episcopal
and Presbyterian Churches is a case in point. I am satisfied that neither

group by accepting the plan would do injury to any of the convictions essential to its own well-being. I am sure that to such fellowship as would result, each constituent can make a notable contribution and that the common life will be immensely strengthened and enriched.

I have come to this conclusion by a process like that which an anthropologist applies in order to find out what we Americans and other races respectively have to contribute to building the world anew after victory has made building possible. A study of this sort has been made by Margaret Mead[1] and she is hopeful that by pooling resources of every sort the people of the world will be able to build "something which combines with all we have learned through the ages, a way of life of which no man has even dreamed." This is like my vision of Church Unity. If I am asked which vision, hers or mine, is more likely to be realized, I answer that mine is, because common devotion to the Person of Our Lord is a more powerful centripetal force than that engendered by fear of other wars or by the hope of attaining some common good not yet expressed in definite terms. If the anthropologist challenges my reply and points to the waning authority of the Church and the loss of its hold on the young, my answer will be that no shortcomings can be charged against the Church that are comparable to the failures of Economics, of Political Science and of Sociology. The bickerings of bishops seem to me less serious than the self-deception of statesmen. It would be unintelligent and most discouraging to assert that a better world order is unattainable; but I deem it neither unintelligent nor discouraging to predict that Church Unity must precede the other. If postwar reconstruction is a vague conception, what the Church has to offer is definite and soul-satisfying. When we come to our senses it will be to our spiritual senses that we come first. So believing, I am consistent in placing the Church at the head of my list of Things That Truly Last.

EARLY EXPERIENCES

It must not be inferred from what I have written that I have outgrown early teachings or in any sense repudiated them. What has come about is an emphasis on affirmatives and a loss of confidence in mere negations. I value my early teaching so highly that I want to share it with all who come my way. The process has been a normal and, as I believe, a wholesome evolution.

[1] *And Keep Your Powder Dry*, by Margaret Mead, William Morrow & Co., New York, 1942.

In my childhood and youth the Church in general and St. Mark's Parish in particular were daily subjects of conversation at my mother's table. Parish boundaries were my ecclesiastical horizon until in 1895 I first sat in the convention of the diocese as a deputy from my parish. I had become a member of the vestry in 1892 and later was made accounting warden. Successive annual re-elections prolonged for a period of forty years my service as a deputy to the diocesan convention. At the time of writing I have been a vestryman for fifty years and rector's warden for more than twenty.

Order, form and color have always made to me a strong appeal. From my boyhood onward I found great satisfaction in the church services and especially in the service of Holy Communion. Both before, during and after college days I made it a practice to attend several early morning services through the week as well as on Sundays. In Lent daily attendance was a fixed habit. For many years I served as an acolyte. I was responsive to the influence of church music but never had enough of a singing voice to be a member of the choir. For a number of years I was its librarian and sat vested in the stalls with the other boys. I readily conformed to the ceremonial practices which became the custom of the parish. For many years genuflections, the making of the sign of the Cross and other ceremonial acts were with me a matter of course. As time passed, however, I became convinced that inward spiritual growth was not keeping pace with proficiency in things symbolic and external. As I seemed unable to "force" the requisite inward growth, I made up my mind to abandon outward practices that were tending to become unreal. I have never regretted this decision, although at the time it was hard to make and harder to carry into effect. This change in religious habits did not in the least diminish my love for services conducted in accordance with ceremonial standards which I personally was unable to reach. I became, however, much more responsive than ever before to the power of services conducted with the utmost simplicity. In my old age, while elaborate ceremonial is still my preference, I can get genuine satisfaction from services conducted in the manner characteristic of the Reformed Churches.

At the same time, I have become sensitive to the presence or absence in the clergy of that spiritual quality without which ceremonial observance is a mockery. Moreover, there are certain ceremonial practices which are affronts to common sense. I refer particularly to the usage which requires the celebrant in the Communion Office to turn his back to the people when reading the Epistle and the Gospel. This accords to the Word of God a treatment less favorable than that which the preacher insists upon for his own sermon. Considerations like these explain, I think, why I have never been a member of a "High Church" or "Anglo-Catholic" *party.* I have been conscious of no affinity with a particular group merely because its members professed certain theological beliefs or conformed to certain ceremonial practices. When the Anglo-Catholic movement was in its early stages one of its enthusiastic leaders pleaded with Francis A. Lewis, who was influential in the councils of the Diocese of Pennsylvania, for the representation of his party on the diocesan deputation to General Convention. "George Pepper is a deputy," was the answer. "What more do you want?" "Pepper!" came the scornful reply. "Why he's not a High Churchman: he's a kind of Methodist."

The convention thus referred to was one of the triennial conventions of the Protestant Episcopal Church which, in accordance with the constitution of that body, has since 1789 met every three years at some predetermined point in the United States. The Convention of 1901 met in San Francisco. One of its duties was to elect for the ensuing triennium the bishops, presbyters and laymen constituting the Board of Missions. This board was the administrative agency of the Episcopal Church for the management and supervision of missions, both domestic and foreign. I was not a deputy to the convention but much to my surprise was elected a lay member of the board. My friend John W. Wood, the Board's executive secretary, satisfied me that acceptance was in the line of duty. Thereafter for more than twenty years I served as a member of the board which, by action of the General Convention of 1919, was converted into the National Council of the Episcopal Church.

The same convention which elected me chose Charles Henry Brent to be Missionary Bishop to the Philippines. I came under his influence shortly after his election and we became friends for life.

WHAT ABOUT MISSIONS?

The mere presence in a household or community of a man like Bishop Brent acts like a spiritual vitamin. In time everybody within reach is vitalized. The oft-discussed question "Are Missions Worth While?" is therefore reducible to a question of fact: Can enough men and women of his type be found to justify an organized effort to send them out? Once on the ground their daily lives can be counted upon to do the rest. My own experience (quite independently of missionary history) compels an affirmative answer to the question. Bishop William Hobart Hare among the Indians, Bishop Peter Trimble Rowe in Alaska, Bishop Channing M. Williams and Bishop Henry St. George Tucker in Japan, Bishop F. R. Graves, Dr. F. L. Hawkes Pott and Edmund Lee Woodward in China, all personal friends of mine,[2] in their time enriched the life and promoted the happiness of untold thousands. The tens of thousands of dollars which during forty years I have raised and given for the work of these men seem to me in retrospect to have been money spent to maximum advantage. In so saying I am referring to the impact of their Christian lives upon those among whom these men lived. The invaluable service of medical missionaries is quite another story. Wilfred Grenfell in Labrador, Rudolph Teusler in Tokyo and Josiah McCracken in Shanghai combined in notable degree the blessings of simple Christian faith and of effective medical and surgical service; but with them their ministrations to the body were incidental to a deeper concern for the inward happiness of the patient.

Sometimes people indict missionary effort as an impertinence. It is a sufficient answer to say that there is nothing impertinent in giving to a disciple of Confucius or of Buddha a fair chance to compare a Christian life with his own. A young Chinese student who had been exposed to Christian teaching put it thus: "If this is not true, no matter; but if it *is* true, nothing else matters." He had detected the element in Christianity which differentiates it from other religions, namely, the fact that it claims to be a direct relationship to God as revealed in the Person of Our Lord. Those who have experienced the reality of the relationship are under a double compulsion to proclaim it. Such men as I have named had heard the inward call to bear witness to their faith and nothing could have held them back from the uttermost parts of the earth. If begged first to minister to people at home they would have had an even more convincing answer than that which our military men can give when urged to defend this continent without crossing the seas. As Bishop Brent was wont to say, "My call is to serve the weakest and the farthest."

THE BOARD OF MISSIONS

To further the efforts of such men seemed to me then and seems to me now a high privilege. The meetings of the Board of Missions were held monthly at the Church Missions House in New York. I found myself a member of an exceedingly interesting group of men over whom my

[2] Except Bishop Williams, who was before my time. He built his Cathedral Church in Tokyo chiefly by denying himself one meal a day for a long series of years. Bishop Schereschewsky, in China, translated the Bible into Mandarin, a work of rare scholarship and of inestimable value.

old friend Bishop William Croswell Doane presided. The greater part of the work was done by committees. I served for years as a member of the Committee on China and Japan, under the chairmanship of Dr. William Nelson McVickar, Bishop of Rhode Island. One of my colleagues on this committee was Captain (afterward Admiral) Alfred T. Mahan, the great naval authority and author of the epoch-making work on *The Influence of Sea Power on History*. Captain Mahan and I became close friends and I profited much by my association with him. His advocacy of imperialism at first impressed me greatly. In later life I have come to regard it with distrust. Incidentally, I acquired through service on this committee much valuable information about life in the Orient and formed many lasting friendships with the bishops, clergy and lay workers who were rendering self-sacrificing and effective service in that part of the world.

Sometimes, at a meeting of the Board, I would try to brighten things up a little by writing a verse or making a sketch and circulating it among the assembled dignitaries. Some of the Bishops stood upon their dignity and liked to be addressed, in the English fashion, by the names of their sees. Not so Bishop Millspaugh of Kansas who was a wholesome, unaffected man with a large head and a big crop of hair. When sitting in a chair with a wide and high wooden back nothing of him was visible to me who sat behind him except the curve of his chair and masses of wiry hair radiating from a common center like the rays of a setting sun. Knowing that he would take it in good part, I one day made a sketch of this phenomenon and wrote under it "What's the matter with Kansas?" As the sketch passed from hand to hand there were successive explosions of laughter and Kansas was as noisy as anybody.

"WHAT'S THE MATTER WITH KANSAS?"

I have made a good many sketches while sitting in meetings. At all sorts of times and in all sorts of places I have jotted down verses and passed them around. If all these were to be assembled they would make a nonsense anthology of considerable bulk.

GENERAL CONVENTION

In 1904 I first went as a deputy to a triennial General Convention of the Episcopal Church. In that year the Convention met in Boston and was made notable by the presence of the Archbishop of Canterbury, Dr. Randall Thomas Davidson. Mrs. Pepper and I had been fortunate enough to spend some time in companionship with him and his wife at Northeast Harbor where in the summer of 1904 he had been the guest of Bishop William Croswell Doane. I recall vividly the sermon he preached at St. Mary's-by-the-Sea, from the text, "None of us liveth unto himself and no man dieth unto himself." As he finished he paused for a moment and said with evident feeling: "Suffer these words, I pray you, from one to whom his first Sunday in your great country is a moving and stimulating occasion brimful of suggestiveness and hope, and accept at his hands a grateful blessing and a brotherly God-speed." These simple words were spoken with such obvious depth of feeling that we were all made conscious of the essential spiritual unity of those who share the Anglican tradition.

At a joint session of the House of Bishops and the House of Clerical and Lay Deputies the Archbishop of Canterbury made a moving address. Under such circumstances one feels in fullest measure the power of an ancient office worthily filled. When he had finished we all rose to our feet. Without prearrangement a deputy near me suddenly began to sing the plain-song *Gloria in Excelsis*. Instantly the whole great assemblage took up the chant and sang with might and main. It was a noble chorus. Many of us, and I among others, felt lifted high above earth for a while as if we were members of an angelic choir. It was one of the great moments of life.

Incidents such as this are rare. Nevertheless, in both Diocesan and General Conventions, even routine business is not without interest. Occasionally there is a brilliant debate and now and then an amusing parliamentary situation.

In 1907 I went as a deputy to the General Convention which in that year met in Richmond. That charming town was not big enough to be indifferent to the Convention. The whole town was thoroughly aroused by the proceedings and tendered true Southern hospitality to everybody. I had the delightful experience of being a guest at Brook Hill, where the Stewart sisters kept open house. Cultivated and witty, unbelievably considerate and thoughtful, these maiden ladies made the stay of each guest a memorable experience. Under their roof I first met their nephew John Stewart Bryan, then an attractive lad and later the talented president of William and Mary. During a later visit to Brook Hill I was quartered in a sort of tower room of unusual shape on the top floor of the big rambling house. They called it "The Prophet's Chamber." In an alcove, concealed by an intervening curtain, was a glorious big four-poster in which, after a strenuous day, one slept like a log. When I appeared at breakfast on the first morning of my visit the sisters in chorus asked how I had slept and almost before I could answer they all began to laugh. Then they explained that the last occupant of the room had been an English archdeacon who had brought letters to them. On his first morning they had asked him the same question and he had answered in evident gloom. Pressed for the whole truth he had finally "come clean." "For the sake of future guests," said he, "I think I ought to tell you that there is no bed in the room." Of a less adventurous spirit than some English explorers, he had not drawn that curtain or discovered the bed and had passed a miserable night in an armchair.

A lot of interesting people attended the Convention. The Bishop of London, Dr. Winnington Ingram, was the most distinguished of the visitors from abroad. He preached a notable sermon at the opening service. Pierpont Morgan, the elder, was a deputy from the Diocese of New York and, as always, the object of much attention. As was his custom, he had leased a house for the period of the Convention and after each day's adjournment he could be seen on his piazza rocking lazily in a big chair.

The three years following the Richmond Convention passed like a watch in the night. In the autumn of 1910, the year in which I had spent so much time and effort in the Ballinger case, I went as a deputy to Cincinnati where the General Convention of 1910 assembled. The two men with whom at this time I was most sympathetic and most closely associated were Robert Hallowell Gardiner who sat as a lay deputy from Maine and Charles Henry Brent, Missionary Bishop of the Philippines. I had known the Bishop ever since his election nine years earlier and had come to revere him as I have revered few other men. We always welcomed him under our roof as a well-beloved guest and our children shared our devotion to him. I zealously supported the work in his field, where without fault on his part ecclesiastical hostilities were unhappily much in evidence; and he, Gardiner and I were consequently filled with eagerness to promote a better understanding among Christians of many names. It was in the hope that the unifying influence of the Episcopal Church might thereby be increased that all three of us favored the omission of the word "Protestant" from the Church's official title.[3] I led the movement in the House of Deputies. After a debate which was happily devoid of all bitterness the proposal for change was defeated by a small margin. This outcome was not without its advantages. Opponents of the proposal would have felt bitterly had it carried. Its advocates were happy over the strength they had developed. The good-tempered discussion of the issue had made everybody happy.

One evening walking back from the convention hall to the hotel we three were reviewing the change-of-name controversy and the whole problem of Christian Unity. Said the Bishop, "There never can be an approach toward unity until we all discuss our differences as well as our agreements. We must drag our differences out of the shadow and bring them into the sunlight." We all three stood still. "Why not agitate for that very thing?" I asked. "Why not advocate a world conference on questions of faith and order?" suggested Gardiner. "We cannot begin too soon," said the Bishop; "there is no time like the present; but we must make it clear that our purpose is to exclude the promotion of any scheme of unity and merely to create better mutual understanding by a frank discussion of different points of view." Before we parted for the night the Bishop had undertaken to open the subject with Doctor Manning, then Rector of Trinity Church, New York, who, we were sure, would be a valuable ally. The next day Bishop Brent reported that Doctor Manning had espoused our cause with heartiness; and immediately thereafter the latter offered in the House of Deputies a resolution for the appointment of a Commission on Faith and Order. Doctor Manning's fellow-deputy from New York, Pierpont Morgan (the elder), was always receptive when a statesmanlike proposal was made and invariably generous in backing it up with an offer of financial support. As soon, therefore, as the Manning resolution was offered Mr. Morgan expressed enthusiastic approval and at once offered $100,000 to meet the expenses incident to effective organization. The proposal to create a Commission

[3] It seemed to us that the Episcopal Church might thus make a more effective approach to the Roman Catholic and Holy Orthodox Churches without appreciably weakening the ties that bind us to the Reformed Churches.

on a World Conference of Faith and Order was welcomed by both
Houses, the necessary resolutions were passed with unanimity and a
Commission of Bishops, Presbyters and laymen was duly appointed. On
this Commission Bishop Brent and Robert Gardiner labored zealously
all the rest of their lives. I was for many years an active member of it
and withdrew only when service in the Senate prevented me from doing
my share of the work. The movement thus begun has already more than
fulfilled the hopes of its originators. It continues to be a power for good
in the Christian world.

"That young man Pepper is an impudent chap," Mr. Morgan remarked
one day during the Convention to my friend Frank Lewis who of course
gleefully reported the remark to me. Mr. Morgan and I were fellow-
members of the Committee on Amendments to the Constitution. At one
of our meetings he had made a suggestion which I thought unsound.
He asked his colleagues on the committee what they thought of it.
Nobody else spoke; so I said, "That seems to me to be well worth considering." "Very condescending of the young man," Mr. Morgan said to
my friend, "to concede that a proposal of mine was worth considering."
The great man was accustomed, I suppose, to have all his proposals met
with a chorus of yeses.

COMMISSIONS AND COMMITTEES

My duties at this period included those of Accounting Warden of St.
Mark's and of a Vestryman of St. James the Less and of the Church of
the Good Shepherd, Rosemont. I carried, too, about a dozen serious responsibilities that resulted from activities in General Convention. Thus
I saw plenty of active service on a number of commissions some of which
were well worth while.[4] My work as a member of the Board of Missions
was continuous and exacting. To the Brotherhood of St. Andrew I gave
freely of effort and substance; as also to the Church Club of Philadelphia
of which later I was president. I became interested in the Federal Council
of Churches, although my enthusiasm for it was later abated when its
officials insisted upon taking sides on the League of Nations issue.

Work on the Prisons Committee of the Church Club was in line with

[4] The list, as nearly as I can recall, was as follows: Christian Unity, Revision
of the Lectionary, Preparation of a Mission Hymnal, Revision and Enrichment
of the Prayer Book, Missionary Organization and Administration, World Conference on Faith and Order, Registration of Communicants, and the Increase and
Development of the Diaconate.

an interest which for a long time absorbed much of my time and energy and continues to absorb some of each. I do not remember just what first led me to concern myself about prisoners in the Eastern Penitentiary, but for many years I was a constant visitor to the prison and took a friendly interest in a considerable number of men among the prisoners. With some of them who became self-respecting citizens I maintained friendly relations as long as they lived. One of these men, an Englishman, while still in jail besought me to visit his parents in a certain city in the north of England. When I was abroad in 1912 I there found an elderly couple, highly respectable and intensely proud, who had managed to conceal from their neighbors the fact of their son's disgrace. I was able to be of some comfort to them and carried back to the boy messages more eloquent than any that letters could convey. "Bob" McKenty, at that time the Warden, was my warm friend and all my work among the prisoners was done with his full approval. It had been his observation that burglars are the most difficult of all criminals to reclaim. I suppose this is because they are at the same time big game hunters and gamblers for high stakes. The thirst for dangerous adventure and the yearning to get something for nothing are appetites not easily controlled.

TRIAL AND ERROR

The current discussion [5] of reunion between the Presbyterian and Episcopal Churches leads me to mention here the "Stonemen's Fellowship." This organization had its origin in a men's club with small membership formed a few years earlier by the Rev. H. Charles Stone, Minister in charge of Holy Trinity Memorial Chapel, an integral part of Holy Trinity (Episcopal) parish in Philadelphia. Under the impetus given by the Billy Sunday Campaign the club grew to large proportions and, during the Lenten season of 1915, its members resolved to increase their enrollment to one thousand. This they did and Stone, somewhat startled at the rapid growth, asked my advice respecting the future of the Club. On Easter Even the members attended a Confirmation service conducted by Bishop Philip M. Rhinelander in Holy Trinity Chapel. After the service I addressed those present, urged the formation of a fellowship upon a definitely religious basis and offered to give any help requested. About seven hundred men subsequently signed a petition asking me to co-operate with Mr. Stone and prepare a plan. Shortly thereafter I submitted to a

[5] 1940-1943.

large representative committee of "Stonemen" a plan which was forthwith adopted as the basis of their future association.

The essence of this plan was to lead men by steps, or degrees, from a simple affirmation of belief in God to a confession of faith in Christ and finally to the Lord's Supper conceived of as the Sacred Rite of the Fellowship. The First Degree was a solemn service of enrollment and of self-dedication. The Second Degree was baptism for the unbaptized and, for those already baptized, a renewal of their baptismal vows. The aim of the Third Degree was to admit men to the Sacred Rite according to a form which, as it seemed to me, should satisfy the religious convictions of all non-Roman Christians.

According to the plan, the form of taking the Third Degree was the Apostolic Rite of Laying on of Hands by the Bishop of Pennsylvania, who was to be the Honorary Chaplain of the Fellowship. An appropriate Third Degree service was planned as well for those who had theretofore received "Episcopal Confirmation" as for those who had not. Emphasis was laid on the fact that men taking the Third Degree did not thereby repudiate their denominational connections. It was not intended that anybody should "become an Episcopalian," or that any Episcopal parish should receive accessions of men drawn from other communions. The Fellowship merely announced that if all men were willing to add to their existing professions a recognition of the *fact* of episcopacy, a way to Corporate Communion would thereby be opened without discussion of denominational differences. It was this conception of common participation in the great rite of the Christian faith that was the essence of the whole plan. If the Fellowship had been merely a league of men who met in order to be exhorted to go back to a multitude of different churches and there make their communions separately, the organization would quickly disintegrate. The same thing would have been true if an attempt had been made to secure in rotation ministers of various churches to officiate at the religious services of the Fellowship. Immediate discussions would have arisen respecting the matters that divide church from church. In order to accomplish its aim the Fellowship had to be content to be called narrow and its leaders had to face the unpleasant fact that some would impugn their motives.

The Fellowship had an amazing growth and soon numbered many thousands of men with an average weekly attendance of 3,000. I had high hopes of its usefulness and I still believe that the central idea has great possibilities. Little pamphlets containing services appropriate to each degree were prepared by me and used with good effect. During my absence in camp at Plattsburg a movement was started inside the Fellowship to use it for the purpose of promoting the political candidacy of one of its members for Mayor. This destructive movement quickly took on an anti-Catholic character and, contrary to anything I had imagined possible, soon so colored the whole organization as to destroy its usefulness. As there was no way to stem the tide of sectarian prejudice thus developed I sorrowfully withdrew and confessed failure. It was nevertheless charged against me in a political campaign ten years later that I had endorsed the Stonemen's Fellowship in a spirit of hostility to the Roman Church.

I have never abandoned the hope that somewhere and under more favorable conditions the plan of the Fellowship might be revived. If it were, and could be kept out of politics, it would be a powerful agency for closer union among Christians of various communions. This, I take it, is the theory upon which reunion between the Presbyterian and Episcopal Churches is now being pressed.

BACK TO CONVENTION

Some exacting legal work and, later, my term in the Senate, led me to decline election as a deputy to General Convention in 1919, 1922 and 1925. In 1928 it seemed best to serve again and to attend the Convention which met that year in Washington. Most of my old friends had passed on but there were two phases of the work which interested me greatly. One was the debate on pending changes in the Book of Common Prayer. The other was the evident tendency among certain of the clergy to assign moral or spiritual significance to secular legislation and to international organization. My views on these and other matters of importance were those of only a minority in the Convention. Most of the measures which I opposed were approved. The suspicion dawned upon me that everybody in the regiment was out of step but me.

I was unable to take part in the 1931 meeting but decided to attend the triennial Convention of 1934 which met in October at Atlantic City. It was to be my seventh and last. My purpose was to find out definitely how great the gulf might be between my view of the nature and mission of the Church and the view of those who are most numerous and most vocal in her councils. The gulf was found to be impassable. There was an obvious determination to use the various agencies of the Church for what seemed to me purely secular purposes. As somebody has acutely observed: "We are the *res*olutionary sons of *rev*olutionary fathers." There had been general recognition, when Prayer Book changes were under consideration, that there was something incongruous in the English system which leaves the final decision respecting such changes to a secular Parliament. It seems to me just as incongruous to stage in church conventions a debate and to pass resolutions on the relative merits of open and closed shop and of membership or nonmembership in the League of Nations. I found the mealymouthed utterances of some of the bishops and other clergy extremely irritating and made up my mind that such a gathering was no place for me.

It is too much to expect that the course of true religion will be any smoother than the course of true love. I had often noted, in studying the law of torts, that many of the early cases on assault and battery had their beginning in English vestry meetings. My own experience with vestries has been a happy one. But there have been many occasions in Convention when I sighed for ordeal by battle. While visiting in Northiam, Sussex, in the summer of 1934, I listened to the tale of woe of a devout member of a neighboring parish who complained that the bishop had appointed an impossible person to the living. It is probable, however, that there was another side to the story; because when the parish finally got rid of him the man of God published an account of his experiences under the suggestive caption, *Five Years of Hell in a Sussex Parish*.

PAROCHIAL LOYALTY

For my part, my own parish church, St. Mark's, will always command my primary allegiance. The church building, erected in 1848, stood at that date almost alone on the western frontier of Philadelphia. Today it is a mid-city church, surrounded by structures which tower above it. They may scrape the sky; but I am sure that the spire of St. Mark's penetrates it. It was built in the days of the Gothic revival. Nottman was the architect. He adapted designs furnished by the Ecclesiological Society of England and produced a churchly building of indescribable charm. It has about it many elements of architectural beauty which, always against my protest, have been marred by some modern and ill-advised changes. As a vestryman for more than half a century and as warden for nearly as long, I have had with the parish the happiest associations. The present Rector, the Rev. Frank L. Vernon, is my very dear friend. To work under his leadership is a most inspiring experience.[6]

[6] Since this was written Doctor Vernon died after an illness induced by overwork. The responsibility of succeeding him has been accepted by Rev. William H. Dunphy, under whose leadership we hope to do useful parish work.

In the early morning communion service at St. Mark's it has always been easy to find refreshment for the spirit. Practically everybody who has made a habit of attendance on such services will, I think, give the same testimony.

While nearly all regular communicants will give such testimony as I have suggested, there is the greatest divergence when you ask them to rationalize their feelings. I here set down the analysis of Holy Communion which I personally have worked out for myself after years of pondering.

Whenever a tangible, external object becomes the symbol of an idea or of a personality, each disciple is apt to interpret the symbol in the light of his own temperament and imaginative power. "The Stars and Stripes" is the symbol of National Unity. To loyal A it is a piece of bunting, pretty to look at and easy to wave. If the symbol is desecrated, A is righteously indignant—but that is all. To loyal B the Flag is a thing so sacred that he not only salutes *it,* but if anyone pollutes *it,* B is transformed into an avenging fury. He thinks lynching is too mild a punishment for the desecration. He identifies the Flag with his Fatherland.

When Our Lord took bread, brake it and said, "This is my body: do this in remembrance of me," He then and there instituted a ceremony which was to be perpetually repeated as a means of vitalizing the spiritual relation between Himself and His disciples. Instantly there arose the possibility on the part of the disciples of a variety of subjective apprehensions of the function of the sacramental bread. The possibility of varying apprehensions doubtless never became a fact while the Lord was still visibly present. Under such conditions the ceremony meant merely that He seemed nearest to them when they were breaking bread together. It was only after the Ascension that occasion for varieties of apprehension could arise.

When the ceremony was performed after the Ascension loyal A found it easier then and there to remember Our Lord than by the mere process of abstract meditation. The bread became in his estimation the equivalent of the sword of a dead hero which the son cherishes as a means of stimulating his memory of his father. The process in each case is wholly subjective: A and the son remember. The bread and the sword are merely precious aids to their memory.

Loyal B, however, was much more imaginative. Performance of the ceremony gave him such a sense of nearness to his Master that memory was forgotten in the actual experience of a present communion between his little self and his great Leader. The bread seemed to him not an aid

to memory of a past transaction or of an absent Person; it was the glow-
ing symbol of a Presence so immediate and real that there lacked nothing but the physical touch of the Master's hand on the disciple's head.

But loyal C was more imaginative still. The Presence was so sensibly
real that the Bread in his estimation must have ceased to be bread and
to have become, as a physical fact, the Body of the Lord. When the consecrated element had thus ceased to be a *symbol* of Reality and had become Reality itself, transubstantiation was complete. That which was
placed in the disciple's hand at the altar rail still looked like bread but
it had ceased to be such and had become Body.

The case of A, B and C which I have thus stated may be expressed as
follows:

A's conception is of a memorial ceremony, corresponding in a general
way to a service in memory of the Father of his Country. Little significance is attached by A to the authority of the celebrant or to the bread
and wine.

B's conception stands between the two extremes of A and C: a transaction much more significant than an appeal to memory but definitely
excluding any miraculous transformation of bread into flesh; a transaction in which emphasis is placed both on the Spiritual Presence and on
the special sanctity of the Symbol of Presence—to wit, the sacramental
bread and wine.

C, on the other hand, conceives of the Sacrament as a miracle in the
physical world, unique in experience and presupposing on the part of the
celebrant an official commission from the Almighty to work the miracle.

A's conception is that of Zwingli and of the other Swiss Reformers.
C's is that of the Church of Rome. B's conception is that of the Church
of England and of the Protestant Episcopal Church in the U.S.A.

This, however, is only a preliminary statement. Within the limits of
B's conception there is much room for further analysis. Imagine a straight
horizontal line, A—C, and imagine B as a point which moves along that
line in either direction without ever reaching either extremity. As B
moves toward A, emphasis on the memorial character of the Eucharist
becomes greater and the sanctity of the symbol tends to disappear. As
B moves toward C, emphasis on the Reality of Christ's Presence increases
and identification of that Presence with the Consecrated Elements approaches its maximum. In the estimation of those most responsive to
Reformation influences, B should always be tending toward A. According
to Anglo-Catholic teaching, B should always be approaching C while

never reaching it, the conception being essentially spiritual and in no degree carnal.

The position of the Church of England and of the Episcopal Church, midway between extremes, is unacceptable to people who by temperament are eager to press a conception to its limit. On the other hand, it is attractive and satisfying to all those who instinctively recoil from extremes and find wisdom in the old Greek proverb "Nothing too much." After all is said, however, it is not in analysis but in actual experience that the power of the Sacrament is to be found. No Christian system that minimizes or ignores this experience will long prove to be soul-satisfying. The Sacrament is the ready instrument for converting mysticism into power.

WASHINGTON CATHEDRAL

Among the most satisfying collects in the Book of Common Prayer is that in which we ask God to grant unto His people that they may love the thing which He commands and desire that which He has promised —"that so, among the sundry and manifold changes of the world, our hearts may surely there be fixed where true joys are to be found." Things commanded surely include service to one's fellows and things promised must certainly comprehend the inward peace which follows service faithfully performed. As for me, I know of no service which more surely "fixes the heart" upon durable satisfactions than to help build a spiritual powerhouse and set it to work for all time to come. This is said not to belittle the social services but to reaffirm my conviction that man's fundamental interest is his relationship to the Unseen.

Mount St. Alban, on which Washington Cathedral stands, is one of those sites which seem preordained for occupation by a great church. The sites of many of the Old World Cathedrals were occupied by earlier Christian churches and in some instances these had succeeded still earlier temples of other faiths. In such cases some principle of natural selection is evidently at work and the elements that determine selection are surely present in the case of Mount St. Alban. It has height and charm and accessibility. It lends itself to the sort of development that emphasizes the natural beauties of a wooded hillside. I find great significance in its relation to the rest of the city of Washington. From the eminence on which the Peace Cross stands one sees the city spread out before him. Stately as is the Capitol and imposing as is the Washington Monument it seems altogether appropriate that the Cathedral should tower above them both.

It was in March of 1899 that I first took an active interest in Washington Cathedral. The Rt. Rev. Dr. Henry Yates Satterlee, first Bishop of Washington, had successfully advocated a change of site for the future structure from the middle of the city to Mount St. Alban. In spite of bitter opposition, he had persevered in his plan and had in 1898 acquired the splendid tract of land which is now the Cathedral Close.

In 1898, to mark the end of the war with Spain, the great Peace Cross was erected on Mount St. Alban and consecrated with appropriate ceremony. President McKinley attended the service and reverently took part in it. Standing beside this Cross one looks down upon the Capital City and his eyes rest at once upon its most conspicuous structures, the Capitol and the Washington Monument. The Psalmist exclaimed in sorrow, "I labor for peace, but when I speak to them thereof they make them ready to battle." When in the thirties statesmen professing a desire for peace were all the while making provocative utterances, I often wished that they would labor in silence. If there had been fewer such utterances and more silent prayer at the foot of the Peace Cross the outlook for the world might now be a happier one. I have a fundamental distrust of the diplomacy of denunciation and a firm belief in the efficacy of prayer.

It has been for me a fascinating experience to watch the transformation which has taken place since I first knew Mount St. Alban. At the outset came the study and work which necessarily preceded actual construction. Instead of seeking competitive designs from various architects Bishop Satterlee and his colleagues wisely decided, first, to determine the style of architecture of the future building and then unhesitatingly to retain the architect who was confessedly master of that style. It was accordingly decided to build in conformity with thirteenth and fourteenth century Gothic and this decision led to the selection of Dr. George F. Bodley, the noted English architect, with whom was associated his pupil Henry Vaughan of Boston. These men are entitled to the credit of the original design. After their death the Cathedral authorities were fortunate in securing worthy successors in the person of Messrs. Frohman, Robb and Little, likewise of Boston.

In 1907 the Cathedral cornerstone was laid. Then the Apse reared itself heavenward and the Great Choir came to its support. Next the dream of the North Transept happily came true. Then were built the Crossing and the beginnings of the Nave and of the South Transept. Meanwhile, beneath the great Church, the three chapels were being completed, little sanctuaries which speak, respectively, of Birth, Death

WASHINGTON CATHEDRAL: DEDICATING THE PILGRIM STEPS

and Resurrection. The great crypts were tunneling their way from the Crossing to the distant point at which the Western Towers will rise. All this construction was the work of masons and sculptors. There is no steel in the vast structure save the rafters that carry the roof.[7] A complete iconographic scheme has been followed throughout. It conforms architecturally to the Gothic tradition; and even John of Damascus himself could find no fault with its theological content. Deep thought, exhaustive study, anxious experiment and earnest discussion have yielded stained glass of which all satisfies some and of which some satisfies me. We have learned that, as far as color is concerned, latitude is a factor of great importance. Glass that satisfies in the latitude (say) of York looks thin and lifeless in the brilliant atmosphere of Washington. It is to glass in the comparable latitude of the Spanish Cathedrals, and particularly of Leon, that we look for suggestion and guidance. Dependence on the primary colors, avoidance or definite subordination of green, grisaille and violet and the elimination of all white or colorless glass have become articles in our stained glass creed. James Sheldon, a lifelong student of the subject, has been an important factor in our education in this field. Behind and above the High Altar a noble reredos has been created. As designed the reredos was surmounted by light and graceful pinnacles which invited the eye to look higher and higher, as is appropriate in a shrine of mystery. Unfortunately the architect was directed to omit these from the final design, with the result that a rigid and confining "sky line" was substituted for limitless aspiration. This serious defect will, I hope, be corrected at some time or other. The notes of a deep-voiced organ reverberate through long-drawn aisle and fretted vault. A massive pulpit, the gift of the Dean and Chapter of Canterbury Cathedral, gives to the preacher a point of vantage from which to proclaim the Living Word. A good beginning has been made in developing a worthy choir. Here is an appealing opportunity to create and maintain a standard of church music equal to that which is the glory of English cathedral worship.

Under the shadow of the Cathedral itself other creations have been brought into being. I have watched the building of the College of Preachers, the beginnings of the Library and the development of St. Alban's School for Boys and of the National Cathedral School for Girls. I have

---

[7] The wooden beams carrying the leaden roofs of Old World Cathedrals are supposed to have been centers of combustion. The number of such churches destroyed by fire is very large.

seen a barren hillside transformed in the course of a few years into a Garden of the Ages. In the open air amphitheater (or, rather, on the hillside which it will some day occupy) I have seen congregations of more than twenty thousand people and on occasion I have actually addressed such. The finished portion of the Cathedral has enfolded nearly four thousand worshipers at a single Easter service and hundreds of thousands of pilgrims have from time to time passed reverently through the great

THE COMPLETED CATHEDRAL—
AS MY GRANDCHILDREN MAY SEE IT

building. Does anyone wonder that to have had a part in the work of bringing all this, and more, to pass seems to me an experience not to be exchanged for any other?

I reckon among the blessings of my life the preservation of a simple faith. Had I been endowed with greater intellectual powers or had I been less fortunate in my early training or if for action I had substituted a habit of speculation, I might have been tossed hither and thither by the winds of strange doctrine. In that event I should have lost the faith of my childhood and gained nothing in exchange. There is something tragic in the spectacle of a man of intellect who has no fixed religious beliefs and rather wistfully confesses his longing for them. Happiness does not appear to be the lot of such. I fancy, for example, that I detect a certain undercurrent of sadness in the writings of Mr. Justice Holmes. Among my friends, irrespective of their age, I often hear the sighful wish expressed that they could share the certainty of my beliefs.

As time sweeps on and comrades fall away and vital energy wanes those who wholeheartedly accept the Christian philosophy of life, no matter how imperfectly their beliefs are translated into action, should be profoundly grateful for an unspeakable blessing. "The consolations of religion" are then perceived to be something much more substantial than a mere form of words. The historic Creeds of Christendom are in that case found sufficient to satisfy all one's yearnings for present peace and all one's cravings for certainty about the future. In particular the inward conviction of personal immortality draws the sting of death and the prospect of reunion with those loved long since and lost a while makes all the difference between gloom and good cheer. I have reflected that the prenatal stage of life was all sleeping and that this present stage is half waking and half sleeping. I expect the next step to be all waking. As birth and death are universal I cannot think of either as an evil. I claim for myself a place in the scheme of things at least as significant as that which this year's spring accords to the bulb which through the winter Mother Earth has conserved. From time to time I have rationalized my beliefs; but all the while I have realized that the beliefs were mine before I assigned a reason for them. I was a loyal American before I studied the Constitution. As shadows lengthen and your cheek feels the evening damp it is a great thing to be able to say with calm assurance:

"I look for the resurrection of the dead and the life of the world to come."

2. OUT OF DOORS

"Out of doors" covers a multitude of delights. Even at my age the mere prospect of a day in the open gives me a thrill. It makes little difference whether the day is to be spent in the woods, on the water or at the farm. It is life under the open sky that brings glee as distinguished from fun. What you do out of doors is second in importance to the mere fact of being there.

Of all promises easy to keep, one that I made to my uncle Doctor Pepper proved to be the easiest. Realizing that by temperament I am enthusiastic and bound to work as hard as I had played, he chose my admission to the bar as the time to give me some wise advice about the conservation of health—advice, I am sorry to say, which in his own case he wholly disregarded. He exacted of me a promise that I would always take a long summer vacation and this I have seldom failed to do.

My engagement to be married was announced in the spring of 1888 after it had in fact existed for four years. My fiancée, her father and I spent our vacation that year at Lake Minnewaska. Thereafter, we made Northeast Harbor our summer home. I think there have been only three summers in fifty-four years when we have failed to visit our beloved Mt. Desert. The first of these exceptional summers we spent at Rye Beach, the second in the Adirondacks and the third in Europe.

Mt. Desert Island was in the old days an ideal vacation-ground for anybody who loved mountains and sea and enjoyed the companionship of people of culture. The island itself was a happy combination of wilderness and civilization. Roughly circular, about fifty miles in circumference, indented by harbors and cut half-way through by an arm of the sea, it is traversed by nine or ten mountainous ridges running north and south, between each two of which there is a deep fresh-water lake. Some of the mountains rise directly out of the sea but none to a greater height than fifteen hundred feet. Precipitous sides, however, offer plenty of opportunity for the adventurous.

My friend Langdon P. Marvin and I were, I believe, the first (in September, 1900) to walk in one day from Bar Harbor to Northeast over nine intervening mountains. This meant about seventeen miles of distance and some seventy-five hundred feet of altitude. Years afterward my daughter Adeline with some companions accomplished the same feat; and at least one group of college boys still later ascended in one day all the peaks on the Island.

Before the advent of automobiles at Northeast, communication between harbors was either by boat or buckboard or, for the more strenuous, on foot or by bicycle. My wife and I got a lot of fun out of a tandem bicycle which we rode in the country around Philadelphia as well as on Mt. Desert Island. In the era before the roads on that island were "improved" by cutting down hills and filling up valleys, it was considered a test of strength to ride the dozen miles from Northeast to Bar Harbor without dismounting. I did this many times.[8]

In the nineties and after the turn of the century the daily life at Northeast Harbor was wholesome and, to me, delightful. Out of doors all day

---

[8] Except in boyhood I have seldom ridden on horseback and then only when a generous aunt enabled me to hire a mount. The bicycle for many years filled a large place in my life. In due time the high 60-inch wheel which I rode in college days was succeeded by the modern type. This I used not merely for sport but for rapid transit. In the city I was accustomed to ride to and fro between home and office.

and engaged, for my part, in strenuous pastime on land and sea, we sometimes devoted our evenings to moonlight sails or buckboard drives, to dances gotten up on the spur of the moment, to impromptu charades or more ambitious theatricals and to round-table games played with pencil and paper. Doctor Huntington's cottage was usually the scene of these games at which he and his son Frank shone brilliantly. There was one game in which two words were assigned to each player and a question asked which he was required to answer in a verse embodying the two words. I remember one evening the question put to Frank was, "What is an impressionist?" and the two words were "beauties" and "ain't." Within the three-minute time limit he wrote:

> "The impressionist artist delighteth to paint
> The beauties of nature in colors she ain't."

Another favorite game was "telegrams." Ten letters, chosen at random, were announced together with the substance of the message to be sent. Thus—a telegram from a father announcing that his daughter had died from eating too much lobster; the letters being S, O, G, S, T, A, L, P, T and E. George W. Norris wrote: "Sally our girl suicided Tuesday— angry lobster pains thus eased." The man who could write that deserved to be Farm Loan Commissioner, Governor of a Federal Reserve Bank, and all the other important things which he in fact later became.

The Maine natives are shrewd and observing folk. Old Captain Hadlock commanded the tiny steamboat which plied among the islands around Mt. Desert. A group of delightful women formed the Cranberry Club and built a clubhouse on Big Cranberry Island to which they resorted for picnics and afternoon teas. A young girl, invited as a guest on one of these outings, stood with the Captain in his little wheelhouse and drank in his pithy sayings. "If I were you," he said, "I'd not jine this club." "Why not?" she asked. "Because," he replied, "I've noticed that them as jines single stays single."

Direct answers Maine men seldom give and they are loth to commit themselves on any proposition. "Who lives on that farm?" I asked of an old chap to whom I was giving a lift. "Willie Richardson," he replied; and then, as if startled by his own definiteness, he added, "Leastways I *think* his name's Willie. He's always been called that since he was a little boy." To a direct question, the reply is apt to be made, "I don't know as I am and I don't know but I am."

"Do you take this woman to be your wedded wife?" the minister asked a somewhat reluctant Maine bridegroom of my acquaintance. "I guess so," was the response.

"Mr. ——," I once said to the man who was supposed to keep my sailboat in condition, "I got caught out alone in that smoky sou'wester yesterday." "Yes," he said; "I see'd ye out in the bay." "When it blew hard," I continued, "I looked at the air chamber and saw it was full of rust holes." "Just like a sieve," he readily assented. "If she had capsized," I suggested, "I should have gone to the bottom." He nodded his head, "Just like a rawk," [9] he said cheerfully, "there weren't nawthing to stop you." "You noticed the holes when you were painting the boat?" I asked. He nodded again. "I suppose it would be easy to close them with solder," I ventured. "Anybody might," was his reply. "Will you do it?" "Sure." And he did; but not on his own responsibility and not till specifically authorized.

Your Maine native is firmly determined to mind nobody's business but his own. At Northeast Harbor a footbridge connects the headlands of Gilpatrick's Cove. In the middle of it is a draw intended to permit the passage of small sailboats. It is very seldom opened. A blind piano tuner was wont to use the familiar bridge in passing from one customer's cottage to another. A local friend of mine kept a dock in the Cove with boats to hire. The bridge leading to his dock bore the classic sign: "Don't too many people get on this bridge at once to avoid breaking down." He told me one day that, not long before, the draw happened to be open and while it was open he saw the blind man start across the bridge. "I says to myself," said my friend, "I shouldn't wonder a mite if he'd walk right off'n that bridge into the water." "What did you do?" I inquired. "Do?" he said, pityingly. "Do? I went about my own business of course. Pretty soon I hear a splash—an' it was him." "What happened then?" I asked, a trifle anxiously. "Oh, I fished him out," he said, "he wa'nt a mite the worse."

My cousin Dr. Perry Pepper employed the local plumber to dig a cesspool near his camp. "But, Mr. Brown," said the Doctor when he inspected the job, "this cesspool is not deep enough." To which the soul-satisfying reply was made, "If it ain't, you'll know it."

Their language is seasoned with spicy metaphor. "That man ain't a contractor," said one of my friends in speaking of a rival carpenter, "he can't even read a blueprint." And then, after a moment's pause, he added impressively, "That man kin no more read a blueprint than a hog

[9] Down-east for "rock."

can sail a sloop in a gale of wind." This same man once summarily disposed of all claims to greatness on the part of Woodrow Wilson and Franklin Roosevelt. "This fellow Roosevelt," said he, "is the same sort of a faker as Wilson. Wilson gets himself re-elected on the slogan 'He kep' us out of war'; then he turns 'round and talks us into war; next he goes overseas to make the world safe; and all that he actually brings back is this d——d daylight saving time. I've no use for either of them."

Maine men seldom betray emotion but they have great depth of feeling. A local captain and I were one day headed out to sea in a sloop. We met and passed an inbound schooner which had on her sails and hull all the marks of heavy weather. I was sailing the sloop. My companion was smoking his pipe. He took it out of his mouth and held it long enough to say to the young man at the wheel of the schooner— "Howdy do?" The latter did the like with his pipe. "Nicely," he said; and each boat held its course. After an appreciable interval my friend observed: "She's been in southern waters. That's my boy. Ain't seen him for nigh onto two years." That was all; but it meant much more than a rapturous greeting or an effusive kiss on both cheeks.

When more than fifty years ago I first knew the people of Mt. Desert Island they seemed to me to be of a finer type than most of those who live there today. While there are still many fine characters, association with "summer people" has done the native folk no good. The necessity for making, during a short summer season, a year's living out of the visitors has developed ways that are dark and tricks that are vain. Standards of honesty have declined. In early days I could leave with perfect assurance tools or other property lying unprotected. Today they would be "lifted" as soon as my back was turned. In like manner the gas will be drained from your car, your woodpile despoiled, your cottage or camp entered when you are absent and the contents pilfered. Occasionally such things are the work of visiting crooks. In the majority of cases this alibi does not hold good. Even when outrageous, however, their transactions often have a grim humor. Two of the local men, in prohibition days, "hijacked" a bootlegger and appropriated his supply of alcohol. Uncertain whether it was or was not poison they decided to make a motor trip to Ellsworth and, en route, to offer a drink to a thirsty friend who ran a filling station. This they did and he took a good long drink. As he was still alive on their return trip they were encouraged to drink the rest of the stuff themselves.

During the nineties we spent our vacations at the Kimball House or in a small cottage close at hand. In 1900 we decided that hotel life was bad

for the two older children and we decided to buy a little land and build
a cottage of our own. This resolve brought disapproval from our older
relatives who thought it madness for young people without capital to
assume such responsibility. But we persevered, bought a few acres on
School House Ledge and built a cottage which proved to be for years
and years a happy summer home. It housed, besides our immediate family of five, my father-in-law, my brother-in-law, Dr. J. Alison Scott, my
sister and their three children. As there were almost always other house
guests, our table was a big one. We were all congenial and had happy
vacations there, summer after summer.

The vacation of 1897 we spent in the Adirondacks. We stayed at the
White-Face Inn and I did a lot of rowing on Lake Placid and climbed
most of the mountains in that beautiful region. From Keene Valley,
whither I had tramped to meet and walk with Walter Lowrie, he and
I climbed Mt. Marcy in a howling autumnal storm. We parted on the
summit, he returning to Keene Valley. Alone, I attempted to follow a
to-me-unknown trail down the opposite side of the mountain. In a clearing encumbered with brush and fallen timber I lost the way. As the
storm continued to rage the situation seemed a bit serious. After thrash-
ing around somewhat frantically in the fashion common to those who
have lost their bearings, I made up my mind to relax a bit, sit down at
the last assured spot on the trail and study the lay of the land in order
to decide how I should proceed from that point if I myself were making
a new trail. This I did and quickly noted a rocky shelf which seemed
like a natural roadbed. Looking along this I descried a great spruce
tree at the far side of the clearing and decided that this must be a land-
mark. Making my way to it through the "blow down" I found on it the
welcome "spot" which assured me that I had rediscovered my route.
After this all went well and drenched and weary I reached the Adirondack Lodge at dusk.

Later in the summer, with four companions, I had another experience
on Mt. Marcy, this one more amusing than the other. We had driven
early from Lake Placid to the Adirondack Lodge and after leaving the
wagon, had there inquired our way through the Indian Pass to that
Marcy Trail which skirts the Opalescent River. Our informant mistakenly told us to take the right-hand fork at a point where the trail
divides. This we did; and persevered in our unconscious error till we
arrived at what we then discovered to be the summit of Mt. McIntyre.
From there we saw the peak of Marcy miles away and beyond the pass

from which we had turned aside. There was nothing to do but plunge down the heavily-timbered mountain side toward Lake Colden, cross the lake and pick up the trail which all along we had intended to take. It was late afternoon when we began to climb Marcy. I was the only member of the party who had been on the mountain before and then my approach had been from the opposite side. I had, however, noted on the ascent with Lowrie a lean-to where the Panther Gorge trail approaches the summit and I undertook to guide my party to it. As darkness fell and no camp was in sight a friendly mutiny was threatened. I pleaded for ten minutes of patience. This was granted; and within that time we spied the gleam of a fire and found some men from Keene Valley camping in the shelter. We made friends with them, shared their fire, pooled our supplies and slept like the dead until it was time to climb to the summit and see a glorious sunrise.

In 1903 I welcomed my first opportunity to climb a mountain in winter. Herbert and Percy Clark, old friends of mine, delightful companions and the keenest of sportsmen, invited me to join them in a winter ascent of Mt. Marcy. I had never tried snowshoeing but I was determined to go. At Keene Valley we met our guides (Ed Phelps and Pete Lamb) and we five made our way to the summit by the John's Brook Trail. The snow was deep and very soft and in some places it was heavy going. We made the grade, however, and then and there resolved that no winter could ever be considered complete without some such expedition.

Fired by the success of the Marcy trip (if a subzero temperature can be said to fire) Percy Clark and I in 1904 made up our minds to tackle Mt. Katahdin in Northern Maine. There are several approaches to this peak which present no great difficulty; but we decided to make an attack upon the south face of the mountain, cross the Pomola Peaks, traverse the "Knife-Edge," and so gain the summit. On a February day we met our guides, Charley Powers and Charles Hathaway, at Millinocket and began our expedition at that point. Powers and I formed a friendship which lasted until his death nearly thirty years later. He was a man of high character and great intelligence. He had learned his woodcraft from the Indians. His resourcefulness in the wilderness was in keeping with the best traditions of frontier days. In later years, when we had come to know one another well, he told me that when, on that first of many expeditions, we started for the mountain he and Hathaway expected Clark and me to quit at the end of the second day. We each carried heavy equipment because we were to camp where we could; and this meant food, sleeping bags and, in general, an arctic outfit. We surprised our guides and on the morning of the fourth day we had reached the timber line at the foot of the East Slide and were ready to make our bid for the summit. The thermometer registered forty degrees below zero. The wind had blown the snow from the Slide, the stony surface of which was covered with glare ice. Charley Powers waited for us at the foot of the Slide. Hathaway went half way up and took shelter in the lee of a great boulder. Clark and I, after a two-hour climb over the ice-covered rock, reached the ridge and were within striking distance of our objective. When, however, we stuck our heads up over the last ledge the northwest wind hit us with such fury that we had sense enough to realize that the Knife-Edge, under such conditions, was a foolhardy venture. We had no rope and no ice-axes. We had, of course, left our snowshoes at the foot of the Slide and our moccasins were as slippery as the rocks. So we ruefully gave up our quest and started back. To the west of the Slide we found a sort of glissade—a steep, snow-covered slope with hardy but stunted spruce-growth piercing the snow at frequent intervals. We sat down and slid, checking ourselves by grabbing spruce-tops as we passed. In less than five minutes we had reached the foot of the Slide which it had taken us two hours to climb. The guides had a roaring fire of birchwood at a spot where heavy evergreen had formed a shelter. To this day I remember with delight the moose-meat which they had cooked for the returning travelers. Charley Powers had shot the moose the preceding November and had hung it on a tree where Nature had ever since kept it in perfect cold storage. I think I have never had such good food either before or since.

On four other winter trips, always with a different companion but always with Charley Powers as one of our guides, I have tried to reach the top by approximately the same route but I have never succeeded. I have been to the summit twice in summer, but hard luck with weather conditions has thwarted me on every winter trip.

Vacations spent in our cottage in Northeast Harbor were delightful but they had not entirely satisfied my craving for out of doors. I was anxious, too, that the children should be taught to take care of themselves in camp and in the woods as well as on the water. We accordingly explored the northwestern (and relatively unsettled) part of Mt. Desert Island and there, in 1907, found a campsite which seemed ideal. Two or three miles north of Pretty Marsh lay Goosemarsh Point, a wooded peninsula jutting out into Blue Hill Bay. Thick woods and thicker underbrush made this point at that time almost inaccessible except by water. It was easy, however, to row or paddle across the cove which lay between the point and the mainland of Mt. Desert. Access to the cove could be had across the land of A. J. Carter, a friendly resident and himself the son-in-law of old Captain Freeman, the owner of the peninsula. The Captain offered to sell for $750 the ten acres constituting the northern end of Goosemarsh Point and two small islands lying northeast of it. I accepted the offer upon condition that a good supply of potable water should be developed. The old man readily acceded to this condition, cut himself a Y-shaped divining rod of alder wood and invited me to go with him on a water hunt. We tramped hither and thither through thick underbrush, he pausing now and then to note the behavior of his rod—the branching ends of which he held in both hands while the shank of the Y was left free. At a certain point he stopped, as the pointing end appeared to be bending downward. "Water here," he remarked in a matter-of-fact tone—and there was. Although we were within thirty feet of high tide, an eight-foot excavation disclosed a gushing spring of pure cold water. The supply has never failed us in thirty years of use. I have no explanation to offer and no theory to advance. Like Truthful James, "I state but the facts."

The Captain was a great character. He had been a seafaring man about whose exploits in outwitting revenue officers there were many legends. We built our cabin on the point bought from him and for years we made expeditions to it from Northeast Harbor, spending one or two nights at a time.

The life story of the well illustrates the evolution of conveniences. At first I drew water by hanging a bucket on a pole with a hook at its end. By grasping with each hand the handles of two buckets just above the rims I was able to lug to the cabin four buckets of water at once. After several years I laid an iron pipe from the well to the cabin and built a tank there. It took 1,500 strokes of the force pump daily to keep the tank full. After a while I bought a small gasoline engine and with it generated enough electricity to light the camp and so do away with candles and kerosene lamps. After about twenty years of pumping by hand I connected up the motor with the pump and, between them, the pump and the current did my work for me. Finally, when the engine had served for ten years, I contracted with the local hydroelectric company to run a wire through the woods and deliver power at the cabin.

And now that all this has been accomplished I pretend that I want to be back in the pole-and-bucket era.

Our navy at the camp consists of an eighteen-foot sloop, a rowboat and several canoes. Our manner of life was and still is simple; but the place has given an immense amount of pleasure to many people. After our daughter Eleanor died in 1930 we seemed to lose interest in the cottage at Northeast Harbor. During subsequent years we rented it and finally sold it. Meanwhile for my wife and me Tern Rock Camp,

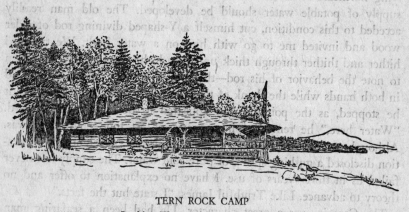

TERN ROCK CAMP
Looking Westward Toward Blue Hill

as we called it, became a summer home. At first we two lived there alone but later we made it a party of three. This happened after my wife had undergone a serious operation. She had faced it with calm courage. The operation, skillfully performed by our old friend Dr. John H. Gibbon, proved eminently successful. Anxiety was quickly replaced by gratitude. When restored to health and shopping, she was greeted with joy by a friendly saleswoman. "Do you mind telling us what was the matter?" was the well-meant inquiry. "Not a bit," Mrs. Pepper replied. "I had a foot taken out of my intestine." "My God!" exclaimed the horrified woman. "How did it get there?"

After her illness I decided to get a Maine forester to help during vacation with the work in camp. We were lucky enough to find in Harvey Williams not only a guide but a philosopher and friend. We three have ever since lived happily during the six weeks' holiday which each year gives me supreme satisfaction. Soon after we acquired our campsite our dear friends the Charlton Yarnalls bought a much larger tract on the Point to the south of us. They too built cabins of which they have regularly made use.

It would be hard for me to overstate the pleasure which I have derived from our camp. The beauty of the outlook, especially at the sunset hour, is wholly satisfying. Many times a day I have been wont to dive into the cold water of the Bay. In my shop there is always work to be done when the weather is bad. Out of doors there is an endless variety of occupations. Night finds one pleasantly weary and the morning brings refreshment. For years and years my first early morning activity, after lighting the fire in the big fireplace, has been to run up Old Glory to the accompaniment of such a rendering of the "Star-Spangled Banner" as I am capable of. Raising the flag in the morning and lowering it at sunset are ritual acts which I really take quite seriously.

Once at camp, and until war came, I have turned a languid eye upon doings in Congress and upon happenings in Europe and in the Orient. The business of the moment, whatever it is, keeps Harvey and me at work early and late, while Mrs. Pepper directs operations and gives advice which we are sometimes wise enough to follow. The only foreign journeys that I make during vacation (excepting the regular Sunday pilgrimages to church) are trips at suitable intervals to a local barber shop to get my hair cut. When people unused to the simple life ask whether in camp time does not hang heavy on your hands, all you can do is to turn upon them a pitying eye, because no explanation could possibly make them understand that in camp you always have to pack into the unforgiving minute a hundred and twenty seconds' worth of distance run.

3. POETRY

In college days I wrote and submitted a required essay on Great Epic Poems. In it I compared the *Iliad*, the *Divine Comedy* and *Paradise Lost*. My thesis was that the *Iliad* was the work of a painter, the *Divine Comedy* of a musician and *Paradise Lost* of a sculptor. Homer had revealed to me a moving picture. Dante had whispered harmonies in my ear.[10] Milton had startled me with a vision in bodily form of God, of Satan

[10] I knew him only in translation, Longfellow's being my favorite. It seemed to me that Dante and his translator had done for the theme of the *Divine Comedy* what Wagner did for German legend.

and of the Angels. Of course it was a crude bit of work; but I am inclined to think that I had chanced upon a basic thought of some value. The thought is that no definition of poetry is adequate unless it recognizes the element of *inclusiveness*. By this I mean that a perfect poem is one that appeals to all one's sensibilities and not merely to a few of them. Poetry, as I apprehend it, implies a worthy thought expressed in words that paint a picture, that make music and that satisfy one's love of rhythm and form.

I agree with A. E. Housman [11] that poetry is music but I cannot accept his implication that poetry consists only in the pleasing sound. I further agree there may be beauty of sound in words that express little or no thought; but I contend that equally beautiful words which express a worthy thought will take me a step nearer the poetic ideal. So also I concede that a worthy thought combined with the music of words may make a powerful appeal; but if the words also bring a picture before my mind and do it in a fashion that satisfies my rhythmic sense, then my poetic ideal is attained—and I am in the presence of perfect poetry.

From the wholeness of the poetic conception there may be subtractions which nevertheless leave much of worth. If a sublime thought is expressed in words that paint a picture the result may be compelling even if there be little music. Much of Browning's verse [12] seems to me to be of this sort. The thought and the picture are present in Walt Whitman's poems but he often leaves my rhythmic sense unsatisfied. And so it is with all the poets: they give us varying degrees of satisfaction ranging from a narrative poem of the ballad type to the utter perfection of *When in Disgrace with Fortune and Men's Eyes*. All poets are "makers"; and I echo Wordsworth when he says "blessings be with them—and eternal praise." But just as there are nine orders of angels so there are many orders among the poets.

The poets, whatever their order, have made a great contribution to my happiness. To what extent my love of poetry is inherited and to what extent acquired I do not know; but, either way, I came by it honestly. Mother took a contagious delight in all forms of poetry. How discriminating my father's poetic taste was I cannot tell; but I remember that during his long last illness he found much satisfaction in Bret Harte's verses then lately published. Naturally enough I became interested in them; and I

---

[11] *The Name and Nature of Poetry*, The Macmillan Co., New York, 1933.
[12] For example, *The Last Ride Together, My Last Duchess, Hervé Riel* and many parts of *The Ring and the Book* and *Pippa Passes*.

Port. James Malone

Pepper

G. PEPPER of Penn. is a model for men;
A bulwark in peace or in war,
With character rounded and solidly founded
  On learning and logic and law.
When Senators bicker of tariff or liquor,
  As Senators will now and then,
The speediest stepper is certainly Pepper,
  George Wharton Pepper of Penn.

Let me further explain that in spite of his brain
  He's an athlete, as every one knows,
And if questions logistic evolve toward the fistic
  He's always right there on his toes.
With these multiple talents of brain power
    and Balance
  Who is there, I ask, in the Sen.
Who can stack up with Pepper, the mental
    Mazeppa,
  George Wharton Pepper, of Penn.!
                    George S. Chappell.

"SUCH IS LIFE!"

scarcely remember a time when I did not know a lot of them by heart. Of course (even with *Dickens in Camp* to his credit) Harte has no claim to greatness. Nevertheless his was not a negligible contribution to the treasury of verse.[13] Neither, I think, was Macaulay's. At the risk of losing the respect of my more discriminating friend, Learned Hand (who shudders at the thought) I must confess to a great liking for the *Lays of Ancient Rome*. They seem to have been a part of my boyhood. I often repeat to myself the account of the homeward flight of "the dark gray charger" after his master Mamilius had fallen at Lake Regillus. In May of 1942, while I was welcoming to Philadelphia the members of the American Law Institute (compelled by war conditions to change their place of meeting) it occurred to me to quote as appropriate these lines from *Horatius*:

> "The harvests of Arretium
> This year, old men shall reap;
> This year, young boys in Umbro
> Shall plunge the struggling sheep:
> And in the vats of Luna
> This year, the must shall foam
> Round the white feet of laughing girls
> Whose sires have marched to Rome."

These ballads of Macaulay's, like Aytoun's *Lays of the Scottish Cavaliers,* unquestionably paint pictures and make them move. Of a far higher order in the realm of ballads are Kipling's *East and West,* Longfellow's *Paul Revere's Ride* and Noyes's *Highwayman.* All have a permanent place in my memory. So I gladly make to these singers a bow of grateful appreciation.

This goes, too, for Conan Doyle: a recitation of his *How the Guards Came Through* can thrill a wartime audience at any time. Kipling's *If—* is a character-making poem if ever there was one. George Henry Boker's *The Black Regiment,* a Civil War poem, might with advantage be widely read today.

Boker's tribute to the Negro reminds me of my debt to James Weldon Johnson for *God's Trombones: Seven Negro Sermons in Verse.*[14] His poetic rendering of these Negro folk sermons has made on me a lasting impression. I particularly admire the way in which he has succeeded in

---

[13] My friend Bob McCracken, a lover of both literature and law, tells me that he has seen a letter from Kipling in which Kipling acknowledged his indebtedness to Bret Harte.

[14] The Viking Press, New York, 1927.

indicating the tempos of the preacher. His version of the prayer by which a sermon was always introduced is as remarkable as the sermons themselves. It must have been a great experience actually to see and hear a typical revivalist in action. Negro oratory is as distinctive as Negro song: there is in it an indescribable something which stirs my emotions as few white speakers can do.

This reference to the Negro and his gifts brings to mind *John Brown's Body*—the Civil War epic with which the late Stephen Vincent Benét electrified us in the twenties. The invocation of the American muse and the prelude (On the Slaver) are fitting introductions to what follows. I learned a few of his passages by heart and thus made the unsuspecting poet one of my young companions.

In college days I developed an enthusiasm for Chaucer. In the *Canterbury Tales* I found plenty of moving pictures set to music. When the Old Kaiser died in 1887 I wrote for the Philadelphia *Press* a description of his summer palace (Babelsberg) which I had visited while abroad. With the honorarium paid me by the newspaper I bought a set of Chaucer which is still a cherished possession.

Two other poets at that time aroused my lasting interest—Matthew Arnold and his friend Arthur Hugh Clough. Arnold, I admit, is often self-conscious and not a little pedantic. But now and then he forgets himself and does something really worth while. In *Thyrsis* (the monody which he wrote after Clough's death) there are some lines that are both picture-painting and music-making. I have in mind particularly these:

> "So, some tempestuous morn in early June
> When the year's primal burst of bloom is o'er,
> Before the roses and the longest day—
> When garden-walks and all the grassy floor
> With blossoms red and white of fallen May
> And chestnut-flowers are strewn—
> So have I heard the cuckoo's parting cry,
> From the wet field, through the vext garden-trees,
> Come with the volleying rain and tossing breeze:
> *The bloom is gone and with the bloom go I!*"

Two of Clough's poems deserve to live—*Qua Cursum Ventus* and *Say Not the Struggle Naught Availeth*. In an address to the Canadian Bar in Toronto, in January of 1941, I recited the latter poem as being peculiarly appropriate in wartime. Not long afterward Mr. Churchill, independently impressed by its timeliness, quoted the poem in one of his stirring international broadcasts.

Years ago, when my son was a small boy, I often used Emerson's *Hypocritic Days* as a warning against waste of time. I would pretend that I was the departing day looking at him scornfully. He would wriggle and grin—but he got the point. *Rhodora* always gave me pleasure. *Brahma* was one of the poems years ago listed by the New York *Sun* as the ten best short poems in English. Among the other nine, as I recall, were *When in Disgrace with Fortune*, Milton's sonnet *On His Blindness*, Blake's *Tiger*, Burns's *Scots Wha Hae*, Scott's *Pibroch of Donald Dhu*, Thackeray's *At the Church-yard Gate*, Tennyson's *Bugle Song* and Kipling's *Gunga Din*. I do not at the moment remember the tenth; but if I were completing the list and were to limit myself (as the *Sun* required) to one poem to a poet, I should add either Shelley's *To Night* or Wordsworth's *Daffodils*. I do not think I would have included either the Thackeray or the Kipling in such fast company. If Kipling were to be included it would be, I think, because of *Recessional* or *When Earth's Last Picture Is Painted*.

I do not remember when my interest in Shakespeare and Milton was first aroused but it must have been in boyhood days. I cannot recall a time when I was not familiar with certain passages in *As You Like It*, *The Tempest*, *Julius Caesar* and *The Merchant of Venice*. Appreciation of the sonnets came later. They now seem to me completely satisfying. Most of them fully realize the poetic ideal. The only two modern writers of sonnets who move me much are Lloyd Mifflin [15] and Santayana. To the former, known to but few, I owe thanks for *At the Gates of Song*.

Milton had a large place in my youthful affections. I early learned the sonnet *On His Blindness*, *Lycidas* and passages from *Paradise Lost*. When lying awake at night I often recite *Lycidas* to myself, taking special delight in the catalogue of flowers culled "to strew the laureate hearse where Lycid lies." I remember as a boy resenting Doctor Johnson's contemptuous estimate of this poem. As the old Doctor was, I believe, tone-deaf the music of Milton's words was probably lost upon him. With sound subtracted, the poem might have small appeal. I concede that it is rather heavy with classical ornament.

Speaking of the classics, I must make my grateful acknowledgment to some of the Greek and Roman poets. Aeschylus, in the *Prometheus Bound* (which we read in freshman year) gave me my first insight into Greek tragedy. Mrs. Browning's translation of the final defiance of Zeus by Prometheus is one of the finest bits of rendering that I know. Aris-

---

[15] Mifflin, a recluse living in Lancaster County, Pennsylvania, was better known in Great Britain than at home.

tophanes was the Gilbert of his day and, like the Englishman, he could make words dance and sing.[16] We read neither Sophocles nor Euripides in college. My acquaintance with them was made later. I have acquired the Loeb Library and I now and then dip into Greek plays with the welcome help of the accompanying translation.

The Aeneid always seemed to me tame in comparison with the *Iliad*. The moving picture was there and the music; but elemental vigor was lacking. The poem was written with a purpose; whereas the *Iliad* was created for its own sake. It is said, I believe, that English does not lend itself to hexameter verse as does the Latin. To my ear, however, parts of *Evangeline* and all of Kingsley's *Andromeda* are in a class with the best hexameters Vergil ever wrote. I rejoiced in Horace and Juvenal, chiefly because in college days Professor Jackson interpreted them so vividly. I am afraid that the venerable professor would have winced at Eugene Field's *The Truth About Horace* but to the class it would have seemed a delicious bit of metrical humor.

Of all ancient poems none ever took hold of my imagination as the Psalms have done. The translation of the Psalter in the Coverdale Bible,[17] as we have it in the Book of Common Prayer, seems to me more beautiful than the later translation as we have it in the King James Version of 1611. This was Mr. Gladstone's view.[18] At one time I began to study Hebrew in the hope of being able to read the Psalms in the original but I never got far enough to realize my dream.[19] The 119th Psalm is an anthology in itself. I have found it more difficult to memorize and retain than any other poem I know. At times I have been letter-perfect in it, but today I find that much of it has escaped me. Of them all, perhaps the 18th Psalm is the most satisfying. The account of the storm in the first fifteen verses is breath-taking. The sudden transition (in verse 16) from the convulsion of nature to God's concern for the individual soul is unsurpassed in dramatic power. In the case of the 91st Psalm I was long puzzled by the seemingly inexplicable interchanges of the first and third persons. I then learned the rabbinical explanation from a Jewish friend of mine who conceived the Psalm to be a "trialogue" between

[16] For an account of our performance of *The Acharnians,* see page 39, *supra.*

[17] The Great Bible of 1539.

[18] Gladstone published a little book (now out of print) containing the text of the Psalter, his own concordance and various groupings of Psalms to answer special needs.

[19] My favorite Psalms are 18, 19, 20, 23, 33, 39, 46, 51, 65, 68, 72, 78, 84, 90, 91, 103, 104, 119, 121, 130, 139, 144 and 145.

King David, the boy Solomon and God Himself. Says the King, "Whoso dwelleth under the defence of the Most High shall abide under the shadow of the Almighty." To which the boy replies, "I will say unto the Lord, Thou art my hope and my stronghold; my God; in him will I trust." Then through a series of verses the King resumes his charge, interrupted once (in verse 9) by another exclamation from the boy; and, finally, in the three closing verses, God Himself speaks and gives His rewarding assurance: "Because he hath set his love upon me therefore will I deliver him; I will set him up because he hath known my Name." When I read Rowland E. Prothero's *The Psalms in Human Life* I was not surprised to learn that the Psalms have in fact filled a unique place in history and that through the ages they have supplied courage and consolation to all sorts and conditions of men.[20]

On my seventy-seventh Birthday [21] I could not honestly apply to myself the lines which Walter Savage Landor wrote on his seventy-fifth:

> "I strove with none; for none was worth my strife,
> Nature I loved, and next to Nature, Art;
> I warmed both hands before the fire of life,
> It sinks, and I am ready to depart."

After some fifty-five years at the bar I am impelled to put my case thus:

> "I strove and strove—and now and then I won;
> Law I have loved, and Nature, too, and Art;
> Life's fire still burns, my work is not yet done:
> Much, much remains before I dare depart."

It would be hard to exaggerate the degree of amusement afforded me by Ogden Nash's *Hard Lines* and by some of his other verse. It is said that General Wolfe, on hearing Gray's *Elegy* for the first time, exclaimed, "I had rather be the author of that poem than take Quebec tomorrow." In transit from the sublime to the ridiculous I can say that I had rather

---

[20] E. P. Dutton & Co., New York, 1905. My copy of this book has on its fly-leaf my name and "from Mother, March 16, 1905." Beneath this inscription I find in my own handwriting the 16th verse of the 18th Psalm: "He shall send down from on high to fetch *me:* and shall take *me* out of many waters." I do not remember writing this but that verse has been in my mind for a lifetime. On two occasions, when I was gravely ill, I kept my mind at rest by reciting this and other Psalms to myself; and often they have supplied a need which nothing else could fill.

[21] March 16, 1944.

be credited with some bits of light verse than be awarded an LL.D. I have
in mind particularly such priceless observations as this:

> "The digestion of John Milton
> Was never up to Stilton:
> He was feeling only so-so
> When he wrote 'Il Penseroso.' " [22]

Or this gem by an author to me unknown:

> "The Queen of Bees—
> A social soul—
> Is much opposed
> To birth control.
> And that is why
> One always sees
> So many, many Sons of Bs!"

In my time I have written scores of "occasional" verses. There have
been toasts and birthday greetings and after-dinner speeches in verse and
limericks by the dozen. Some years ago we had a walking club. A dozen
friends, men and women, used to spring into action on holidays and
Saturday afternoons. We tramped six or eight miles from the place of
assembly to the home of the member who was feeding us on arrival.
James M. Willcox and his lovely wife, Jean, Anna and Charlton Yarnall,
Marjorie and John Gibbon and Tom and Honora Newhall were among
the bright particular stars in the firmament of that club of blessed memory. Jim Willcox and Charlton Yarnall wrote clever light verse and their
recitations were often a feature of our meetings. Jean Willcox hailed from
California. I find in an old file a jingle which I addressed to this Girl from
the Golden West. Here it is as I recited it at a Thanksgiving dinner at
about the time when "Wally" and the King were front-page stuff:

CALIFORNIA JEAN [23]

I

At this happy time of year—when the turkey brings us cheer—
We remember all the blessings that we share:

[22] This was quoted to me by my friend William Hamilton Coulson. He thinks
the author is E. C. Bentley.

[23] With acknowledgments to Kipling for the versification and the swing of the
lines.

And, of blessings, sure the best is the Girl from Farthest West—
With the tender eyes and devastating hair.
    Hollywood! Hollywood! They had kept her if they could!
    They are always snooping round to find a queen:
    They are sick of Painted Harlots—they can get them by the car-lots—
    But the modest dames are few and far between.

2

It was California's loss: it was Pennsylvania's gain
When across the open spaces traveled Jean.
Tho' the sun was moving west, it was eastward that she pressed
And she spurned the eager States that lie between.
    Hollywood! Hollywood! You had kept her if you could;
    You are always looking out to find a queen.
    You are sick of Movie Stars shooting 'round in private cars,
    But a truly lovely Beauty's rarely seen.

3

There was heard a dismal moan when she passed through Arizone—
As she shook her pretty head when begged to stay:
There was plenty of bravado when the men of Colorado
Feigned contentment as she hurried on her way.
    Colorado! Colorado! You may talk of El Dorado
    And the charms of lofty mountains capped with snow:
    But the beauty of your scene couldn't touch the heart of Jean:
    So she laughed at all her Colorado beaux.

4

It was just the same in Ute—where they thought she looked so cute
That the ghost of Brigham Young returned to leer:
When she crossed the Mississippi all the river-men were dippy
And they lined the banks to greet her with a cheer.
    Brigham Young! Brigham Young! Could you find your oily tongue
    To your harem you would surely try to add her!
    But you'd shortly have to take to the bottom of Salt Lake
    As your other gals got mad—and then grew madder.

5

Illinois and Indiana—in their most seductive manna—
Sought to check her in her tantalizing flight:

But she spied the broad Ohi—and she raised a joyful cry
For the shores of Pennsylvania were in sight!
   Middle West! Middle West! She would far outshine your best!
   Were you wise you'd never try to capture Jean:
   You would ship her from Chicago—parcel post or special cargo—
   Lest she make your native beauties look too mean.

6

When she neared the hoarse Atlantic, Oh! she nearly drove us frantic
Lest she'd pass us by and travel further east!
But she found us to her liking—so she quit her further hiking:
And *that* is why Thanksgiving means a feast.
   Hollywood! Hollywood! Your allurements she withstood:
   How you'd love to sign a contract with our Jean!
   I suppose you think her silly to be satisfied with Philly
   When she might have made her fortune on the screen.

7

There are plenty who will say—had she kept her eastward way—
That for *her* the Coronation Bells would ring:
And we'd all declare, by golly, she could cramp the style of Wally
And steal away the boyish English King!
   Hollywood! Buckingham! Oh! we do not give a damn
   For the things that happen east or happen west:
   We are happy in between, drinking healths to Lady Jean—
   Of all the gals we pledge her as the best!

As president of the American Law Institute it has long been my job
to sign the warrants which authorize salary payments to various people
working on the Restatement of the Common Law. Among these are the
lady secretaries and stenographers many of whom I never saw but whose
warrants I regularly signed. Hence this lament:

     Day by day I sign my name
     To a warrant for cash for an Unknown Dame;
     And the worst of it is that the Fair Payee
     Is quite unaware what she owes to *me*.
     I'd like her to know who it is—by heck!—
     Without whose order she'd get no check:
     I'd like her to know that it's *I* each day
     Who tells the Treasurer whom to pay.

I am the Boy Friend, if you please,
Who issues the order to pay *Louise.*
I am the lad who cuts the melon
And starts a slice on its way to *Helen.*
Not one cent would *Dorothy* see
If it weren't for poor forgotten *Me.*
Eleanor's nails would be ghastly white
If I my name should omit to write—
Don Eden's tears were a mountain torrent
If *I* should refuse to sign her warrant;
And if I suddenly acted mean
Who would buy "pretties" for poor *Arlene?*

Enough of this: I'll accept what Fate meant—
And turn my thoughts to Sublime Restatement:
Conscious that Dames whom I never saw
Have fewer charms than the Common Law!

And here is part of a greeting to the stenographers of my firm at an office Christmas Party held many years ago:

Fair Eve (they assure us) was best of all girls:
But how can they possibly tell?
She never was tried—as stenographers are—
By the petulant tap of the bell.
She could sit at her ease—or recline, did she please,
On a bank that was mossy and green,
Without the vexation of taking dictation
From Pepper—or Stokes—or Bodine.

In Eden there never were dressmaker's bills
For the gowns to appear in on Sundays:
Nor charges for furbelows, ribbons and frills,
Or slippers or stockings or undies.
Eve's raiment of leaves was both modern and chic
And well within pocketbook reach:
With a bough from a tree—which of course she had free—
She was all fitted out for Palm Beach.

Instead of six mails to be answered each day
She had but one male—that was Adam:

And if she insisted on having time off
And hours of rest—why, she had 'em.
And Eve had her Adam well trained, you can bet;
One droop of a lid and he'd come:
A contrast quite painful to manner disdainful
—The haughty demeanor of some.

No: Eve couldn't stand what stenographers can—
The strain—it would age her and break her;
And if she applies for a place in our gang
I'll counsel the firm not to take her.
Our girls are the best of the feminine bunch
—Their service we never forget.
And we gladly admit that you ladies are IT
For you've put the whole firm in your debt!

The association of a poem with a picture suggests the close affinity between all manifestations of Art, whether Poetry, Music, Painting or Architecture. If Schelling could describe Architecture as "frozen music" I may perhaps make bold to characterize Poetry as the other three forms of Art all melted into one. I am sure that there is in my own case a close relation between the pleasure I take in Poetry and my deep interest in the other three Arts. I have had no formal education in any of them but all three fill a large place in my life. Since childhood I have always done a lot of sketching. On journeys to Europe and elsewhere I have never been without a sketchbook. The drawings have little merit and they seem particularly crude when compared with what my father did and what my son does so well. But the mere fact of making a sketch increases appreciation of its subject matter and serves to record it permanently on the tablet of memory. My part in the evolution of Washington Cathedral has been an education in Gothic architecture.[24] It was a great satisfaction to me when my son chose architecture as his profession and I have ever since taken proper pride in his professional achievements.

In 1938 I decided to try my hand at painting in oils. I quickly developed a keen interest in this new hobby. One of my first efforts was a canvas styled "Trophies and Toys"—a portrait of our cocker spaniel Winkie, with a display of his show ribbons and cups and a collection of his play-

[24] In 1940 I delivered at Wilmington, Delaware, a lecture on "Gothic Architecture as Exemplified in Washington Cathedral."

things. This was hung in the annual exhibition of the Chester County Art Association at West Chester. Two of my landscapes were given a place in one of the art exhibitions at the Century Club in New York. It is practically impossible, except during vacation, to find time for what has now become a hobby. Of course I realize how crude my efforts are but I mean to persevere and perhaps get out of the duffer class. "Oh, Mr. Pepper!" say some indulgent friends, "we didn't know you had so delightful a talent." Over against this laudation I set a comment by my sister Frances. "George dear," said she, "you are ruining your house." This did not discourage me (sisters being what they are) but I confess to a sense of hopelessness when I contemplate the technique of my friend Cameron Burnside [25] and note his capacity to make of a portrait a living picture.

I have several times tried a combination of painting and handicraft by mounting one of my ship models against a painted background. The rocks and trees on the coast of Maine lend themselves to this form of decoration. One of my models thus treated was awarded a blue ribbon in a hobby show. My good friend the late Samuel Vauclain used to say that modelmaking is the sign of an unbalanced mind; that it is better to do nothing than to make something that can't be used. I wonder. Perhaps the catch is in the word "used." Possibly a visible reminder of the open sea is really useful, something that enables you to feel again the freshening breeze, to see again the unnumbered smiles on the face of the ocean and to hear the slap-slap of water under the bow. At the end of anxious days I have found it possible to make voyages of this sort in my little shop when to keep imagination on shore would have meant fretting over a client's troubles or sulking over a disappointing decision.

If I am right in conceiving Poetry to be all the Arts melted into one it is natural that I should accord it first place in my affections. It seems to me that no niche in a Hall of Fame is so much to be coveted as a place in an anthology. Such a volume records the perpetual succession of the poets. I have a deep sense of personal gratitude to the compiler every time I open his book and come upon that which delights me. There is always something responsive to whatever my mood happens to be.

[25] For the Philadelphia Bar Association he painted a portrait of me which Mrs. Pepper liked so well that I sat for him a second time. His portraits of William I. Schaffer and of Mr. and Mrs. Roland Morris are works of art of unusual excellence. After having their studio for twenty years in Paris he and his artist-wife were driven out by the German invasion and returned to Pennsylvania, his ancestral home.

Do I need to be aroused from listlessness? Sir Walter or Bobby Burns will do the trick. Do I need to be recalled from devious byways and headed in the right direction? If so, Francis Thompson's *Hound of Heaven* will sound the recall. Do I wish to leave sullen earth for a while and play with planets or sojourn among the stars? Shelley can readily arrange the journey. Is it the soothing concordance of sweet sounds that I crave? Tennyson's harp is ready at hand. *In Memoriam* has on occasion stood me in good stead. *Crossing the Bar* has given me needed confidence and *Ulysses* has more than once roused my old spirit to the pitch of action. Speaking of Tennyson, let me thank him for the marvelous sequence of vowel sounds in *Break, break, break on thy cold, gray stones, O Sea*,[26] for the echoing music of the *Bugle Song* and for the exquisite pathos of *Home they brought her Warrior dead*. When I speak of pathos I inevitably think of Coventry Patmore's *My little son that looked through thoughtful eyes* and of Eugene Field's *Little Boy Blue*.

These anthologies! How seductive they are! I turn their pages forward and backward: everywhere I find friends, Spenser, Jonson, Lovelace, Blake, Byron, Keats, the Coleridges, Wordsworth, Browning, Alice Meynell, Emerson, Poe, Lloyd Mifflin, Field, Riley, Kipling and a host of others—I salute them all as they pass. They do not seem to know me and are quite indifferent to my greeting. But I know them well and I am content merely to touch the hem of the garment of any passing poet. And the mention of Kipling's name reminds me that the caption of this chapter was an unconscious plagiarism from him:

"Still the pine-woods scent the noon; still the cat-bird sings his tune;
  Still autumn sets the maple forests blazing.
Still the grape-vine through the dusk flings her soul-compelling musk;
  While the fire-flies in the corn make night amazing!
    They are there, there, there with Earth immortal
    (Citizens I give you friendly warning)
    The things that truly last when men and times have passed,
    They are all in Pennsylvania this morning."

[26] a — a — a
o — i — o; a — o; o — e!

The Quest of Justice

(A TREATISE FOR LAWYERS ONLY)

"The law is unknown to him that knoweth not the reason
thereof and the known certaintie of the law is the safetie of all."

—LORD COKE

I F the wages of sin be death and if all lawyers are as wicked as some
people assert, there must be by this time a considerable amount of
death to my credit. I must have been living in sin, and quite happily at
that, for much more than fifty years.

Certainly there is today much greater public dissatisfaction with lawyers and the law than there was when I came to the bar. Lawyers as a
class have always been unpopular. Hogarth's classic picture of a lawsuit is a bit of eighteenth century testimony to this effect.[1] But it is
also true that as individuals lawyers are as much trusted by their own
clients as are any other men I know. They receive as many confidential
communications as ministers or doctors and, in addition, are often entrusted with the unsecured custody of millions of dollars in cash and
securities. However this may be, the class unpopularity of lawyers is
evidently increasing.

The law itself, both as an uncharted wilderness of principles and rules
and as an undigested mass of statutory enactments, is certainly putting
democracy to a severe test. Justinian and Napoleon could, with the
stroke of a pen, give immediate authority to reforms in the law which

[1] In his cartoon a lawsuit is represented by a cow. The plaintiff is pulling her
by the horns and the defendant by the tail. The lawyer meanwhile is milking her.
(See sketch on page 76.)

with us must be worked out slowly and painfully by a democratic process. It is this democratic process to which the American Law Institute is addressing itself. Recent books, such as *The Law and Mr. Smith*,[2] *Look at the Law*[3] and *Woe Unto You Lawyers*[4] purport to specify recognized evils and to suggest appropriate remedies. The difficulty of the subject becomes evident when critics of the law, like the authors of the two books last mentioned, have with bitter words confirmed your own conviction that there is much amiss and then have grievously disappointed you when you turn hopefully to their remedial proposals.[5]

It seems to me that in all this welter of criticism and abuse there has been pretty general failure to distinguish between two entirely different sins of the lawyer. The professional ideal is fidelity to the court, as representing the public, and to the client for whom the attorney is trustee. The so-called "corporation lawyer," when he deserves to be scolded, is one whose offense does not consist in representing a corporation or in being disloyal to his client but in allowing fidelity to that client to dim or black out entirely his sense of public duty. Bad as this is, it is, after all, an overgrown and distorted virtue and, as such, not so bad as the far more subtle and more common vice of regarding the client as a suitable subject for exploitation. Those who are indifferent to public interest are relatively few and can readily be identified. Those seemingly incapable of grasping the conception of trusteeship are legion and they are the microbes, working in secret, who threaten the life of the bar. By "trusteeship" I mean the fixed principle that there *cannot* be any conflict of interest between the trustee and his beneficiary. The instant a question arises between them the trustee must yield. The instant that the attorney's interest becomes inconsistent with the client's, the attorney's interest must be forgotten. My guess is that a majority of the whole number of young men who come to the bar in our big cities think of the client as the merchant does of his customer. The two deal at arm's length and the young attorney proceeds on the vicious assumption that the client is quite able to take care of himself. The source of

[2] *The Law and Mr. Smith*, by Max Radin, The Bobbs-Merrill Co., Indianapolis and New York, 1938.

[3] *Look at the Law*, by P. E. Jackson, E. P. Dutton & Co., New York, 1940.

[4] *Woe Unto You Lawyers*, by F. Rodell, Reynal & Hitchcock, Inc., New York, 1938.

[5] The best part of *Look at the Law* is the foreword by Mr. Arthur Garfield Hays. He does his best to answer by anticipation the criticism that the author's treatment of his subject is Exhibit A of intellectual dishonesty in the handling of evidence and the presentation of a case.

the evil should be sought in the young man's background and environment. Everybody admits that to secure a good trustee you must resort
to a highly selective process. Few realize that to admit young men to
the bar with no other than an educational test is to give a respectable and
intelligent young fox easy access to the hen roost. I also hazard the suggestion that not only law but all callings once deemed respectable are
now under attack. Physicians, bankers, insurance men, operators of public utilities, captains of industry and many other groups are bitterly as-
sailed by writers who have a flair for this sort of thing but who themselves hold no passport to public confidence.

Having eased my mind by these observations, I need to be reminded
that an autobiography is not the best medium for a discussion of such
issues. My immediate job is merely to chronicle my own professional
experiences—as teacher, practitioner and adventurer in the cause of law
reform.

TEACHING

Upon admission to the bar I at once became both teacher and practitioner. The Fellowship in the Law School to which on graduation I had
been appointed made me a member of the teaching staff. The course
in common law pleading was assigned to me. I prepared it with very
great care but became increasingly dissatisfied with the lecture and textbook method of instruction which was then in general use. As to the
lecture, the wit was right who described it as the process by which material on the notes of the lecturer is transferred to the notes of the student
without passing through the mind of either. I was constantly recasting
my material and during the academic year 1890-1891 went to Cambridge
to make a systematic study of the inductive method, or case system of
instruction. This system had been introduced into the Harvard Law
School by Dean Christopher C. Langdell and was effectively applied by
John Chipman Gray in Property; by James Bradley Thayer in Evidence
and Constitutional Law; by James Barr Ames in Torts, Trusts and
Pleading; and in contracts by the then "baby member" of that great
faculty, Samuel Williston. I look back to this experience with peculiar
satisfaction, not merely for its educational value, but because I then laid
the foundations of lifelong friendships with Gray, Thayer and Ames and
established with Williston a contact which, happily for me, has continued to the present day.[6]

[6] His recently published autobiography (*Life and Law*, Little, Brown & Co.,
Boston, 1941), with an appreciative Foreword by Learned Hand, is a delightful
addition to the literature of the law.

Other courses were assigned to me from time to time, including partnership, corporations and insurance. In 1893 I was elected to the then newly-created Algernon Sydney Biddle Professorship of Law, an honor which I appreciated all the more because the chair had been endowed in memory of a preceptor and friend.

After teaching partnership and corporations for several years as separate courses it dawned upon me that multitudes of problems are common to both fields of activity. This led to the discovery that much was to be gained by placing primary emphasis upon the problem itself and only a subordinate emphasis upon the type of association in connection with which the problem happened to arise. The two courses were accordingly consolidated into one, which I styled the Law of Association. In it I dealt with all the situations which arise when two or more people are associated, either as mere holders of property or as members of groups organized for business or other purposes. If associates are mere co-owners of property no one of them has the representative authority to bind his fellows. If, as co-owners, they launch their property in trade as co-proprietors of a business, they are said to be partners. Each partner represents his fellows and within the scope of the common enterprise may by his acts impose liability upon them. When, however, the associates so organize themselves that no representative action may normally be taken except by elected officials, the associates are regarded as having reached the stage of "incorporation"; and this is usually sanctioned only when there is a statute under which such a form of organization is regularized. This latter fact (back of which there is a long and interesting history) accounts for the common superstition that "the corporation" is a fictional person "created" by the state. Of course the state no more "creates" corporations than it "creates" marriages. In both instances people associate themselves pursuant to a law. In the one case their association is a domestic, in the other a business, relation. If, in either case, their association is bona fide but in fact irregular, interesting questions present themselves respecting the legal consequences of their conduct. In the domestic field, are their children legitimate or bastards? In the field of business, shall the associates be accorded the immunities which regularity would have insured? Or shall their irregularity be penalized?

I make this passing reference to my favorite law school course because I am certain that the line of development thus briefly indicated is the line which a student of this subject should follow. Had my life been devoted to teaching, my confidence in my own conclusions would have led me to write a treatise on the Law of Association. As it is, that delightful task must be left to others; but sooner or later somebody will do some worthy exploration in this (to me) most beckoning of all the fields of the law.

Another course which interested the students was based upon Smith's Leading Cases. The object of this course was to give the class facility in the use of authorities. This (then) well-known collection of cases was chosen because each of them dealt with a different branch of the law and all had been decided by judges of repute. The analysis of a decision in order to determine the precise point decided and to distinguish between dicta and what the court said on the very point in issue was one of the ends in view. The accurate, short and clear statement of the case itself was another. The handling of authorities in brief and in oral argument was a third. Methods of research, the use of the lawyer's tools and emphasis on the supreme value of thoroughness in investigation received a large share of attention. I believe that such a course has definite educational value. It gives the student a basis of experience which is bound to be useful to him in every department of his work at the bar. Give me an associate who is thorough and I can easily forgive him for not being brilliant.

During my twenty-one years of teaching I had happy relationships with faculty colleagues and with men who were teaching courses similar to mine in other schools. Ernst Freund in Chicago was making important contributions to the study of the corporation as was Professor Maitland of Cambridge. With both men I had agreeable contacts and stimulating correspondence. Monroe Smith, working at Columbia in the field of Roman Law, often gave me a helping hand. With Jeremiah Smith of Harvard I formed a warm friendship.[7]

All these men were agreeable companions. I cannot, however, say the

[7] There is a story that one morning he said to his class, "Gentlemen, this is a sad day for me: my only brother died 125 years ago today." He proceeded to explain that his father, a soldier in the Revolutionary War, had married when scarcely more than a boy; that both his young wife and the son who was born to them died; that after being a widower for fifty years the father married again; that Professor Smith himself was a child of this marriage and, being seventy-five years old when he made the statement, could count the lapse of a century and a quarter since the death of his father's first son.

same of Justice Holmes's friend and correspondent, Sir Frederick Pollock.[8] Because of his association with Maitland and of his delightful *Leading Cases Done into Rhyme* I looked forward with keen anticipation to meeting him at a dinner given in New Haven in his honor during one of his visits to the United States. His host, Edward Avery Harriman, had included me in his list of guests. Seated at the right of the host the distinguished visitor grunted in monosyllables when addressed and made no effort whatever to be entertaining. When called upon to speak he made a few perfunctory remarks, settled down in his chair and went conspicuously to sleep. While the Chief Justice of Connecticut and other speakers paid tribute to the value of his books he gave no signs of life. Being irritated by his behavior I picked up a siphon of soda water and shot the contents into a glass with as much noise as possible. Sir Frederick woke up, perceived that all was well and quietly went to sleep again. If passive misconduct following lawful entry could be a trespass *ab initio* he surely could have been treated as a trespasser. But unhappily the Six Carpenters' Case decides otherwise—as appears from Sir Frederick's own rhythmic record of the futile attempt of John Vaux to recover in trespass against the Six Carpenters who had paid for the first but declined to pay for the second round of drinks!

> "Sed per totam curiam 'twas well resolved
> (note, reader, this difference)
> that in mere not doing no trespass is
> and John Vaux went empty thence.
> The birds on the bough sing loud and sing low,
> no trespass was here *ab initio*."

During my teaching days there was a steady trend in the direction of the law school training of students and away from the office system. This resulted from the fact that in the law school a greater variety of courses can be better co-ordinated and more effectively taught and from the further fact that the highly-organized modern law office is no place for quiet study. While this process has been inevitable two regrettable evils incident to the change await a cure. One is a growing estrangement between cloistered teachers and the lawyers of the arena. The sec-

---

[8] The published correspondence between Sir Frederick Pollock and Mr. Justice Holmes (*Holmes-Pollock Letters,* Cambridge, Harvard University Press, 1941) is good reading, but I have a suspicion that each was posing a bit and trying to outdo the other in erudition and phrasemaking.

ond is the removal of the student from the civilizing influence of a responsible preceptor and a consequent substitution of business for professional standards.

These evils are remediable. Since law is made in the arena, judges and practitioners will always have the last word. But since it is essential to its coherence and clarity that law should pass through the schools, the teaching scholars are indispensable factors in any sound evolutionary process. All that is needed to insure mutual respect is to enlist all three groups in a common undertaking, as has been done in the American Law Institute and in the sessions of the Advisory Committee on Federal Rules of Procedure. Stop long-range sniping at and by teachers, practitioners and judges, substitute association in a worthy task, and effective intellectual fellowship between all three groups will naturally and inevitably result.

If the student is to develop a sense of trusteeship he must be exposed to the influence of a preceptor whom he respects and who himself has the right point of view. In big cities the problem is especially difficult but it is there that its solution is most imperative. To attempt an arbitrary limitation of the number of lawyers is unwise; but to refuse admission to the bar to all except candidates for whom acceptable preceptors have been found, will have a tendency not only to raise quality but to reduce numbers.

As to the purely educational phase of the problem I have some definite ideas which someday will be recognized as sound. They were suggested in the address made when I became president of the Pennsylvania Bar Association. I had intended to include the address in this volume in an effort to keep the subject before the profession, but limitation of space forbade.

When in 1910 I reluctantly resigned my professorship in the Law School I may have been helping to prove that practice and teaching do not mix. Certainly a point had been reached at which choice was inevitable. To continue for an indefinite time to do two men's work was impracticable. It is equally certain, however, that if I could go back to the classroom my experience as an active practitioner would add much value to my teaching. While, therefore, it may be for most men impracticable to practice and teach simultaneously, a very considerable amount of past practice ought to be required as part of the equipment of the future teacher. Under classroom conditions the teacher is what a county court judge would become if there were no appeal from his decisions.

In the arena the practitioner who is always right and who proclaims the courts to be wrong except when they agree with him is not apt to get very far in his profession. A similar attitude in the classroom, however, often gains political recognition and appointment to public office. A reasonable amount of licking is good for both practitioner and teacher. It helps him to substitute reality for dream-stuff. It makes him a wiser adviser to the client and a safer guide to the student.

On the other hand it is also true that past experience as a teacher may be an asset of considerable value in practice. The exploration of authority and the habit of thoroughness are far less common at the bar than they ought to be. A teacher who has mastered the technique of classroom exposition may have a justifiable feeling of confidence before the court, unless indeed his method is school-masterish, an attitude which most judges are quick to resent.

A lot of time is wasted discussing the merits and demerits of the "case system." This is the discussion of a false issue. The true choice is between doctrine and self-development. If the teacher's objective is to stimulate the student's self-development he certainly will not do it by talking *at* him or by injecting textbook doctrine into him. The teacher will, if he is wise, say no more than is necessary to make the students discover the problem and isolate it for study. Later he may with advantage "sum up" after the students themselves have carried the discussion to its end. The extent to which and the manner in which the teacher will utilize decided cases will vary according to his type of mind and habit of thought. But that he *must* make large use of them is self-evident, first because nothing but a concrete fact-situation can give reality to the problem of which the law supplies the solution; and, second, because the decided cases are the record of the very controversies with which our social order has concerned itself. I make these observations with some confidence because I studied with increasing uneasiness under a lecture and textbook system, attempted to follow it in teaching, became dissatisfied with it as an educational process, investigated and adopted the laboratory method of stimulating the self-development of the student and for a score of years applied it at least to my own satisfaction. When I had resigned my professorship my colleagues gave me a welcome evidence of their regard. It took the form of a minute signed by the eight professors who at that time constituted the faculty. In this minute they expressed appreciation of my work, especially in the fields of Corporations, Partnership and Insurance, and recorded the fact that I had been "the first man in this community to demonstrate the possibilities of modern scientific methods of law teaching."

PRACTICING

In the line of my profession I have enjoyed unusual opportunities. The list of important cases of all sorts in which I have had a part is an impressive one. These cases have brought me into friendly contact with most of the great American lawyers of the last fifty years and with not a few judges and advocates of other countries. Among lawyers from abroad none can ever rank with Sir Norman Birkett [9] as a companion and friend. I recall with interest Lord Birkenhead, who was Lord Chancellor in England's coalition government during World War I. In Lord MacMillan's volume *Law and Other Things* [10] there is an appreciative sketch of this remarkable man. The description of him there given squares in some respects with the impression he made on many of us when he visited this country as the guest of the American Bar Association. I suspect that Lord MacMillan's loyal friendship has led him to rate Birkenhead a bit too high. Unquestionably, however, he rendered useful service during his term of office. Under the English system, it is the function of the Lord Chancellor to nominate for appointment by the Crown lawyers who he thinks would make good judges. Owing to the war turnover, Birkenhead had been called thus to nominate (as I recall the figures) for about forty judicial vacancies in the higher courts and for many hundreds in the courts of inferior jurisdiction. He told me that in no case had he known the political affiliation of his nominees. He added that in three hundred years no responsible leader of the Opposition in the House of Commons had ever charged a Lord Chancellor with making nominations for political reasons. He that hath ears to hear, let him hear.

In earlier chapters I have referred to such of my legal cases as seemed to have an integral relation to my life-story.[11] Here are recorded some which perhaps have elements of interest for lawyers and a few which have I believe a genuine public interest. These cases at least illustrate the fascinating variety of an American lawyer's practice. I have included jury trials of different sorts as well as a variety of cases in state and federal appellate courts. Some of these I have won and some I have lost.

[9] See *supra*, page 291.   [11] See, for example, *supra*, pages 82, 95, 99, 226, 243.
[10] Cambridge University Press.

They are scattered through more than a half-century of practice, beginning with the nineties and running through 1943.

The first of my cases to attract public attention was an adventurous attempt, based on the alleged invalidity of the trusts under his will, to secure for the kin of Benjamin Franklin money which the City of Philadelphia had in 1890 been holding for a hundred years. Russell Duane, himself a Franklin descendant, had been one of my fellow-

"WHO STOLE THE PARISH BELL-ROPES, YOU SCAMPING RASCAL?"

Lawyers may refer to *Jackson v. Adams*, 2 Bingham's New Cases 402 (1835).

students in the Biddle & Ward office. In connection with our course on the law of future interests in property we had been led to study Franklin's will and we had come to the conclusion that its provisions violated the rule against perpetuities. I still think that our legal theory was sound; but I had not then learned what I now so well know—namely, that there are occasional situations which time and sentiment have immunized from successful attack. It is altogether proper that this should be so but only maturity teaches the lesson.

Doctor Franklin, dying in 1790, left one thousand pounds to Philadelphia to be accumulated for a hundred years. A similar gift to Boston we were not concerned with. He anticipated that in 1890 the fund would have grown to $655,000, of which $500,000 was then to be given to the City and the residue accumulated for a second hundred years. He figured that in 1990 there would be some twenty millions to divide between City and State. The method of accumulation which the City

was to employ from the outset was the making of interest-bearing loans
to deserving artisans. When, however, in 1890 it came time for the
beneficial interest of the City to take effect, the fund amounted to only
$100,000 and it was this fund that we claimed for the next of kin. We
alleged that the loan scheme was not itself a charity and that the final
gifts had been held in suspense beyond the period permitted by the
common law.

The defendants in the suit, the Board of City Trusts, were represented
by F. Carroll Brewster, an able and adroit lawyer of long experience.
In a way that was maddening to youthful opponents, he successfully
ignored the vital legal questions, adroitly suggested that the Orphans'
Court, in which the proceedings had been brought, lacked jurisdiction
and cleverly pictured the case as an attempt by greedy and ungrateful
relatives to defeat a worthy charity. The Orphans' Court ignored the
jurisdictional objection but decided the case against us on the somewhat
remarkable ground that the City of Philadelphia, being both trustee and
beneficiary, had by accepting the trust and administering it over a long
period of years entered into a contract with the testator which was binding upon him as well as upon those succeeding to his estate. Not a bit
discouraged we appealed to the Supreme Court of Pennsylvania. With
youthful ardor we betook ourselves to Boston, laid our case before John
Chipman Gray (then the greatest living authority on this branch of the
law) and invited him to help us, both with our brief on appeal and in
oral argument. He studied the record carefully, agreed that we were
right and, while warning us that we could not win, accepted a tiny
retaining fee and threw himself into the case with vigor. The Supreme
Court treated us with great consideration, extended our time for oral
argument and listened with the utmost attention. In due time, however,
an adverse decision was announced. The court ignored the ground upon
which the lower court had rested its decision but sustained the contention, ignored below, that the Orphans' Court had no jurisdiction of the
case. Here was another test of our determination but we were equal to
it. If the Orphans' Court lacked jurisdiction then the Common Pleas
would surely do us justice. We accordingly filed a bill in equity. Again
we were met by a demurrer, a type of defense which a wag once described as an equity pleader's idea of a joke. Again we argued with zeal
and again we were defeated. The court sustained the demurrer in an
opinion the substance of which was that the whole scheme was charitable
and that charity covers a multitude of sins. This failed to convince us

that we were wrong; but by this time it had dawned upon us that we had attempted the impossible. We had sense enough not to appeal.

I shall never forget my bitter disappointment, not merely at the outcome of the litigation, but at our inability to get a decision upon what we regarded as the real point in controversy. However, the experience gained was of enormous value. Among other things I learned that in any human system for the administration of justice there must be a reserved judicial right to refuse in exceptional cases to stretch beyond the breaking point a legal principle that is sound enough for everyday use. Half a century later the Orphans' Court appointed me Master to determine a question arising under the provisions of Franklin's will. Thus I was called upon as a judge to facilitate the administration of the trust which as a youthful advocate I had tried to set aside.

TRIAL BY JURY

In early days at the bar I tried a lot of cases for the Union Traction Company—the company which controlled the Philadelphia surface transit system. Accidents were many and a large force of trial lawyers was required to represent the company in the resulting damage suits. Thomas Leaming was in charge of the company's legal department and the trial staff worked under his direction. He was a capable lawyer and a most agreeable companion. He had begun life as an artist and had switched to the law. He wrote a book called *A Philadelphia Lawyer in the London Courts*, and illustrated it himself. It is a most readable little volume.

The trial of accident cases, whether for plaintiff or defendant, tends to develop a technique of its own. Perjury is plentiful and the imagination of witnesses runs riot. Juries, albeit predisposed to favor plaintiffs, are nevertheless rather quick to detect fraud and are prompt in condemning it when detected. Jurors may also be counted upon to sympathize with anybody who has acted under provocation. They are apt to resent the conduct of the man who was provocative. I remember a case which illustrates this perfectly. An irritable and irritating passenger had given a tongue-lashing to a conductor who, quite properly, had refused to honor an unavailable transfer ticket. After thus easing his mind the passenger had paid his fare. The conductor had then meekly resumed his place on the platform and the incident appeared to be closed. However, what the passenger had said to him rankled and suddenly the conductor's anger flamed. He re-entered the car and dared the passenger

to repeat what he had said. This the passenger readily did and in a somewhat aggravated form. Thereupon the conductor laid his coat aside,
sailed into the other fellow, punched him good and hard and gave him
a pair of black eyes. Then the conductor rang the bell, stopped the car,
called in the motorman and directed him to help eject the passenger—
which was done. Breathing threatenings and slaughter, the outraged
plaintiff demanded fifty thousand dollars of the company not merely
as compensation but as exemplary and even vindictive damages. The
company offered $15,000 in settlement, which was rejected with scorn.
When the case came on for trial I had not a single witness. In the interval the conductor had died. There had been only a few people on the
car and they had been subpoenaed by the plaintiff. In cross-examination,
however, I led the plaintiff through the transaction step by step and the
more vividly he recalled it the angrier he became. He even blurted out,
with some satisfaction, that he understood the conductor had died. This
was a great help because there was no other way of establishing the fact
and I wanted the jury to know why he was not being called as a witness. By the time the plaintiff left the stand it looked as if several of the
jurors had themselves been irritated by him and rather sympathized with
the conductor. My adversary had counted upon the closing speech to the
jury but when the defendant offered no testimony he was taken by
surprise because I thereby became entitled to the last speech. What he
had prepared to say was intended as a closing appeal and was quite
ineffective as an introduction to my speech. I had asked the court to
instruct the jury to find for the defendant on the ground that the company is not liable for injuries done by a servant who, after properly discharging his whole official duty, picks a private quarrel. The trial judge,
Mayer Sulzberger, was an acute and learned lawyer. He refused my motion and directed me to proceed with my closing speech to the jury. At
the end of it he delivered an interesting charge. He told the jury that
the defendant was right as to everything that had happened before the
conductor summoned the motorman. When he did that, the trial judge
explained, the conductor resumed his function as captain of the ship
and thereby subjected the company to liability for his subsequent conduct. The court therefore instructed the jury that they must disregard
the private quarrel but that they might find a verdict for whatever damage the plaintiff had sustained in the process of his ejection from the
car. The jury found a verdict for $500. What thereafter became of the
plaintiff I do not know; but when he and his lawyer left the courtroom
they were as angry a pair as I ever saw.

WHAT IS AN ISLAND?

Another case of more than usual interest was one called *Houseman v. International Navigation Company.* The International Navigation Company was in possession of a tract of land in South Philadelphia near the confluence of the Delaware and the Schuylkill. Although this tract was a part of the mainland at the time of the suit, my client Houseman contended that originally it had been an island (called Cabin Island) and that he was successor in title to one to whom a patent for the island had been issued by the Commonwealth under the terms of an early statute. I had the unusual experience of bringing an action of ejectment on an original land title for land situated in a metropolitan area. The case came on to be tried before Judge Robert von Moschzisker and a jury. The important question of fact in the case was whether, at the date of the patent, the land in question was an island. If so, the authority given to the land office by the act of 1806 had been properly exercised when the patent was issued to my client's predecessor. My contention was that there had originally been a channel called the "Back Channel" separating the island from the shore and that it was only long afterward that the island had become part of the mainland in virtue of gradual and imperceptible accretions. By a happy chance I found in the Philadelphia Library an ancient map which not only showed the back channel but indicated that neglect to recognize its existence and protect it by fortification had been an important factor in Lord Howe's capture of Philadelphia in the Revolutionary War. I was accordingly able to argue to the jury that the present defendant was making the same mistake as the defenders of Philadelphia had made more than a hundred years before. I asked for a verdict that the premises in question had been an island at the date of the patent and the jury so found. The case was afterward appealed to the Supreme Court of Pennsylvania. That tribunal held no error had been committed by the trial court and refused to disturb the verdict.[12]

"YES; WE HAVE NO BANANAS"

In the winter of 1915-1916, while the World War was raging abroad, bloodless battles continued to be fought in the courts at home. Among the cases which at this time made a heavy demand upon my time and vitality was one called *Bluefields Steamship Co. v. United Fruit Company.*

[12] 214 Pa. 552 (1906).

I was retained by Moorfield Storey of Boston and his partner Robert G. Dodge to appear with them for the United Fruit Company which was alleged to have brought about the ruin of the plaintiff's business by all sorts of attempts to monopolize and restrain the trade in growing bananas in Nicaragua and transporting them into the United States. The claim was for actual damages of $5,000,000, which, had the plaintiff obtained a verdict, would have been automatically trebled by the terms of the Sherman Anti-trust Act. It was a jury trial and lasted from the 9th of November to the end of the ensuing January. In the course of preparation and trial I became as familiar with the geography of Nicaragua as if I had been a native and I acquired as much knowledge of banana raising in general and of the plantations on the Escondido River in particular as if I myself had been a planter. The case was hotly and even bitterly contested throughout and ended in a verdict for our client, the defendant. Up to that time this was the longest jury trial that had ever taken place in the United States District Court for the Eastern District of Pennsylvania. The Court refused a new trial and the Circuit Court of Appeals affirmed the judgment. Years afterward at a diplomatic dinner in Washington, a rather dull affair, I found myself next to the then minister from Nicaragua. In order to enliven the proceedings a bit I asked him whether navigation was still impeded by the bar at the mouth of the Escondido. He looked at me in astonishment and asked what I knew about that river. I told him with becoming modesty that I could name the plantations on both sides of the river all the way from its mouth to Rama and added that as a member of the Foreign Relations Committee in the Senate it was our business to be thoroughly posted about the geography and commerce of the different nations with which the United States has friendly relations. He took the matter seriously and with unfeigned astonishment remarked that this seemed to him an incomprehensible evidence of practically universal knowledge. Before I could enter a disclaimer our conversation was interrupted and the good man went on his way—doubtless with a wholly unjustifiable admiration for the omniscience of senators of the United States.

My association with Mr. Storey in the Bluefields case was to me a most interesting experience. He had a wide reputation not only as a lawyer but as a reformer and as a promoter of all good causes. He was an earnest advocate of the rights of the Negro. His admiration for the race was unbounded. In the Bluefields case, however, it so happened that in an attempt to rebut some important evidence introduced by us the plaintiff had put on the stand a string of colored witnesses brought up from

Nicaragua for the purpose of testifying. Fortunately for us, the jury were not much impressed by the testimony of these visitors. But what was said in private by Mr. Storey about the individuals in question was distinctly less favorable than his estimate of the race as a whole. Association in this case with that sound lawyer and stimulating companion Robert G. Dodge laid the foundation of an enduring friendship. The late Walker B. Spencer of New Orleans likewise proved himself to be an able and congenial colleague.

THE NATIONAL GAME

Another treble-damage suit under the Sherman Act called for quick transition from bananas to baseball. In 1915 the Federal League Club of Baltimore brought a suit in equity in the United States District Court for the Northern District of Illinois against the two older Leagues, their several officers and all their constituent clubs. The prayers for relief included a declaration that the Major Leagues constituted a conspiracy and monopoly in violation of the common law, statute law and all laws whatsoever. An injunction was sought, preliminary until hearing and final thereafter, which if granted would have brought the mechanism of organized baseball to a standstill. Argument on the motion for the preliminary injunction was to be heard by Judge Kenesaw Mountain Landis.[13] I suspect that his jurisdiction had been selected by the plaintiff because the Judge had acquired the reputation of a trust-buster and it was thought that he would find satisfaction in busting this one. My aid was sought by the National and American Leagues and by the individual officials. I went out to Chicago and with able local assistance opposed the granting of the preliminary injunction. My contention was that there was in fact no such combination or conspiracy or monopoly as alleged by the plaintiff; but that in any event the federal court was without jurisdiction because organized baseball was not interstate commerce and the federal anti-trust statutes were therefore inapplicable. After protracted argument Judge Landis refused to grant the preliminary injunction and ordered the case to stand over for trial. The plaintiff never brought it on for trial, however, and thus the Federal League was repulsed with loss. Four years later, however, the issue which had been thus mooted before Judge Landis was revived in an action under the

[13] Six years later Judge Landis, no longer on the bench, became Baseball Commissioner. See page 359, *infra*.

Sherman Act against the Major League Clubs and their individual officers. The forum selected by the attorneys for the plaintiff was the
Supreme Court of the District of Columbia. The case came on for trial
before Judge Stafford and a jury. Again with able local support I appeared for the defendants. The trial began on March 25th and ended on
the 12th of April, the Court obligingly recessing for the day on April
10th to enable me to debate in Philadelphia with Senator Hitchcock.[14]
The atmosphere of the Washington courtroom was unfriendly to my
clients. I raised at every opportunity the objection that a spontaneous
output of human activity is not in its nature commerce, that therefore
organized baseball cannot be interstate commerce; and that, it not being
commerce among the states, the federal statute could have no application. The court, however, ruled against me and the jury found an
$80,000 verdict for the plaintiff which the statute automatically trebled.
This was the first stage of a three-round fight and it was unquestionably
the plaintiff's round. The story of the other two was destined to be
different.

The second round was fought in the middle of October, 1920. My
clients had appealed from the judgment on the verdict entered against
them in the court below and the case came on for argument in the
Court of Appeals of the District of Columbia on October 15th. I mention the date because of the coincidence that on the same day there was
being played the final game in the World Series of that year. While
all of America was experiencing this annual thrill, a court was being
called upon to decide whether these great sporting events would have
to be discontinued. In due course a decision was rendered in our favor
so that the second round in the fight was ours. A third round became
necessary, however, because the Federal League at once appealed to the
Supreme Court of the United States.

While this appeal was pending the opportunity came to me to review
and revise the many contracts which hold Organized Baseball together.
These included the agreements which determine the relation of player to
club, of club to club, of club to league, of league to league and of major
league to minor league. The several existing contracts had been amended
from time to time and the result was like an old lady's will with a maze
of codicils. The task of revision required a study of every detail of the
system. Most important of all, it required something like statesmanship
to secure for the game its proper place in public estimation and give club

[14] See page 127, *supra*.

owners and players the feeling that they are public servants. The club owners were willing enough to have rules and regulations made to control the players but they were not so ready to set their own houses in order. The situation called for a sporting dictatorship; an official who could exercise between games the same sort of undisputed authority that belongs to the umpire during play. Judge Landis, for a number of reasons, was the obvious man for the job and he was fortunately willing to take it. After protracted conferences and much correspondence the whole system was recast; every contract was redrawn and wholesome declarations of policy were exacted from all concerned. The declaration signed by all the club owners in January of 1921 was as follows:

> "We, the undersigned, earnestly desirous of insuring to the public wholesome and high class baseball, and believing that we ourselves should set for the Players an example of the sportsmanship which accepts the umpire's decision without complaint, hereby pledge ourselves loyally to support the Commissioner in his important and difficult task; and we assure him that each of us will acquiesce in his decisions even when we believe them mistaken and that we will not discredit the sport by public criticism of him or of one another."

Later a volume was published embodying the entire series of agreements. I wrote for it a foreword under the caption: "Play Fair, Play Hard, Play for the Team."

Everybody interested in baseball realized that reform had come none too soon because there were many signs that the public was losing confidence in the integrity of the sport. It was an additional satisfaction to be assured of the hearty appreciation of the clients. John Heydler, president of the National League, wrote as follows:

> "The 'Foreword' is fine. It presents a new viewpoint, which to an old-timer like myself, steeped in the traditions of old laws and procedures, is unique and refreshing. To my mind you have taken care of the sportsmanship as well as the business side of the game in a very few words. I feel confident Judge Landis and Mr. Johnson [15] will likewise endorse this Alpha of our new Baseball Bible."

Both Johnson and Judge Landis heartily approved and Organized Baseball thereafter found less quick water in the channel.

There still remained the overhanging cloud represented by the litigation which had now reached the Supreme Court of the United States.

[15] B. B. Johnson, President American League of Professional Baseball Clubs.

While I was confident of the ultimate outcome, I awaited the third and final round of the fight with no little anxiety. This round came while I was in the midst of my first preprimary campaign for the Senatorial nomination. The case was set for argument before the Supreme Court of the United States on the 19th of April, 1922. The situation was dramatic. The courtroom was full of interested onlookers who realized that the continuance of the World Series games was at stake. Counsel for the Federal League made the grave mistake of minimizing the real point in the case (the question, namely, whether interstate commerce was involved) and sought to inflame the passions of the Court by a vehement attack upon the evils of organization, a few of which were real and many, as I thought, imaginary. I argued with much earnestness the proposition that personal effort not related to production is not a subject of commerce; that the attempt to secure all the skilled service needed for professional baseball is not an attempt to monopolize commerce or any part of it; and that Organized Baseball, not being commerce, and therefore not interstate commerce, does not come within the scope of the prohibitions of the Sherman Act. In due course the Court decided in accordance with this contention and affirmed the judgment of the court below. The opinion of Mr. Justice Holmes as it appears in 259 U.S. p. 207 is a model of conciseness. Conceding that the Leagues "must induce free persons to cross state lines and must arrange and pay for their doing so" he observed that "the transport is a mere incident, not the essential thing. That to which it is incident, the exhibition, although made for money would not be called trade or commerce in the commonly accepted use of those words. As it is put by the defendants, personal effort not related to production is not a subject of commerce." [16]

So ended an interesting and long-drawn-out fight. The position of Judge Landis, the Commissioner, was made secure and everybody realized that the way had been cleared for an administration characterized by good sportsmanship and good sense.

Baseball controversies in the courts have produced some interesting decisions in the domain of equitable remedies. When the civil war in Organized Baseball first began, an "outlaw" club sought to entice "Rein-

[16] The analogy of the practice of medicine or law at once suggests itself. In *Am. Medical Association vs. U.S.*, 317 U.S. 519 (1943), the Court has decided that an organization not for profit employing physicians at fixed salaries is engaged in trade. It may be that the baseball decision will be upheld as to the conduct of the individual but will in time be modified as respects the activity of the associations which exploit the service of the individual.

deer" Killifer to forsake the Philadelphia Club and enter the service of the enticer. Killifer's playing contract with Philadelphia had expired but by its terms he was bound to give his employer a fair chance to bargain with him for the ensuing season. Tempted by the big salary offered to him he had neglected to do this and had signed up with the outlaw. Thereupon the Philadelphia Club offered him a still larger salary which he accepted, returned to his first love and was ready to play. The outlaw club immediately filed a bill to restrain him from violating his negative covenant. I was retained to represent the defendants. The suit was brought in Michigan, where Killifer lived and was tried in the United States District Court in Grand Rapids. I conceded that Killifer had broken his contract with the plaintiff and that, as a theoretical matter, he could be held liable in a common law action for damages, but urged that the plaintiff had done an inequitable thing in persuading him to disregard his "reserve clause" and that as the plaintiff came into court with unclean hands no equitable relief should be decreed. The Court took this view and dismissed the bill. The Circuit Court of Appeals for the Seventh Circuit affirmed the decree and Killifer played with the "Phillies."

PUBLIC SERVICE AND PRIVATE PRACTICE

While I was in the Senate I maintained contact with my law office and argued as many cases as possible. This was essential not only in fairness to my partners but to earn my daily bread. The volume of my Senate work was so great that an office force had to be maintained largely at my own expense. Thus my entire salary was spent and as much again. And this without counting living expenses at a small hotel where (somewhat to the disgust of socially-important friends) we lived with simplicity but in great comfort. One of my cases at this time was *Frick v. Pennsylvania,* in which my senatorial colleague David Reed and I found ourselves on opposite sides. Henry C. Frick died domiciled in Pennsylvania. Part of his estate was an immensely valuable collection of pictures and other objects of art which were permanently located in New York. Pennsylvania, in computing the state inheritance tax, included the value of this collection on the theory that these assets were taxable where the owner lived. On behalf of Frick's executors I contended that the collection had acquired a tax-situs in New York and was not subject to taxation in Pennsylvania. The Supreme Court of Pennsylvania decided against me but on appeal the Supreme Court of the United States reversed the judgment and sustained my contention. This decision blazed a new trail in the forest of taxation and "Frick's Estate" became a leading case.

Another case which came up during my Senate term was *Myers v. United States*. This I argued as *amicus curiae* at the invitation of the Supreme Court of the United States. The case presented for judicial decision the question which sixty years earlier had been involved in the impeachment of President Johnson. Congress had passed an act creating the office of postmaster of a certain grade and had provided in substance that an official appointed to the office by the President and confirmed by the Senate should be removable by the President only with the Senate's consent. President Wilson, a sturdy defender of executive prerogative, had removed Myers (a duly qualified postmaster) although the Senate had not given its consent to his removal. Myers sued for his salary in the Court of Claims. That tribunal decided against him and the case came before the Supreme Court of the United States on appeal. After hearing an argument, that Court was of opinion that the issue thus raised between President and Congress deserved further consideration. They accordingly restored the case to the list, ordered a reargument and invited me to appear on behalf of the Congress. Solicitor General Beck and I presented our opposing views. The Court, by a 6-3 vote, decided that the requirement by Congress of the consent of the Senate was an unconstitutional restriction upon the President's power of removal.

PRO BONO PUBLICO

This was one of many important cases in which I charged no fee and considered the work done as a bit of public service. It was therefore particularly gratifying to receive the thanks of the Court, which were expressed by the Chief Justice in the following words:

> "Before closing this opinion, we wish to express the obligation of the Court to Mr. Pepper for his able brief and argument as a friend of the Court. Undertaken at our request, our obligation is none the less if we find ourselves obliged to take a view adverse to his. The strong presentation of arguments against the conclusion of the Court is of the utmost value in enabling the Court to satisfy itself that it has fully considered all that can be said."

This recognition was the more highly appreciated because, as I am told, it was the first expression of this sort in the Court's history.

The majority opinion was a vindication, after the event, of the position taken by President Johnson with respect to the Tenure of Office Act in 1867. Since, however, the powerful dissent by Justices Holmes, McReynolds and Brandeis, suggests future reconsideration, it may not be out of place to make some comments upon it.

A postmaster is clearly an "inferior officer" within the meaning of Section 2 of Article II of the Constitution, which empowers the Congress to vest the appointment of such officers in the President alone, in the courts of law or in the heads of departments. When, therefore, the Congress in creating the office of postmaster vested the power of appointment in the President, it should seem that restrictions upon the right of removal might be made applicable to the chief executive as well as to any other officer of government in whom the power of appointment might have been vested. The three dissenting Justices insisted that the only question before the Court was whether, as to the removal of such an inferior officer, the President might invoke an unlimited prerogative. Without hesitation they answered this question in the negative. The Chief Justice, however, speaking for the majority, rested his decision upon reasoning broad enough to make it applicable to the case of superior officers as well. The unnecessary breadth of the view thus taken turned up as an embarrassment to the Court when in 1933 President Franklin Roosevelt undertook to remove a member of the Federal Trade Commission. In this later case Commissioner Humphrey had received from the President the following extraordinary communication:

> "You will, I know, realize that I do not feel that your mind and my mind go along together on either the policies or the administering of the Federal Trade Commission, and, frankly, I think it is best for the people of this country that I should have a full confidence."

Of course the Commissioner had declined to resign and had subsequently received notice of an executive removal. The Court of Claims, in a suit by the Commissioner to recover his salary, certified to the Supreme Court a series of questions which in effect called for a definite utterance by the appellate court respecting the exact limits which were to be placed on the *Myers* decision. The Court naturally shrank from conceding to the Executive the power to pack such a tribunal as the Federal Trade Commission with men who should recognize no will but his. The distinction was accordingly drawn between, on the one hand, a purely executive officer such as a postmaster and, on the other hand, a member of a "quasi-legislative or quasi-judicial agency"; and it was held that the Presidential power of removal extended only to the former. That the view of the

majority in the *Myers* case had proved to be a trouble maker is indicated
in the concluding paragraph of the opinion of the Court in the *Humphrey*
case, which is as follows:

"To the extent that, between the decision in the *Myers* case, which
sustains the unrestrictable power of the President to remove purely
executive officers, and our present decision that such power does not
extend to an office such as that here involved, there shall remain a field
of doubt, we leave such cases as may fall within it for future consideration and determination as they may arise." [17]

Another case of very considerable public importance came on for
argument several years after my Senate term was over. As in the *Myers*
case I had upheld the rights of the Senate and House, so in this, the
George Otis Smith case, it became my duty to vindicate the constitutional rights of the President as against the Senate. It so happened that
I had been invited by a committee of senators (headed by Senator Walsh
of Montana) to represent the Senate in this controversy. It seemed clear
to me, however, that the Senate was in the wrong and the honor was
therefore declined. Subsequently Attorney General Mitchell asked me
to take the other side of the controversy and this I was glad to do. It
was another case, by the way, in which there could be no pecuniary
compensation for the vast amount of labor and effort involved. It was
taken, as were many others both before and since, from a sense of professional or civic obligation.

In this case President Hoover had appointed George Otis Smith and
others to be members of the newly-created Federal Power Commission.
The appointments were duly confirmed by the Senate and the President
was formally notified of the confirmations. In due course he proceeded to
issue their commissions. Thereafter the appointees, in effecting the organization of the Commission, incurred the wrath of Senators Wheeler
and Norris by removing several persons from the staff left by the old
Commission. At the instance of the aggrieved Senators the Senate by
resolution sought to recall the confirmations and requested the President
to return the papers. "I cannot," replied Mr. Hoover, "admit the power
of the Senate to encroach upon the Executive functions by removal of a
duly appointed executive officer under the guise of reconsideration of
his nomination." The Senate thereupon caused proceedings in quo war-
ranto to be instituted in the Supreme Court of the District of Columbia

[17] *Humphrey v. United States,* 295 U.S. 602 (1935).

on the theory that under the terms of its own rules the Senate might within a limited time lawfully insist upon a return of the papers and might reconsider its act of confirmation even after commissions had been issued to the appointees and they had begun to function. That able lawyer and cultured gentleman John W. Davis represented the Senate. Each of us explored the records of Senate action from the beginning of the government. I spent days in the Library of Congress and thoroughly enjoyed the opportunity for research. We argued the case in the first instance in the Supreme Court of the District of Columbia. That court sustained the President. After an appeal by the Senate to the Court of Appeals of the District the cause was by that Court certified to the Supreme Court of the United States. Both on account of its inherent importance and because of its political implications the controversy aroused widespread interest. We argued the question in a crowded courtroom. In due course the Court, in an opinion by Mr. Justice Brandeis,[18] affirmed the judgment appealed from and vindicated the position taken by President Hoover.

A LEGAL NIGHTMARE

During the time that I was working on the *George Otis Smith* case I had my first professional contact with the Movie industry. The Warner Brothers, producers, distributors and exhibitors of pictures, became involved in a controversy with the American Telephone and Telegraph Company, with a subsidiary of which Warner Brothers had a license contract. The controversy turned upon the interpretation of the contract and upon the making of certain alleged discriminations against Warner Brothers and in favor of their competitors. Many millions of dollars were involved in the outcome of the controversy. The contract contained a provision making arbitration the compulsory remedy in the event of dispute. The wise rules of the common law discouraging such agreements had been set aside by a New York statute and recourse to the regular courts for redress of grievances had thus been effectually blocked by the legislature. The mania for arbitration, heralded as a New Deal in judicial procedure, is a good illustration of public readiness to cure one evil by resorting to a worse. Whatever judicial abuses there may be, the courts, in my opinion, are much to be preferred to tribunals of arbitration. In this case the parties at the outset fondly imagined that by fixing

[18] *United States v. Smith,* 286 U.S. 6 (1932).

high per diem compensation they could secure eminent arbitrators who would dispose of the controversy in short order.

At the time I came into the case three such arbitrators had been sitting intermittently during a period of two years at $1,000 per day apiece and all expenses paid. Forty-five hundred printed pages of testimony had been taken and, as far as I could judge, the case was no nearer a decision than at the opening session. Shortly after I appeared, Samuel Untermeyer (the arbitrator who had been chosen by the Warners) discovered that he had agreed to represent a client with an interest adverse to the American T. & T. and that he was therefore disqualified from serving further in a judicial capacity. He accordingly withdrew, retaining the fees already paid to him for attendance at sessions. Under the New York law not only was it necessary to begin the proceedings *de novo* but it was forbidden to the parties to stipulate that testimony theretofore taken might be accepted by the new tribunal. The months already spent had to be forgotten, the arbitrators' fees and the heavy stenographic, printing and legal expense had to be charged off—and the reformed procedure had to take a new start. By the time all this was accomplished another year had elapsed. Even so we made no real progress because of those infirmities which are inherent in all such arbitration proceedings. One is the difficulty of agreeing on dates for sittings. Another is the psychological unfitness of arbitrators to discharge a judicial duty. When three judges hear a case in the regular way counsel have three open minds to deal with. When, however, an arbitrator is chosen by each party and the two choose a third, it is a practical impossibility for either of the first two to ignore the circumstances of his selection. A man with an unusually delicate ethical sense will lean backward, thus doing injustice to the party who named him. It is much more likely, however, that each of the two original arbitrators will act as an unofficial advocate for the side that named him. In that event the two compete for the ear of their third colleague. This creates a situation unsatisfactory to the arbitrators themselves and highly unsatisfactory to the litigants and their counsel. I have several times served as arbitrator and have appeared before a number of such tribunals. As a result I always strongly advise a client never to make an arbitration contract.

In the Warner case, in spite of all efforts to expedite the proceedings, less than thirty sessions were held during the winter of 1931-1932. By the spring of 1932 the expenditures of Warner Brothers alone in the two arbitrations had amounted to about $300,000. A request by the Warners made to the arbitrators to withdraw was promptly refused by two of them. The Warners then, as a measure of desperation, filed a bill in the Chancery Court of Delaware (the domicile of one of the corporations concerned in the controversy) ignoring the arbitration and invoking the jurisdiction of the courts of a State in which compulsory arbitration is wisely discouraged. The Chancellor entertained the bill and entered a decree favorable to the Warners. This, however, was reversed by the Supreme Court of Delaware substantially on the ground that the plaintiffs, by breaking their arbitration contract in New York, had disqualified themselves to seek equitable relief elsewhere. In other words, there was here applied against me the doctrine which I had successfully invoked in the Killifer case. This meant that the Warners had no alternative but to negotiate for a settlement of their claim. At this stage, Untermeyer, without notifying counsel on either side, reinjected himself into the case, brought the parties together behind the backs of their attorneys, effected the inevitable settlement and received the compensation which, according to our way of thinking, the labors of others had earned. Shortly after this achievement had come to my knowledge I was one day called on the telephone by a member of a Philadelphia reception committee formed to meet and greet Untermeyer on the occasion of a projected visit to the city. I was invited to act as chairman of this reception committee. I said that I should be glad to act if at liberty to frame my own greeting. "What would that be?" was the next question. "I want to be at liberty," I answered, "to say on the arrival of the distinguished guest, 'Sammy, get the hell out of here.'" There was a gasp over the wire and the invitation was not further pressed.

Looking back over the course of this litigation I am certain that never in any other case have I spent a comparable amount of time and effort with so little advantage to the client. I *did* get a good fundamental education in the making and production of motion pictures and in the intricacies of that remarkable industry.

UNEMPLOYMENT RELIEF

Now that unemployment relief has come to be regarded as a normal governmental function it is interesting to recall that this has not always been the case. The term "unemployment relief" was first used, I believe, in 1880. Relief had not previously been thought of as a function of the federal government and in the states it was not unemployment but poverty of which the legislatures took cognizance. From the time that unemployment resulting from the depression of 1929 first required governmental action two distinct policies have been in evidence—Mr. Hoover's policy of emphasizing nonpolitical local responsibility and Mr. Roosevelt's policy of appropriating federal funds not without political benefit to himself. In Pennsylvania, prior to the Roosevelt regime, fiscal stringency led Governor Pinchot to deprecate direct state appropriations for relief out of existing resources. He attempted to place upon municipal units responsibility for providing relief funds and to vest their administration in a State Commission to be created for the purpose. He conceived of an amendment to the State Constitution under which the State might borrow money for relief and ultimately repay those who in the interval had made relief loans to the State commission. In the fall of 1931 he accordingly convened the legislature in special session and sought to limit the agenda to a consideration of his plan. The legislature rejected the plan and appropriated $10,000,000 to be distributed through the Department of Welfare to the various pre-existing local boards for poor relief. Then ensued a struggle between the executive and the legislature. A proceeding was begun in the Dauphin County Court by the Governor through his Attorney General to test the constitutionality of the appropriation. The Governor's contention was that the legislature had gone beyond the terms of his call when they substituted their own plan for his. He also urged that the appropriation was invalid for various other reasons, including a contention that it was a prohibited increase of the indebtedness of the Commonwealth and an appropriation to individuals in violation of a certain constitutional restriction. I was asked by a group in the legislature to intervene in the proceeding as *amicus curiae* and both to file a brief and to take part in the oral argument, opposing the Governor's position. This I did first in the Dauphin County Court and (after a decision in our favor) in the Supreme Court of Pennsylvania to which the Governor had appealed. This was another important case in which I worked without a fee. As the controversy had a political as well as a constitutional aspect the argument (which took place in Pittsburgh) was a rather heated one and the atmosphere of the courtroom a trifle tense. The Court divided on the issues raised but the majority took the view which I had urged and sustained the validity of the appropriation.

It was in the midst of presidential excitement in 1936 that the rumored use in Pennsylvania of federal money to influence or reward Democratic activity necessitated some form of authoritative investigation. The Pennsylvania State Senate, with a slim Republican majority, appointed a committee to take testimony and ascertain what legislative steps might be taken to check the evil. The idea of such an investigation by a state authority was repugnant to federal officials and a bill in the name of the United States was filed in the United States District Court for the Middle District of Pennsylvania to restrain the removal of the lid. Somewhat reluctantly, because of the large amount of unpaid though arduous professional work I had already done, I joined William A. Schnader in representing the Senate Committee. The argument took place at Harrisburg before Judge Johnson. The federal government was ably represented by John Dickinson. The Court accepted his contention that somehow federal sovereignty was involved, the preliminary injunction was made permanent and no investigation took place. This proved to be a political boomerang for the Democrats who in 1939 were faced by criminal prosecutions for political misuse of federal funds. The incidental revelations of corruption of the electorate constitute a powerful argument against this form of governmental relief.

STATE COURTS TO THE RESCUE

While New Deal battles have in most instances been fought in federal courts there have been some significant engagements in the state courts as well. A case in point was the litigation resulting from a legislative attempt in Pennsylvania to destroy an important Philadelphia court. Franklin Roosevelt's hostile attitude toward federal courts and judges naturally encouraged his admirers in Pennsylvania to imitate him. In Philadelphia, in addition to the Orphans' Court, there had been for many years five Courts of Common Pleas, each manned by three judges. There was also the Municipal Court, with eleven judges, the broad jurisdiction of which includes, among other things, domestic troubles and juvenile delinquency. Official hostility came to a head in the winter of 1936-1937. A Democratic legislature, under pressure from Governor Earle, created in Philadelphia two additional courts of Common Pleas, thus giving the executive six important places to fill and also undertook to set up a so-called Family Court with five judges to be appointed. At the same time a bill was passed abolishing the Municipal Court in the middle of the terms for which its judges had been elected by the people. The Municipal Court judges asked a small group of lawyers to represent them. I was included in the group—another *pro bono publico* service. We took the proper steps to determine the validity both of the Family Court Act and the Municipal Court "ripper." The Supreme Court of Pennsylvania took original jurisdiction of both cases and we argued them with vigor, while the politicians crowded the courtroom and the public waited to learn whether the judiciary has any rights which the legislature is bound to respect. The Court decided both cases in our favor, declaring the Family Court Act invalid for palpable disregard of certain constitutional limitations and holding that the "ripper" had been intended to take effect only if the Family Court were upheld. This latter theory was sound enough and one which all the justices of the Supreme Court could accept. The decision, however, leaves open the really important question whether the legislature may, if it so determines, destroy a court which it has previously created and do it while judges, elected by the people for terms as yet unexpired, are sitting and discharging their judicial duties. Possibly the Supreme Court would have divided on this question, which remains to be faced if the present "open season" on courts is not soon closed.

When in June of 1939 the cornerstone of a new home for the Municipal Court was to be laid I accepted the Court's invitation to lay the stone and make the dedicatory address. Since I had helped to preserve the Court's existence, it seemed fitting that I should also have a part in giving it a permanent place of abode.

TRIUMPH AND DISASTER

Every advocate enjoys the thrill brought by victory after a hard fight. He also knows the sinking of heart that comes when an anticipated victory is turned into a defeat. These are the cases in which he tries to take his licking like a gentleman. This oft-quoted phrase I first heard years ago from the lips of John Chipman Gray after my young heart had been wrung by losing the Franklin will case,[19] Again and again I have reminded myself of it when a disappointing decision tempted me to curse out the court. I think one of the characteristics that make many of the New Dealers seem so unlovely is their entire lack of sportsmanship. They are the world's poorest losers. When Congress takes an unwelcome stand or the Supreme Court renders an unpalatable decision there arises in Washington a howl of mingled wrath and agony. The President makes caustic and even abusive statements to the press. Cabinet members break out with irritating and intemperate criticisms; and all the lesser frogs in the puddle croak themselves hoarse in a chorus of protest. I think I could respect even their most sophomoric views on law

[19] See *supra*, page 350.

and other things if they sometimes doubted a little of their own in-
fallibility and were willing to concede that there may have been brave
men before Agamemnon.

This is not to advocate a servile acceptance of adverse decisions as
ultimate revelations of truth. But there is a vast difference between conviction that a court has erred and passionate clamor for the umpire's
scalp.

I here record four interesting cases lost of which the first and last are in
my judgment bad law while the other two are (in my perhaps mistaken view) illustrations of decisions determined by the atmosphere surrounding them.

Of all the law suits I have lost (and there have been many) the one
over which I grieved most was the case of a college student who had
been, I thought, a victim of gross academic injustice. While an undergraduate at Bryn Mawr she had been suspected of stealing money from
fellow students. The then president of the college, Miss M. Carey
Thomas, had dealt with the case in a way that I regarded as essentially
unfair and had finally expelled the girl. I satisfied myself that the suspicion was entirely groundless and my partner Isaac Pennypacker and I
willingly undertook the task of seeking reinstatement. We applied for a
writ of mandamus and pressed our claim with great earnestness. It was a
difficult case to win because the defense was not that justice had been
done but that what had happened was nobody's business. The president, who was as flinty as anybody I ever met, coolly took the rigorous
position that under the terms of a student's contract with the college
the student might be dismissed as an "undesirable" at the will of the
president and without the preferment of charges and without a trial.
This position was approved both by the trial court and by the Supreme
Court of Pennsylvania in what seems to me one of the most unjust decisions that I know of. To guarantee to the faculty of even a public college unrestricted academic freedom is altogether proper and may be
even essential; but to deny to a student in any college the ordinary elements of fair play impresses me as a monstrous inconsistency. I find it
hard to understand how any court could have been content to put the
seal of approval on what was in fact the murder of a reputation.

In the Warner case I had striven fruitlessly in the service of one producer. Four years later I took up the cudgels for another, but with no
better success. In *Paramount Publix Corporation v. American Tri-Ergon*

Corporation [20] the Supreme Court of the United States brought up on certiorari a patent case decided by the Circuit Court of Appeals for the Second Circuit. The Paramount Corporation had been using a process for making a combined sound and picture positive film widely acclaimed as the "Western Electric Sound System." The Tri-Ergon Corporation, the stock of which was owned by William Fox, contended before the lower court that this use was an infringement of a valid patent belonging to Tri-Ergon. This contention was sustained and a decree duly made that the patent was valid and infringed. The aggrieved infringer petitioned for certiorari and the Supreme Court, as is usual under such circumstances, refused to review the decision and dismissed the petition. Then the victorious Fox made his big mistake. If he had waited until the period had elapsed during which under the rules of the Supreme Court a rehearing can be applied for, his patent would have been unassailable in that proceeding and he might have proceeded at his leisure to garner the fruits of victory. What he actually did, while still within the shadow of a possible review, was to begin infringement suits against various concerns who were using the patented process. Instantly the Paramount Corporation filed a new petition adroitly suggesting that the patented process was of such commercial necessity that, unless the decision below were reversed, the entire industry would be brought under Fox's domination. Since no new ground of invalidity was shown, this was tantamount to a suggestion that Fox's patent should be adjudged invalid merely because it was so valuable. The Supreme Court, seemingly impressed, granted the relief previously refused, brought the case up for review and caused it to be set down for argument. At this stage I was retained by Fox to help in the preparation of a brief and to take part in the oral argument. My colleagues and I satisfied ourselves that the decision appealed from was sound and that the patented invention was not only technically valid but highly meritorious. It solved a theretofore unsolved problem and made possible a combined sound and picture positive which the public would listen to. If, however, we had had any doubt about the mental attitude of the Supreme Court toward the patent it would have been dispelled by the atmosphere of the courtroom when the case was called. I have argued in some chilly atmospheres but this one was subzero. I felt as if I were addressing myself to nine penguins sitting on ice blocks. We never had a chance: the case had been in

[20] 294 U.S. 464 (1935).

effect decided when the petition for rehearing was granted. When shortly after the argument a reversal was formally announced it merely gave official confirmation to our surmise. It cannot of course be said that the decision thus made was wrong. The case, like multitudes of other patent cases, might have been decided either way. Whether the lower court would have been reversed if the Supreme Court had not been alarmed by the petitioner's prediction of grave commercial consequences is, of course, anybody's guess. My guess is that it would not have been; and that is why I list the decision as the product of an atmosphere so cold that no legal argument could live in it. Certainly mine was frozen to death and the efforts of two able colleagues met the same fate.

Guth v. Loft, a decision of the Supreme Court of Delaware,[21] was another case in which I was retained to accomplish the impossible. In that case my client Charles G. Guth had been given an opportunity to buy cheaply the trademark and formula for a soft drink known as Pepsi-Cola. He seized the opportunity and in an astonishingly short time convinced a great part of the American public that their physical welfare if not their eternal salvation depended upon drinking Pepsi-Cola. An asset costing some $12,000 thus came in the course of about eight years to have an estimated value of some $30,000,000. This great accession of wealth suggested some thoughts to the stockholders of the Loft Candy Co., of which Guth had been president at the time he seized the Pepsi-Cola opportunity. They brought suit against him in the Chancery Court of Delaware and charged that the original opportunity to purchase had been offered him as a company officer and not for his own benefit, that he had used company resources to finance both the purchase and the development and that he was therefore bound to account to the company for all that he had fondly supposed was his own. At the end of a protracted trial the Chancellor decided the case against Guth and in favor of the company. The Chancellor made findings of fact deemed by him sufficient to sustain his decree. I was retained to carry the case on appeal to the Supreme Court of Delaware. A reading of the voluminous record satisfied me that Guth had made a poor witness and must have aroused the Chancellor's antipathy because a number of the points found against him might easily have been decided the other way. However—there stood the findings and on appeal there was not a Chinaman's chance of upsetting them. It accordingly seemed wise not to dispute Guth's liability to account but to insist that it arose only be-

[21] *Guth v. Loft,* S. C. Del., January, 1939, No. 1.

cause of his use of company resources. On this theory advantage could be taken of the Chancellor's refusal to find that the original opportunity had been offered to Guth in his capacity as president. It might then be consistently argued that the court should apply an equitable measure of liability proportionate to the company's contribution; and such a yardstick would in fact have enormously reduced the size of the decree. This plan was followed in oral argument. The Supreme Court of Delaware is a delightful tribunal before which to appear. No fixed limit of time is imposed upon counsel. The five judges are able men. Chief Justice Layton was one of my students in law school days and I am proud of having had something to do with his development. The number of cases on the court's docket is usually small; and the attention given to the arguments in each case is always close and sustained. This particular case received the fullest measure of consideration. While my able opponents, Messrs. Podell and Southerland, did full justice to their case I almost persuaded myself that my argument had persuaded the Court that the decree appealed from was too rigorous. I say "almost" for though somewhat responsive to my own oratory I could not quite believe that the impossible had actually been accomplished. And it had not been. In due course the decree appealed from was affirmed. It was interesting, however, to observe that the Chief Justice thought it necessary to find (as the Chancellor had refused to do) that the original opportunity had in fact been offered to Guth in his capacity as president and not to him as an individual. This departure of the appellate court from the Chancellor's theory indicated to me that the atmosphere of the case was such that Guth was bound to lose—if not on one ground then on another. Every practitioner knows how often this proves to be a litigant's fate. When you are young at the bar you fondly imagine that judges are as impersonal and relentless as adding machines, registering mathematical results irrespective of whom it may concern. Long experience teaches that this fortunately is not the fact. Rules of law and even the more flexible doctrines of equity are most likely to produce a wholesome result when applied by human beings who can not only temper justice with mercy but weigh the relative social consequences of the opposing views that are urged by counsel.

No list of typical lawsuits is nowadays complete unless it includes an income tax case. Of this sort was *Deputy v. duPont*, decided by the Supreme Court of the United States in January of 1940. It involved the determination of the sum properly payable by the taxpayer for the year

1931. In it I took a licking. The comment which I here make upon the decision comes perilously close to a squeal.

The Federal Revenue Act at that time in force authorized the deduction from gross income of "all the ordinary and necessary expenses paid or incurred during the taxable year in carrying on any trade or business." During 1931 Pierre S. duPont in fact paid to a creditor, who had lent him a big block of stock, $647,000.00 which was the annual payment for which the lender had stipulated. The loan had been running for some years and the deduction of similar payments in each of those years had been approved by the Bureau of Internal Revenue. In 1931, however, there came a change of mind on the part of the federal government. A tax undiminished by the deduction was accordingly demanded. The demand was complied with, the money paid and the taxpayer in the usual way sued the collector to recover it. Likewise in the way that has now become usual the trial court rejected his claim. I was retained by the taxpayer to take the case on appeal to the Circuit Court of Appeals of the Third Circuit. In oral argument I urged that the payment to the creditor was deductible not only as an ordinary and necessary expense of the taxpayer's business but (under another provision of the Revenue Act) as "interest paid on indebtedness." The Court decided in favor of the taxpayer on the first point and accordingly was not required to determine the second. If the decision had been the other way and the unlucky taxpayer had petitioned the Supreme Court of the United States to review the decision, he would have had, in my judgment, a slim chance to succeed. When, however, the government was the loser a review was sought and promptly granted. The case came on for argument and I put all I had into the presentation of my client's case. I was moved to do this by personal friendship for him and by a conviction that his cause was just. I had detected in the judicial atmosphere that sort of prepossession which had led to the grant of certiorari. A situation like this always puts an advocate on his mettle.

Both the trial court and the Circuit Court of Appeals had agreed in finding that the taxpayer was engaged in the business of conserving and enhancing his estate. As all the multitudinous tax settlements made by the Bureau during an eighteen-year period had proceeded on the theory that there *is* such a business, there was some ground for hoping that even new and inexperienced judges would hesitate to disturb such a well-settled administrative practice. That the expense of carrying a loan is both ordinary and necessary is a fact likely to be discovered even by the most naïve borrower. That the obligation to repay a loan (whether of money or money's worth) is an indebtedness and that the annual charge for carrying it is interest has been recognized by all the authorities since Justinian's time. These considerations I urged upon the eight sitting Justices with all the energy at my command. After the argument many listening lawyers in the courtroom expressed the confident view that the case was "in the bag." I, however, had my doubts. Several days later an admiring friend wrote from Washington that at a party which he had attended one of the young Justices had been loud in his praise of my argument. I at once called up my client and told him to prepare for the worst as judicial compliment is the usual precursor of a swift kick. So it proved to be in this case. By a six-to-two vote [22] the Court reversed the Circuit Court of Appeals and reinstated the judgment of the District Court. Four of the six Justices were willing to concede (without so deciding) that the taxpayer was engaged in business. Two of the six regarded this concession as a "litigation-breeding assumption" and thought they were showing "appropriate regard for administrative practice" when they declared that "*any* trade or business" is an expression applicable only to the limited class of business in which goods or services are sold. Four found significance in the fact that the pending loan had been incurred in order to repay an older loan by another lender which seven years before had been made to enable the taxpayer to cover a short sale. They concluded that the annual payments on the later loan, although perhaps "necessary," were not "ordinary" because it did not appear that the taxpayer had engaged in a short sale transaction more than once. All of the six were of opinion that the obligation to return a loan of stock is not an "indebtedness" and that the stipulated price of a creditor's forbearance is not "interest" as the term is used by Congress unless the loan is of money—although Congress itself in its usury legislation has made a contrary declaration. But the six all agreed that the taxpayer must lose and that the government must win, the divergences in the rationalizing process being relatively immaterial. The two dissenting Justices thought that the certiorari ought never to have been granted but that, having been granted, the judgment appealed from should be affirmed.

I indulge myself in the (for me) unwonted luxury of critical comment in this case not merely because the decision seems to me to be wrong but because it is one that nobody with a truly liberal mind can approve. It contradicts the impression, entertained by many, that the Court has

---

[22] *Collector of Internal Revenue v. duPont*, 308 U.S. 488 (1940).

been "liberalized" by recent changes in its personnel—unless, indeed, it is liberal to construe a tax act most strongly against the taxpayer and to resolve all possible doubts against the citizen and in favor of the Sovereign. Such a definition of liberalism, if it could be tolerated, would require us to classify Hampden as an ultraconservative.

So much for a running commentary on a few of the many causes which have fallen to the lot of an active practitioner during a long career at the bar. As I review them there come to my mind some lines from a Scotch ballad [23] which I memorized when I was a boy:

> "There's fighting on the mountainside—there's war within the blast:
> Old faces look upon me—old forms go trooping past.
> I hear the pibroch wailing amid the din of fight
> And my old spirit wakes again upon the verge of night."

ADVENTURES IN LAW REFORM

Seldom introspective, I *do* now and then try to account for the impression of many that I am a rather pronounced case of standpatter, opposed to reforms in general and particularly to those which aim to promote social welfare. Perhaps this impression prevails because when I was in public life it suited the purposes of opponents so to picture me. A deal of caricature can be popularized in this way. When as a person unknown to the public I suddenly appeared in the Senate, unprepared editors in different parts of the country simply had to publish immediately a picture and a biographical note. The cuts supposed to be pictures of me which forthwith appeared in the South, East and Northwest accordingly ranged from pictures of an anemic middle-aged failure with walrus-tusk mustachios to a bull-necked, cleanshaven and formidable-looking prize fighter. The stories varied in somewhat the same way, making a lifelike portrait a bit difficult. It is true, of course, that a lot of my acquaintances, representatives of old Philadelphia families, are as I am supposed to be; and what more natural than that I should be thought like other peas in the same pod? If I have never worn spats or carried a cane, or if my prejudice against gloves was the despair of Maine guides on winter trips, how should these facts be known to cartoonists who wanted to depict me as a son of privilege softened by luxury and with no concern for the welfare of my fellow man? A still more persistent source of misconception has been my political philosophy. This has often led me, after failing to

[23] "The Execution of Montrose," *Lays of the Scottish Cavaliers,* by Aytoun.

get my views accepted, to "go along" with the Party—on the theory that since parties are essential to our form of government a citizen's support of his party should not evaporate every time he and his party leaders fail to agree.

Whatever the explanation and in spite of impressions to the contrary, the fact is that I am now and always have been deeply and often vitally interested in social reforms of all sorts and among others, in all movements for the improvement of the law, its practice and its administration. The amount of time, effort and money I have spent in promoting many of these has been prodigious.

To round out the development of law students I worked ceaselessly to bring the Law School into closer contact with the life of the University as a whole and to modernize a curriculum which had become outmoded. In the approach to legal problems I have constantly sought the solution most consistent with the principles of social evolution. In constitutional law (as, for example, in so-called "New Deal" cases) I have remained true to the conviction that human relationships and social reforms are most wholesomely promoted in neighborhoods and in states. I hold that what seems to be gained by central efficiency is more than offset by the decline of local and individual responsibility. Outspoken opposition to the use of injunctions in labor disputes [24] and effective insistence upon justice to political prisoners [25] were factors in my defeat when I tried to remain in the Senate. I have made passing reference to my efforts to raise standards of admission to the bar.[26] As far as concerns the improvement of the law itself and of methods of legal procedure, I have found welcome outlets for effort in the American Law Institute and the Federal Advisory Committee.

THE AMERICAN LAW INSTITUTE

Following World War I, when everybody fondly imagined that an era of peace and prosperity was assured, my friend and former colleague William Draper Lewis conceived the idea that the time was ripe for an authoritative formulation of the principles underlying our unwritten law. Some men would have contented themselves with a bare suggestion that something be done or, having attempted to do it, would have been baffled by many and great difficulties. Lewis was of a different sort. He was—

[24] *Supra,* page 213.   [26] *Supra,* pages 65, 347.

[25] *Supra,* page 194.

and is—a remarkable combination of legal learning, scientific imagination and tireless tenacity of purpose. He formulated a plan for accomplishing his aim and succeeded in arousing the interest of Elihu Root. This projected restatement of the common law in all its more important phases was an ambitious undertaking for such an unofficial group as the plan contemplated. However, with Lewis in the engine room and Root on the bridge a voluntary organization was effectively launched and chiefly through Root's influence the necessary financial support was pledged by the Carnegie Corporation. The need for a restatement of the law had long been great and was growing greater because the chaotic mass of judicial decisions had become such as to defy the most daring attempts of individual scholars to systematize them. The aim of the Institute has been to produce in each field a formulated restatement of the existing law, with the expectation that this restatement will ultimately be accepted as authoritative by courts of last resort. I share with my colleagues the view that gradually a unifying influence will thus be exerted and that this will be all the more effective because the process is evolutionary and free from legislative compulsion. The method of attacking this formidable problem was carefully worked out by Lewis and Root. George W. Wickersham was happily induced to accept the presidency of the Institute. Selected "Reporters" in the several fields of the law, assisted by working groups of advisers, submitted from time to time to the Council of the Institute tentative drafts of restatements. After several years of study and discussion each of these drafts was perfected and referred for consideration to the seven hundred members of the Institute in annual meeting assembled. These men are representatives of all parts of the country and all branches of the profession. I became a member of the Council in 1930 and a vice president two years later. I threw myself into the work with zeal and after Mr. Wickersham's death was elected president by the Council.

I have greatly enjoyed the experience of presiding at the meetings of the Council of thirty-three and at the annual meeting in May. The members of the Council are well-known judges and practicing lawyers from all parts of the country. They represent all varieties of social and political opinion and differ widely in their approach to legal problems. To sit on the bench in the "trial room" of the Bar Association in New York and look into the faces of these men is to confront as able and intelligent a group as can be found anywhere. They are seated in a big semicircle, each with a desk before him. The reporter whose work is under consideration sits on one side of the presiding officer while the Director sits on the other. Everybody is keenly interested and there is lively debate. To encourage full discussion, to check it when irrelevant, to cut it off when time presses, to give the reporter adequate support and always to take account of sensibilities and known peculiarities, is the moderator's interesting task. I have found it wise to stick by the rules of parliamentary law in guiding the discussion but to go to the limit of effort in trying to get as many problems as possible settled without division. This is relatively easy because every man in the group is blessed with good manners and a spirit of co-operation.

The big meeting in May must be conducted with more formality; but the same general principles apply. Ever since the birth of the Institute it has been the custom for the Chief Justice of the United States to open the proceedings with an address of welcome. In 1939 Chief Justice Hughes, to whom we always extended a hearty greeting, was kept away by a slight illness. Mr. Justice Butler took his place. He made a great hit with his audience. "I understand," he observed, "that so far you have not undertaken a restatement of constitutional law. If and when you *do* attempt to restate it, you will find that our Court has occupied the field before you." His smile guaranteed the good humor of this reference to decisions from which he had felt impelled to dissent.[27]

In such a large gathering there are always a few men who would waste time if permitted to do so and occasionally one or two who have ulterior reasons for obstruction. The course to be steered by the presiding officer is between undue attention to minor features of the work and, at the other extreme, such a superficial discussion as would render the approval of the meeting really worthless. If the moderator could combine a clear perception of the precise issue under discussion, a familiarity with parliamentary law, enough humor to keep everybody smiling and an inexhaustible supply of patience he would be ideally fitted for his job.

Until recently the annual banquet, always a feature of the meeting, had been tending to become intolerably dull. With effective co-operation from Judge Learned Hand, the Director and Judge Goodrich, I have managed to brighten up the event. The formula is to have only two

[27] The annual meeting in May of 1942 had to be held in Philadelphia because of congested hotel conditions in Washington. Chief Justice Stone felt bound to decline our invitation and for the first time we lacked the benediction of the Court. In 1943, Mr. Justice Rutledge accepted an invitation to speak but at the last moment was unable to appear. His manuscript address was read by Judge Goodrich. In 1944, Mr. Justice Jackson represented the Court and was warmly welcomed.

speeches and these brief and in lighter vein. A high level of entertainment was reached when Professor Barton Leach, of the Harvard Law School, proved that he can play the accordion and sing original comic songs with as much skill as he can thread his way among powers in trust and the mazes of the rule against perpetuities.[28]

The task of the Institute as originally undertaken has been completed. The publication of nineteen weighty volumes [29] will have redeemed the Institute's pledge and fully justified the Carnegie Corporation's generous support. Whether or not the organization shall be permitted to dissolve is a question as yet unanswered. Some scholarly work akin to the restatement [30] has been undertaken by the Institute with the financial backing of the Carnegie Corporation and some with backing from other sources.[31] The effective co-operation of the three branches of the profession—the Bench, the Bar and the Schools—has made of the Institute a most useful instrument for scholarly work of the highest class. If the organization is dissolved it will leave a record of notable achievement. Its continued existence would be justified only if its work were to proceed on the same high plane as heretofore.[32]

THE FEDERAL ADVISORY COMMITTEE

Contemporaneously with American Law Institute work I have been doing my share in a different but related field of professional activity. The year 1937 brought to an end at least one stage in a labor of love which several years previously the Federal Advisory Committee had undertaken. This was a group of fourteen lawyers appointed by the

[28] Under war conditions it has been found expedient to omit these features of our annual meetings.

[29] The following volumes have appeared: *Agency* (2), *Contracts* (2), *Conflict of Laws, Property* (2), *Restitution, Torts* (4), *Trusts* (2) and *Judgments.*

[30] A proposed Code of Criminal Procedure and a model act to Provide for Contribution among Joint Tort-Feasors.

[31] Special reference is made to systematic proposals for the reform of criminal procedure in the treatment of youths convicted of crime.

[32] As I write (July 1944) it has been determined that the Institute, with the co-operation of the Commissioners on Uniform State Laws, will undertake the formidable task of formulating a Code of Commercial Law suitable for adoption by Congress and by the legislatures of the several states. This has been made possible by a liberal grant from the Maurice and Laura Falk Foundation of Pittsburgh.

Supreme Court of the United States to formulate a new body of rules of civil procedure for the federal District courts throughout the United States. Congress in 1934 had passed an act giving to the Supreme Court, upon certain conditions, the authority to prescribe such rules and the committee was called into being to assist the Court in the discharge of this onerous duty. I was made a member in virtue of my succeeding Mr. Wickersham as president of the American Law Institute. My colleagues, drawn from all parts of the country, are lawyers in active practice, former judges and distinguished professors of law. The chairman is William D. Mitchell, former Attorney General of the United States. Our secretary is Colonel Edgar B. Tolman of the Chicago bar, and our "reporter" is Professor Charles E. Clark, formerly Dean of the Yale Law School and now a judge of the Circuit Court of Appeals for the Second Circuit. He is a specialist in the field of procedure. We met for periods of a week at a time and at inconveniently frequent intervals. Our sessions were held in the new Supreme Court Building at Washington. We were wont to meet at ten, or earlier, each morning and we sat until ten at night or later. Drafts of rules submitted by the Reporter were subjected to a fire test of criticism. Many of the rules were redrafted a number of times. It is literally true that every word in them was a subject of study and nearly every sentence was a battleground. Tentative drafts were submitted for the scrutiny of bench and bar. When agreement on substance had been reached I was appointed chairman of a subcommittee on style with the responsibility of making all the rules readable and clear. The sessions of this subcommittee took place alternately in New Haven and in Washington. Finally our work was made as perfect as we could make it and the Court ordered spread upon its minutes an appreciation of our services. The rules, with some minor exceptions, were approved by the Court, transmitted to the Attorney General and by him reported to Congress. Under the terms of the act they became effective in the fall of 1938. Our committee did not actually disband but we separated with a sense of regret that at least for the time being happy companionship in a worthwhile undertaking had come to an end. We had had a lot of fun out of our meetings as well as an immense amount of hard work. Witticisms were plenty and humorous verses not infrequent. It remains to be seen whether rules prepared with so much study and care will actually work well in practice. The prescription of a single form of action as a substitute for separate proceedings at law and in equity is a big departure from a procedure to which many of us have been for a lifetime accustomed. Particular innovations, urged as reforms, may justify themselves in use.

THE NEW POOH-BAH.

Uncle Sam. "Who the hell are you?
Advisory Committee "I'm the President, the Congress
and the Supreme Court"

As to the outcome of the whole experiment I am somewhat hopeful; but much will depend upon the willingness of bench and bar to adopt a co-operative rather than an obstructive attitude. At any rate, we rendered a public service to the best of our ability—and even lawyers can do no more.

EMOLUMENTS

I suppose that no record in the life of a lawyer would be complete were nothing to be said about fees. There is a general impression that practicing lawyers exact enormous sums for their services and that clients as a class are bled white. I greatly doubt whether a really thorough study of the subject would justify any such sweeping statement. The first step in such a study would be to determine what factors the lawyer may properly take into account when fixing his fee. Among them the following should certainly be included: the nature of the service performed, i.e., whether ordinary or requiring an unusual output of skill and effort; the time consumed in conference, in study and in court; the amount of money involved; the degree of responsibility assumed by the attorney; the result obtained for the client. These factors, and others, are of course imponderable but when fairly estimated it is remarkable how just the result reached usually is. The value assigned to each varies from generation to generation along with other price levels; and at any given moment differs in different centers of population.

I have in my possession the book in which my grandfather George Mifflin Wharton with scrupulous care recorded his professional earnings from October 1844 to October 1866. He began to practice in 1827 and died in 1870; but the records for the first sixteen years and the last three are unfortunately missing. At the time when the available record begins he was apparently well established. He had a growing local practice and had been admitted to the bar of the Supreme Court of the United States.[33] For the seventeenth year the aggregate of his fees was $4,326.76. For the thirty-ninth year it was $19,260.34. In the interval the yearly aggregates show a gradual although, of course, not a uniform increase. His biggest year was the twenty-ninth of his practice when his professional receipts totaled $25,117.94. This included a $10,000 fee, which appears to be the largest ever paid him. Nobody can read his record of professional earnings without being convinced that his was a practice which grew steadily and in wholesome fashion. The figures are indeed small when compared

[33] December 29, 1843, on motion of John Sergeant, Esq.

with those that are familiar today but the purchasing power of the dollar was many times as great then as at present—and there was no income tax!

I find from my own records that in my first year of practice my fees amounted to an even $2,000; and during the five years thereafter (in round figures) to $3,000, $6,500, $10,000, $9,000 and $10,500. From that point onward there has been a much more gradual increase, with fluctuations up and down. I estimate that through the years about half of the whole amount of my activity has been gratuitous nonlegal service to the Church, to the University, to the Profession, to the Community and to individuals; and that of the other half, which represents my legal work, about a quarter has been done without charge. In other words my earnings have come from about three-eighths of my total output of time and effort. Relations with clients have been happy and in the rare instances where there have been discussions about fees the outcome has always been a friendly adjustment. The size of one of the largest fees I ever received was due to the fact that the client insisted upon paying twice as much as I had charged.

These statements will seem strange to those who have credited rumors of great sums received by me for professional work. In the Agricultural Adjustment Act case (*United States v. Butler*) [84] I was reported to have received a million dollars. In point of fact no fee whatever was paid to me. It was arranged in advance that I should argue the case without charge to Butler and his coreceiver. This I was willing to do because of the advantage which would accrue to other clients of mine who had cases depending on the result. I argued before the Supreme Court of the United States two other notable cases (*Myers v. United States* [85] and *United States v. George Otis Smith*) [86] without fee and merely as a public service. The same is true of some well-known cases before the Supreme Court of Pennsylvania, including those which involved the constitutionality of the Municipal Court "Ripper Bill," and of the State Appropriation for Unemployment Relief. A good illustration of popular misapprehension of the fees received by individual lawyers was an allowance [87] made by the United States District Court to my colleagues and to me for services in the reorganization of the Philadelphia Rapid Transit Co.—now the Philadelphia Transportation Co. I was congratulated on every side upon the receipt of $300,000. In point of fact my share of the allowance was $50,000, which was of course paid to my firm. The service for which

[84] See page 244, *supra.*   [86] *Supra,* page 363.
[85] *Supra,* page 361.   [87] February 1940.

the fee was paid extended over a period of five years. My individual share finally figured out to be about $5,000 a year, which, of course, I was happy to divide with Uncle Sam. Indeed that Grand Old Man has come out pretty well in his fiscal relations with me. He has been my silent partner these many years and I have never begrudged the large proportion of my earnings that I have paid him. But I admit that it has been at times a bit irritating to realize that our Uncle has not been permitted to keep what I have paid him but has been compelled by his noncontributing partners to hand it out in ways that have done the old gentleman no good. As a joint result of income taxation and a habit of subscribing freely to worthy causes I am still, at seventy-seven, dependent on daily earnings for daily bread. Provision for some dependent friends and relatives, and the kin of those who have served me, more than consumes the net income yielded by the investments into which I have put my savings. The present federal income tax policy virtually prohibits the citizen from putting his surplus earnings into productive enterprise and, instead, first appropriates them and then pipes them into the treasury. Thence they are pumped out and made to flow into channels the direction and destination of which is determined by men who themselves may never have been able to earn more than a precarious living. This process cannot long continue. Either productive enterprise will be starved to death or the piping, pumping and diversion of earnings will have to be brought within reasonable limits. The widely-proclaimed doctrine that "government" may be depended upon to supply industry with capital is based upon a mistaken conception of what "government" is, has and does. "Government" *is* a miscellaneous collection of men few of whom, as individuals, are competent to launch or run any sort of business. "Government" *has* only what these men by taxation and borrowing can take from those who have the ability and energy to do what they themselves cannot do. What "Government" *does,* therefore, is to appropriate the resources of the competent, thus preventing them from determining the destination of their earnings, and instead to entrust that vital function to the incompetent. There is probably some high-sounding name for this process but we might as well be honest about it and call it damn foolishness.

What the psychologists call "the suggestion of opposites" probably explains why, after commenting thus upon the New Deal, I am reminded of a Scotch experience in the matter of fees.

Many years ago a Philadelphia bank requested us to collect from a local debtor a sum due to a creditor living in Scotland. With the usual amount of trouble the collection was made. As a matter of international courtesy no fee was deducted and the remittance of the full amount was made to the Scotch bank which had forwarded the claim for collection. A letter from this institution expressed high appreciation of our courtesy but explained that the creditor was in a large way of business and quite able to afford a fee. The bank had therefore taken the liberty of suggesting to the creditor that five dollars be sent us by way of compensation. The next mail brought a polite letter from the creditor, referring to the fact that the bank had suggested the payment of a fee, suppressing all mention of five dollars as an appropriate amount and enclosing two United States one dollar bills, which we were asked to accept with the sender's compliments. This we were happy to do. For the encouragement of other clients I had the correspondence mounted and framed and the precious two dollars displayed as part of the exhibit. This was hung in our reception room. At the end of forty-eight hours it disappeared. Up to that point the joke had been on Scotland; thereafter the only conclusion to draw was that if the Scotch are thrifty, American office cleaners cannot always be trusted under the strain of great temptation.

I have been told by members of the London Bar that barristers in leading practice there make more money than men in the same relative position here and do it with less effort. On the other hand there is some evidence that the balance of trade is the other way. The Association of the Bar of the City of New York on West 44th Street is a large and impressive structure. Its marble halls contain statues and busts and the walls of the various rooms are hung with portraits. Mr. Wickersham once told me that a distinguished English judge to whom he was showing the building was greatly impressed and remarked that it was a magnificent home for the American Bar. "Not the American Bar," said Mr. Wickersham, "only the New York Bar." "The Bar of the State of New York?" queried the visitor. "No," said Mr. Wickersham, "merely the lawyers practicing in the City of New York." "Dear, dear," exclaimed the visitor, "what a suggestion of comfortable emoluments!"

Looking backward over my own professional life and that of many, many other busy lawyers I am really amazed to see the amount of work that has been done with no thought of financial return. When highly-paid public officials declaim from time to time about the selfishness and greed of the bar it would not be improper to remind them that many of us have been doing all our lives without pay more real work than they have ever dreamed of doing to earn their generous salaries.

In my seventy-eighth year law work excites me as much as it did when

I was young. Had I in youth had the privilege of corresponding with Mr. Justice Holmes he might have written to me such a letter as the enthusiasm of another young correspondent called forth. "I like your rapture over the law," he wrote. "I only fear that it may be dimmed as you get into the actualities (in the sense of the hard side) of life. But if, as I hope, and as what you write indicates, you bear the fire in your belly, it will survive and transfigure the hard facts." [38]

[38] Oliver Wendell Holmes, *Book Notices and Uncollected Letters and Papers,* page 159.

13

Glancing Astern

"For who to dumb Forgetfulness a prey,
This pleasing anxious being e'er resigned,
Left the warm precincts of the cheerful day
Nor cast one longing lingering look behind?"
—GRAY's *Elegy*

WHEN I turn my back on the future and cast a lingering look astern it takes in the whole of life in a moment of time.

Surveying work done, I am inclined to think that my law school teaching days were the happiest of all although the practice of law has combined plenty of thrills and much quiet satisfaction. As for public service, while life in the Senate was intensely interesting my sojourn there was ended at about the time I had learned how to be really useful. As far as tangible results go my Senate term was a waste of time and effort. If I were to live the experience over again I should devote much more attention to building up a political organization with a view to re-election. To serve a single term is hardly worth while. Browning best expresses my thoughts on this subject in those well-known lines:

"Look at the end of work: contrast
The petty Done—the Undone vast
This present of theirs with the hopeful Past—" [1]

Congenial office relationships have made the practice of law a continuing delight but there is no great professional achievement to which I can look back with pardonable pride. The award to me in 1941 of the medal

[1] *Their Last Ride Together.*

388

of the American Bar Association "for conspicuous service to American jurisprudence" seems justifiable only on the theory that I personified the work of the American Law Institute. After all, it is in the home that my greatest happiness has been found. The self-sacrificing devotion of my wife, the love of my children and the companionship of my grandchildren have been blessings which in retrospect fill me with gratitude.

All my life I have taken a deep interest in people, as such. The exploring of human personality seems to me an absorbing pursuit. I can say with confidence that never in my life have I been bored. Now and then friends have charged me with feigning an interest in others which I did not really feel. They were wrong. The interest was genuine and its manifestation spontaneous and natural. An incident of this attitude is, I suppose, a tendency to rate people more highly than they deserve. This is a dangerous quality for an executive or anybody charged with the selection of subordinates. Among friends, however, it tends to put others at their best, since the other fellow is apt to try hard to live up to your favorable estimate of him. Indeed you may thus sometimes make another aware of some really great capacity which he himself did not know he possessed. It may be that all this has something to do with the making of fast friends. As I review the friendships of a lifetime I am impressed with their number and diversity. Classmates, fellow parishioners, teammates, companions in out-door life, faculty colleagues, students, professional brethren, fellow workers in community enterprises, friends made in the Senate and during political campaigns, members of our office family, people in all walks of life to whom I have been drawn through the rendering of needed service, men and women found to be congenial in the contacts of social life—together they make a goodly company, marching as it were in endless column. I individualize them as they pass and thank God for the unspeakable satisfaction they have brought me alike in times of sunshine and of shadow.

Most of these friends of a lifetime are dead but I have the inward assurance of reunion with them all. Birth and death are the only two experiences which all men share; and the Universal Order of which they are a part cannot on the whole make for happiness unless each of them is itself a good. There is only one way in which this can come to pass— and that is if birth and death are each mere gateways to a larger life. The preservation of personal identity and the possibility of communion beyond the grave are essential to the conception of a happy death. It is therefore with calm confidence that I look for the resurrection of the dead and the life of the world to come.

This is all that need here be said about my faith in the future for at the moment I am looking backward, not forward. It interests me to list the men who during my life have in one way or another impressed me most. In such a list I should include my uncle Provost Pepper for his charm, my father-in-law Doctor Fisher for his culture and urbanity, Bishop Brent for his simple godliness, John G. Johnson, one-time leader of the American bar, for his prodigiousness, President Arthur Hadley of Yale for his omniscience, Marshal Foch for his compelling personality, Professor F. W. Maitland of Cambridge for his scholarship and Herbert Hoover for his comprehensive grasp of public questions. The five friends of my own generation whose deaths have made me most eager for re-union are my fellow law student, William Wharton Smith; my two brothers-in-law, Joseph Alison Scott and William Forbes Fisher; my class-mate and "best man" Charles C. Townsend; and my cousin and partner Benjamin Franklin Pepper. Bill Smith was one of the finest men I ever knew. He and Ned Stewardson, a sculptor of great promise, were drowned at Newport when their sloop capsized and sank in a gale on Brenton's Reef. This happened shortly after we had graduated from the law school and it was my first poignant grief. Al Scott meant as much to me as one man can mean to another. It is more than thirty years since he died but his place in my affections has never been filled. Billy Fisher had every quality which inspires affection. Companionship with Charley Townsend both at work and at play was a delightful experience, whether as a faculty colleague, as a fellow traveler abroad or as a comrade on fishing and camping trips at home. The honor roll of those who gave their lives for their country contains the name of no more gallant gentle-man than Franklin Pepper.

My glance astern takes in institutions as well as people and four stand out above all the rest. These are Washington Cathedral, the University of Pennsylvania, the Franklin Institute and the American Law Institute. My lifelong association with St. Mark's, as parishioner, vestryman and warden, has been the source of unspeakable satisfaction. If under such rectors as Doctor Nicholson and Doctor Vernon I did not develop strength for the journey, the fault was not theirs but mine.

Recollections of people met, work done and causes served are matched by memories of sporting events and of days and nights spent in the open. Indeed my glance astern takes all outdoors in its sweep. I am not sure whether my happiest experiences have been on water or on land. On the whole I think that experiences ashore are the more satisfying. As between summer and winter, happy summer days have been the more numerous but the greatest thrills have attended life in the woods in sub-zero temperature. I look back to my days and nights on Mt. Katahdin with real delight. If the flash of daffodils upon the inward eye can make the heart dance, think what can be done by driven snow, dazzling-white birch trunks which cast upon it purple shadows, laden evergreens bowing low under unaccustomed weight and, back of all, a sky of matchless blue, a sunshine that seems to pour from high heaven and all about you an atmosphere that makes you thrillingly grateful for the mere fact of life. Moving through the wilderness on snowshoes upon a crust strong enough to hold you, you see all around you the evidences of that teeming animal life which in summer is a mere suspicion. Every sort of creature, from field mouse to moose, has left his footprints for your edification; and by following the big game tracks you can often overtake their departing maker and mystify him by taking his photograph as he stands there shoulder-deep in snow.

On what authority I do not know, but I have heard it said that it is the summit of Mt. Katahdin which among eminences in the Western Hemisphere first catches the beams of the rising sun. At any rate, as I look shoreward from the open sea that grand old mountain is the thing that I see last—this time with a sunset glory upon his head.

THE END

APPENDIX

AMENDMENTS TO THE COVENANT OF THE LEAGUE OF NATIONS

Suggested by me to Lord Robert Cecil. (See page 178, *supra*.)

A

The Preamble. As at present.

Article 1. As at present.

Article 2. As at present.

Article 3. As at present.

Article 4. As at present, with the amendment already made.

Article 5. As at present.

Article 6. As at present with the amendment already made.

Article 7. As at present.

Article 8. Amend by inserting at the beginning thereof an additional paragraph to read as follows:

> "The Members of the League recognize that war between any two or more States not only entails social and economic loss upon the combatants but is likely to disturb the peace of the world, to undermine universal standards of morality and to impair respect for the sanctity of human life. They, therefore, declare war in general to be an evil so great that severally and collectively they are ready to use all efforts and to make all sacrifices consistent with national honor and self-preservation, to make its recurrence unlikely or impossible."

Article 9. As at present.

Article 10. Strike out and renumber subsequent Articles accordingly.

Article 11. Amend by inserting a period after the word "League" where
(New 10) it first occurs in line 3; and striking out the words "and the

393

League shall take any action that may be deemed wise and effectual to safeguard the peace of nations."

Article 12. Strike out and renumber subsequent Articles accordingly.

Article 13. As at present with the amendments already made.
(New 11)

Article 14. As at present.
(New 12)

Article 15. Strike out and substitute a new Article to read as follows:
(New 13)

"If there should arise between Members of the League any dispute likely to lead to a rupture which is not submitted to arbitration or judicial settlement in accordance with Article 13 (new 11), the Council at the request of either party to the dispute or upon its own initiative shall endeavor to effect a settlement of the dispute and if such efforts are successful a statement shall be made public giving such facts and explanations regarding the dispute and the terms of settlement thereof as the Council may deem appropriate.

If the dispute is not thus settled the Council either unanimously or by a majority vote shall make and publish a report containing a statement of the facts of the dispute and the recommendations which are deemed just and proper in regard thereto except that if the dispute is found by the Council to arise out of a matter which by international law is solely within the domestic jurisdiction of one of the parties, the Council shall so report and shall make no recommendation as to its settlement.

Any Member of the League represented on the Council may make public a statement of the facts of the dispute and of its conclusions regarding the same.

The Council may in any case under this Article refer the dispute to the Assembly. The dispute shall be so referred at the request of either party to the dispute provided that such request be made within fourteen days after the receipt by both the parties of formal notice that the Council has taken cognizance of the dispute.

In any case referred to the Assembly all the provisions of

this Article relating to the action of the Council shall apply to the action of the Assembly.

Each Member of the League agrees with all the others that in case the report of the Council or of the Assembly and the recommendations therein contained are adverse to the contentions of such Member in the dispute then pending, such Member will in no case resort to war until three months after the date of such report."

Article 16. Strike out and substitute a new Article to read as follows: (New 14)

"Should any Member of the League be found by the Council to have resorted to war in disregard of its covenants under Articles 13 (new 11) or 15 (new 13), it shall ipso facto be deemed to have committed an act of war against all other Members of the League.

In deliberations of the Council on the question whether or not such an act of war has been committed, the votes of Members of the League alleged to have committed such an act and of Members against whom such action was directed shall not be counted.

It shall thereupon become the duty of the Council to recommend that all Members of the League shall immediately sever all trade or financial relations with the Member in default, shall prohibit all intercourse between their nationals and the nationals of said State and shall prevent all financial, commercial or personal intercourse between the nationals of said State and the nationals of any other State whether a Member of the League or not.

The Members of the League agree, further, that they will mutually support one another in the financial and economic measures which are taken under this Article, in order to minimize the loss and inconvenience resulting from the above measures, and that they will mutually support one another in resisting any special measures aimed at one of their number by the covenant-breaking State, and that they will take the necessary steps to afford passage through their territory to the forces of any of the Members of the League which are co-operating to protect the covenants of the League.

Any Member of the League which has violated any covenant of the League may be declared an outlaw nation by a vote of the Council concurred in by the representatives of all of the other Members of the League represented thereon."

Article 17. Amend by striking out in the first paragraph the numerals
(New 15) 12 to 16 and substituting 13 (new 11) to 16 (new 14).

Further amend by inserting in the third paragraph after the numeral 16 the following: "(new 14)."

Further amend by striking out in the fourth paragraph the last clause thereof and substitute the following:

". . . , The Council may make such recommendations as will in its judgment tend to prevent hostilities and to effect a settlement of the dispute."

Article 18. As at present.
(New 16)

Article 19. As at present.
(New 17)

Article 20. As at present.
(New 18)

Article 21. Strike out and substitute the following:
(New 19)

"Nothing in this Covenant shall be deemed to affect the validity of international engagements such as treaties of arbitration or regional understandings for securing the maintenance of peace. If the United States of America becomes a Member of the League it shall not be deemed to have assumed any obligation inconsistent with its traditional policy known as the Monroe Doctrine."

Article 22. As at present.
(New 20)

Article 23. As at present.
(New 21)

Article 24. As at present.
(New 22)

Article 25. As at present.
(New 23)

Article 26. As at present with the amendment already made.
(New 24)

B

1. Amend Article 1 by inserting before the final paragraph a new paragraph to read as follows:

   "Any such fully self-governing State, Dominion or Colony may become an Associate Member of the League if its admission is agreed to by two-thirds of the Assembly and any Member of the League may at any time terminate its membership and become an Associate Member by depositing with the Secretariat a declaration of intention to that effect. Associate Members shall have such rights and be subject to such obligations as are defined in Article 10."

2. Amend by inserting a new Article to become Article 10 (Associate Members), subsequent Articles to be numbered accordingly:

   "Associate Members shall have the rights and privileges of other Members but shall not be subject to the obligations resulting from any of the following articles in this Covenant: (new numbering) 11, 12, 13, 16 and 17."

3. Amend Article 18 (new number) by inserting at the end thereof a new paragraph to read as follows:

   "In the event of a dispute between an Associate Member of the League and a State which is not a Member, the State not a Member shall be invited to accept the provisions of Article 14 (new number). If a State so invited shall refuse to accept the obligations of said Article for the purposes of such dispute and shall resort to war against an Associate Member of the League, the Council may recommend to the Members and Associate Members such action as will tend to prevent hostilities and to result in the settlement of the dispute."

4. Amend Article 22 (new number) so that the same shall read:

   "Nothing in this Covenant shall be deemed to affect the validity of international engagements such as treaties of arbitration or regional understandings for securing the maintenance of peace. If the United States of America becomes a Member or an Associate Member of the League it shall not be deemed to have assumed any obligation inconsistent with its traditional policy known as the 'Monroe Doctrine.'"

Article 22. As at present, with the amendment already made.
(Now 24)

B

1. Amend Article 1 by inserting before the final paragraph a new paragraph to read as follows:

"Any such fully self-governing State, Dominion or Colony may become an Associate Member of the League if its admission is agreed to by two-thirds of the Assembly and any Member of the League may at any time terminate its membership and become an Associate Member by depositing with the Secretariat a declaration of intention to that effect. Associate Members shall have such rights and be subject to such obligations as are defined in Article 10."

2. Amend by inserting a new Article to become Article 10 (Associate Members), subsequent Articles to be numbered accordingly:

"Associate Members shall have the rights and privileges of other Members but shall not be subject to the obligations resulting from any of the following articles in this Covenant: (new numbering) 11, 12, 13, 16 and 17."

3. Amend Article 15 (new number) by inserting at the end thereof a new paragraph to read as follows:

"In the event of a dispute between an Associate Member of the League and a State which is not a Member, the State not a Member shall be invited to accept the provisions of Article 14 (new number) if a State so invited shall refuse to accept the obligations of said Article for the purposes of such dispute and shall resort to war against an Associate Member of the League, the Council may recommend to the Members and Associate Members such action as will tend to prevent hostilities and to result in the settlement of the dispute."

4. Amend Article 22 (new number) so that the same shall read:

"Nothing in this Covenant shall be deemed to affect the validity of international engagements such as treaties of arbitration or regional understandings for securing the maintenance of peace. If the United States of America becomes a Member or an Associate Member of the League it shall not be deemed to have assumed any obligation inconsistent with its traditional policy known as the Monroe Doctrine.

INDEX